Jim Scrivener
& Mike Sayer

Straightforward

Elementary Teacher's Book

MACMILLAN

Macmillan Education
Between Towns Road, Oxford OX4 3PP
A division of Macmillan Publishers Limited
Companies and representatives throughout the world

ISBN-13: 978-1-4050-1076-4
ISBN-10: 1-4050-1076-2

Original design by eMC Design. This edition designed by Mike Brain Graphic Design Limited.
Illustrated by Lisa Buck pp38, 52 and 68, Mark Duffin pp 51
Cover design by Macmillan Publishers Limited
Cover photographs courtesy of: Top line (left to right) Zefa/Masterfile/Roy Ooms, Peter Titmuss/Alamy, Al Rod/Corbis, Gallo Images/Getty Images (and lower half of front cover right), LWA-Stephen Welstead/Corbis, IMAGINA/Atushi Tsunoda/Alamy (and lower half of front cover left).
Bottom line: Stone/Getty, John Powell Photographer/Alamy, Metronap, Zefa/K.H.Haenel, Stockbyte, Rex Features/Eye Ubiquitous.
Back cover photos: John Marshall Cheary III, Metronap, Stockbyte.

The publishers would like to thank Jim Scrivener for his hard work on the Resource Materials and for his limericks.

The authors and publishers would like to thank the following for permission to reproduce their material:
Girls Just Want To Have Fun Words and Music by Robert Hazard copyright © Sony/ATV Music Publishing Limited 1979, reprinted by permission of the publishers. All Rights Reserved; *Sailing* Words and Music by Gavin Sutherland copyright © Island Music Limited. Universal/Island Music Limited 1972, reprinted by permission of Music Sales Limited. All Rights Reserved. International Copyright Secured; *Fields Of Gold* Words and Music by Sting copyright © Steerpike Limited/EMI Music Publishing Limited, London, WC2H 0QY 1993, reprinted by permission of the publishers; *I Say A Little Prayer* Words by Hal David Music by Burt Bacharach copyright © Blue Seas Music Incorporated/Casa David Music Incorporated USA, Windswept Music (London)/Universal/MCA Music Limited 1966, reprinted by permission of Music Sales Limited and Windswept Music. All Rights Reserved. International Copyright Secured; *I Believe I Can Fly* Words and Music by R Kelly copyright © Zomba Songs Incorporated, USA/Zomba Music Publishers Limited 1997, reprinted by permission of Music Sales Limited. All Rights Reserved. International Copyright Secured

Printed and bound in Spain by Edelvives

2010 2009 2008 2007 2006
10 9 8 7 6 5 4 3 2 1

Contents

Introduction

A straightforward approach

Approaches to language teaching come and go. When I first taught English, over twenty years ago in a Moroccan high school, I and most of my colleagues used a grammar-translation approach. Since then, in a variety of institutions in many different countries, I have used audiolingual techniques in a Direct Method school, a functional-situational approach, 'hard' and 'soft' versions of the communicative approach, a lexical approach, a task-based approach and a number of combinations of all of these. Over the years, it became increasingly clear that the grail of the 'perfect' approach was elusive and unobtainable. Different things work with different students in different educational contexts. We live, as the US-based educationalist Kumaravadivelu has put it, in a 'post-method condition'. The best approach to any language teaching situation will be eclectic, drawing on a multitude of approaches and techniques, choosing and shaping them in ways that are appropriate to our own particular classrooms. The approach in *Straightforward*, therefore, is eclectic and seeks to incorporate elements from many different approaches to language teaching.

Coursebooks, of course, reflect changing fashions and in recent years we have seen examples that follow a task-based approach, a lexical approach or approaches that are driven by an analysis of computer databases. With *Straightforward*, we did not want to be restricted in this way. As students develop their language competence and their autonomy as learners, their needs will change and our approach to teaching will need to change, too. Because of this, our approach to syllabus and task design changes through the levels of the course. All of the levels share the same basic design, but the approaches to the teaching of grammar and the assumptions about students' independence, for example, are not exactly the same from one level to the next.

The features of *Straightforward* that are common to all the levels include the following:
- All lessons include a balance of language learning and language using (language work and skills work).
- There is a stronger than usual focus on vocabulary development. This involves both the learning of words and phrases and attention to how these items are used (i.e. the grammar of vocabulary). For our research, we have used the same database as the *Macmillan English Dictionary*.
- The grammatical syllabus will be familiar but it is also contemporary, reflecting insights from the analysis of language corpora.
- Every unit (up to and including intermediate level) contains one lesson that focuses on functional or situational English.
- In every lesson, language is contextualized and presented in either a spoken or written text, and every lesson includes opportunities for either reading or listening. Word lists are provided at the end of every unit in the *Language reference* sections.

- There is a wide variety of types of text, both in terms of content and source (articles, newspaper cuttings, brochures, websites, emails, etc.). The topics are varied and the approaches to them are lively.
- Many of the texts focus on aspects of culture in the English-speaking world and encourage intercultural comparison. This work is reinforced by regular *Did you know?* sections that contain further cultural information.
- Every lesson contains opportunities for communicative practice. There are a wide variety of these speaking tasks, so that students have the opportunity to develop a range of communicative skills.

As teachers, we face many challenges in our working lives and finding the time for all that we have to do, let alone what we would like to do, is often difficult. *Straightforward* sets out to make life for teachers as easy as possible. Each lesson is presented on a double page in a clear, easy-to-use way, with each section labelled so that students know exactly what they should be focusing on. The exercises and activities are designed and written so that teachers may go into their classrooms with a minimum of preparation and come out at the end without having encountered any unpleasant surprises along the way. They do not need to spend valuable time figuring out in advance what a particular activity involves.

It would be wrong, however, to pretend that a coursebook can provide all of the answers all of the time. Particular students, particular classrooms and particular schools vary too greatly for it to be possible to provide one 'route map' that will be appropriate to everybody. For this reason, the *Straightforward Teacher's Book* provides a wealth of suggestions for ways of adapting, extending and abridging the material in the Student's Book. Even when things work very well, we still need to vary our approach from time to time so that we keep fresh, so that we keep experimenting and learning, and so that we continue to develop ourselves. So even though it won't matter if you forget to bring the Teacher's Book into class with you, I am sure that you will come to value the Teacher's Book highly as a tool for professional development.

Philip Kerr

The Common European Framework

The *Common European Framework of Reference for Languages: Learning, teaching, assessment* (CEF) of the Council of Europe is a long and commonly misunderstood document. The *Framework* is being used in many different ways in many different educational contexts around the world, but it was never intended to tell teachers what to do or how to do it. As the authors of the *Framework* point out, its objective is to raise questions, not to answer them. It is intended to describe, rather than to prescribe or proscribe. It is, in other words, exactly what it says:, and is a document for reference. It was devised and written so that users could adapt its scaling system and descriptors critically, adapting them to the needs of their own educational contexts. Indeed, it is such a long and unwieldy document that it would be impractical and unrealistic to attempt to apply it to any educational context without adaptation and modification.

The most well-known part of the Framework is the scale which describes a learner's language proficiency. There are six points on this scale (A1, A2, B1, B2, C1 and C2) and these range from a very low-level beginner to a very sophisticated language user with a level that is approximately equivalent to the Cambridge Proficiency examination, for example.

These levels do not correspond to years of language learning or academic study, nor are they intended to. The vast majority of learners never reach level C2 and they do not need to either, whether it is for work or examination purposes. This majority can expect to reach the fourth or the fifth level (B2 or C1), but it will typically take them more than four (or five) years of school study to get there. What is more, progress in language learning does not proceed in an orderly, predictable year-by-year fashion: improvements will be more marked at some stages of learning than at others. For these reasons, it is not possible or desirable for a coursebook (which represents a year's study in most educational contexts) to correspond exactly to the Council of Europe's levels – whatever some books may claim to the contrary! Having said that, it is possible to establish broad equivalences between the levels of *Straightforward* and the Council of Europe levels.

Straightforward level	Council of Europe level
Beginner	A1
Elementary	A1 – A2
Pre Intermediate	A2 – B1
Intermediate	B1
Upper Intermediate	B2
Advanced	C1

The levels in the Council of Europe Framework are described in terms of competences – what learners *can do* with the language. These *can-do* statements are extremely useful in determining course objectives, and we kept these closely in mind when we planned and wrote *Straightforward*. There are, however, two important points to bear in mind. The *can-do* statements are too numerous and too detailed for a course to attempt to work towards all of them. Some selection and modification is necessary and inevitable. Secondly, the organization of the syllabus cannot only be informed by descriptions of what a student should be able to do. The *can-do* statements are intended to describe and help

in evaluation, not to determine the structure of a learning programme.

Although there can be no exact correspondence between the *can-do* lists and the organization of a coursebook, *Straightforward* reflects both the detail and the philosophy of the *Framework* in many ways. Here are a few examples:

- In line with the *Framework*, *Straightforward* takes an approach to language learning that balances the importance of knowing about the language with the need to do things with it.
- The functional/situational language lessons directly reflect the communicative needs that are outlined in the *Framework*.
- Grammar and vocabulary are always presented and practised in such a way that the communicative value of this language is transparent to the student.
- In line with the *Framework*, *Straightforward* gives much greater prominence to the development of speaking skills than it does to writing skills.
- Students are encouraged to develop their sub-skills and strategies in using the four language skills of reading, writing, speaking and listening in ways that also directly reflect the *can-do* statements in the *Framework*.
- Learning tasks that provide opportunities for students to practise the four skills, reflect the variety of text-types and interactions that are outlined in the *Framework*.

Besides the scales and the descriptions of competences, the *Framework* emphasizes the aims of language learning. Among these is the need to become independent and autonomous as a learner, and the recognition that language learning can encourage cooperation and other social values. Our approach in *Straightforward* to the development of autonomy is a gradual one and recognizes that, at lower levels especially, many students actually want or need to be dependent for a time. We believe that independence cannot be imposed on anyone: it must be acquired. However, from the very start, we encourage students to work cooperatively in pairs and groups. In our selection of topics, texts and tasks, we have attempted to promote a knowledge of other cultures, to encourage open-mindedness and to foster respect for others.

The complete text of the *Framework* is available in print in at least eighteen languages. It is also freely available online in English and a number of other languages. For further information, go to the Council of Europe's website at www.coe.int

Straightforward Elementary – a summary

Straightforward is a general English course aimed at adults and young adults. The Student's Book contains material for approximately 90 hours of classroom study. Extra material for practice, revision, homework and tests are found in the other components (see below).

Student's Book

There are twelve units in the Student's Book, each of which contains four lessons (A, B, C and D) and two pages of language reference. The lessons contain two pages each. Each double-page is designed for approximately 90 minutes of classroom study.

Each unit contains:
- two to three grammar sections
- two to four vocabulary sections
- one functional language section
- two pronunciation sections
- four to seven speaking skills sections
- two reading skills sections
- two listening skills sections
- one *Did you know?* section

In addition, there is one page of review exercises for each of the twelve units.

Scripts for all listening exercises are found at the end of the book.

Class CDs

The two CDs contain recordings of all the listening and pronunciation exercises in the Student's Book. The track listings are shown in the instructions for exercises in the Student's Book.

Workbook (includes audio CD)

For each lesson of two pages in the Student's Book, there is one page of exercises to provide further practice of the grammar, vocabulary and functional language.

The Workbook also contains supplementary reading material. There is a reading skills page for each of the twelve Student's Book units. There is also a Dr Jekyll and Mr Hyde short story at the back of the book which provides an opportunity for extensive reading skills practice.

The *Straightforward* writing course consists of twelve double-page lessons, linked in topic to the Student's Book units and designed to develop students' abilities to deal with a variety of written genres.

The Workbook audio CD contains recordings of all the Workbook reading texts and most of the Student's Book reading texts. Students are encouraged to listen and read simultaneously. In the process, they gain self-confidence and develop their ability to tackle longer texts. Dictation exercises from the Workbook are also included on this CD.

The Workbook is available with or without the answer key.

Teacher's Book (includes two resource CDs)

The Teacher's Book provides step-by-step notes for each lesson. These include:
- short lesson summaries
- answers to all exercises and explanatory language notes
- suggestions for alternative procedures
- suggestions for supplementary activities and extra discussion questions
- advice for different class types (stronger/weaker students, older/younger students, etc.)
- supplementary cultural notes
- ideas for homework and further study
- model answers for the writing tasks in the workbook

The Teacher's Book also includes one photocopiable worksheet for each of the 48 lessons (including six songs). These provide further communicative practice of the language from the lesson.

Throughout the Teacher's Book, there are short *Teaching One Step Beyond* sections. See below for further information.

The two resource CDs contain:
- twelve unit tests
- four progress tests
- twelve self-assessment checklists
- Council of Europe checklists
- recordings of the six songs
- listening material for the tests

The two resource CDs are at the back of the Teacher's Book. CD 1 contains the test and self-assessment checklists, both of which can be adapted and customized to suit teachers' particular needs. CD 2 contains the audio material for the tests and recordings of the six songs from the photocopiable worksheets.

There is a test for each of the twelve units in the Student's Book. These unit tests focus on the grammar, vocabulary and functional language that has been presented in the unit.

The four progress tests (after every three units) contain separate sections to test the four skills as well as a section that focuses on language.

CD 1 also includes twelve self-assessment checklists, one for each of the Student's Book units. After they have completed a unit, the students can use the checklist to assess themselves on how well they think they can do specific actions in English.

Grammar

The approach to the presentation of grammar in *Straightforward* varies, depending on a number of factors. Generally speaking, students are shown the grammatical rules and patterns before being asked to practise them. However, when the language can be considered to be 'revision', rather than 'new', a guided discovery approach is taken. Sometimes, these approaches are combined when a grammar section contains both 'revision' and 'new' language. The teacher's book contains suggestions for alternative approaches.

At the start of many units, the Teacher's Book suggests some optional *Test before you teach* tasks. Although it may feel strange to set tasks that are specifically designed to allow students to use language items that will only be presented later in the coursebook unit, these tasks have two main purposes. Firstly, they are diagnostic: they allow you to get an idea of how much the students can do with the items you plan to teach. This may lead you to change what you do later in some ways. Secondly, they are motivational: they help students to realize for themselves what they can or can't do. They will help students to see the purpose of the language items when they come to study them.

Every lesson with a grammar focus includes a reference box, which shows the basic rules and patterns. More detailed explanations can be found in the *Language reference* pages at the end of each unit. The teacher's book contains further useful language notes for the teacher.

A sequence of grammar practice exercises always follows the presentation. These include mechanical manipulation of grammatical forms and patterns, as well as more communicative practice. There are plenty of opportunities for students to personalize their use of this language. Many teachers will want to provide further practice. This can be found in the review pages, in the corresponding pages of the workbook and in the suggestions and photocopiable pages in the teacher's book.

Vocabulary

We believe that vocabulary development is probably the most important task that language learners face, and, for this reason, there are more vocabulary sections in *Straightforward* than in most other coursebooks.

In *Straightforward Elementary* much of the vocabulary presented is topic-based, i.e. a set of words or phrases around a certain theme, e.g. food, clothes, furniture, etc. There are also awareness raising activities about lexical features such as collocation, verb patterns, key verbs, etc.

In the same way that students are always asked to do something with the grammar that they have studied, vocabulary sections always include exercises that require students to use the new words. New vocabulary items are also recycled in texts, other exercises and in the Workbook material.

In the *Language reference* sections at the end of each unit, you will find a word list that contains the vocabulary items that have appeared in the unit. A simple coding system indicates how common, and therefore how useful to learn, the words are. Both students and teachers will find the word lists useful for revision purposes.

Functional/situational language

Each unit of *Straightforward Elementary* contains one lesson that concentrates on situational or functional language. The lessons that focus on situational language provide students with the language that they need to cope with common, everyday situations in an English-speaking environment – what is sometimes called survival English. The lessons that focus on functional language provide students with the language that they need for basic communicative purposes – making requests or offers, for example.

This language is presented through dialogues and the students are helped towards producing similar dialogues of their own. You will see that a small group of characters appear in all of these dialogues, and the relationships between these characters develop as the course progresses. The story of these characters, however, is episodic, so that it does not matter if you choose to deal with the language in one of these lessons in a different way. These lessons do not depend on the students knowing what happened to the characters in previous lessons. In the lesson notes of the Teacher's Book there are summaries of the situations in each lesson.

Pronunciation

Each unit of *Straightforward Elementary* contains two pronunciation sections. There is no general agreement in the world of English language teaching about the best order in which to teach the various features of English pronunciation, and we cannot expect students to become perfect overnight. The primary aim, therefore, of these sections is to raise students' awareness of pronunciation and to give them some opportunities to produce English sounds, stress and intonation patterns.

In addition to the time that is spent on pronunciation work in these sections, many teachers will want to integrate work on pronunciation at other times during the course. The Teacher's Book offers many suggestions for how to go about this.

Reading and listening

Language is best understood when it is seen or heard in context and every lesson in *Straightforward* contains either a reading or a listening text. The tasks that accompany these texts encourage students to get to grips with the meaning of the text before they focus on the details of the language that the texts contain. In their mother tongue, students use a range of strategies and techniques when reading or listening, and the tasks in *Straightforward* are intended to encourage students to transfer these strategies and techniques to English.

The tasks are designed so that they can be achieved without the students understanding every word of what they read or hear. It is important that students learn to tolerate not understanding everything they come across.

Scripts for the listening texts can be found at the back of the book, and these can be used to direct the students' attention to particular language items once the sequence of comprehension tasks has been completed. The scripts will also be useful in some mixed ability classes and with students with very little confidence. But, as far as possible, students should be encouraged to approach the listening exercises without referring to the written version.

Speaking

A language is learnt, at least in part, through the student's attempts to use it. When students attempt to communicate meanings in English, they have the chance to practise what they have learnt and to experiment with what they have not learnt (or only partially learnt). The many speaking sections in *Straightforward* are intended to provide opportunities for students to do both these things.

We know from research that different kinds of speaking tasks make different requirements on the learners. So it is important that students are given a variety of speaking tasks in order to be challenged in different ways. Some tasks encourage students to work together towards finding a solution to a problem (convergent tasks), others allow for a greater divergence of views and opinions and do not have any fixed 'end point'. Some tasks require students to say quite a lot in one go (extended turns), others require more frequent shorter turns in dialogues and conversations. Some tasks require students to work in groups, some in pairs, and some to make individual presentations. In order to provide opportunities for this variety, *Straightforward* contains a great variety of task types: discussing and arguing, brainstorming and putting things in order, telling stories and personal anecdotes, describing and evaluating, roleplays and conversations, solving problems, etc.

Writing

Students benefit from written consolidation and practice of the language that they have studied, but they also need to develop their ability to communicate in English in written form. The writing syllabus for *Straightforward Elementary* is in the Workbook and consists of twelve double-paged lessons. These relate in topic to the twelve units of the Student's Book. These lessons can be used either in the classroom or for self-study.

Each lesson focuses on one written genre (e.g. a phone message, an invitation, a card for a special occasion, a letter of application, a discursive composition).

The writing lessons begin by showing students a model of a particular genre. Before producing a similar piece of writing, the students will look at a range of features of written English: paragraph organization, linkers and clause structure, spelling, etc. In addition, there is a bank of useful phrases for written English at the back of the book. The Teacher's Book contains model answers for each of the tasks that the students do at the end of each writing lesson.

Did you know?

Every lesson contains one *Did you know?* section. These are short texts that contain cultural information about the English-speaking world. Besides being informative and interesting, these sections are designed to encourage cross-cultural comparison and to provide further opportunities for speaking.

Further study

(including homework, web research, extensive reading)

It would be wonderful if we could reach a high level of language proficiency just by attending a few hours of lessons every week. Sadly, this is not the case and our students must be encouraged to do everything possible to extend their learning opportunities outside the classroom.

The Workbook provides further practice of language that has been presented in the lessons and, although this can be used in the classroom, many teachers will prefer to set this as homework.

It is well known that regular extensive reading is also of enormous help. The Workbook contains a Dr Jekyll and Mr Hyde short story that can be used for this purpose, but the students who make the fastest progress will be those who use their own initiative to find and read material that interests them.

For many students nowadays, the easiest and cheapest source of material is online. The Teacher's Book contains *Web research tasks* that will encourage students to become more autonomous in their learning. It suggests particular words and word combinations that are appropriate for web searches, and students can do these individually, in pairs or in small groups. One way of organizing these activities is by giving students a time limit (e.g. ten minutes), during which they have to find out as much as possible about a particular topic. They then share the information they have gathered in this way (they could also be asked to write short reports as a follow-up).

Methodology guidelines

Methodology guidelines: Discussion starters

Many units of this teachers' book include a number of suggestions for 'discussion starters'. These usually take the form of questions intended to get students to start thinking and talking, often at the start of a new lesson, when a new topic or theme is being introduced. This section suggests a range of possible ideas for using these in class.

N.B. There are often a lot of ideas for discussion starters in the units. Remember that you are definitely not intended to use them all! The idea is to offer you a range of possible ideas – so that you can pick ones that you like or which might appeal to your class.

Typical use: working in 'whole-class' mode.
Ask the questions randomly around the class.
Make sure you pay more attention to the meaning of what students say rather than focusing too much on accuracy. Respond to the ideas and views students state. As far as possible, turn it into a conversation. Get them interested and involved.
Encourage students to listen to each other and respond to each other – rather than having all interaction going via you. A few don'ts: avoid asking questions routinely person by person round the class (predictable and dull); avoid constant correction (students may say less in an attempt to avoid error); avoid letting one or two strong students dominate to the exclusion of most others.
Try to give all students a chance to speak. If a loud student talks over a quieter one, try not looking at and not hearing the loud one and wait patiently for the quieter one to have their say.

Other ideas
Pairs/groups: Choose one question or statement that you think is particularly interesting. Write it on the board. Put students into pairs or small groups to say what they think about it. After a few minutes a spokesperson from each pair/group reports back to the whole room.
Starting with individuals: choose a number of the questions and write them on the board (or prepare handouts with them printed on). Ask students to work on their own and write two or three sentence in response to each question/statement. After sufficient thinking and writing time, gather students together in small groups to compare.

Notes
Discussion starters are typically intended to be used in fairly short stages of the lesson. They are mainly for leading into other more substantial later stages. However, occasionally you may find that a topic really takes off and is itself stimulating to students. Symptoms will be lots of argument and discussion and a real enthusiasm on students' part for stating their views. In such cases you may want to avoid cutting an exciting activity off in its prime, so it's often a good idea to allow an extended time for the stage.
You can often seamlessly segue (i.e. link smoothly) from the discussion starters directly into the activity, text or exercise following.

Methodology guidelines: Test before you teach

At the start of many units, the Teacher's Book suggests some optional *Test before you teach* tasks. Although it may feel strange to set tasks that are specifically designed to allow students to use language items that will only be taught later in the coursebook unit, these tasks have a number of purposes. Firstly, they are diagnostic, i.e. they allow you to get an idea of how much the students can do with the items you plan to teach. This may lead you to change what you do later in some ways. For example, if you realize that students know a lot about one aspect but little about another, you might decide to plan a lesson that spends more time on the latter. Secondly, they are motivational, i.e. they help students to realize for themselves what they can or can't do. By asking students to do a task which they perhaps can't yet achieve with full success, they may realize that there is some language that they don't yet have full command of. This may help them to see the purpose of the language items when they come to study them.

Methodology guidelines: Web research tasks

This Teacher's book includes many ideas for extension tasks using the internet. They are presented in the following way: (1) a *Web research task* (2) A list of *Web search key words*

All web tasks provide work on relevant reading skills work. This is true not only of the final web pages students find, but (because web search engines may find thousands of results) students also have to quickly scan read the summaries in order to select the most relevant for their needs.

Web research tasks may also lead to a lot of speaking and negotiation between students working together.

Setting up Web research tasks

To allow all students to work simultaneously, you will ideally need to have enough internet-connected computers so that a maximum of three students work per computer. If this is not possible, you will need to allow some students to work on the task while others do other work, e.g. allowing a six-minute time slot at the computer for each pair of students.

Running Web research tasks

The tasks all involve students using the internet to find information, pictures, ideas, etc. These will not work if students are not familiar with basic web protocols. Although many students nowadays are very computer literate, you may need to teach:

- How to use a search engine such as Google, e.g. remember to put multi-word items inside quotation marks, e.g. *"Great Barrier Reef"* not *Great Barrier Reef*
- The tasks usually give suggestions of useful *web search key words*. We have given these (rather than actual internet addresses) because web addresses tend to change suddenly, whereas these search words are likely to produce good results at any time.
- How to use *hot-links* between pages (often underlined items) – and how to get back to where they started from
- How to store or print favourite pages.

With all the *Web research tasks* it may be important to emphasize that students are trying to catch specific answers to tasks. It's very easy to get distracted and diverted on the net and just start browsing. If this is a problem with your students, set tight time limits to find answers. For many web tasks in this book, six to ten minutes should be enough to find a useful amount of information.

Methodology guidelines: Grammar boxes

In every lesson of the Students' Book in which new grammar or functional language is introduced you will find a Grammar box. These boxes summarize information about the new language being studied. In most cases, no methodological instructions or exercises are offered, so the teacher has many options about how to use them. This section suggests a number of typical ideas for using these as well as a few more unusual possibilities. In every case you can mix and match ideas to suit your class.

- Ask students to quietly read through the information to themselves.
- Ask one or two students to read the information aloud to the rest of the class.
- Ask students to work in pairs and read the information aloud to each other.
- Ask students to work in pairs, read and then discuss or ask each other questions about the contents.
- The teacher reads aloud the information to the class.
- The teacher allows quiet reading time and then asks questions based on the material in the box.
- The teacher uses material in the substitution tables (which feature in many of the Grammar boxes) to give students simple repetition or substitution drills.
- Ask students in pairs to drill each other.
- Books closed: before students look at the Grammar box, read it aloud to them. At various key points, pause and elicit what the next word or words might be. Clearly confirm right answers. When you have finished, allow students to open books and read the information through quietly.
- Books closed: write the information from the Grammar box on the board, trying to keep the same layout as the book. Leave gaps at key places. Ask students to either copy the diagram and fill it in, or come to the board and fill in the information there. Allow students to discuss the suggested answers before they check with the printed version.
- Books closed: use the information in the Grammar box to inform your own question-making. Elicit the information item by item, example by example, from students and note it on the board. When the information is complete, allow students to open their books and find the same content printed there.

Methodology guidelines: Key methodology

You will find *Key methodology* sections throughout this Teacher's book. They introduce you to a number of essential teaching techniques and give practical, immediately usable ideas that you can try out in class to extend the range of your teaching. These sections aim to be both informative and inspiring. They can help you find new ways to really exploit material and get the most out of your learners.

Basics 1

WHAT THE LESSON IS ABOUT

Theme	Learning the basics
Vocabulary	International English; Numbers 1–10;
Functional	Introductions 1 & 2: introducing yourself
language	Alphabet

IF YOU WANT A LEAD-IN …

Test before you teach: international English

◗ *Methodology guidelines: Test before you teach, page xiii*

- Find out how many words students already know in English. Put students in pairs and ask them to write ten words they know in English. Elicit their words and write them on the board.
- This is a confidence-building exercise. It aims to show students that they actually already know lots of English words as well as allowing you to find out what your students already know.

▣ Key Methodology 1
▣ Elementary learners 1: language levels

- *If this is your first time teaching this level, you may be wondering what elementary level students look like and how to deal with them.*
- *The first thing to note is that* Elementary *is quite a broad description. It's useful as a general way of referring to a group of people and their course, but it's important to understand that this shorthand also covers up as much as it reveals.*
- *Every class, whatever its name, is a mixed-level class. Students will know different things and be good at doing different things. This is true even if students are at the same school and have studied all their English together. This should remind us as teachers that, even though it is a comforting simplification to visualize the class as a single entity, it is always mainly a group of individuals – who need different kinds of input, practice and help.*
- *But for the moment, to keep with the generalization, an average elementary learner is one who has made that big step forward from knowing little or nothing about a language to one who is able to do quite a number of basic things. We could say that they have a survival level, i.e. if thrown in the deep end, they could ask questions, state problems, etc. and usually get their message across, though with many mistakes and misunderstandings. In other words, they have just enough to get by.*
- *For a detailed look at what an elementary learner might be able to do, see the description given as part of the* Common European Framework on page ix or on the Council of Europe *Website at* www.coe.int.

INTERNATIONAL ENGLISH

◗ *Language reference, Student's Book page 11*

1
- Ask students to look at the international English words and tick the ones that they know.

Extra task
- If you have a monolingual class, you could add to this list by using mime or pictures to elicit other English words that you know the students will be familiar with.

2 **1.1**
- Play the recording. Students listen and point to the words they hear.

```
 1 – E  bus
 2 – C  taxi
 3 – A  hotel
 4 – F  hospital
 5 – D  police
 6 – B  tea
 7 – B  coffee
 8 – B  pizza
 9 – H  airport
10 – E  football
```

◉ **1.1**

```
 1  Oh no, the bus! The bus!
 2  Taxi! Taxi! TAXI!
 3  'The hotel.'
 4  Two units to the hospital. To the hospital.
 5  I say, stop! Police! Police!
 6  A: Tea?
    B: Ooohh, yeah.
 7  Ahh. Coffee.
 8  A: Pizza?
    B: Yeah. A pizza. OK.
 9  A: The airport, Charles.
    B: Yes, sir.
10  Yeah. I love football.
```

3 ◉ **1.2**
- Play the recording for students to listen and repeat.

◉ **1.2**

```
bus
taxi
hotel
hospital
football
airport
pizza
coffee
police
tea
```

NUMBERS 1–10

❯ *Language reference, Student's Book page 11*

1 & 2 1.3

- Play the recording. Students read and listen to the numbers.
- Play the recording again. Students listen and repeat.
- Ask students to listen and repeat after you model each number, so that by watching how you form the words, they can copy the way you move your mouth to make the words.

🔘 1.3

1, 2, 3, 4, 5, 6, 7, 8, 9, 10

Language notes: pronunciation /θ/, /f/ & /v/

- Some students may find it difficult to produce the /θ/ sound in three, and the /f/ and /v/ sounds in four, five and seven.
- Show the way the tongue goes past the teeth when making /θ/, and the lower lip is slightly bitten when making /f/ and /v/.

3 🔘 1.4

- Play the recording. Students listen and write the numbers they hear. They can compare their answers with a partner. Then write the correct numbers in order on the board.

See tapescript below for answers.

🔘 1.4

4, 8, 9, 6, 3, 7

4

❯ *Communication activities, Student's Book page 137*

- Pairwork. Put students in A and B pairs and ask them to turn to page 137 at the back of the Student's Book.
- Model the activity by saying a number. Tell students to point to the correct number. Then say two or three more numbers.
- Students then take it in turns to say and point to numbers.

Extra task

- Dictate five sets of numbers to the students. For example:
  794823   794923
  785623   795723
  974843
- Let students check their numbers in pairs.
- Ask two students to come up to the board. Give them a marker pen or chalk. The rest of the class must read out the numbers in order, and they must write them on the board.
- Ask a few students in the class to read out a number. The other students must say which number they read. Or put students in pairs to read and say which number.

INTRODUCTIONS 1

1 & 2 🔘 1.5

- Ask students to look at the picture. Ask: *What does he say? What does she say?*
- Play the recording. Ask students to read and listen to the dialogue.
- Play the recording again and pause after each line for students to listen and repeat, both chorally and individually.

🔘 1.5

W = woman   F = Frank
W: Hello.
F: Hi.
W: What's your name?
F: My name's Frank.
W: Nice to meet you.
F: Nice to meet you.

3 🔘 1.6

- Ask students to look at the pictures. Ask: *What does he say?* for both pictures.
- Play the recording. Students match the dialogues to the pictures.

Picture A = Dialogue 1
Picture B = Dialogue 2

🔘 1.6

1   C = computer   A = astronaut
C: Hello.
A: Hi.
C: What's your name?
A: My name's John.
C: Nice to meet you, John.
A: Nice to meet you.
2   SC = ship's captain   C = castaway
SC: Hello.
C: Hello.
SC: What's your name?
C: My name's Robinson.
SC: Nice to meet you.
C: Nice to meet you.

4

- Walk round the class and say, *Hello … What's your name? … Nice to meet you.* Try to sound positive and exaggerate your intonation pattern. Shake hands with students or wave at them as you walk round. Encourage students to respond. Eventually, most of the class should be responding to what you say.
- Put students in pairs to say *hello* and practise the dialogue.
- Tell all the students to stand up and walk round, practising the dialogue with as many people as they can in the class.

ALPHABET

❯ *Language reference, Student's Book page 10*
❯ *Key Methodology 28: Pronunciation – phonemes, page 124*

1 & 2 1.7

- Play the recording. Students read and listen to the alphabet.
- Then play the recording again for students to listen and repeat.

🔘 1.7

A B C D E F G H I J K L M N O P Q R S T U V W X Y Z

Language notes
- Some of these letters are difficult to say. Notably G /dʒiː/, J /dʒeɪ/ and Q /kjuː/. Write the phonemic script on the board to show that these sounds are made by combining consonant sounds.
- Note also the pronunciation of W: double /juː/.
- N.B. Z is pronounced /zed/ in British English, but /ziː/ in American English.

3 💿 1.8
- Ask students to look at the first circle. Play the recording. Students listen to the sound and the letters, and point to them as they listen. Then play the rest of the recording. Students listen and point at the letters in each circle.

💿 1.8

/eɪ/	A, H, J
/iː/	B, C, D, E, G, P
/e/	F, L, M, N, S
/aɪ/	I
/əʊ/	O
/ɑː/	R

Alternative procedure
- You could also write the letters on the board (in circles) before doing this exercise. Then you can point to them as you play the recording.

Language notes
- The letters have been divided into sound groups according to phonemic script.

4 & 5 💿 1.9
- Students add letters from the box to the correct circles in exercise 3. They can then compare their answers with a partner.
- Play the recording. Students listen and check. If you wrote the letters in circles on the board, then add to them.
- Finally, play the recording again for students to listen and repeat.

/eɪ/	/iː/	/e/
A, H, J, K	B, C, D, E, G, P T, V	F, L, M, N, S X, Z

/aɪ/	/əʊ/	/ɑː/	/uː/
I, Y	O	R	Q, U, W

💿 1.9

/eɪ/	A, H, J, K
/iː/	B, C, D, E, G, P, T, V
/e/	F, L, M, N, S, X, Z
/aɪ/	I, Y
/əʊ/	O
/ɑː/	R

6 💿 1.10
- Play the recording. Students listen and write the letters they hear. They can check their answers with a partner.
- Play the recording again. Write the answers on the board as you listen.

See tapescript below for answers.

💿 1.10

1	CNN
2	BBC
3	USA
4	DVD
5	CD

INTRODUCTIONS 2

1 & 2 💿 1.11
- Point to the photo and ask: *What do they say?* Elicit ideas.
- Students put the lines of the dialogue in the correct order. Allow them to compare their answers with a partner.
- Play the recording. Students listen and check.
- Play the recording again. Pause after each line for students to repeat.

2, 5, 4, 3, 1

💿 1.11

L = Lindsay K = Katy
L: Hello.
K: Hi. My name's Katy. What's your name?
L: My name's Lindsay.
K: Oh. How do you spell that?
L: L-I-N-D-S-A-Y.

Extra task
- Tell the left hand side of the class they are Katy. The right hand side are Lindsay. Gesture to the right and say *hello*. They repeat. Then gesture to the left, and say the next line of the dialogue. And so on. Then do it again, but this time just gesture – the class must remember and say the dialogue. Do this until the class have memorized the whole dialogue.

3
- Groupwork. Put students in groups of four. Model the task with a strong student. Students take it in turns to ask each other to spell their names.
- You could do this as a class mingle – if your class isn't too big. That way students get to walk round and meet students they don't often talk to.
- Managing a mingle is straightforward. First, ask all the students to stand up, and make sure there is a clear space for students to circulate, (perhaps by moving some desks and chairs). Tell students to talk to at least five people they don't know very well. Give a five-minute time limit. Circulate and join in with the class.

Extra task
- Ask students to stand up and spell out their name. The rest of the class must listen and write it down. Then ask a confident student to come to the board and write it down. Check whether it is right with the first student.

Stronger classes
- Tell students to imagine they are a famous person. They must ask and answer the questions, and spell out the name of their character.

Key Methodology 2
Elementary learners 2: students in class

- In Key Methodology 1, we looked at the language level of elementary learners. But what does this mean for the teacher in the classroom? It suggests that you can speak entirely in English to the class (and it's probably best if you do), but you need to grade your language – which means that you generally avoid vocabulary that you think is too far above the learners' current level. Also be careful about using complex grammar. Keep sentences relatively short. But note that grading your language doesn't mean babytalk. Everything you say needs to be real English, said with natural rhythm and normal connected speech features. If you slow down the speed of your delivery, make sure you retain these natural features.

- The students are learning to communicate in their new language. They will make lots of mistakes. Make sure that you don't kill their self-confidence by constantly correcting every error. Remember that successful communication is just as important a goal as accurate use of grammar.

- The students will not learn things on a single meeting. Don't get discouraged if you have a great lesson and you think they've really learnt something – but next time they come, there's no sign of the item ever having been taught. This is absolutely normal. It's not you or your teaching. The process of learning is quite slow and untidy!

- The students are more than just a language level. Although they can only communicate in a limited way in English, they still have all their adult (or adolescent) intelligence, skills and interests. It's sometimes easy to forget this and falsely equate a low language level with limited other abilities or childlike interests. Keep alert to the people trying to use the language. As far as possible, empathize with their successes and frustrations when trying to say what they want to, though they don't yet have all the language they need.

  ❯ Key Methodology 7: Accurate speaking and fluent speaking, page 21.

IF YOU WANT SOMETHING EXTRA …

❯ Photocopiable activity, page 188
❯ Teacher's notes, page 171

Basics 2

WHAT THE LESSON IS ABOUT

Theme	Learning the basics
Vocabulary	Days of the week; Colours; Numbers 11–100; Things around you
Grammar	*A/an*; Plurals
Functional language	Classroom English 1 & 2: asking questions in class

IF YOU WANT A LEAD-IN ...

Test before you teach: basic vocabulary

> *Methodology guidelines: Test before you teach, page xiii*

- Draw simple pictures of the 10 to 15 objects you think students might know on an OHT; e.g. a key; a sandwich; a mobile phone; a TV; an apple; an orange; a pen; a pencil; a pizza; a cup; a glass; a book; a CD.
- Tell students they have one minute to look at and remember the objects.
- Remove the OHT. Students must write down all the words they remember. Find out who has the most words.

■ **Key Methodology 3**
■ **Classroom English: teacher language**

- *It can be hard to get some instructions across at elementary level, and you may feel that using the students' mother tongue will save time and stress. That's fine occasionally, but if you mainly use the students' own language to instruct or explain, the students are missing out on their most important source of exposure to English.*
- *Students can learn most instructions quite quickly. If they don't understand 'Get into pairs' the first time, they will after three or four times. If you're nervous about using only English, try saying the instruction in English – and then after a second or two repeating it a little more quietly in your students' language. After a few times, drop the translation and simply say the English version on its own.*
- *Here are a few common wordings for typical classroom instructions:*

  Basic instructions
  Turn to page 27.
  Look at exercise 3 in the Students' book.
  Look at the picture at the top of the page.
  Don't start yet.
  Read the instructions carefully.
  Read the text.
  Do exercise 4.
  Write your answers.
  Don't write your answers – tell your partner.
  Listen and answer the questions.
  If you've finished, do exercise 5.
  If you've finished, check your answers on page 45.
  If you've finished, wait quietly until everyone has finished.
  30 seconds!
  Please stop now!
  Close your books now, please.

Groupings
Get into pairs.
In your pair, one of you is the customer. One of you is the shop assistant.
In your pair, decide who is 'A' and who is 'B'.
Talk to your partner.
Don't show your picture/text to your partner.
Change places. Find a new partner to work with.
Work in a group with two other people.
Stand up. Walk around and meet a new partner.

Questions after a task
What's the answer to question 7?
What do you think?
Do you agree with her?
Which answer is correct?
Does anyone have a problem?

Language focus
How do you say this word?
What word is missing in this sentence?
Where's the stress?
Can you translate this sentence into your language?
Look it up in your dictionary.

Keeping order
Sshhh!
Listen!
Please stop talking now.
Don't shout. Talk quietly please.

CLASSROOM ENGLISH 1

> *Language reference, Student's Book page 11*

1
- Students match the pictures to the verbs in the box.
- In feedback, point to the picture, say the verb, and ask students to repeat.

A	listen to	E	read
B	open	F	write
C	close	G	look at
D	talk		

2 & 3 ◉ 1.12
- Students listen to the recording and then complete the phrases with the verbs from the box in exercise 1. They can then compare their answers with a partner.
- Play the recording again. Students listen and check their answers.
- You could play the recording one more time for students to listen and repeat.

1	Open	5	Look at
2	Close	6	Read
3	Write	7	Listen to
4	Talk		

🔘 **1.12**

1	OK, <u>open your books.</u> Open your books!
2	Now, <u>close your books.</u> Yes, close your books.
3	So, <u>write the words.</u> That's right. Write the words. Good.
4	Not me. <u>Talk to a partner.</u> Talk to a partner.
5	Now … <u>look at the picture.</u> I know, I know …
6	<u>Read the text.</u> Read the text.
7	<u>Listen to the CD.</u> Listen – to – the – CD!

Extra task: mime game

- Mime the instructions in exercise 2, e.g. mime *Open your books* by opening an imaginary book. Students copy your mime. Then give the instruction for each activity followed by the mime. The students must again copy the mime. Finally, give instructions (at random). The students must do the correct mime to each instruction.
- In pairs, students take it in turns to give an instruction. Their partner must mime the instruction correctly.

COLOURS

🔵 *Language reference, Student's Book page 11*

1
- Students match the words in the box to the colours. They can compare their answers with a partner before you check with the whole class.

1	red	5	brown
2	green	6	white
3	yellow	7	black
4	blue		

2 🔘 1.13
- Play the recording for students to listen and repeat.

🔘 **1.13**

red   green   yellow   blue   brown   white   black

DAYS OF THE WEEK

🔵 *Language reference, Student's Book page 11*

1 🔘 1.14
- Copy the abbreviated days of the week onto the board in a column. Point to a few abbreviations, and say, *What day is it?* Test whether students can tell you the days.
- Play the recording. Students listen and complete the words. They can compare their answers with a partner.
- Play the recording again. Write the correct words on the board as you listen.

See tapescript below for answers.

🔘 **1.14**

Monday – M O N D A Y
Tuesday – T U E S D A Y
Wednesday – W E D N E S D A Y
Thursday – T H U R S D A Y
Friday – F R I D A Y
Saturday – S A T U R D A Y
Sunday – S U N D A Y

2 🔘 1.15
- Tell students to cover the words so that they are not reading as they listen. Play the recording. Students listen and repeat.
- N.B. it is important that students listen and repeat without looking at the words. This avoids errors like trying to pronounce the silent *d* in *Wednesday*.

🔘 **1.15**

Monday   Tuesday   Wednesday   Thursday   Friday   Saturday   Sunday

Language note

- Days of the week always start with a capital letter in English.
- Note the /tʃ/ sound in *Tuesday*, and the /θ/ sound in *Thursday*. For the latter, show that students must start with the tip of their tongue in front of their teeth when they say the word.

3 🔘 1.16
- Play the recording. Students listen to five conversations, and underline the day of the week they hear. They can compare their answers with a partner before you check with the whole class. N.B. Tell students to listen for the days of the week only, and not worry about understanding other words.

1	Monday	4	Saturday
2	Thursday	5	Friday
3	Saturday		

🔘 **1.16**

1
A: What day is it today?
B: It's <u>Monday</u>.
A: I thought so.
2
A: When is English class?
B: It's on <u>Thursday</u> this week.
A: OK.
3
A: Do you want to go out this Saturday?
B: *This* <u>Saturday</u>?
A: Yes.
4
A: So, what did you do last <u>Saturday</u>.
B: Nothing much. And you?
A: No. Nothing.
5
A: Hello, class. What day is it today?
B: It's <u>Friday</u>!
A: Yes, Friday.

Extra task

- Mime activities that are typical of certain days, e.g. praying, watching football, playing tennis, washing clothes, going to work on the tube (looking bored), dancing. Students must shout out which day of the week is being mimed.
- Put students in small groups to mime activities and guess the days.

NUMBERS 11–100

> *Language reference, Student's Book page 11*

1

- Students match the words to the numbers. They can check their answers with a partner.

eleven	11
twelve	12
thirteen	13
fourteen	14
fifteen	15
sixteen	16
seventeen	17
eighteen	18
nineteen	19
twenty	20

2 **1.17**

- Tell students to cover the words in exercise 1. Then play the recording for students to listen and repeat.

1.17

11 12 13 14 15 16 17 18 19 20

3

- Students write the numbers for the words. They can compare their answers with a partner before you check with the whole class.
- In feedback, ask students to listen and repeat the words after you.

forty-seven	47
fifty-nine	59
sixty-one	61
seventy-five	75
eighty-eight	88
ninety-one	91
one hundred	100

Extra task

- Write pairs of numbers on the board. For example:

13	30
46	36
70	17
14	15
95	99

- Read out one word in each pair. Students must listen and write the correct number.
- N.B. this is trickier than it looks for low level students.

Language notes

- Saying numbers is not easy, e.g. pronouncing /θ/ (as in *thirty-three*), and /f/ and /v/, as in (*fifty-four* and *seventy-seven*). Take time to model producing the /θ/ sound, (show students how to start with the tip of their tongue past their teeth), and the /f/ and /v/ sounds, (show students they must start by biting their bottom lip gently).
- Getting the stress correct is also important. With 'teen' numbers the stress is generally on the 'teen', (fif'teen). With 'ty' numbers, it's on an earlier syllable, ('fifty). It's important to model and practise this. Otherwise, students will have difficulty differentiating between these numbers.
- N.B. There will be more detailed work on word stress in lesson 2B.

Extra task: colours bingo

- Give students a blank piece of paper each, and ask them to divide it into two halves – a red half and a blue half. (You could ask them to colour in the two halves.) Tell students to write six different numbers from 11 to 20 in the red half, and six different numbers from 41 to 50 in the blue half. Go round the class and make sure everybody completes their cards correctly.
- Write 11, 12, 13, etc. up to 20 on the board in a line. Under it, do the same with numbers from 41 to 50.
- Then read out the numbers below. Mime for students to tick the number. Continue until someone shouts Bingo. Tell students to change their numbers and play the game two or three times.

Red 12	Blue 42	Red 18	Red 20
Blue 43	Blue 50	Red 13	Blue 46
Red 16	Red 15	Blue 42	Blue 47
Blue 45	Red 17	Blue 41	Red 19
Red 11	Blue 49	Blue 44	Blue 48

- You could extend this task by putting students in groups to play bingo. This time ask them to complete a green card with six numbers between 61 and 70, and a brown card with six numbers between 91 and 100. Again model it carefully, as above, and write the lists of numbers on the board.
- Put students in groups of five or six, and nominate a bingo caller. Students play bingo as before. By writing the numbers on the board, you (hopefully) avoid students repeating numbers or forgetting to say them.
- Monitor as they play, and correct pronunciation.

Cultural note

- Bingo is very popular in the UK. There are Bingo Halls in most British towns, and large numbers of people turn up to play for large cash prizes. Bingo callers read out the numbers very quickly, and use funny names for the numbers, e.g. '*legs*' 11, '*two fat ladies*' 88, and '*key to the door*' 21.

THINGS AROUND YOU

> *Language reference, Student's Book page 11*

1 **1.18**

- Ask students to look at the picture. Point to the different objects, and say: *What is it?* Find out which words students already know.
- Play the recording again. Students listen and repeat.

1.18

an ID card
an earring
an apple
coins
keys
photos
a pen
sweets

2 **1.19**

- Play the recording. Students read and listen to the words.
- Ask: *What things are in your classroom?* Tell students to put a tick or a cross.

1.19

> a TV
> a board
> a door
> a window
> a CD player

3 **1.20**

• Play the recording. Students listen to words from exercises 1 and 2. Tell students to point to the object on the page or in the class and say the word.

 1.20

> a board
> a door
> an ID card
> a window
> an earring
> an apple
> coins
> a CD player
> keys
> photos
> a pen
> sweets

4

• Model the activity by asking a confident student the questions first. Then put students in pairs to take it in turns to ask and answer.

Grammar: *a/an*, plurals

❯ *Language reference, Student's Book page 10*
❯ *Methodology guidelines: Grammar boxes, page xiii*

1

• Students follow the rules to make the words plural. Allow them to compare their answers with a partner. Then write the correct answers on the board.
• Model the pronunciation. In particular, point out the /ɪz/ sound in buses /bʌsɪz/.

> 1 wallets
> 2 buses
> 3 taxis
> 4 hotels
> 5 mobile phones
> 6 sandwiches

Language notes

• Nouns ending in *s*, *ss*, *sh* and *ch* add *-es* in the plural, e.g. *buses, sandwiches, churches*.
• Nouns ending in *y* become plural by changing *y* to *i* and adding *es*, (*lorry* ➤ *lorries*). That is, unless there is a vowel before the final *y*, (*key* ➤ *keys*; *toy* ➤ *toys*).
• Words ending in *o* vary: *photos, heroes*.
• Note also that some common nouns have irregular plurals: *man* ➤ *men*; *woman* ➤ *women*; *child* ➤ *children*; *person* ➤ *people*; *sheep* ➤ *sheep*. N.B. these irregular plurals will be taught later in the course.

2

• Students write *a*, *an* or *nothing*. Allow them to compare their answers with a partner. Then write the correct answers on the board.

1	<u>an</u> ID card	5	<u>an</u> airport
2	<u>a</u> bus	6	<u>a</u> key
3	– apples	7	– hotels
4	– taxis	8	a hospital

Language notes

• Note that *a* and *an* are pronounced with the weak-stressed schwa sound /ə/. And there is linking between *an* and the first letter of the noun, *an‿apple*. Actually, a more accurate rule here is that *a* is followed by a consonant sound, and *an* is followed by a vowel sound. So, we say, *a hospital* but *an honest man*. The silent *h* in *honest* means that the word begins with a vowel sound. Similarly, compare *an umbrella* and *a uniform*.

Stronger classes

• Play a memory chain game. Write on the board: *I've got … and …* Say: *I've got a key and an apple*. The next student says, *I've got a key, an apple and a mobile phone*. The next student says: *I've got a key, an apple, a mobile phone, and …* And so on. Nominate students round the class. See if they can remember all the words in the list and keep adding one.

Classroom english 2

1 **1.21**

• Play the recording. Students listen and complete the questions and sentences with a word from the box.
• Play the recording again. Students listen and repeat.
• If you have a monolingual class, translate the phrases.

1	mean	3	don't
2	say	4	don't

 1.21

> 1 What does *apple* mean?
> 2 How do you say *merci* in English?
> 3 I don't know.
> 4 I don't understand.

Alternative procedure for stronger classes

• You could let students look at the sentences and guess which words go where before they listen to the recording.

2

• Students look at the pictures on page 8 and 9 and model the activity.
• Pairwork. Tell students to work with a partner and ask questions.
• Here are a couple of ideas to remind students of useful classroom English during their lessons.
  1 It is a good idea to put useful classroom English on the wall – next to the board perhaps.
  2 Type the following on to paper, then laminate them or stick them on cardboard, and fix them to the walls:
    What does _____ mean?
    How do you say _____ in English?
    Can I say _____?
    I'm sorry, I don't understand.
    Could you repeat, please?

Key Methodology 4
Classroom English: student language

- *It's certainly worth teaching your students a small number of classroom sentences so that they can, for example, ask common questions correctly. Students will be able to use these throughout their years of English studies.*

Questions about language
What does miracle *mean?*
How do you say kifli *in English?*
How do you pronounce/say this word?
How do you spell coffee?
What's the difference between bread *and* loaf?
What's the past of go?

Requests for help
Could you help me please?
Could you repeat that please?
I don't understand.
Could you say that slowly please?
Am I pronouncing fussy *correctly?*
What's the right answer?

Announcing
I've finished. / We've finished. *
I / We got seven answers right.
I / We chose the third picture.
I / We think that …
I know.
I don't know.

Politeness
Sorry.
Thank you.

How could you teach these?
- *Pick out a few you think are particularly useful and do a short input and practice – just as if they were any other phrases.*
- *When someone uses any wrongly in class, clearly but unobtrusively repeat and correct it (without necessarily making the student repeat it). Keep a list of problem phrases and later teach a few together based on these actual problems.*
- *Write (or get students to write) a number of these phrases on a large poster clearly visible at the front of class. When a student says one wrongly, walk over to the poster and point to the correct one (you don't need to say anything!). After a few times of doing this, simply walking towards the poster should produce a reaction and instant self-correction!*

* *If you only teach one phrase, please make it this one! Otherswise, students go often on saying 'Finish' or 'I am finish', etc. through to Upper Intermediate level. Don't worry that they haven't studied the present perfect yet. Teach 'I've finished' as a fixed phrase – like a vocabulary item – without any further grammatical explanation – and think of it as a useful pre-exposure to the tense.*

IF YOU WANT SOMETHING EXTRA …

❯ *Photocopiable activity, pages 191 – 192*
❯ *Teacher's notes, page 171*

1A | The new person

WHAT THE LESSON IS ABOUT

Theme	Introducing yourself
Speaking	Guided conversation: introductions
Reading & listening	Conversations: the first day at a new job
Vocabulary	Objects 1
Grammar	Verb *to be* – affirmative; Possessive adjectives
Pronunciation	Contractions
Functional language	Survival English: saying hello & goodbye

IF YOU WANT A LEAD-IN ...

Test before you teach: introducing yourself

⊙ *Methodology guidelines: Test before you teach, page xiii*

- Write the following words and phrases at random all over the board:
  Hello.   Hi.   What's your name?   How do you spell that?
  My name's ...   Nice to meet you.   Bye.   See you later.
- Put students in pairs. Tell them to have a quick conversation using the words and phrases on the board. Model it if you have to.
- Ask students to change pairs and tell them to have a conversation with their new partner.

READING & LISTENING

The Reading and Listening text is about Alyssa, who has just started a new job and is meeting her colleagues in the office. The text presents common phrases for introducing yourself.

⊙ *Key Methodology 5: Dialogues 1, page 11*

1
- You could read the text aloud to the students while they listen and read.

2 & 3 **1.22**
- Tell students to look at the pictures. Ask: *Where is Alyssa? What does she say?* Point to various characters in the pictures and ask: *Where is he/she? What does he/she say?* Elicit as much as possible from the students.
- Students match the dialogues to the pictures. They can then compare their answers with a partner.
- Play the recording. Students listen and check their answers. Point to the correct pictures as students listen.

1 D	2 C	3 B	4 A

🔘 **1.22**

> **A = Alyssa C = Charles J = Julien E = Eric M = Margaret**
> **Ca = Carla**
> **1 Picture D**
> **A:** Hello.
> **C:** Good morning.
> **A:** My name's Alyssa.
> **C:** You're new. Hello, I'm Charles. I'm the manager.

> **2 Picture C**
> **C:** Good morning, Julian.
> **J:** Good morning, Charles.
> **C:** Julian, this is Alison. She's new.
> **J:** Nice to meet you, Alison.
> **A:** I'm not Alison.
> **J:** What?
> **A:** My name isn't Alison. It's Alyssa.
> **J:** Nice to meet you, Alyssa.
> **C:** Sorry.
> **3 Picture B**
> **E:** Alyssa!
> **A:** Hello, Eric!
> **E:** How are you?
> **A:** I'm fine, thanks. How are you?
> **E:** Fine. Good to see you. Goodbye.
> **A:** Yeah. Bye
> **4 Picture A**
> **M:** She's new.
> **C:** What's her name?
> **M:** Alyssa.
> **C:** Alyssa? How do you spell that?
> **M:** I don't know.

Alternative procedure with stronger classes

- With stronger classes, do the listening task before students read. Ask them to look at the pictures and guess what the people are saying. Then ask them to cover the written dialogues, and listen to each dialogue and match them to the pictures. Finally, let them read the dialogues to check.

Extra tasks

1
- You could set a true or false specific information task. Write the following statements on the board, and ask students to write *T* or *F* next to them as they listen.
  1 Alyssa is new. (T)
  2 Charles isn't the manager. (F)
  3 Charles says Good afternoon to Julian. (F)
  4 Eric is fine. (T)

2
- Divide the class into two halves. Point to the first dialogue. Tell the right half they are Alyssa. Tell the left half they are Charles. Play and pause each line of the dialogue. Students repeat, playing their roles. You could then ask them to repeat the dialogue, playing their roles, without listening to the recording or looking at the dialogue in their books.
- Do the same with the other dialogues. For dialogue 2, the right half will have to play both Charles and Alyssa.

4
- Pairwork. Put students in pairs to practise the dialogues. Let them read the dialogues first from the book and then ask them to cover the dialogues, look at the pictures, and practise from memory.
- At the end, ask different pairs to stand up and roleplay each dialogue for the class.

<table>
<tr><td>

Language note

- The dialogues use shortened forms or contractions (*I'm*, *isn't*, *don't*, etc.) from the outset, as this is natural English. This may confuse some students. It will be taught later in the *Grammar* section. However, if any student queries the use, a good way of simply showing what's going on is to hold up your forefinger and thumb, and say *I am*, then push them together and say *I'm*. This also serves as a useful correction technique if any student insists on separating the words.

</td><td>

VOCABULARY: objects 1

❯ *Language reference, Student's Book page 21*

1 🔘 **1.23**
- Play the recording. Students listen and repeat the words.

🔘 **1.23**

</td></tr>
</table>

▪ Key Methodology 5
▪ ▪ Dialogues 1

Reading dialogues aloud yourself

- *As an alternative way of introducing coursebook dialogues, rather than playing the recording, you might sometimes want to read one aloud yourself. This can have the advantage of making the conversation sound more live and immediate to students. You don't need to be a great actor to do this, but it will help if you can make some distinction between characters as you read. Easy ways to do this are:*

  1 *Change the place you stand for each character as you read it, e.g. move one step left or right for each character.*

  2 *Write the character names on the board. Use a pen to point to the character speaking. As each new person speaks, move the pen.*

  3 *Bring in large colourful photos of people's faces cut out from a magazine. Introduce them by holding each picture up one at a time and saying the name of a character in the dialogue. Stick them on the board. When you read the dialogue point at the appropriate character's picture.*

- *When you read a dialogue aloud, try to make sure that it sounds reasonably natural:*

  Don't slow down too much or over-pronounce.
  Don't decontract contracted words (e.g. don't say I am *instead of* I'm*).*
  Don't speak with flat intonation or without stresses.

Ways of working on dialogues after they have been studied

- *After doing all the coursebook exercises on a dialogue, you may decide that you would like to exploit the conversations a little more. Here are a few ideas:*

  1 *Books closed. Give students one minute to study and try to remember the dialogue.*

  2 *Pairwork. Students see how much of the dialogue they can remember and write down. Check with the book after finishing.*

  3 *Pairwork. Students look at the text and see if they can make a few changes to create a very similar – but slightly different – dialogue. Early on in the book, students can change small things such as people's names, place names, etc. Later on, after students have studied more language, they could be more adventurous in what they change.*

| a desk |
| a computer |
| a chair |
| a pen |
| a coffee |
| a piece of paper |
| a phone |
| a book |

2
- Ask students to look back at the picture on page 12 and find the words from exercise 1.
- You could play the recording again for students to listen, repeat, and point to the words in the picture.

3 🔘 **1.24**
- Play the recording. Students listen to Alyssa and Margaret, and tick the words from exercise 1 they hear. They can then compare their answers with a partner. You may need to play the recording a second time.

The following words should be ticked:
desk; computer; phone; paper

🔘 **1.24**

M = Margaret A = Alyssa
M: Hello.
A: Hi. My name's Alyssa.
M: Yes. I know. I'm Margaret.
A: Nice to meet you.
M: Umm. You're new, so I'll explain. This is our <u>desk</u>.
A: Great.
M: This is your <u>computer</u>.
A: Yes.
M: And this is my computer. Don't touch.
A: OK. I understand.
M: This is my <u>phone</u>. You don't have a phone.
A: And this?
M: Your paper. This is my <u>paper</u>. And this is my cup. And that's it.
A: OK. Thank you.

Alternative procedure for stronger students

- Before playing the recording in exercise 3, tell students to close their books. Tell them to draw a rectangle on a blank sheet of paper. This is a desk. Tell the class to listen to the recording and draw simple versions of the objects that Margaret says are on the desk.
- Let them compare answers with a partner before looking at the tapescript.

Extra task

- Ask students to tell you what objects they can see on their desk and in the classroom.

GRAMMAR: verb *to be*; possessive adjectives

❍ *Language reference, Student's Book page 20*
❍ *Methodology guidelines: Grammar boxes, page xiii*

1
- Students complete the sentences with *is/are/am*. They can compare their answers with a partner before you check with the whole class.
- In feedback, remind students that when we write, we often use long forms, but when we speak, we usually contract, e.g. *Her name is Alyssa* (written). *Her name's Alyssa* (spoken). This reminder will help students with exercise 2.

1	is	5	are
2	is	6	is
3	are	7	are
4	am	8	am

2
- Students say the sentences in exercise 1 with contractions. They can then write them down in their exercise books.

1	Her name isn't Alison.
2	Her name's Alyssa.
3	You're new.
4	I'm the manager.
5	They're in the office.
6	He's in the hotel.
7	Eric and Julian aren't managers.
8	I'm fine, thanks.

Language notes

- The verb *to be* is unique in English. That's why, at this level, it tends to be taught first in isolation. *Have* is its only rival.
- Here *to be* is a linking verb followed by an adjective or noun complement. It can, of course, also be used as an auxiliary verb in progressive and passive forms.
- *To be* changes its form depending on person, tense and aspect. Actually, this feels quite normal to most language learners, whose L1 probably has verbs that conjugate much more than English, but it does mean that students have a lot to learn and memorize.
- Note the following forms:

  I am …   *I'm …*
  He is/She is/It is …   *He's/She's/It's …*
  You/We/They are …   *You're/We're/They're …*

  I'm not …
  He/She/It isn't …
  You/We/they aren't

- Be aware that there is quite a lot of manipulation involved in these forms, e.g. *I'm* becomes *I'm not* in the negative, but *He's* becomes *He isn't*. (*He's not* and *You're not* are possible, but less commonly used, and usually only to emphasize *not*.)
- It may surprise students that English only has one *you*, whereas most languages have a singular and a plural *you*, (and a polite one, too, sometimes). So, *You're tall* may sound odd when referring to one person.
- Nouns in most languages have gender, so using *It* with everything except people will be a new idea.
- Some languages regularly miss out pronouns when the meaning is clear, so expect errors like, *Is tall*.

3
- Students underline the correct word in each sentence. Do the first as an example to get students started. They can compare their answers with a partner before you check with the whole class.

1	your	3	His	5	our
2	my	4	her	6	Her

Extra task
- Get students to write sentences about people and objects in the classroom and then read them out.

Language notes
- Notice the form and pronunciation of possessive adjectives:
  my /maɪ/   *your* /jɔː/   *his* /hɪs/   *her* /hɜː/   *its* /ɪts/
  our /aʊə/   *their* /ðɜː/
- Possessive adjectives go in front of nouns. As English nouns have no gender, the adjectives do not change because of this. This may be a revelation to students. Similarly, unlike many languages, possessive adjectives do not change their form according to whether the noun they describe is singular or plural. So, English uses *our book* and *our books*. Note that most languages would have two variations of *our* here. *Your* can describe singular and plural nouns.
- In terms of pronunciation, the long vowel sounds and diphthongs of *your* /jɔː/, *their* /ðɜː/, *we're* /wɪə/ and *our* /aʊe/ are challenging for students. Notice that *your* and *their* sound the same as *you're* and *they're*, which causes spelling errors among native speakers. To many language learners, *his* /hɪs/ and *he's* /hiːz/ sound the same, as do *our* /aʊə/ and *are* /ɑː/ – so you may need to practise these sounds.

SPEAKING

1
- Groupwork. Put students in groups of three (A, B and C). Hold up the page with the dialogue prompts, point to the first prompt, and say *Hello*. Point to the next, and say *Hello*. And so on until you think the students have got the idea.
- Students work in threes to write a dialogue from the prompts. Monitor and help.
- Then tell them to practise the dialogue.

2
- Students change roles and repeat the conversation. Tell them to practise without looking at what they have written.

Stronger classes
- Students should be able to improvize the conversation without the initial written preparation stage.

Extra task
- Make this a mingle. Put students in pairs. They must walk round the class, find another pair, and introduce themselves. They then move on to find another pair.

IF YOU WANT SOMETHING EXTRA …

❍ *Photocopiable activity, page 193*
❍ *Teaching notes, page 171*

1B | Personal profile

WHAT THE LESSON IS ABOUT

Theme	Asking for personal information
Speaking	Roleplay: making a phone call to a language school
Listening	A phone call to a language school
Vocabulary	Countries & nationalities
Grammar	Verb *to be* – negative & questions
Did you know?	*They aren't American!:* Hollywood stars from other countries

IF YOU WANT A LEAD-IN ...

Introducing the theme: asking for personal information

- Find three or four magazine pictures of well-known people and put them on the board. Ask: *What is his/her name? Where is he/she from? What's his/her nationality? What's his/her first language?* If you haven't got pictures, just write the names on the board.

Test before you teach: countries

❯ *Methodology guidelines: Test before you teach, page xiii*

- Write lots of 'products' on the board, e.g. *hamburgers, coffee, BMWs, Ipods, Gucci clothes, Dior perfume, vodka, Rolls Royce, whisky, tacos, salsa,* etc. Ask students: *Where's it from?*

VOCABULARY: countries & nationalities

❯ *Language reference, Student's Book page 21*

1

- Tell students to look at the flags. Read through the names of the countries to model the pronunciation. You could ask students to listen and repeat.
- Students find the correct flag or flags that go with each sentence.

1 I and D   2 E   3 B

2 & 3 💿 1.25

- Students write the nationalities for the countries in the correct column. They can compare their answers with a partner.
- Play the recording. Students listen and check their answers.
- You could either transfer this table (completed) on to an OHT to enable you to feedback on answers quickly and easily, or draw the table on the board and ask individual students to come up and write a nationality.
- It is a good idea to mark the stress on the words in the table. You could also put a schwa /ə/ symbol above weakly-pronounced syllables where appropriate.
- Play the recording again. Students listen and repeat.

-(i)an	-ish	-ese	other
□ *Russian*	□ *British*	□ *Chinese*	*Greek*
/ə/□ Brazilian	□ Polish	□ Japanese	French
□ German	□ Turkish		
Italian	Irish		

💿 1.25

Russian
Brazilian
German
Italian
British
Polish
Turkish
Irish
Chinese
Japanese
Greek
French

Language note

- English uses capitals with countries and nationalities.
- Note the strong stress, and, in particular, the weak-stressed schwa (/ə/) sounds in the names of the countries:

/ə/□ Brazil	□/ə/ Italy	□ France	□ Russia
□ /ə/ China	/ə/ □ Japan	□/ə/ Poland	□ Turkey
□ /ə/ Britain	/ə/ □ /ə/ Argentina	□ Greece	

- Note the shifting stress with some words:
  Italy ➝ It□alian; Ch□ina ➝ Chin□ese, Japan ➝ Japan□ese.
- N.B. There will be more work on word stress in lesson 2B.

Cultural note

- Students are sometimes confused between *Britain* and *England*, particularly if their L1 does not differentiate.
- Britain or Great Britain describes the island, which comprises the three countries of England, Scotland and Wales. So, if you come from London, you are English and British, but if you come from Edinburgh, you are Scottish and British, but definitely not English!
- The full, official name of the country is the United Kingdom of Great Britain and Northern Ireland. Hence, UK. The Republic of Ireland (or Eire) is a separate country.
- N.B. People from Wales are Welsh and British.

4

- You could put students in pairs to describe the other flags in the picture, using the nationality words from exercise 1.

A – The Brazilian flag is green, yellow, blue and white.
C – The French flag is blue, white and red.
F, G, H – The Japanese, Polish and Turkish flags are white and red.
J – The Greek flag is blue and white.

5

- Model the questions with a student. You could briefly drill the two questions round the class to make sure students can pronounce them appropriately.
- Pairwork. Put students in pairs to practise the dialogue.

Multilingual classes

- If you have a range of nationalities in your class, you could extend this into an interesting, 'finding out' exercise.
- Make sure everybody knows how to form and pronounce their country and nationality. Then put students in groups of five or six to ask and answer the questions from exercise 5. You could do this as a class mingle.
- In feedback, ask individuals to try to remember where different students come from.

LISTENING

In this listening, a receptionist, who works for the company Language Link, takes down information on the phone from a language student, so that Language link can put this person in touch with other students who are studying the same language as him.

1

- Students read the advertisement, and answer the gist question.

Language Link is a website where you can practise your English (or other languages) with other students.

2 **1.26**

- Play the recording. Students listen to a telephone call to Language Link, and underline the correct answer.

1 language student
2 German
3 English
4 26
5 Australian
6 London

 1.26

R = receptionist M = Mark
R: Good afternoon, Language Link.
M: Hi. I would like to register for Language Link, please.
R: Of course. What's your name?
M: My name's Mark.
R: What's your last name?
M: Richards.
R: How do you spell that?
M: R-I-C-H-A-R-D-S.
R: Thank you. Are you a language teacher?
M: No, I'm not.
R: <u>Are you a language student?</u>
M: <u>Yes, I am.</u>
R: What is your language of study?
M: <u>I'm a German student.</u>

R: German … OK. We have lots of German students for you on Language Link.
M: Great.
R: How old are you?
M: Um, <u>I'm 26 years old.</u>
R: Twenty … six. Good. Where are you from?
M: I'm from Sydney.
R: <u>Are you Australian?</u>
M: <u>Yes, I am.</u>
R: I love Australia. Nicole Kidman is my favourite actress.
M: Where are you from?
R: Me? <u>I'm from London.</u> OK, what's your email address?
M: Mark at mail dot com.
R: Thank you.

3 **1.26**

- Read through the form carefully as a class to focus students on the task. Play the recording again. Students listen and complete the form for Mark. They can compare their answers with a partner before you check with the whole class.
- In feedback, ask questions to elicit answers, e.g. *What's his name? What's his first language?* As well as eliciting answers, this models questions.

Language Link – Personal Profile

First name: *Mark*	Sex: male ✓ female ☐
Last name: *Richards*	

	Age:	
Language student ✓	13–16	☐
Language teacher ☐	17–25	☐
Language of study: *German*	26–35	✓
First language: *English*	36–45	☐
Nationality: *Australian*	46–55	☐
Email address: *mark@mail.com*	over 55	☐

GRAMMAR: verb *to be* – negative & questions

❯ *Language reference, Student's Book page 20*
❯ *Methodology guidelines: Grammar boxes, page xiii*

1

- Students read the text about the Language Link member. Ask a few questions to establish understanding, e.g. *Is Ben a student? Is he American?*
- Put students in pairs to write questions and answers about Ben.
- When students have finished, ask them to ask and answer the questions across the class. Nominate a student to ask, *Is Ben Canadian?* Nominate another student, who answers, *No, he isn't.*

3 Is his last name Stark? Yes, it is.
4 Is he from New York? No, he isn't.
5 Is he a language student? Yes, he is.
6 Is he 43 years old? No, he isn't.

2 & 3 **1.27**

- Students put the words in the correct order to make questions. They can then compare their answers with a partner.
- Play the recording for students to listen and check their answers.

- Play the recording again. Students listen and repeat the questions.

See tapescript below for answers.

 1.27

1	What's your name?
2	What's your last name?
3	Are you a language teacher?
4	Are you a language student?
5	How old are you?
6	Where are you from?

Language notes

- The verb *to be* forms questions with a simple inversion:
  I am … → Am I …?   You are … → Are you …? etc.
- This is fairly straightforward. However, in many languages there is no inversion. The statement and question have the same form – the question is expressed by means of rising intonation. Watch out for errors such as:

  ✗ *You are tired?* and ✗ *Where you are from?*
- *Yes/no* questions tend to have rising intonation:

  Are you a student?
- In contrast, *Wh-* questions generally have falling intonation:

  What's your name?
- Short answers have falling intonation:

  Yes, I am.
- N.B. In the affirmative, short forms cannot be abbreviated: ✗ *Yes, he's.* Students (and some teachers!) often want to respond to *yes/no* questions with long answers, e.g. *Are you a student? Yes, I am a student.* Correct this as it is not a natural use of English.
- For other problems connected with the verb *to be*, see the language note in lesson 1A.

Extra practice for stronger students

- Put students into pairs to ask and answer the questions in exercise 2.
- Monitor and correct errors of form and pronunciation.
- Students change pairs. Students must ask each other about the person they have just spoken to. They must ask: *What's his/her name? Is he/she a language teacher?*, etc.

Speaking

❯ *Key Methodology 7: Accurate speaking & fluent speaking, page 20*

1 & 2

- Tell students to copy the Language Link – Personal Profile form in the Student's Book into their exercise books.
- Pairwork. Put students into A and B pairs. Model the conversation briefly with an A student, asking questions and pretending to fill in the form. Then tell students to roleplay the interview.
- Monitor and help if necessary.

Did you know?

1 & 2

- Students read the text about Hollywood stars from other countries and discuss the questions with their partner. You could then ask students to discuss the questions in class.

Extra task

- You could bring in pictures from magazines of well-known film stars and ask questions about them: *Where is he from? How old is he?*, etc.

Cultural note

- Some non-American Hollywood stars:
  British: Orlando Bloom, Anthony Hopkins, Sean Connery, Kate Winslett, Jude Law, Hugh Grant, Euan MacGregor.
  Australian: Mel Gibson
  Canadian: Mike Myers, Dan Aykroyd
  Spanish: Antonio Banderas, Penelope Cruz
  Mexican: Salma Hayek
  Oh, and Keanu Reeves was born in Beirut!

Web research task

❯ *Methodology guidelines: Web research tasks, page xiii*

- Write the names of four or five Hollywood stars, of different nationalities, on the board. Tell students to choose two to research on the web.
- Students must find the following information: Where are they from? What is their nationality? How old are they?

Web search key words

- name/biography/information

If you want something extra …

❯ *Photocopiable activity, page 194*
❯ *Teacher's notes, page 172*

1c Personal possessions

WHAT THE LESSON IS ABOUT

Theme	Decribing posssesions
Speaking	Game: *What's this in English?*
Reading &	A conversation: talking about
Listening	possessions
Vocabulary	Objects 2
Grammar	*This, that, these, those*

IF YOU WANT A LEAD-IN ...

Test before you teach: objects

❯ *Methodology guidelines: Test before you teach, page xiii*

- Put five or six small objects from this lesson, e.g. keys, a pen, a mobile, a CD, etc. in a soft cloth bag, (or carrier bag). Pass it round the class. Students must feel the bag, but not look inside. They must write down which objects they think are in the bag.
- At the end, reveal the objects, and find out who got most right.

VOCABULARY: objects 2

❯ *Language reference: Student's Book page 21*

1 & 2 1.28

- Tell students to look at the pictures. Ask: *What can you see?* Elicit as many words as you can.
- Students write sentences for each of the pictures, using the words in the box.
- Play the recording for students to check their answers.
- Then play the recording again. Students repeat the sentences.

1.28

```
 1  It's an umbrella.
 2  It's a mobile phone.
 3  They're keys.
 4  It's an alarm clock.
 5  It's a bottle of water.
 6  They're pens.
 7  It's a camera.
 8  They're glasses.
 9  It's a newspaper.
10  It's a book.
```

Language note
- Note the weak stress in these words:
  um'brella, 'camera, a'larm /ə/ /ə//ə/ /ə/
- Note the linking and weak stress in *bottle of*: /bɒtələv/.

LISTENING

1 & 2 1.29
- Ask students to look at the picture.
- Play the recording. Students listen and tick the objects they hear.

- Students then check their answers with tapescript 1.29 on page 140.

The following things should be ticked:
book; camera; keys; alarm clock; mobile phone; glasses

1.29

```
M = man  W = woman
1
M:  What's this?
W:  It's my book. My private book.
M:  OK. OK. Relax.
2
M:  Wait a minute. Is that a camera?
M:  Err ... yes. Just one photo please, Mr Pott.
M:  No cameras! No cameras!
3
M:  Excuse me.
W:  Yes?
M:  I think these are your keys.
W:  Yes, they are! Thank you.
M:  You're welcome.
4
W:  Is that the alarm clock, James?
M:  No, that's my mobile phone. Hello?
M:  Hello, Mr Bond.
5
W:  Are those your glasses?
M:  Huh? What? Where?
W:  Oh, David! Those are your glasses.
M:  Oh, nooooo.
```

3
- Pairwork. Put students in pairs. Tell them to practise reading the dialogue.

◼ Key Methodology 6
◼ Dialogues 2

Whole class reading a dialogue aloud

- *It's often useful to give the whole class a chance to read a dialogue aloud themselves. It can also help students to memorize certain patterns, phrases, words and sounds. When reading en masse, you need to take care that you don't all sink into that monotonous one-tone one-rhythm style that is all too easy to do when a large group of people read together. Try these ideas to avoid this:*
- *1 Read the dialogue aloud yourself a few times and ask students to read along with you. Keep up your original speed, rhythm, etc. If students are quiet, use gestures or facial expressions to encourage them to speak up more. As you get to the end of each reading, simply start again at the beginning. Go through the dialogue two or three times in this way – then half-way through one reading, start speaking more quietly and not saying a few words here and there. Do this more and more, making sure that students keep going. After a while, students should be able to maintain the dialogue on their own with minimal help from you.*

2 Write the dialogue up on the board. Read it aloud once with students. Then with the students watching, erase two or three words from the written text. Read through the text again with students, and if all goes well, they will be able to recall the missing words and say them just as if they were still visible. Now erase three or four more words and start reading again. Go on like this until the whole dialogue has vanished! Ask students to say the dialogue to each other. Can they remember it all?

Students in pairs reading a dialogue aloud

- Getting students working in pairs to read dialogues aloud themselves seems like a good idea, but often doesn't work as well as teachers expect. Worse, if you invite one or two unprepared victims to the front of class to inaudibly stumble and muddle their way through a conversation, it can be embarrassing and make you wonder if it really was a sound idea. But reading aloud can be really good and useful. The secret is to prepare carefully rather than throwing students in the deep end. Try one of these ideas:
  1 Generally, it's best to do pair work reading aloud after you have practised reading in the whole class (see section 1 above).
  2 One of the best ways to get reading aloud sounding good is to pay attention to the stresses. Use the board to go through a written dialogue text, marking all the stressed syllables. Practise reading it line by line, taking care to encourage students to punch the stresses, i.e. really make them sound different from the syllables around them.
  3 Sometimes students just find there is too much to concentrate on at once. Saying it aloud, with words in the right order and with good pronunciation, and taking note of what your partner says – it's all too much! One way round this is to ask students to start by just mouthing through the whole dialogue once, i.e. not actually speaking, but moving their mouths as if they are saying the words. This can help students to get familiar with the words and the mechanics involved in saying them. Second time, ask students to read whispering. Third time, normally. Students may find that alongside the increase in volume comes a growth in confidence. They also have a number of opportunities to try the dialogue in unthreatening ways.

GRAMMAR: *this, that, these, those*

❯ *Language reference, Student's Book page 20*
❯ *Methodology guidelines: Grammar boxes, page xiii*

1
- Students underline the correct words in the dialogues. They can compare their answers with a partner before you check with the whole class.

1	this
2	that
3	these
4	that
5	those

Extra task
- Walk round the class with a bag, and collect objects from the students, (pens, keys, mobile phones, bottles of water). Put all the objects in the bag.
- Pull out an object, look at a student, and say: *Is this your book/pen?* or *Are these your keys?* Encourage students to say *Yes, it is* or *No, they aren't.*
- Put students in small groups. Tell everybody to put two objects on the table in front of them. Students take it in turns to ask *Is this...?* or *Are these...?* questions.

Language notes
- We use the demonstrative adjective *this* to describe people and things that are physically close (here), whereas *that* describes people and things that are further away, (there). *These* is the plural of *this*, and *those* is the plural of *that*.
- The voiced /ð/ sound of these words is a bit of a tongue-twister for students. Remind them that the tip of the tongue must start past the teeth when saying these words.

2 & 3 1.30
- Students complete the sentences with *this/that/these/those*. They can then compare their answers with a partner.
- Play the recording for students to listen to and check their answers.
- Play the recording again. Students listen and say the sentences.

See tapescript below for answers.

1.30

1	Is <u>that</u> a taxi? Yes, it is.
2	<u>These</u> are your keys.
3	Is <u>this</u> your ID card?
4	Look. <u>Those</u> are English buses.

SPEAKING

1 & 2
- Groupwork. Divide students into groups of three to play the game. They should sit around one desk.
- Each person puts three personal possessions from their bag on the desk.
- Model the activity carefully. Point to something across the room (board, window, chair), and say: *What's that in English?* Elicit a response. Then pick up something from the table, and ask: *What's this in English?*
- Once students have the idea, leave them to play the game in their groups.

Alternative procedure
- You could make the *Speaking* activity above competitive by dividing the class into two groups, Team A and Team B.
- Team A must point to or hold up an object and say, *What's this/that in English?* If Team B know the answer, they get a point. If they don't, then Team A get a point so long as they can say what it is. Then Team B ask a question.
- Put marks up on the board as they play.
- This game works best with small classes.

IF YOU WANT SOMETHING EXTRA ...

❯ *Photocopiable activity, page 195*
❯ *Teacher's notes, page 172*

1D | In person

WHAT THE LESSON IS ABOUT

Theme	Ordering drinks: offers and responses
Speaking	Roleplay: at a welcome party
Reading	An email from a tour guide inviting people to a welcome party
Listening	Conversations at a welcome party
Vocabulary	Drinks
Functional language	At a party: offers & responses

IF YOU WANT A LEAD-IN ...

Pre-teach key words: drinks

- Use a mime game to elicit drinks. Mime drinking lots of different drinks, e.g. *tea* (by lifting the cup with your finger in the air and sipping); *beer* (by drinking from a bottle and wiping your mouth); *wine* (by holding the glass up and saying cheers then sipping it); *water* (by pretending you're exhausted, pouring it on your head, then drinking it thirstily).
- Write the words on the board as you elicit them.
- Put students in pairs, one facing the board, one with his/her back to the board. Write the words you elicited in a list on the board. The student facing the board must mime the words in the correct order. The other student must guess them. Which pair is the quickest?

READING

In each unit of *Straightforward Elementary* Student's book, there is a listening story. These are usually in Lesson D of each unit. The story is about the events that happen to a group of tourists visiting England with the Explore London Tour Company. We are first introduced to Valerie Hudson, a tour guide who works for the Explore London Tour Company in this reading text. She has sent an email to Mr Curtis, who has just joined the tour, introducing herself and inviting him to a welcome party.

1

- Tell students to look at the email. Set the scene by asking: *What is it? Who is it from? Who is it to? What is the subject?* Students read the email. Ask: *What is it about?*

> It's about a welcome party for a tour group.

2

- Students read the email again and answer the questions.

> 1 It's a tour company.
> 2 She's a tour guide.
> 3 At the Regent Hotel, London
> 4 It's on Sunday, May 14 at 7.30pm.

LISTENING

In this episode of the listening story, we meet the various members of the Explore London tour group.
In conversation 1 we meet Rob and Meg from Australia, who are booking in at the reception desk.

In conversation 2, Herb (Mr Curtis from the email in the Reading section) and Hannah (his wife) order tea at the bar. In conversation 3, the tour guide Valerie, introduces herself to Sam, another member of the tour group, at reception. In conversation 4, Sam has a mysterious phone conversation in his room with a man who wants to know where he is. In conversation 5, the new tour group have all met in the bar for the welcome party and are introducing themselves to each other.

1 1.31

- Ask students to look at the pictures. Point to each one and ask *What is it?* Elicit the words or point to the different places. Drill the words for pronunciation.
- Play the recording. Students listen to the conversations, and underline the correct place for each conversation.

> 1 reception
> 2 bar
> 3 reception
> 4 hotel room
> 5 bar
> 6 bar

🔘 1.31

Re = Receptionist R = Rob M = Meg He = Herb
Ha = Hannah Wr = Waiter S = Sam V = Valerie Vo = voice

1
Re: Good afternoon.
R: Good afternoon. We have a reservation.
Re: What's your name?
R: Rob and Meg Sherman.
Re: How do you spell that?
R: S H E R M A N.
Re: Sherman, yes. Are you with the tour?
M: Yes, we are.
Re: Room 34. These are your keys.
M/R: Thank you.

2
He: <u>Is this the bar?</u>
Ha: Yes, sweetheart, <u>I think it is. Look ... BAR.</u>
He: It's very English!
Ha: I know!
Wr: Good afternoon. Would you like a drink?
He: Yes, please. <u>A beer.</u>
Ha: <u>Tea, please.</u>
He: Well, darling. We're here. We're in London. Listen to that. That's London.
Ha: Wonderful.
W: Tea?
Ha: Here.
He: Beer over here. Thanks.
W: You're welcome.

3
Re: And these are your keys, Mr Moore.
S: Thank you.
V: <u>Hello, are you Sam Moore?</u>
S: <u>Yes, I am.</u>
V: Hi. <u>My name's Valerie. I'm the tour guide for your tour.</u>
S: Oh, hello. Nice to meet you.
V: Nice to meet you. Would you like a drink? Our welcome party is in the bar.
S: No, thank you. I'm tired, and I'll just go to my room.
V: Really? OK then. See you tomorrow.
S: Thank you again. Goodbye.

4

S:	Hello?
Vo:	Hello, Sam. Where are you?
S:	In the hotel.
Vo:	<u>Are you in the bar?</u>
S:	<u>No, I'm not. I'm in my room.</u>
Vo:	Is he in the hotel now?
S:	No, he isn't. Not at the moment.
Vo:	Stay in contact.
S:	Alright.

5

V:	Hello! My name's Valerie.
He:	Well, hi Valerie! I'm Herb Curtis. This is my wife, Hannah.
V:	Nice to meet you.
Ha:	Nice to meet you.
V:	<u>This is Rob, and Meg. They're on your tour.</u>
R:	Hello.
He:	Where are you from Rob?
R:	<u>We're Australian.</u>
Ha:	<u>Australia! Wow!</u>
He:	<u>Hannah and I are from Dallas, Texas.</u>
Ha:	<u>That's in the United States of America.</u>

6

V:	Would you like a drink, Rob?
R:	Yes, please, coffee.
V:	Meg? Would you like a drink?
M:	Yes, please. A mineral water, please.

Extra task

- Listening is demanding at this level, so it is a good idea to predict as much language and context as you can before asking students to listen. Here are three ways you could do this for this listening.
  1 Write: *reception*, *bar*, and *hotel room* on the board. Say: *Where am I?* Then mime various actions, e.g. drinking a beer, carrying a suitcase, ringing the reception bell, having a shower. Students say where you are. This prepares them, hopefully, to listen for the situational clues on the recording.
  2 Do the same – but with words. So, mime ringing a bell and say: *We're with the tour group. We have a reservation*, etc. Again, students tell you the situation, so that they are prepared for listening.
  3 If you have a strong class, you could elicit phrases. Point to *bar* on the board and ask: *What do you say in a bar?* Elicit phrases and write them on the board.

Cultural note

- There are a variety of accents on this recording. Herb and Hannah have American (Texan) accents. Their vowel sounds are noticeably longer than the short, clipped vowels of the waiter and receptionist, who speak with standard British RP (received pronunciation) accents.
- Rob and Meg are Australian. The most noticeable feature of their accent is the rising intonation at the end of sentences, even statements.
- Herb mentions *English beer*. Real English beer, called *bitter*, is darker, flatter and warmer than the paler beer served in most countries. It has a strong, bitter taste.

2 💿 **1.31**

- Play the recording again. Students listen and put a cross or a tick by the underlined information. They can compare their answers with a partner before you check with the whole class.

1 ✓   2 ✗   3 ✓   4 ✗   5 ✗   6 ✓   7 ✗   8 ✗   9 ✓   10 ✗
11 ✓   12 ✗

Extra task for stronger students

- Tell students to rewrite the incorrect sentences to make them correct.
  (Answers: 4 He has <u>beer</u>. She has tea.
                  5 <u>His</u> name is Sam Moore.
                  7 He <u>is</u> in his room.
                  8 He <u>isn't</u> in the bar.
                  10 Rob and Meg are from <u>Australia</u>.)

VOCABULARY: drinks

> *Language reference, Student's Book page 21*

1

- Students match the words to the pictures.

A wine
B mineral water
C beer
D tea
E (orange) juice
F coffee

2 💿 **1.32**

- Play the recording. Students listen and repeat the words.

💿 **1.32**

A:	Tea.
B:	Coffee.
A:	Wine.
B:	Orange juice.
A:	Mineral water.
B:	Beer.

Alternative procedure

> *Key Methodology 10, 11 & 12: Flashcards 1, 2 & 3, pages 37, 40 & 43*

- Use flashcards to elicit and drill these words. Draw simple pictures to represent the different drinks on A4 paper, and paste them on to cardboard. Stand at the front of the class, and show each flashcard. Elicit or model the word. Ask students to repeat chorally and individually.
- Show the cards at random to individuals. Can they remember and say the word?

Language note

- Note the diphthong in beer /bɪə/, and /ɪ/ sound in orange /ˈɒrɪndʒ/.

3

- Pairwork. Put students in pairs. One student covers the words. The other points to a picture and tests their partner.

FUNCTIONAL LANGUAGE: offers & responses

 Language reference, Student's Book page 20

1 & 2 🔘 1.33
- You could put students in pairs to complete the words in the box to make phrases.
- Play the recording for students to listen and check their answers.

See tapescript below for answers.

🔘 1.33

> **A:** Would you <u>like</u> a drink?
> **B:** Yes, <u>please</u>.
> **A:** No, <u>thank</u> you.
> **B:** No, <u>thanks</u>.

3 🔘 1.34
- This is a prompt drill. Play the recording and pause after each word. Students listen to the words and make offers as in the example. Get the whole class to say the phrase chorally after the prompt. Then nominate two or three confident students to repeat individually.

🔘 1.34

> 1 a coffee
> 2 a drink
> 3 a mineral water
> 4 a pizza
> 5 a sandwich
> 6 an apple
> 7 a glass of wine

4
- Write five or six drinks (*beer, water,* etc.) on the board. Put students in A and B pairs. Tell Student A to offer drinks, using the prompts on the board. Tell Student B to respond. Change roles after a minute or two.
- Monitor and correct if necessary. Make sure students are pronouncing *would* /wʊd/ correctly, and that their intonation is rising when making an offer.

Alternative procedure: eliciting & drilling from a situational context
- You could bring this off the page by using the board and eliciting and drilling the dialogue, using visuals and mime.
- Draw a drinks menu on the board. You could copy the one in exercise 6. Next to it draw a stick figure carrying a tray with two glasses on it. Point to the menu, and say, *What's this?* Point to the figure, and say, *What's his/her job?*
- Point to *coffee* on the drinks menu, then to the waiter/waitress. Say: *What does he/she say?* Elicit: *Would you like a coffee?* If you can't elicit it, just model it.
- Drill the phrase: *Would you like a coffee?* round the class, chorally and individually. Make sure students are pronouncing would /wʊd/ correctly, and that their intonation is rising.

- You could back chain if students find it hard to say, as follows:
Say: *a coffee*. Students repeat.
Say: *like a coffee*. Students repeat.
Say: *Would you like a coffee?* Students repeat.
- Point to the other drinks. Elicit and practise the phrase. Then get students to ask and respond across the class in open pairs. So, nominate Student A and point to beer on the menu on the board. Student A says: *Would you like a beer?* Nominate Student B, across the class, who say: *Yes, please* or *No, thanks*. Do this a few times. Then put students in pairs to play waiter and customer, and practise the mini-dialogue.

Roleplay

5
- Groupwork. Put students in groups of three. Read through the instructions carefully as a class. Tell students to decide on roles. Give students three or four minutes to prepare conversations. Remind them to use the *Useful language* box to help them.

Stronger & weaker classes
- Stronger students may be ready to improvise.
- Weaker students may need to write the conversation down first.

6

⦿ *Key Methodology 7: Accurate speaking & fluent speaking , page 20*

- Ask a few groups to act out their conversation for the class.

Extra task
- If your classroom situation allows, it is a nice idea to physically act this out. Move desks, tables and chairs around so that the classroom is a fair imitation of a café. That means that four students should be sitting round a table. So, if you have sixteen students, then you should have four café tables with four students round each.
- Ask one student from each table to stand up and come to the front of the classroom. Tell the class that they are waiters. Give each waiter a drinks menu, (which you made and photocopied earlier). Tell them to take it to a table and hand it out, then take the customer's order.
- By making it real, hopefully, students are encouraged to improvise and play with the language they have.

> ### ■ Key Methodology 7
> ### ■ Accurate speaking & fluent speaking
>
> - *This course incorporates a lot of speaking work. Sometimes the tasks focus on helping students to become more accurate at using grammar or other language points. In other tasks the aim is primarily fluency – encouraging students to feel more confident and adventurous in speaking freely. Some tasks fall somewhere between these two. Make sure you are clear about the purpose of each task before it starts, because the different aims may mean that you need to change your role as a teacher.*

Accurate speaking

- *If a task is mainly helping students to practise language points, then it is important and valuable to help students get better at using the items. The teacher has an essential role in:*
  1 *drawing the students' attention to errors.*
  2 *helping them to notice errors themselves.*
  3 *encouraging students to think about possible corrections.*
  4 *encouraging students to try out corrections.*
  5 *encouraging students to give feedback to each other.*
- *If you don't do any of these things, then students will tend to stay at their current level of competence rather than improving.*

❯ *Key Methodology 16: Helping students say it better, page 66.*

Fluent speaking

- *Many tasks are primarily communication activities which, although incorporating recently studied items, are mostly aimed at giving students chances to use all the language they have studied so far – to try (as far as possible) to integrate the items together and actually communicate using their English. In these tasks, the students are aiming to speak as fluently and confidently as they can without long pauses or breakdowns in communication.*
- *Try not to create a classroom atmosphere where students feel they need to get everything correct all the time.*
- *Many students will benefit from active permission to not worry about getting everything right in some activities. If an activity has a mainly fluency aim, introduce it by saying something like 'Don't worry about making mistakes. Try to give a clear message'.*
- *The best way to encourage students to not worry about being correct is to visibly not worry yourself. Don't hover over students frowning or nodding when they get something wrong. If you monitor and note down errors, do this discreetly so that students don't see you scribbling every time they speak.*
- *Once a fluent speaking activity is under way, you might consider vanishing, i.e. disappearing into a quiet corner of the room. You can still keep an eye on the room, but not be a dominant presence.*

❯ *Key Methodology 8 & 9: Spoken Errors – fluency tasks 1 & 2, pages 29 & 35.*
❯ *Key Methodology 17: Finger feedback, page 69*

IF YOU WANT SOMETHING EXTRA ...

❯ *Photocopiable activity, page 196*
❯ *Teacher's notes, page 172*

Answer key

1 REVIEW

❯ Student's Book page 147

1

A	a computer
B	a bottle of water
C	a clock
D	a phone
E	a newspaper
F	a chair

2

1 Her
2 his
3 Their
4 their
5 her
6 His

3

2 Is she Brazilian? No, she isn't.
3 Is her last name Janeiro? No, it isn't.
4 Is she a language teacher? Yes, she is.
5 Is she Irish? Yes, she is.
6 Is she 21 years old? No, she isn't.

4

1 Julian, this <u>is</u> Alyssa. She's new.
  Nice to meet you.
2 How <u>do</u> you spell your name?
  A-L-Y-S-S-A.
3 Are you <u>a</u> language teacher?
  Yes, I am.
4 Where is she from?
  She<u>'s</u> from Warsaw. She's Polish.
5 Are these your keys?
  No, <u>they</u> aren't. My keys are here.
6 Would you like a drink?
  No, thank <u>you</u>.

5

1 How are you
2 I'm fine
3 Would you like
4 Yes, please
5 No, it isn't

1 WRITING

❯ Workbook page 65

Registration form

First Name: _Tom_
Last Name: _Butler_
Age: _28_
Sex: Male ✔   Female ☐
Nationality: _Scottish_
Home town: _Glasgow_
email address: _tombutler@totalmail.org_

Registration form

First Name: _Natalie_
Last Name: _Smith_
Age: _19_
Sex: Male ☐   Female ✔
Nationality: _South African_
Home town: _Cape Town_
email address: _nats@hotmail.com_

Registration form

First Name: _Sophie_
Last Name: _Givet_
Age: _33_
Sex: Male ☐   Female ✔
Nationality: _French_
Home town: _Lyon_
email address: _sgivet@freeserve.net_

2A | The expat files

WHAT THE LESSON IS ABOUT

Theme	Expats – people living in foreign countries
Speaking	Talking about life as an expat
Reading	*The expat files*: an article about Britons living abroad
Listening	A Briton talking about living abroad
Vocabulary	Common verbs 1
Grammar	Present simple affirmative & negative

IF YOU WANT A LEAD-IN ...

Test before you teach: the present simple affirmative

◗ *Methodology guidelines: Test before you teach, page xiii*

* Write the name of four or five famous people on the board. Choose people of the same sex that both you and your students know a bit about, e.g. Nicole Kidman; Madonna; Beyoncé; Jennifer Lopez; Penelope Cruz, and write on the board:
  She comes from …
  She lives in …
  She speaks …
  She …
* Describe one of the people using the words on the board, e.g. *She comes from Australia. She lives in the USA. She speaks English. She makes movies.* Students must guess who you are describing. (Answer: *Nicole Kidman.*)
* Put students in threes. They must take it in turns to describe one of the people on the board, using the prompts.

VOCABULARY: common verbs 1

◗ *Language reference, Student's Book page 31*

1

* Ask students to look at the verbs in the box. You could check some of them by miming, e.g. say: *read* and then mime reading a book.
* Students write a verb from the box in each space. Do the first as an example. They can compare their answers with a partner before you check with the whole class.

1	live	5	read
2	drink	6	speak
3	go	7	work
4	eat	8	have

2

* Students add the words to the correct list in exercise 1. Do the first as an example. They can compare their answers with a partner before you check with the whole class.

1 – live <u>in Britain</u>
2 – drink <u>water</u>
4 – eat <u>hamburgers</u>
6 – speak <u>Italian</u>
7 – work <u>in a hospital</u>
8 – have <u>a dog</u>

3 1.35

* Play the recording. Students listen and underline the words from exercises 1 and 2 that they hear.

See tapescript below for answers.

 1.35

My name's Sabrina. I'm from Cardiff, Wales. I <u>live in a flat</u>. I don't <u>have a cat</u> or <u>a dog</u>. I <u>go to school</u>. I <u>speak English and Italian</u>. I <u>drink coffee</u>, lots of coffee.

READING

This article is about three British people who have left Britain to live in another country. They compare living in their new country with living in Britain.

1

* Read through the introduction as a class. Check that students understand 'expat'. You could ask, *Where do 'expats' from your country go?*
* Students read the article and answer the questions about the people.

1 Sandra is from London. Carl and Anna are from Liverpool.
2 Sandra is in Seattle, USA. Carl and Anna are in Malaga, Spain.
3 Yes, they are all happy: Sandra likes it. Carl and Anna love it.

Cultural note

* An *expat* or *expatriate* is someone who lives in a foreign country. It is particularly used to describe people who retain aspects of their own culture, or even live among people of their own culture, e.g. American expats who live in Saudi Arabia may well live and work there for years without learning Arabic or adopting a local lifestyle. To that extent it has a different meaning from *emigrant* – someone who lives abroad, but adapts to that society.
* *Seattle* /siːjætl/ is a modern city on the Pacific northwest coast in Washington State, USA. Located on the shore of sparkling Elliot bay, with Lake Washington behind and the snowy peak of Mount Rainier in the distance, the city has a magnificent setting. It's the home of Starbucks and Microsoft.
* *Mexican-American fast food* is food made in America but of Mexican origin, e.g. *tacos*.
* The city of *Malaga* is on the Costa Blanca coast in Spain. The Costa Blanca coast is an area of attractive beaches, though it is very heavily developed. Malaga has some historic buildings, dating from Spain's Moorish period, but its importance is as a commercial city and a transport hub for the region. Large numbers of British people retire to the resorts of southern Spain because of the sun and lower property prices.
* *Liverpool* is a city in north-west England. Home of the Beatles and European City of Culture, 2008.
* *The BBC* (British Broadcasting Corporation) is a non-commercial TV and radio broadcaster in Britain. It is the most commonly watched TV station in Britain.

2

- Students read the article again and find the names to complete the sentences. They can compare their answers with a partner before you check with the whole class.

1	Carl and Anna
2	Sandra
3	Sandra
4	Carl and Anna
5	Sandra
6	Carl and Anna

3

- Students close their book, and write down everything they can remember about Sandra or Carl and Anna. They then compare what they have remembered with a partner.
- Have a brief class discussion. Ask different students to give you a sentence about either Sandra or Carl and Anna.

Extra task

- Write *Who …?* on the board. Ask: *Who lives in a flat? Who has a dog?* Students respond. Then put students in pairs to ask and answer *Who …?* questions.

4

- Pairwork. Students discuss the question in pairs.
- You could then find out from the class who would like to live in another country and where.

LISTENING

In this listening, Nathan Mackinnon, who is originally from Scotland, talks about living in Istanbul. He describes the things that are similar to and the things that are different from his life in Scotland.

1 💿 **1.36**

- Play the recording. Students listen and underline the correct information.

Name: MacKinnon
From: Scotland
New home: Istanbul
Job: Teacher
Opinion: I like it

💿 **1.36**

My name's David MacKinnon, that's M-A-C-K-I-N-N-O-N. I'm from Scotland, but now I live in Istanbul. My life is very different here. I live in a flat, not a house. I only eat Turkish food now. I still read English newspapers, and I have the BBC on the internet in my flat. Oh yeah, I go to football matches here in Istanbul. That's different, because in Scotland I don't like football! I work at a university. I'm an English teacher. I speak Turkish, because I have a Turkish girlfriend! I really like it here, it's great.

2 💿 **1.36**

- Play the recording again. Students listen and mark the sentences true or false.

1	F	(He lives in a flat.)
2	F	(He only eats Turkish food now.)
3	F	(He still reads English newspapers.)
4	T	
5	T	
6	T	

3

- Pairwork. Put students in pairs to discuss the questions.

Extra questions for stronger students

- *What do you eat/drink/read/watch on TV?*
- *Where do you go at the weekend?*
- *Where do you work/study?*

GRAMMAR: present simple affirmative & negative

- ▶ *Language reference, Student's Book page 30*
- ▶ *Methodology guidelines: Grammar boxes, page xiii*
- ▶ *Key Methodology 17: Finger feedback page 68*

1

- Students make sentences in the present simple.

1	She works in Germany.
2	We live in a big flat.
3	I don't speak English.
4	He has a dog.
5	They don't eat a lot of pizza.
6	He goes to an American school.

Language notes

- The present simple affirmative can seem very simple to most language learners. Unlike most languages, the verb almost never changes depending on person or plurality, (*I go, you go, we go*, etc.) The exception, of course, is the *s* in *he* and *she* forms, (*He goes*).
- Lulled into a false sense of security, a very common and repeated error, therefore, is to fail to add *s* to the *he* and *she* forms. It is very easy for students to get into the habit of saying *he speak* or *she eat*. Students need lots of practice and correction in this area.
  N.B. be aware of the slightly irregular changes of *go/do* (*goes/does*) and *have* (*has*).
- In introducing negative forms, students come across the auxiliary verb *do* for the first time. Other languages don't use it. They express *I don't speak English*, for example, in ways that translate as, *No(t) speak English, I no(t) speak English, I speak not English*. Consequently, provide lots of practice, and expect the errors above.
- Notice the form: *don't* is a shortened form of *do not*. Let curious students be aware of this, but correct if students are saying *do not*, as it is an uncommon usage. The third person form of *don't* is *doesn't*. A common error for students is to over-apply rules and say, for example, *He doesn't lives …* and some students may attempt to add *s* to make a plural, *They don't lives …*, – watch out for this.

- The /əʊ/ sound in *don't*, and the /ʌ/ sound in *doesn't* are difficult and need repetition practice. Note that in some varieties of English, *doesn't* is pronounced /dʊz(ə)nt/. Point out that *don't* and *doesn't* are strongly stressed in sentences.
- *Have* conjugates like other verbs in the present simple, (*I have …*, *I don't have …*, *Do you have …*, etc.). However, you may wish to point out that British English *have got* can be used as an alternative to *have* when talking about possessions and states. *Have got* conjugates like present perfect forms, e.g. *I've got …*, *I haven't got …*, *Have you got …?*
- N.B. students will do more work on *have got* in lesson 9.

2

- Students complete the text. Do the first sentence as an example. They can compare their answers with a partner before you check with the whole class.

1	is	5	works
2	is	6	lives
3	lives	7	don't speak
4	is	8	drinks

3

- Students complete the sentences with a positive or negative verb so that they are true for themselves.

1	live/don't live
2	drink/don't drink
3	work/don't work
4	have/don't have
5	speak/don't speak

4

- Pairwork. Put students in pairs. They read out their sentences to each other and compare them.
- In feedback, ask students to summarize their findings, e.g. *I live in a house, but Juan doesn't live in a house. We don't drink coffee*, etc.

Extra practice: using drills

❯ *Key Methodology 14: Drilling 1 – basics, page 55*

- At this level, students need to do some oral repetition work to be able to manipulate the form and pronunciation when speaking. Here are two suggestions:
1 Make a set of flashcards, showing pictures of a house, a flat, tea, coffee, beer, wine, hamburgers, a dog, a cat, a newspaper, books, and the words English, French, Japanese. Obviously, you can add to or change these. In class, hold up each flashcard, and say, for example, *I live in a house, I don't live in a flat*. Get students to repeat chorally and individually. Then hold up different pictures and get students to make true sentences about themselves from the flashcard prompt.
Once you have done this for a while, hold up a flashcard, point to a student, then nominate another student to remember and speak for that student, e.g. hold up *cat*, point to Maria, and nominate Tomas. Tomas says, *She doesn't have a cat*. Go round the class,

eliciting more sentences in this way.
2 Put a picture of a woman on the board. Write a set of words round the picture: *coffee, tea, orange juice, tennis matches, the university, a flat, a house*, etc. Put a cross or tick next to each word. Then point to the words and make sentences about the woman, e.g. *This is Rose. She drinks coffee but she doesn't drink tea …*
Model and drill the sentences round the class chorally and individually. Then nominate students to make sentences from the word prompts. At the end, take the picture off the board, and write: *My best friend …*
In pairs, students must tell each other about their best friend, using the word prompts.

SPEAKING

1

- Students read the text and say where the American expat is.

He's in Paris, France.

2

- If you are an expat, model this activity by telling students about your new life in the students' country.
- Students must prepare a text about their new life. You could write prompts on the board to help students prepare:
I'm … I live … I drink … I eat …

3

- Pairwork. Put students in pairs. They must tell their partner about their new life. Their partner must then guess the country they are talking about.

4

- Pairs join up with another pair to make groups of fours. Students must introduce their partner to another student, and use the third person.
- Monitor and note errors for feedback at the end.

Alternative procedure to exercise 3 & 4

- Make this a mingle activity. Hand out to every student a piece of paper with the name of a country on it. They must prepare to describe their imaginary life there. Students then mingle for five minutes and tell everybody they can about their lifestyle. After five minutes, stop the activity. Tell students to mingle again, but this time tell students to talk about other people they have met, not to talk about themselves.

IF YOU WANT SOMETHING EXTRA …

❯ *Photocopiable activity, page 197*
❯ *Teacher's notes, page 173*

2B | Typical friends

Theme	Friends
Speaking	Talking about things you do with your friends
Listening	A radio interview about men and women and friendship
Vocabulary	Common verbs 2: free time activities
Grammar	Present simple questions & short answers
Pronunciation	Word stress 1

IF YOU WANT A LEAD-IN ...

Introducing the theme: friends

- Draw on the board, the following diagram:

- Tell students to copy the diagram. Then write the names of two of your men friends and two of your women friends next to the appropriate circles. Point to one, and say, for example, *This is Jill. I go dancing with Jill. She likes music.* Point to another. *This is Joe. I play football with Joe.*
- Tell students to write the names of four friends. Then put them in pairs to talk about them with their partner.

Pre-teach key words: freetime activities

- Use flashcards to elicit and practise key words from this lesson. Before the lesson, get a pile of sheets of paper or (better) card, and draw lots of quick sketches to represent activities: watch TV, listen to music, go dancing, go shopping, etc.
- Hold up the flashcards, and elicit and drill the vocabulary. Then write the days of the week on the board (Sunday – Saturday). Say, for example, *On Saturday, I play sports. On Friday, I go dancing.* Ask students to make sentences from the flashcards and the days of the week.
- Put students in pairs to describe a typical week.

VOCABULARY: common verbs 2

> *Language reference, Student's Book page 31*

1

- Students match each picture A–D with a phrase from the box.
- Check the other words by miming them or by showing visuals, (see the flashcard idea in the *Pre-tech key words* section).
- In feedback, model and drill the words for pronunciation.

A	go shopping	C	watch TV
B	listen to music	D	study

Language notes

- Note the pronunciation of TV /tiːˈviː/ and restaurant /ˈrestərɒnt/.
- Note *listen **to*** – students often forget to say *to* here.

26

2

- Model the activity by asking the questions briefly in class, and eliciting a few responses.
- Pairwork. Students work in pairs to ask and answer the questions.

Alternative procedure

- You could do this as a class survey. Ask students to list the activities in exercise 1 vertically on the left side of a blank sheet of paper. Tell them to draw six columns. Then tell students to stand up, walk round, and ask six people about their activities, using the questions in exercise 2. Tell them to write the person's name at the top of a column, then put a tick, a cross, or the letter A (to represent 'alone') in the column, next to the different activities.
- It would be a good idea to write the form up on the board first, and model a couple of questions with a student, so that they are clear about what they have to do.
- In feedback, ask students to summarize their findings: *Three people go to restaurants, Juan studies alone,* etc.

LISTENING

This listening is a radio interview with a psychologist. He talks about the way typical friendships between men and friendships between women differ.

1

- Students read the website, and say what it is about.

> The webpage is about the things men do with their men friends and the things women do with their women friends and how they are different.

2 1.37

- Play the recording. Students listen to the interview, and tick the words they hear. They can compare their answers with a partner before you check with the whole class.

> *The following words should be ticked:*
> sports; football; feelings; personal; movies; politics

🌐 **1.37**

> **I = interviewer P = Dr Palmer**
> **I:** What about women? Do women talk about <u>sports</u>?
> **P:** No, no, they don't. Not like men. Women friends are more <u>personal</u>. They talk more about personal things. They talk about their <u>feelings</u>.
> **I:** What other things are different?
> **P:** Well, women listen to their friends a lot more.
> **I:** Really?
> **P:** Yes. That's why women know more about their friends.
> **I:** Do men know a lot about their friends?
> **P:** No, they don't. Ask a man what he knows about his friends and he can say 'My friend likes this music, and this sport, and this <u>football</u> team, and this kind of woman ...', but after that, not much.
> **I:** Very interesting. What about you, Doctor? Do you have a lot of friends?
> **P:** No, I don't. I have one or two friends.
> **I:** Do you play sports with your friends?
> **P:** No, no, I don't. I'm seventy years old. But we talk about <u>movies</u>, and <u>politics</u>. ...
> **I:** Thank you, Dr Palmer.
> **P:** You're welcome.

Language note

- When you talk about your feelings, you talk about your emotions about something, i.e. things that make you angry, happy, sad, etc.

3 🌑 **1.37**

- Tell students to read through the sentences and decide which symbol(s) refer to men (M), women (W) or both (MW). Then play the recording again. Students can then compare their answers with a partner before you check with the whole class.

3 M	4 W	5 W	6 W	7 M

4

- Ask students if they agree or disagree with what Dr Palmer says about men and women. Students put a tick if they agree and a cross if they disagree with the statements in exercise 3.

5

- Model what you want students to say, e.g. *I think men talk about sports and women don't talk about sports, but I don't think women listen more to their friends …*
- Pairwork. Put students in pairs or small groups to compare their answers.

GRAMMAR: present simple questions & short answers

❯ *Language reference, Student's Book page 30*
❯ *Methodology guidelines: Grammar boxes, page xiii*

1

- Students make questions in the present simple.

Part 1
3   Do they talk about personal things?
4   Does he have women friends?
Part 2
5   Does she have a lot of friends?
6   Do they talk about personal things?
7   Do they do things together?
8   Does she have men friends?

Language notes

- Manipulating the auxiliary verbs *do* and *does* to form questions is a strange and difficult thing for many students new to English. In many languages, questions are formed by a simple transposition of subject and verb. Other languages, don't even transpose, and merely use rising intonation to express the question. So, expect errors like ✗ Play you football? And ✗ You play football?
- Students may over-apply rules, e.g. ✗ Does she has a lot of friends?
- It is a good idea to draw a simple table on the board to show students how questions are formed:

do/does	subject	infinitive
	I	
Do	you	
	we	
	they	play sports?
Does	he	
	she	
	it	

- When making the question, remind students that the full verb is usually stressed while *Do you* /dəjə/ and *Does he* /dʌzɪ/ is contracted. You will need to do plenty of drilling to get students to approximate this.

2 🌑 **1.38**

- Play the recording. Students listen to a man and a woman talk about their friends. They mark the questions in exercise 1 with a tick or a cross.

1 ✗	2 ✓	3 ✗	4 ✗	5 ✓	6 ✓	7 ✓	8 ✓

🌑 **1.38**

I = Interviewer   T = Tom   J = Jane
I: <u>Do you have a lot of friends?</u>
T: <u>No, I don't.</u> Not really. I have one good friend at the sports club, Tony.
I: The article says men do activities together. <u>Do you play sports with your friends?</u>
T: <u>Yes, I do.</u> Tony and I play tennis. Sometimes we watch the football together, but that's always at the sports club.
I: <u>Do you talk about personal things,</u> feelings, with your friends?
T: <u>No, I don't.</u> We don't talk a lot, if we do, we talk about sports.
I: <u>Do you have women friends?</u>
T: <u>No, I don't.</u> My wife wouldn't like it I think, if I had women friends.

I: <u>Do you have a lot of friends?</u>
J: <u>Yes, I do.</u> I have a lot of friends, yes.
I: <u>Do you talk about personal things?</u>
J: <u>Yes, we do.</u> We talk about problems, love life, things like that.
I: <u>Do you do things together?</u>
J: <u>Yes, we do.</u> Of course. But not typical things like shopping if that's what you mean. We go out for a drink, or to a disco.
I: <u>Do you have men friends?</u>
J: <u>Yes, I do!</u> A lot of my friends are men friends. They talk about all their problems to me.

3

- Pairwork. Model the activity briefly with a confident student. Then put students in pairs to ask and answer the questions in exercise 1 about the man and woman in the recording.

Alternative procedure

❯ *Key Methodology 14: Drilling 1 – the basics, page 55*

- Do this as a whole class activity as a sort of drill first. Ask the first question, and get the whole class to respond. Then ask the same question to one or two individuals. Then move on to the next question, and so on. At the end, put students in pairs to practise again. At this level, students need lots of practice in manipulating these forms.

Language notes

- Short answers do not come naturally and students are likely to want to say: *Yes, he plays* or *Yes, he plays football*, etc. Again, use drills to get students used to manipulating these forms.

4

- Pairwork. Model the activity carefully with a student. Then put students in pairs to ask and answer the questions.

Extra practice

- Write the following prompts on the board. Ask students to make questions from the prompts and then ask a partner.
  1 you/play sports with your friends?
  2 you/talk about personal things?
  3 you/go to the cinema with your friends?
  4 you/go on holiday with friends?
  5 you/meet your friends often?

Extra drill for short answers

❯ *Key Methodology 15: Drilling 2 – substitution, page 58*

- Draw two stick figures on the board, one clearly male, one clearly female. Write a large tick and a large cross on the board.
  Say: *Does he have a lot of friends?* Point to the male stick figure and the tick. Students say, *Yes, he does.*
  Say: *Do they play sports?* Point to both stick figures and the cross. Students say: *No, they don't.*
- Continue with the prompts below, asking *Do you/Does he/ Does she/Do they* questions. Students have to manipulate their short answers.

    Play football?
    Go dancing?
    Go shopping?
    Watch TV?
    Listen to music?
    Go to restaurants?
    Travel?
    Study?

PRONUNCIATION: word stress 1

1 **1.39**

- Play the recording. Students listen to the words in the chart.
- Play the recording again. Students listen and repeat.

🔘 **1.39**

> sports; watch; go; play; live
> travel; shopping; music; football; study; restaurant;
> personal; politics; cinema; hospital

2 🔘 **1.40**

- Play the recording. Students listen and put the words into the chart in exercise 1.

☐	☐▫	☐▫▫
have	English	hamburger
friend	coffee	newspaper

🔘 **1.40**

> hamburger
> have
> English
> newspaper
> coffee
> friend

3

- Ask students to say the words in the chart. Alternatively, put students in pairs to say the words to each other. Monitor and correct errors if necessary.

Extra task

- Ask students in pairs to look back in the Student's Book, Workbook and their exercise book to find two words that they could add to each column.

Language notes

- English is a stress-timed language, so strong stresses are very stressed and weak stresses are not stressed at all. This is a challenge for speakers of syllable-timed languages who want to give equal stress to each syllable.
- It is a good idea to exaggerate stress when modelling and drilling such words.
- Also, point out the prevalence of the schwa /ə/ sound in weak-stressed syllables, e.g. ☐ /ə/ /ə/ ***personal***.

SPEAKING

1

- Tell students to look at the words in the circles and ask students what things they do with their friends. Elicit a few responses from students. Then put students in pairs to ask each other the question.

2

- Pairwork. Students work in pairs to interview their partner about what they do with friends. Again, it is a good idea to model this first by asking a few *Do you* questions round the class. Monitor and correct errors if necessary.

■ **Key Methodology 8**
■ **Spoken errors: fluency tasks 1**

- *When students are working on communication tasks in pairs or small groups, many teachers like to discreetly monitor (i.e. not overtly helping, correcting or interfering) in order to note down errors made by speakers. In this way, they can collect a list of perhaps ten to fifteen errors that may be useful to work on with the class after the activity is finished.*
  What can you do with such a list? Here are some ideas:

The 'Classic' technique

- *The simplest (and perhaps classic) way is simply to write the errors on the board, and invite comments and corrections from students.*

Variations

Vary the classic technique by:

1 *allowing pair work discussion time before the whole class feedback.*
2 *including some correct sentences as well as incorrect ones. Ask students to decide in each case if sentences are wrong before they correct, i.e. tell them:* Some may be good – some not – decide! *This work involves more thinking, and also celebrates what was achieved in the task, as well as focusing on what they got wrong,*
3 *occasionally including a whole list of only correct sentences. Let students review and discuss them in the usual way – and by the end, they'll discover that all were correct. Congratulate the class on making so many excellent sentences!*

3

- In the same pairs, students discuss the question.
- In feedback, ask students to say whether their partners are a 'typical' man friend or a 'typical' woman friend, and why.

IF YOU WANT SOMETHING EXTRA ...

❯ *Photocopiable activity, page 198*
❯ *Teacher's notes, page 173*

2c | He still lives with his parents

WHAT THE LESSON IS ABOUT

Theme	The family: living at home
Speaking	Describing how old people are when they do things; talking about your family
Reading	*An Englishman's Home ... is his Castle!*; an article about a man who lives at home with his parents
Vocabulary	The family
Grammar	*Wh-* questions; Possessive *'s*
Pronunciation	Final *-s*
Did you know	*The family in Britain*: changing family life in the UK

IF YOU WANT A LEAD-IN ...

Test before you teach: family trees

> *Methodology guidelines: Test before you teach, page xiii*

- Draw a family tree on the board. Put your name on it. Then write the names of four or five family members next to it in a list. Tell students about your family, e.g. *Jean is my mother. She's 62 and Scottish. She's very nice. She lives in Glasgow.* At the end, tell students to copy and complete the family tree. They can ask you any questions to help them.

Discussion starters

> *Methodology guidelines: Discussion starters, page xii*

- *How old are you?*
- *Do you live with your parents? Why? Why not?*

SPEAKING

1
- Pairwork. Students discuss the question with a partner.

Multilingual classes

- If you have a variety of nationalities in your class, this activity becomes more of a 'finding out' information gap. You could put students in groups to discuss. Then, in feedback, find out differences between countries.

READING

The reading text is about Andy Castle, a 37-year-old man who still lives with his parents. Andy's mother and father are interviewed and give different opinions about what they think of their son still living with them, and then Andy is interviewed, giving his point of view about the situation.

1
- Ask students to look at the photo. Ask: *Who can you see? How old is he?* etc.
- Students read the interviews with three people from the Castle family. They then say what they think the problem is.

> Andy is 37, but he lives at home. His mother is happy, but his father isn't.

Alternative procedure

- You could break this reading into sections if you think it is a bit long for students to read in one go. Students read 'The Castle Family'. Then ask: *What is the problem?* Students then go on to read 'Doris Castle'. Ask: *Is it a problem for Doris?* Students read 'Jack Castle'. Ask: *Is it a problem for Jack?* Finally, students read 'Andy's point of view'. Ask them: *Is it a problem for Andy?*

Language notes

- **An opinion** says what you think about something or someone.
- **A point of view** is when you give an opinion from the way you see the situation.

Cultural notes

- In Britain, people usually go to university at eighteen, and it is very common for students to go to a university far from home, so they have to live away from home. Compared to other Europeans, young Britons are more likely to live away from home in flatshares with young friends. However, rising house prices have resulted in a recent upsurge of young people continuing to live at home.
- **An Englishman's home is his castle** is a well-known saying. Here it is a play on the family's name, *Castle*.
- **Brighton** is an attractive, seaside town on the south coast of England.

2
- Students read the article again and underline the correct word.

1	isn't
2	has
3	wants
4	doesn't live
5	isn't
6	loves
7	likes

3
- Put students in pairs or small groups to discuss the questions.
- Then have a brief class discussion.

> *Possible answers to why Andy lives at home:*
> He doesn't have a girlfriend. He doesn't want to live alone. He is happy to live with his parents. He likes the house. A lot of friends live at home. He doesn't want to spend a lot of money on his own house.

VOCABULARY: the family

> *Language reference, Student's Book page 31*

1
- Students look back at the text on page 26 and find all the family words. They can compare their answers with a partner before you check with the whole class.

> daughter; son; father; grandfather

2

⦾ *Communication activities, Student's Book pages 134 & 136*

- Pairwork. Put students in A and B pairs. Student A turns to page 134, and Student B turns to page 136. They then ask and answer each other's questions in order to complete Emily's family tree.

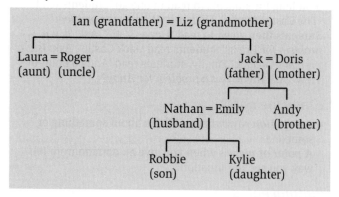

GRAMMAR: *Wh-* questions & possessive *'s*

⦾ *Language reference, Student's Book page 30*
⦾ *Methodology guidelines: Grammar boxes, page xiii*

1

- Students complete the questions with a question word from the box. They can compare their answers with a partner before you check with the whole class.

1	Where
2	Who
3	Why
4	How
5	What

Language notes

- Questions like *Who does he live with?* can confuse, as many languages cannot end sentences with prepositions in this way. *With whom does he live?* is correct English, but considered over formal and old-fashioned nowadays.
- Note that the spelling and pronunciation of question words are at odds: *Where* /weə/, *Who* /huː/.

2

- Students put the words in order to make questions. They can compare their answers with a partner before you check with the whole class.

1	Where do you live?
2	Who do you live with?
3	What are their names?
4	How old are they?

Language notes

- The major problem that students will have here is remembering the correct order of words when forming questions, and remembering to use auxiliaries. Watch out for errors like, ✗ *Where you are from?* and ✗ *Where he lives?*

3

- Pairwork. Put students in pairs to ask and answer the questions in exercise 2.

Extra task

- Draw the table below on the board, or use an OHT.

	live?
	live with?
	live there?
What	*do there?*
When	*work?*
Where	*work with?*
Who	*work there?*
Why	*do there?*
	go at the weekend?
	go with?
	go there?
	do there?

- Model questions from the table, e.g. *Where do you live? Who do you live with? Why do you live there? What do you do there?* Ask students to listen and repeat.
- Choose a student and interview him/her. Ask the set of questions above, and encourage the student to respond quickly. They can say *I don't know* if they can't think of an answer quickly enough.
- Put students in pairs to interview each other, using the prompts in the table.

4

- Students add 's or ' to make possessives. They can compare their answers with a partner before you check with the whole class.

2	John's cousin
3	the teachers' room
4	Andy's books
5	his brother's birthday
6	those families' houses

Language notes

- We use *'s* (possessive *'s* or the saxon genetive) to show possession. It is a use unique to English, and therefore new and strange to students. They will make errors like ✗ the mother of Andy and ✗ Andy mother.
- N.B. we only use possessive *'s* with people. Compare *John's head* and the *head of the river*.
- As possessive *'s* looks the same as the abbreviated form of *is* or *has*, this can confuse. Compare *John's tired* and *John's friends*. At this level, it's best to avoid these uses in the same sentence.

5

- Students work in groups of three, A, B and C. Instruct the activity carefully, and model it briefly.

Alternative procedure

- You could do this in larger groups, say six. One student covers his/her eyes. The others place objects on the table. The student then has to guess who the objects belong to. They get a point for each one they guess right. Students take it in turns. At the end, find out which student has the most points.

PRONUNCIATION: final -*s*

1 & 2 1.41

- Play the recording. Students read and listen to the pronunciation of the final -*s* in the words. Sometimes the final -*s* is pronounced as an extra syllable.
- Play the recording again for students to listen and repeat.

 1.41

> go goes
> computer computers
>
> watch watches
> house houses
> class classes

Language notes

- In the third person, verbs end with -*s* (or -*es*), which is pronounced /z/ after vowels and voiced consonants: *goes* /geʊz/, *lives* /lɪvz/, but /s/ after unvoiced consonants: *speaks* /spiːks/.
- There is an extra syllable /ɪz/ when words end with *sh*, *ch*, *ss* or *s*, (*watches* /wɒtʃɪz/, *buses* /bʌsɪz/, etc). Also when it ends with /dʒ/, (*languages* /laŋgwɪdʒɪz/).

3 & 4 1.42

- You could put students in pairs to say the words to each other. Do the first two as examples.
- Play the recording. Students listen to the recording to check their answers.
- You could play the recording again. Students listen and repeat.

> There is an extra syllable in *Charles'*, *buses* and *sandwiches*

 1.42

> **no extra syllable**
> do does
> listen listens
> study studies
>
> **extra syllable**
> Charles Charles'
> bus buses
> sandwich sandwiches

Extra task for stronger classes

- Tell students in pairs to write three sentences. Each sentence must contain at least two words from exercises 1 and/or 3, e.g. *He goes to Charles' Yoga classes*.
- Ask students to read out their sentences for the class.
- Alternatively, write a few sentences on the board yourself, and ask students to read them out as tongue twisters.

Language notes

- Notice *John's* /dʒɒnz/ but *Charles'* /tʃɑːlzɪz/. When a name ends in *s*, only a comma is added, but the pronunciation adds /ɪz/.
- Students may say that *studies* has an extra syllable. It doesn't because *study* already has two syllables.
- N.B. *goes* /geʊz/ but *does* /dʌz/.

DID YOU KNOW?

1 & 2

- Pairwork. Ask students to read the text about the typical British family, and then discuss the questions with a partner, comparing typical families in their own country to that in Britain.
- In feedback, find out whether there is a consensus of opinion in the classroom.

Multilingual classes

- If you have a range of nationalities in your class, do this in groups, so students can compare their countries.

Language notes

- *1.62* is pronounced *one point six two*.
- *31%* is pronounced *thirty one per cent*.

Web research tasks

❯ *Methodology guidelines: Web research tasks, page xiii*

- Students find out statistics about the changing family in their country on the web. Or they could choose a different English-speaking country (USA, Canada, New Zealand, etc), and find statistics for that country.

Web search key words

- country/statistics/census/family

IF YOU WANT SOMETHING EXTRA ...

❯ *Photocopiable activity, page 199*
❯ *Teacher's notes, page 173*

2D | Tour group

WHAT THE LESSON IS ABOUT

Theme	Describing physical appearance
Speaking	Communication: describing famous faces past & present
Listening	A phone call: describing people arriving at the airport
Vocabulary	Adjectives: describing people
Grammar	Adjectives
Functional language	Describing people

IF YOU WANT A LEAD-IN ...

Test before you teach: describing physical appearance

❯ *Methodology guidelines: Test before you teach, page xiii*

- Find two interesting and contrasting magazine pictures of a man and a woman. Put them on the board, and ask students to tell you about them. Find out how many descriptive words they know, but avoid teaching any at this stage.
- A nice follow-up to this is to put students in A and B pairs, and give all the A students a magazine picture of a man or woman. Student A says: *This is my boyfriend/girlfriend*. Then both students describe the person in the picture.

VOCABULARY: adjectives

1 & 2   1.43

- Students match the adjectives in the box to the pictures and complete the sentences.
- Play the recording. Students listen and check their answers.
- Play the recording again. Students listen and repeat.

See tapescript below for answers.

🌐 1.43

1 He's <u>tall</u>; He's <u>short</u>.
2 She's <u>young</u>; She's <u>old</u>.
3 He's <u>fat</u>; He's <u>thin</u>.
4 He's <u>handsome</u>; She's <u>beautiful</u>; They're <u>ugly</u>.
5 She has <u>fair</u> hair; He has <u>dark</u> hair.

3

- Students put the adjectives in the right category. They can compare their answers with a partner before you check with the whole class.

age: middle-aged
height: medium height
looks: average-looking; pretty

Language notes

- Connotation plays large role with these words.
- **Thin** and **fat** both have negative connotations, and are rude if used to describe someone face to face. You may want to introduce *slim*, which means *thin* but in a positive, attractive sense. Similarly, *ugly* is a very negative word.

- **Fair** hair can mean any hair colour from light brown to Swedish blond. **Blond** is used to mean very fair.
- **Middle-aged** is usually used to describe people in their fifties and sixties. However, when exactly it starts and ends depends on the point of view (and age) of the person using the word.
- N.B. we can say, He is *of medium height*.

GRAMMAR: adjectives

❯ *Language reference, Student's Book page 30*
❯ *Methodology guidelines: Grammar boxes, page xiii*

Language notes

- In English, adjectives never change their form, and always go before the noun. N.B. in many languages adjectives go after nouns and change their form to match the gender of the noun they are describing, or to match whether the noun is singular or plural.
- Note the collocations: *handsome man; beautiful woman; pretty girl*. You may want to introduce *attractive* or *good-looking* which are adjectives that can be used to describe any person.

1

- Students think of a famous person for each category, and write their names in the circle. They can compare their answers with a partner.
- In feedback, ask for examples from around the class.

2

- Pairwork. Put students in A and B pairs. They take it in turns to say names and guess categories.

Extension task

- On the board or on a sheet of paper (photocopied and handed out), write a list of ten to fifteen categories. For example:

A handsome film star	A fat comedian
A young pop star	An old TV personality
A beautiful singer	A middle-aged film star
An ugly politician	A tall sportswoman

- Ask students in pairs to write an example for each. Make it a competition – who can find examples the quickest.
- In feedback, students read out their examples. The rest of the class must guess the category.

LISTENING

In this episode of the listening story we meet Brian, who works with Valerie for Explore London Tours. He has gone to the airport to pick up some people who are joining the tour: Delilah Williams, Patti Owen and Dave Matthews. Valerie phones Brian up to tell him which planes the tourists are arriving on and to describe what they look like.

1

- Put students in pairs to describe Valerie and Brian in the pictures.
- In feedback, elicit lots of descriptive adjectives and phrases from students.

Valerie:	She's young. She's pretty/beautiful. She has fair hair/short hair.
Brian:	He's middle-aged. He's fat. He has dark hair/short hair.

2 💿 **1.44**
- Play the recording. Students listen to the conversation and answer the questions.

> 1   At the airport.
> 2   Brian is at the airport to meet people on the Explore London Tour. Valerie describes what they look like.

💿 **1.44**

> **V = Valerie   B = Brian   D = Dave**
> **B:** Hello?
> **V:** Hi, Brian? It's Valerie. <u>Are you at the airport?</u>
> **B:** <u>Yes, I am.</u>
> **V:** I'm sorry I'm not there. Is the plane from New Zealand there?
> **B:** Yes, it is. Who's on the plane?
> **V:** You have to meet two women, <u>Delilah Williams and Patti Owen.</u>
> **B:** Fine. Delilah and Patti. What do they look like?
> **V:** Hold on, I have their photos here. OK, <u>Delilah is short and pretty. She has long dark hair.</u>
> **B:** <u>How old is she?</u>
> **V:** <u>Around 30.</u>
> **B:** OK. And Patti?
> **V:** <u>Patti's also around 30 years old. They're friends. Patti's tall. She has fair hair.</u>
> **B:** Hello? Hello? …
> **V:**   Hello?
> **B:** Hi, it's Brian again. Sorry about that, my mobile phone. OK, Patti and Delilah. Who else?
> **V:** There's also Dave.
> **B:** Dave?
> **V:** Yes, <u>Dave Matthews.</u> He's on the plane from Canada.
> **B:** OK, what does he look like?
> **V:** <u>He's around 25. He's a little fat. He has dark hair. Oh, he has glasses.</u>
> **B:** OK. Wait a minute. I think I see Dave now.
> **V:** Great. Call me when you meet everyone.
> **B:** Sure. Bye. Excuse me. Are you Dave Matthews?
> **D:** Yes, I am. Hi!

3 💿 **1.44**
- Play the recording. Students listen again and match the people to the pictures.

> A   Delilah Williams – from New Zealand
> B   Patti Owen – from New Zealand
> D   Dave Matthews – from Canada

Extra task
- In pairs, students choose and describe a person in one of the pictures. Their partner must guess and point to the person they are describing.

FUNCTIONAL LANGUAGE: describing people

❯ *Language reference, Student's Book page 31*

1 💿 **1.45**
- This is a drill. Read through the examples carefully. Point out *She's* + adjective, and *She has* + noun. Then play the recording. Students listen to the prompt word then make a sentence using *She's* or *She has*.

- You could play the recording once, getting students to make sentences chorally, then play it again, nominating individuals to produce sentences.

> 3   green eyes – She has green eyes.
> 4   young – She's young.
> 5   twenty years old – She's twenty years old.
> 6   black hair – She has black hair.
> 7   beautiful – She's beautiful.
> 8   short – She's short.
> 9   pretty – She's pretty.

💿 **1.45**

> 1   glasses
> 2   tall
> 3   green eyes
> 4   young
> 5   twenty years old
> 6   black hair
> 7   beautiful
> 8   short
> 9   pretty

2
- Students correct the questions and sentences by adding one word. They can compare their answers with a partner before you check with the whole class.

> 1   What do they look <u>like</u>?
> 2   Delilah is short <u>and</u> pretty.
> 3   How old <u>is</u> she?
> 4   Patti is around 30 years <u>old</u>.
> 5   What <u>does</u> he look like?
> 6   He's <u>a</u> little fat.
> 7   He has dark <u>hair</u> and glasses.
> 8   She <u>has</u> blue eyes.

Alternative procedure

❯ *Key Methodology 14: Drilling 1 – basics, page 55*

- It is a good idea to introduce *What does he look like?* by means of a board presentation. This allows you to drill and practise the language fully, and it is a fun, whole class activity.
- Put a picture of a woman and a picture of a man on the board. Point to the pictures and elicit lots of adjectives: *tall, short, old, young, beautiful,* etc. Write the adjectives on the board next to the relevant pictures.
- Point to the picture of the woman, and say: *What does she look like?* Repeat the question two or three times. Then ask students to repeat chorally and individually.
- Model the dialogue. Point to the picture and say: *What does she look like? She's tall and young.* Point to a student and get them to say: *What does she look like?* Point to another student and get them to say: *She's tall and young.* Do this a number of times, getting students to ask and answer across the class.

• Repeat the procedure with the picture of the man.

Language notes

• *What does he look like?* is a form that students find confusing and difficult to say. Students may want to say, *How is he?* to mean *What does he look like?* N.B. in many languages this form can be used to ask for physical description. Here, *like* is a preposition not a verb.

• Students may confuse this question with *What does he like?* Students may want to use *look like* in the answer: ✗ *He looks like tall.*

• We use *She's* + adjective and *She has* + noun when describing people.

3

• Pairwork. Put students into A and B pairs. Give Student A a minute to think of how to describe the person in the class they have chosen. Give Student B a minute to prepare the questions.

• Student B asks questions and Student A describes someone in the class.

• When Student B has guessed the person, they change roles.

SPEAKING

1

◗ *Communication activities, Student's Book, pages 132 & 135*

• Lead in by checking that students know the famous people in the task. (See *Cultural notes* below.) Write the people's names on the board, and ask students to tell you what they know about them.

• Pairwork. Put students in A and B pairs. Student A turn to page 132 in the Student's Book and Student B turns to page 135.

• Model the activity briefly by describing Student A's first picture to the class. Then tell students to take it in turns to describe their famous people.

• In feedback, find out which pictures of the famous people are the same, and which are different.

Same: Madonna, Halle Berry

Cultural notes

• **Elvis Presley** (American 1937–1977). Known as the king of rock and roll. When young, in the 1950s, he was tall and slim, but in middle age he became fat because of beer, drugs and fast food. He died of a heart attack.

• **Madonna**: Italian-American queen of 1980s pop. She is still singing and acting, and now also writes children's books. She is married to the British film director Guy Ritchie and lives in England.

• **Diego Maradonna** from Argentina, was considered the best footballer in the world in the 1980s. In recent years, he has had a lot of health problems and became overweight, partly because of a cocaine addiction.

• **Halle Berry**: American film star who won an Oscar in 2001 for *Monster's Ball* and appeared in the James Bond movie *Die Another Day* in 2002.

• **Sean Connery**: Scottish film star. He was the first actor to play James Bond in *Dr No* (1962). He is now in his seventies and is still acting.

▪ Key Methodology 9
▪ Spoken errors: fluency tasks 2

• *Here are some further ideas for working on errors after a fluent speaking task has finished.*

1 Student teacher

• *Write the errors on the board. Get a student to come to the board and be the teacher. Their job is not to decide about what is correct or incorrect themselves, but to get the class to agree and note their decision on the board. For this reason, don't choose the strongest student to do this task. Instruct 'the teacher' and class that you will go to the back of the room, and tell the teacher that you don't want them to call you until they are satisfied that they have got all the correct answers on the board. While the class is working together force yourself to vanish a little. Restrain yourself from the urge to constantly help and correct.*

2 Split lists

• *This idea takes a little time to prepare – but it's worth it. Use two sheets of paper headed A and B and make a list of numbers 1–20 down each page. While monitoring students doing the fluency activity, write each error you hear randomly on either sheet A or B. Where there is an error on A, leave a blank space on list B next to the corresponding number, and vice versa.*

• *When you have time (or after class), go through the list and where there is an error in list A, write a corrected version of the sentence next to the same number in list B (and do the same for errors in list B). For example:*

A	**B**
1 What's your name?	1 What your name is?
2 Is he teacher?	2 Is he a teacher?

• *Photocopy enough sheets so that half the students can have A and half B.*

• *In class, give A to all the students in one part of the room and B to the other half. Tell them that the sentences are ones you heard while they were speaking. Make sure they understand that some sentences are correct and some are not.*

• *Put students in pairs (both with the same worksheet). They must study their sheet and decide which are correct – and then correct the incorrect ones.*

• *When they have finished, reorganize the pairs so that everyone now has an A and a B in their pair. They should compare worksheets. Do they match? Do both students think a sentence is incorrect – or correct? Which one is the correct answer? Students may find that they need to rethink their original decision at this stage.*

Web research tasks

◗ *Methodology guidelines: Web research tasks, page xiii*

• Students must research a famous person, and find pictures of them now and when they were younger. They must write a comparative description of them

Web search key words

• name of person/biography/images

IF YOU WANT SOMETHING EXTRA …

◗ *Photocopiable activity, page 200*
◗ *Teacher's notes, page 174*

Answer key

2 REVIEW

◆ *Student's Book page 148*

1

1 live
2 have
3 go
4 work
5 speak
6 eat

2

3 She drinks beer.
4 She doesn't speak Spanish.
5 She has lots of friends.
6 She doesn't have a boyfriend.
7 She goes dancing.
8 She doesn't live with her parents.

3

1 uncle
2 grandfather
3 mother
4 aunt
5 brother
6 daughter

4

1 He's my mother's husband. He's my <u>father</u>.
2 He's my brother. He's my parents' <u>son</u>.
3 She's my mother's/father's daughters. They're my <u>sisters</u>.

5

1 We ~~doesn't~~ <u>don't</u> work now.
2 No, he ~~don't~~ <u>doesn't</u>.
3 Do you ~~has~~ <u>have</u> lots of friends?
4 She ~~speak~~ <u>speaks</u> French and Spanish.
5 I don't ~~lives~~ <u>live</u> in London.
6 ~~Is~~ <u>Are</u> you married?

6

1 Do you have lots of friends?
2 Do you live with your parents?
3 How is your life different?
4 What do you do?
5 What is your name?
6 Where are you from?
7 Who do you live with?

7

a) 5   b) 6   c) 2   d) 4   e) 3   f) 1   g) 7

8

1 young
2 thin
3 tall
4 beautiful
5 fair

Model answer
Hi, my mother's name is Gill. She has long brown hair and brown eyes. My father's name is Mark. He is tall. He has blue eyes and blond hair. My sister's name is Maggie. She is short and has long blond hair and blue eyes. My brother's name is John. He is tall and thin. He's average-looking.

| 35

3A | Houseswap

WHAT THE LESSON IS ABOUT

Theme	Places to live; swapping homes
Speaking	Game: Class houseswap – exchanging information; describing & 'swapping' houses
Reading	*Welcome to Houseswap.com*: a website describing houses to swap for the holidays
Vocabulary	Describing where you live
Grammar	Prepositions of place

IF YOU WANT A LEAD-IN ...

Test before you teach: describing houses

> *Methodology guidelines: Test before you teach, page xiii*

- Draw a simple block of flats on the board. Point to one of them and say: *This is my home. It's a flat.* Then describe the flat in simple terms:
  It's an old flat. It's in England. It's near the city centre. It's small. There is a balcony. It has two bedrooms. It's beautiful. I like it.
- Now say: *This is your home.* Nominate a student to describe it, using any language that they have. It's fine if they only have one or two sentences to offer.
- Ask one or two other students to describe their home. Then put students in pairs to describe their homes.

Pre-teach key vocabulary: swap

- Go round the class, saying, e.g. *Can I swap my pen/book for your pencil/mobile?* Make a few *swaps* with students in the class. Then elicit what *swap* means. Ask: *What things do you swap with friends?*

Language notes

- **Swap** means to exchange one thing for another with somebody. It is usually used with small, simple exchanges rather than swapping houses. Common collocations: *swap seats, swap places, swap stories, swap clothes.*
- **Houseswap** means you give someone your house for the holidays, and they give you their house.

VOCABULARY: places to live

> *Language reference, Student's Book page 41*

1

- Students match the adjectives in A to their opposites in B.

A		B
big	≠	small
new	≠	old
noisy	≠	quiet
lovely	≠	horrible

Extra practice

> *Key Methodology 10: Flashcards 1 – the essentials, page 37*

- Use flashcards to practise the words. You need to find a fairly large picture of a busy city, and one of a quiet village in magazines. Hold up your picture of a city. Say: *It's big.* Spread your arms to show the meaning of the word. Ask students to repeat after you as a class. Then nominate two or three individuals to repeat. Point to the village and say: *It's small.* Push your arms towards each other to mime the meaning. Ask students to repeat. Do the same with all the words. And try to mime the meaning, e.g. screw up your face and cover your ears to show *noisy*; put your finger to your lips for *quiet*; smile and do a thumbs up for *lovely*.
- Once students have listened and repeated, point to pictures and nominate individuals to give you a sentence, e.g. point to the picture of the city and nominate a student. The student must say: for example, *It's new and it's noisy*.
- End the practice by putting the pictures on the board, and asking students in pairs to point to and describe the pictures.
- When doing this sort of controlled practice be strict on pronunciation. In particular, make sure students pronounce *quiet* /kwaɪət/ as two syllables, and watch out for the pronunciation of /ɔɪ/ in *noisy* and /ɔː/ in *small*.

2 1.46

- Ask students to read the text in the speech bubble carefully first before you play the recording.
- Students listen to the recording and underline the words that they hear. They can compare their answers with a partner before you check with the whole class.

> *See underlined answers in the tapescript below.*

1.46

> I live in a <u>small</u> flat on Herbert Street. It's in the centre of Dublin. It's a <u>lovely</u> flat, but the street is <u>noisy</u>. I <u>like</u> it.

3

> *Key Methodology 7: Accurate speaking & fluent speaking, page 20*

- Ask students to look at the gapped text in the speech bubble. Model the activity by saying a sentence to describe where you live.
- Pairwork. Put students in pairs. Give them a moment or two to think what they are going to say. Then ask the pairs to tell each other about where they live. Monitor and check that students are producing (reasonably) accurate sentences. Ask two or three individuals to tell the class where they live in feedback.
- Ask students to write sentences to describe where they live in their exercise book.

Extra task

- Ask students to imagine they are millionaires and live in a dream house. Ask them to write a sentence then read it for the class, e.g. *I live in a big house on Tropical Beach. It's in Barbados. It's a lovely house. I like it.*

READING

The first reading text is the homepage of an internet site, Houseswap.com. In the introduction it explains that it is a company which helps people find other people who would like to swap their home with them for the holidays.
The second text contains five descriptions of homes people are trying to swap on the site.

1

- Before class, find three very different pictures of luxury holiday homes from magazines. Put them on the board and ask students to describe them: *It's big, old, lovely*, etc. Tell students, *You can go on holiday to one of these houses. Which one and why?*
- Write *Houseswap* on the board. Ask: *What is Houseswap?* Remind them of the Lead-in *Pre-teach key vocabulary* task if you did it. Students read the introduction to the *Houseswap* webpage, and say what 'swap' means.

> ### ■ Key Methodology 10
> ### ■ Flashcards 1: the essentials
>
> - *Flashcards are pictures (or sometimes words written in large letters) that you can hold up and show to the class or pass around for a variety of activities. If you regularly teach lower level classes, one of the most useful ways of investing your preparation time is in building up your own personal stock of flashcards. If you choose pictures carefully and prepare the cards well, they will go on being useful to you for years to come.*
> - *Scour glossy magazines for good pictures. Alternatively, you can draw simple images yourself. Or persuade an artistic friend to draw a few for you!*
> - *If you teach a largish class, you need to choose pictures big enough to be easily seen even at the back of class. Anything smaller than half an A4 page will be too small.*
> - *A good basic set of flashcards will include:*
>   *1 striking different faces showing people of different ages, backgrounds, etc.*
>   *2 people doing different things: work, relaxing, sports, etc.*
>   *3 everyday objects.*
>   *4 landscapes and city views.*
> - *Don't try to build a whole set of flashcards in one go. Allow it grow slowly alongside your teaching work.*
> - *It is vital that you maintain your pictures in good condition. Magazine pages tear and fall apart very easily. If you hope to get a few years' use out of them, spend a little time on ways of mounting them:*
>   *1 if you have the opportunity, laminate your pictures, i.e. encase them in a plastic envelope.*
>   *2 as an alternative to laminating, put pictures into A4 transparent file pouches (pochettes). This has the advantage of allowing you to store them in a standard ring binder file.*
>   *3 a third alternative is to glue pictures onto a cardboard backing. This has the advantage of preserving their life a little longer than otherwise – but the pictures tend to look a little more wrinkled.*
> - *When you have a set of flashcards, they can be used in a variety of ways to spice up your lessons.*
>
> ❍ *Key Methodology 11 & 12: Flashcards 2 & 3, pages 41 & 44*

2

- Ask students to look at the six small photos on page 33.

Ask them to describe the houses, and say which one they like. Ask: *Where do you think the houses are?*
- Students read about some of the homes on *Houseswap*, and match each home to a picture. Remind students that there is one extra picture. They can compare their answers with a partner before you check with the whole class.

1	photo A	3	photo C	5	photo D
2	photo F	4	photo E		

Cultural notes

- **Cambridge** is a small city in eastern England. It is famous for its old and prestigious university.
- A **cottage** is a small, traditional house in the countryside.
- **Santa Monica** is an expensive, exclusive resort town on the coast of California near Hollywood. It is popular with the rich and famous. The house on offer is likely to be a large villa with a swimming pool.
- **Notting Hill** is a busy, cosmopolitan quarter of central London, near Hyde Park. It is famous for its bars and restaurants. Portabello market is in Notting Hill, where you can buy food, clothes and antiques.
- **Heathrow** is London's largest airport and one of the world's busiest.
- **The Champs Elysees** is the main, wide, tree-lined thoroughfare in Paris. Its main monument is the huge arch of the Arc de triomphe.

3

- Students read about the homes again and mark the sentences true or false. They can compare their answers with a partner before you check with the whole class.

1 T	2 F	3 F	4 F	5 F	6 T	7 F	8 F

4

- Pairwork. Put students in pairs. Students discuss the questions with their partner.
- In class feedback, ask some students to say which home they have chosen and why, (*It's in the centre of Paris, It's big*, etc.).

Web research tasks

❍ *Methodology guidelines: Web research tasks, page xiii*

- Ask students to find their dream home on the web. Tell them to decide where they want to live, (ideally, make sure they choose an English-speaking country). They should also decide whether they want a flat, cottage or house.
- Tell students to go online and find their home. They must find the following information: where it is, its description, and how much is it.

Web search key words

- name of city or country/house/home/property
- home swap/home exchange

GRAMMAR: prepositions of place

❍ *Language reference, Student's Book page 40*
❍ *Methodology guidelines: Grammar boxes, page xiii*

1

- Ask students to look back at the five descriptions of houses on the *Houseswap* webpage on page 32. They must underline all the prepositions of place and the nouns that follow them.

1 <u>in</u> a small, white house.
   <u>in</u> Cambridge.
   <u>next</u> to an old restaurant ...
   <u>close</u> to the university.

2 <u>in</u> Scotland.
   <u>in</u> the mountains.
   <u>far from</u> other people ...

3 <u>on</u> the beach.
   <u>in</u> Santa Monica ...
   <u>near</u> our house!

4 <u>in</u> the centre of London.
   <u>in</u> Notting Hill.
   <u>behind</u> a market.
   <u>close to</u> a hospital ...

5 <u>at the end</u> of the Champs Elysées <u>in</u> Paris.
   <u>opposite</u> the Arc de Triomphe.

Extra task: in, on & at

- Write *in*, *on* and *at* on the board. Build up a list of 'rules' under each preposition.

in	*on*	*at*
a house	streets	the end ...
towns/cities	the beach	home
countries	floors	
the mountains		
the centre ...		

Extra task: opposite, behind, next to, *etc.*

- You could check students' understanding by drawing a simple street map (as shown) on the board and ask them where the school/hospital, etc. is and elicit responses using prepositions of place, e.g. *The school is opposite the big house. The car park is behind the university.*

school	supermarket	hospital
		bus stop

High Street

	university	small house
big house	car park	

Language notes: prepositions of place

- ***In*, *on*** and ***at*** are difficult for students if and when they are used differently in the students' L1 from English. If you have a monolingual class, predict errors by checking which of the uses in the grammar box are similar and which are different from the students' L1.
- You could show the difference between *in*, *on* and *at* by drawing the following symbols on the board:

  in ⊗   *on* ___✗   *at* ●✗

- We generally say *at school*, *at university*, *at work*. No article is used. However, when we want to stress the specific location we can say *in the*, e.g. *John isn't outside. He's waiting in the school.*
  N.B. We say *at home* not ✗ *in home.*

- ***Opposite*** and ***in front of*** are often confused. You can check the difference between them by drawing faces on the board:

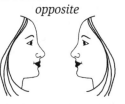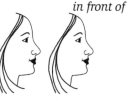

opposite	*in front of*

- Watch out for stray uses of *of*, e.g. ✗ *It is behind of my house.*
- N.B. *near* and *near to* are both correct, e.g. *I live near London. I live near to the centre.*

2

- Students complete the texts with prepositions.

1	in	4	on	7	to
2	in	5	in	8	from
3	on	6	in		

3

- Model the activity briefly by describing someone in the class, using the sentence prompts. The students must guess who you are describing.
- Students choose a person in the class, and complete the sentences with information about that person.

4

- Pairwork. Put students in pairs. Each partner must read their sentences from exercise 3, and their partner must guess who they are describing. Monitor and help if necessary.

SPEAKING

1

- Tell students to close their eyes and imagine their home. Say: *Where is it? Is it a flat or a house? Is it big or small; new or old; lovely or horrible? Is it close to the city centre? Is it far from the shops?*
- Tell students to open their eyes, and write a short description of their home on a piece of paper. Give them a time limit of four minutes. Remind students to look back at the webpage descriptions on page 32 to help them.

Alternative procedure

- Ask students to imagine and describe their 'perfect' house rather than their own house. You could get students to draw the house as well as write a description.

2

- Ask students to stand up and walk round the class. They must find another student and take it in turns to describe their homes. They must then make a note whether they are interested in swapping houses with that person.
- Make it a rule that they must speak to at least three people before they can make a final decision which of the houses they want to swap with.
- Monitor, prompt and correct where necessary.

3

- When all or most students have swapped, ask them to sit down. Ask a few students to describe their new home.

IF YOU WANT SOMETHING EXTRA ...

❯ *Photocopiable activity, page 201*
❯ *Teacher's notes, page 174*

3B | 1600 Pennsylvania Avenue

WHAT THE LESSON IS ABOUT

Theme	Famous houses (the White House)
Speaking	Presentation: giving a virtual tour of your home
Listening	A radio documentary programme about the White House
Vocabulary	Parts of a house
Grammar	*There is/there are; How many*
Did you know	*Number 10 Downing Street*

IF YOU WANT A LEAD-IN ...

Pre-teach key words: parts of a house

- Write *parts of a house* in the middle of the board. Say: *Where am I?* Then mime the act of cooking food. Try to elicit *kitchen*. Say the word, ask students to repeat, then write it on the board. Repeat this to elicit the following words:
  Dining room (mime eating)
  Bedroom (mime sleeping)
  Bathroom (mime showering)
  Living room (mime watching TV)
- Rub the words off the board, then ask students to come to the front of the class and mime an action. The other students must guess the room.

LISTENING

This listening is the introduction to a documentary about the White House. An official at the White House talks about what other names the building has, where it is and who lives there. He goes on to give more details about the house: how old it is; how many rooms there are; whereabouts in the building the President works; how many people work there and information about public visits.

1

- Ask students to look at the photos. Tell them to work silently on their own and answer the questions. If they don't know the answers to some of the questions, tell them to guess.
- Ask students to describe the house: *It's big; It's old; It's beautiful; It's white.*

---

1 It's more than 200 years old.
2 Its common name is the White House.
3 The President of the United States and his family live there.
4 Yes, there are.
5 There are 132 rooms.
6 Washington DC, USA.

---

2 🔘 1.47

- Now play the recording. Students listen out for the questions from exercise 1, and put the questions in the order that they hear them.
- Then play the recording again for students to check their answers to exercise 1 and 2. They can then compare their answers with a partner before you check with the class.

4, 1, 3, 6, 5, 2

🔘 1.47

V = visitor O = official
V: What is the name of the house?
O: There are at least <u>four names</u> for the house at 1600 Pennsylvania Avenue, including the President's Palace, the President's House and the Executive Mansion. But this famous building's common name is <u>the White House</u>.
V: Where is it?
O: The White House is in the centre of <u>Washington, DC</u>, the capital of the <u>United States of America</u>.
V: Who lives there?
O: <u>The President of the United States and his family</u> officially live in the White House. But there are hundreds of people who work there, and there are thousands of visitors every day.
V: How old is it?
O: The White House was built in 1800. <u>It's now more than 200 years old</u>.
V: How many rooms are there?
O: There are <u>132 rooms</u> in the White House. There are 16 family bedrooms, three kitchens and <u>32 bathrooms</u>. There are also six floors, <u>seven staircases</u>, three elevators, 147 windows and 412 doors. There is a games room, a mini golf course, a tennis court, two swimming pools, a bowling alley and even a small cinema.
V: <u>Are there public visits?</u>
O: <u>Yes, there are.</u> Public visits are available for groups of <u>ten people</u> or more from Tuesday to Saturday, from 7:30 am to 12:30 pm. Please note that there aren't any public telephones or public bathrooms on the tour of the White House.

Language notes

- ***Elevators*** = US English; *lifts* = UK English
- ***The bathroom*** (US English) is a room with a toilet. In UK English, it is just called *the toilet*, whereas a *bathroom* contains a bath or a shower and a place to wash your hands, and often includes, but not always, a toilet. In US English, *restrooms* are bathrooms in public places, whereas in UK English, the terms *Public toilets* or *Ladies* and *Gents* are used.

Cultural notes

- ***The White House*** at 1600 Pennsylvania Avenue was completed in 1800 by Irish immigrant James Hoban. He modelled it on the neoclassical Georgian manors of Dublin. It was burned down by the British in the War of 1812, then rebuilt and painted white, hence its name. Every US president since 1800 has lived there.

3 🔘 1.47

- Read out the numbers and ask students to repeat them.
- Then ask students to read through the sentences and remember or guess which number goes in which space.
- Play the recording again. They can compare their answers with a partner before you check with the whole class.

---

1 4   2 200   3 32   4 7   5 10

4

- Pairwork. Students discuss the question briefly with a partner. They can then tell the class about their opinion.

VOCABULARY: parts of a house

❯ *Language reference, Student's Book page 41*

1 🔘 **1.48**

- Play the recording for students to listen and repeat the words in the box.
- Then read out the words in the box, and ask students to repeat them again. Make sure students are approximating the weak stress in *kitchen* /ˈkɪtʃən/ and *balcony* /ˈbælkənɪ:/.
- Students match the words to the numbers on the map. They can then compare their answers with a partner.

🔘 **1.48**

living room   hall   kitchen   balcony   bedroom
bathroom   dining room

> ■ **Key Methodology 11**
> ■ **Flashcards 2: presenting vocabulary**
>
> - *Instead of using coursebook illustrations to introduce vocabulary, try using your cards to do a books-closed presentation.*
> - *The simplest way is to stand at the front of the class, hold up a card, e.g. a picture of two eggs, and invite students to name the object(s) shown. If they can't produce the word, you can model it yourself.*
> - *You could say the item once clearly in a sentence, e.g.* The Queen's standing on the balcony. *Then isolate the word and say it clearly two or three times, e.g.* balcony … balcony. *Try to leave a longish pause between each time you say the word – allow time for the word to 'echo' in students' minds before they hear it again. If you repeat too quickly, each new hearing simply drowns out the one before. Also, don't repeat too many times – three or four is sufficient. If you do it more, students may relax and not pay the attention that is needed.*
> - *Now get students to repeat the word. First of all, gesture to get the whole class to repeat the word, two or three times – then gesture to ask individuals to say it one by one with feedback.*
> > ❯ *Key Methodology 16: Helping students say it better, page 66*
> > ❯ *Key Methodology 12: More ways of presenting vocabulary, page 44*

2 🔘 **1.49**

- Play the recording for students to check their answers.

1   hall
2   bedroom
3   dining room
4   living room
5   kitchen
6   bathroom
7   balcony

🔘 **1.49**

M = man   W = woman

1
M: So, come in, come in.
W: Wow. So, this is your new flat.
M: Yeah. Look, this is the hall. These are my pictures, here and … here.
W: Mmmm.

2
M: The bedroom.
W: Nice and big.
M: Yes. Look out the window. You can see the park …
W: Ooohh.

3
W: What's this room?
M: It's the dining room. I don't go in here really, there's only me.

4
W: Is this the living room?
M: Yes, I'm here a lot of the time.
W: I like your TV.
M: Thanks.

5
M: Would you like a drink?
W: Umm, yes, please. What do you have?
M: Come into the kitchen. Let's see.

6
W: Where's the bathroom?
M: Next to you. Right here.
W: I see.

7
W: Look at this balcony. You have a nice flat.
M: Thanks, it's not exactly the White House, but it's home.

3

- Model the present simple question forms. Ask students to listen and repeat. Pay particular attention to the weak /ə/ stress and the intonation pattern in these sentences.

      /ə/ /ə/   □
  Where do you watch TV?

- Nominate individual students to ask and answer the questions across the class in open pairs.
- Pairwork. Put students in pairs to ask and answer the questions. Monitor, prompt and correct as necessary.

GRAMMAR: *there is / there are; How many*

❯ *Language reference, Student's Book page 40*
❯ *Methodology guidelines: Grammar boxes, page xiv*

❯ *Key Methodology 15: Drilling 2 – substitution , page 58*

1

- Read through the examples with the class, then elicit the answer to number 3 to make sure students know what to do. Students make sentences about the White House using the prompts. Monitor and help if necessary. They can compare their answers with a partner before you check with the whole class.
- In feedback, you could ask a confident student to come up to the board. Ask the rest of the class what the answer is. The student at the board must write it up. Change the student after two sentences.

3 There are two swimming pools.
4 There isn't a restaurant.
5 There are three kitchens.
6 There are seven lifts.
7 There aren't any public telephones.

Extra task: a substitution drill

- Now turn this writing task into a simple substitution drill.
- Write ' + ' and '–' on the board. Say: *a cinema*, point to ' + ', and nominate a student. The student must say: *There's a cinema*. Continue round the class, saying *seven floors, a staircase*, etc.
- Alternatively, if you have time, you could draw simple pictures to represent *two tennis courts, a restaurant*, etc. Make about ten pictures. Then use these visual prompts to prompt sentences from students. They work better than verbal prompts.

Language notes

- *There is* and *there are* do not translate literally into the students' first language. If you have a monolingual class it is worth briefly exploring what phrase is used in their language, and whether they have a singular and a plural phrase (like English) or just one phrase for both singular and plural.
- Using *any* with negative and question forms may well be a new concept for students. In many Latin languages, for example, there is no need to use a word like *any*, so students are likely to avoid it, e.g. ✗ There are not swimming pools.

2

❯ *Key Methodology 29: Pronunciation – don't avoid intonation!, page 126*

- Ask students to look at the table. Then model the activity carefully by reading out two or three questions. Make sure that students have grasped the idea of *Is there a* + singular noun, and *Are there any* + plural noun.
- Elicit sentences from around the class.
- Now model the stress and intonation pattern carefully. Show that the main strong stress is on the noun in column 4, and that the voice rises at the end. Show the falling intonation on the short answer.
  For example:

  Is there a bathroom in your house?

  Yes, there is.
- Ask students to listen and repeat your model.

Language notes

- At this level, students may find it difficult to manipulate these forms. They will need lots of practice.
- **There is** + singular noun and **There are** + plural noun is a fairly simple idea to grasp. However, be aware that transposing the word order to make questions and adding the abbreviated *not* may well be unfamiliar and will therefore lead to errors, e.g. using the same word order when making a statement or asking a question, such as, ✗ There is a bathroom? with rising intonation.

- *There is* and *There aren't* are not easy to pronounce accurately! You will need to do lots of repetition work to get students to approximate these phrases. Note the following in particular.
  Weak stress and linking and the pronunciation (or not) of *r*:
  There's a …/ðeəzə/
  There isn't a … /ðərɪz(ə)ntə/
  There are …. /ðeərə/
  The strong and weak stress of *are*:
  There are … /ðeərə/
  There aren't … /ðeərɑːnt/
  Are there …/ɑːðeə/

3

❯ *Key Methodology 7: Accurate speaking & fluent speaking, page 20*

- Pairwork. Put students in pairs. Students ask and answer the questions from exercise 2. Monitor, prompt, and make sure that students are both manipulating the forms and pronouncing them correctly.
- You could copy the table in exercise 2 on to the board (or use an OHT). That way students will have their attention on you and the board when you elicit and drill the questions.

4

- Read the example, and elicit the answer to number 2 to make sure students know what to do. Students make questions using the prompts. Monitor and help where necessary. They can compare their answers with a partner before you check with the whole class.
- When they have finished, model and drill some of the questions. Then ask students to ask and answer the questions across the class.

2 How many students are there in class today?
3 How many bathrooms are there in your house?
4 How many teachers are there at your school?
5 How many books are there in your bag today?

5

- Pairwork. Put students in pairs to practise asking and answering the questions in exercise 4. Monitor and prompt if necessary.

SPEAKING

1

❯ *Key Methodology 9: Spoken errors – fluency tasks 1, page 28*

- Draw a basic map of your house or flat on the board. Label the rooms, or ask students to guess which room is which, then label them. Make a short presentation about your home, using the words in the *Useful language* box.
- Students draw a map of their house or flat. Then they prepare a short presentation using the words from the lesson and the *Useful language* box to help them. Monitor and help if necessary.
- Put students in groups of three or four. They take it in turns to make their presentations.

Alternative procedure

- If you have an OHP, ask students to draw the plan of their house on OHTs. The students can then take it in turns to come to the front of the class and make their presentations while pointing to the various rooms on their plan on the OHT.

DID YOU KNOW?

1 & 2
- Ask students to read about Number 10 Downing Street.
- Groupwork. Divide students into groups of four or five. Tell them to work on their own and find two interesting facts from the text to tell their group.
- Students discuss the questions in their groups.

Alternative procedures

- In a class where the students are from the same country, get them to discuss the questions and pool their knowledge in order to prepare and present a short description of the famous house. Alternatively, they could discuss then write the description individually for homework.
- In a class with a variety of nationalities, make sure they are in groups with a good mix of nationalities. The students must find out as much as they can about each other's leader's house. In the feedback, ask each group what they can remember about one of the houses described, e.g. *Group A – tell me about Maria's president's house.*

Cultural notes

- Downing Street is a row of tall, narrow terraced houses. From the front, 10 Downing Street looks very small, but it actually goes back a long way. The Prime Minister usually lives in a flat at Number 10, and the Chancellor (or Finance Minister) usually lives in a flat next door at Number 11, which is in fact bigger than the one at Number 10. At the time of writing, the Prime Minister Tony Blair lives at Number 11 with his wife Cherie and four children. The flat at Number 10 was too small for the Blair family, so they swapped flats with the Chancellor Gordon Brown.

Web research tasks

❯ *Methodology guidelines: Web research tasks, page xiii*

- Find out where the presidents of the following countries live: France, Germany, Italy, Russia, Brazil, Mexico, etc. (Tailor this to suit your students.)
- Find: the address/what rooms and facilities there are.
Web search key words
- president/address/the country concerned
- Alternatively, ask students to find out more information about the White House. Go to: www.whitehouse.gov.

IF YOU WANT SOMETHING EXTRA ...

❯ *Photocopiable activity, page 202*
❯ *Teacher's notes, page 174*

3c | My first flat

WHAT THE LESSON IS ABOUT

Theme	Describing rooms
Speaking	Communication: asking questions to find differences between two rooms
Reading & listening	A conversation about moving into a new flat
Vocabulary	Furniture
Grammar	*A, an, some, any*

IF YOU WANT A LEAD-IN ...

Introducing the theme: describing rooms

- Write *There is…* and *There are…* on the board. Look around the classroom, and make two or three sentences, e.g. *There is a whiteboard. There are eight tables.* Tell students to look around the classroom for a few seconds then ask them to give you as many sentences as they can to describe the room.
- An alternative to this is to ask students in pairs to write three sentences about the classroom. Two must be true, and one false. Ask each pair to read out their sentences. The rest of the class must say which one is false.

VOCABULARY: furniture

> *Language reference, Student's Book page 41*

1
- Students look at the pictures and say what the rooms are. Elicit answers and model good pronunciation for students to repeat.

Flat A – living room; Flat B living room
Flat B – bedroom; Flat A – kitchen

---

2 & 3 ● 1.50
- Students match the words to the numbers in the picture.
- Play the recording. Students listen and repeat the words.

---

a fridge – 14
a stereo – 3
a chair – 7
curtains – 11
a clock – 4
a sofa – 2
a television – 1
a cupboard – 12
a desk – 8
plants – 10
a wardrobe – 5
a cooker – 13
pictures – 9
a bed – 6

● 1.50

---

a fridge; a sofa; plants; a bed; a stereo; a television; a chair; a cooker; a wardrobe; curtains; a cupboard; a clock; a lamp; pictures

---

Language notes
- Pay particular attention to the words below, which have specific pronunciation problems:

/ə/ sounds on the final syllable:

  /ə/   /ə/   /ə/   /ə/   /ə/
sof**a** mirr**or** cook**er** curt**ai**ns cupb**oa**rd

problem sounds:

  /dʒ/   /ʃ/   /ɔː/ /əʊ/   /tʃ/
fri**dg**e televi**si**on w**ar**dr**o**be pi**c**tures

Extra idea
- Revise *there is/are* by asking students to give you sentences from the pictures on page 36 using these forms, e.g. *In picture 2, there are two plants./There is a cupboard.*

■ Key Methodology 12
■ Flashcards 3: more ways of presenting vocabulary

- *Here are two different ideas for introducing or revising vocabulary using flashcards.*

Picture lists
- *Collect a set of cards that show the words you want to teach. Write the list of words in a column on the left-hand side of a piece of paper, and photocopy it or write it on the board for students to copy.*
- *Now distribute the cards randomly around the room. Each pair of students gets one card. Pairs must decide which word they think the picture shows and copy a simple version of the picture onto their own list next to the word. If they don't know a word, they draw the picture at the bottom of the page.*
- *When pairs have seen all the cards, ask them to look at other pairs' answers and see if there are any words they can learn – or maybe answers they disagree with.*
- *At the end, go through the pictures one by one at the front, and confirm the words.*

Hidden answers
- *Before students arrive, write the words you want to teach in various positions around the board, and then use tape or sticky-tack to put flashcards with the corresponding pictures on the board covering the words, i.e. the picture of a station hides the word station underneath it.*
- *In the lesson, ask pairs of students to look at the board (they could come up for a close look), and write down what the words are for the objects they can see.*
- *When students have finished, ask a pair to choose one word they think they really know. They come to the board and write it below the picture. Don't say if it's correct or not. Ask other pairs if they agree or not with what they have written. If they don't, ask them to come up and also write their answer below the flashcard.*
- *When everyone has written their words, you can dramatically remove the picture and reveal the real answer underneath. You could give points to the teams that were correct if you wished.*
- *Continue with the other pictures in the same way.*

4 **1.51**

- Read the introduction as a class and explain that Shelly and Claudia are students. Ask students which flat they think they will rent – Flat A or Flat B?
- Play the recording. Students listen and say which flat Shelly and Claudia decide to rent.

Flat A

🔘 **1.51**

> L = landlord S = Shelly C = Claudia
> **L:** OK, this is the flat. Bedroom here … and here. The beds are a little old.
> **S/C:** Oh.
> **L:** Here's the living room. You have a window, a sofa and a TV. The TV's Japanese. It's in good condition. It's my mother's TV.
> **S:** That TV isn't new.
> **L:** The kitchen. I know it's dirty, but look – the cooker works perfectly, and the fridge, too. Look, oh … a sandwich. What's that doing there?
> **C:** Yuk.
> **L:** Anyway, it's £50 per week. Do you want it or not.
> **C:** Ummm.
> **S:** Yes, we do, thank you.

READING & LISTENING

Students read and listen to a dialogue in which Shelly (from *Vocabulary* exercise 4) phones her father up to tell him about her new flat and tries to assure him that everything is fine. Her father would like to see it, but Shelly makes an excuse why he can't come and ends the phone call. Students will need to 'read between the lines' to infer that Shelly is not actually telling the truth.

1 🔘 **1.52**

- Read through the questions with the class. Tell students to read and listen to the dialogue at the same time.
- You could put students in pairs to discuss the answers to the questions and then discuss them as a class.

> 1 Shelly tells her father that she likes her flat, but she probably doesn't.
> 2 She's from Italy.
> 3 No. She says, *This week isn't good.* (Probably because she wants to clean her flat before they see it.)

🔘 **1.52**

> S = Shelly F = father
> **S:** Hello?
> **F:** Hello, Shelly?
> **S:** Oh, hi, Dad.
> **F:** How are you?
> **S:** I'm fine. Fine.
> **F:** How's your new flat? Do you like it?
> **S:** Yes, I do. <u>It's … perfect.</u>
> **F:** Well, tell me about it. Is it big?
> **S:** <u>Yes, it is.</u>
> **F:** And what about furniture? Is there any furniture?
> **S:** Yes, <u>I have a desk</u> and a bed in my room.
> **F:** Would you like a lamp? We have an extra lamp at home.
> **S:** No, thanks, Dad. <u>Claudia has a lamp for the living room.</u>
> **F:** Who's Claudia?
> **S:** She's my flatmate. She's Italian. Don't worry, there aren't any boys here.

> **F:** Good. Your mother has some old curtains. Do you want them?
> **S:** No, that's fine. <u>We have curtains.</u>
> **F:** Really?
> **S:** Yes.
> **F:** Oh. So, when do we come and see the flat?
> **S:** This week isn't good. <u>We don't have any chairs.</u>
> **F:** No chairs? What does that mean, no chairs?
> **S:** I don't know. Sorry, that's the door. Talk to you later, OK, Dad? Bye.

2

- Tell students to look back at Flat A on page 36 and underline false information in the dialogue. They can compare their answers with a partner before you check with the whole class.

> It's … perfect.
> Claudia has a lamp for the living room.
> We have curtains.
> We don't have any chairs.

Language & cultural notes

- Shelley's father uses the markers *Really?* And *Oh* which suggest that he is surprised by what she is saying – and probably doesn't believe her. You may wish to point these out to students.
- *Dad* and *Mum* are common abbreviations for mother and father. Younger children say *Mummy* and *Daddy*. Americans tend to say *Mom* rather than *Mum*.

3

▶ *Key Methodology 5 & 6: Dialogues 1 & 2, pages 11 & 16*

- Pairwork. Put students in pairs. Ask them to play the roles of Shelley and her dad, and to practise reading the dialogue.
- Monitor carefully and help with any problems.
- At the end, you could ask one or two pairs to read out parts of their dialogue.

GRAMMAR: *a, an, some & any*

▶ *Language reference, Student's Book page 40*

▶ *Methodology guidelines: Grammar boxes, page xiii*

1

- Ask students to look at the picture of Shelley's bedroom. Ask: *What can you see?* Elicit answers from the students.
- Students look at the picture and complete the sentences. They can compare their answers with a partner before you check with the whole class.

1	any	4	a	7	a
2	a	5	any	8	any
3	some	6	some		

Language notes: a, an, some & any

- Here, at this level, the use of *some*, *any* and *a/an* is kept nice and simple. It looks at the use with single and plural countable nouns only. Basically, the rule here is, use *some* in positive sentences, and *any* in negative sentences and questions.
- If you have a monolingual class, think about how *some* and *any* are expressed in L1. In some languages they are missed out where English tends to use them, and the same word is used for both *some* and *any*. At this level, whenever L1 differs from English, it takes lots of practice before students can grasp and manipulate new forms.

- Be aware that *some* and *any* gets more complicated with uncountable nouns, e.g. *I have some money.*
- *Some* is also used with a question form when making offers and requests, e.g. *Would you like some biscuits? Can I have some bread?* No need to share this with your students at this level though!

2

❯ *Key Methodology 7: Accurate speaking & fluent speaking, page 20*

- Ask students to look at the table. Then model the activity carefully by looking round the room and reading out two or three true sentences.
- Elicit sentences from around the class.
- Now model the stress and intonation pattern carefully. Point out the weak pronunciation of *are* in *there are* /ðeərə/, and the long /ɑː/ sound in *there aren't* /ðeərɑːnt/. Show that the main strong stress is on the noun in column 4, and that the voice falls at the end. Ask students to listen and repeat your model.
- Put students in pairs or threes to make true sentences from the table.

SPEAKING

❯ *Communication activities, Student's Book pages 132 & 136*

1

- Pairwork. Put students in A and B pairs. Student A turns to page 132 and Student B turns to page 136.
- Students look at their pictures of a room. They ask and answer questions to find six differences between their rooms.

Alternative procedure

- A good way of doing this activity is to divide it into two stages.
- Divide the class in half. One half looks at the picture for Student A on page 132 and the other half looks at the picture for Student B on page 136. Allow three or four minutes for the students to look at their pictures and then ask them to describe it to another student in their group.
- Then redivide the students so that a Student A pairs up with a Student B. Tell the new pairs to ask and answer questions to find six differences between their pictures.
- Ask students to tell you the differences in feedback.

IF YOU WANT SOMETHING EXTRA ...

❯ *Photocopiable activity, page 203*
❯ *Teacher's notes, page 175*

3D | Tate Modern

WHAT THE LESSON IS ABOUT

Theme	Museums & art galleries; giving directions
Speaking	Roleplay: giving directions in a building
Reading	Information about the Tate Modern
Listening	Five conversations at the information desk of an art gallery asking for directions
Vocabulary	Ordinal numbers
Functional language	In a building: giving directions

IF YOU WANT A LEAD-IN ...

Introducing the theme: art galleries

- Tell students that they are going to submit a piece of artwork to an art gallery. Ask them to draw their picture on a blank piece of A4 paper. Tell them that it is modern art and they can be as creative as they like. Encourage students to use different coloured pencils or pens. Give them three minutes.
- If possible, ask students to attach their art to the wall nearest to them. Go across to one piece of artwork, and describe it imaginatively as if you were a critic, e.g. *Oh yes ... very interesting ...; It's lovely ...; It's red and green ...; there are some trees ...; and an animal here ...; I like it ... .*
- Tell students they are critics. They must walk round the room and describe the works of art to each other.

READING

1 & 2

- Ask students to look at the photos. Ask: *What type of building is it? What can you see there? Would you like to go there?*
- Read the questions as a class. Then ask students to read the text and find answers to the questions. Let them check their answers in pairs They can compare their answers with a partner before discussing as a class.

> 1 It's next to the Millenium Bridge in London.
> 2 Modern art.

Cultural note

- The **Tate Modern** houses the British collection of international modern art, i.e. art since 1900. International pre-1900 painting is found in the National Gallery in Trafalgar Square.
- The Tate Modern is situated on the Thames, in the centre of London, and is linked to St Paul's Cathedral by the Millennium footbridge.
- There are three other Tate galleries in Britain. Tate Britain, which displays British art from the sixteenth century to the present day; Tate Liverpool and Tate St Ives, in Cornwall.

3

- Pairwork. Put students in pairs or threes to discuss the questions.

Extra task

- Write the following table on the board:

My favourite	museum art gallery	is ...	because ...

- Model the activity by producing a couple of sentences, e.g. *My favourite museum is the Louvre because it is big and there are interesting paintings*.
- Give students two minutes to think of their favourites, then put them in pairs or threes to discuss.
- Have a brief class feedback.

Web research tasks

> ❯ *Methodology guidelines: Web research tasks, page xiii*

- Ask students to visit the Tate Modern website or another museum or art gallery in Britain and find more about what is on display there.

Web search key words

- museum/art gallery/name of city

VOCABULARY: ordinal numbers

> ❯ *Language reference, Student's Book page 41*

1

- Students match the words to the ordinal numbers.
- In feedback, ask students to listen to and repeat the words after you.

1st	first
2nd	second
3rd	third
4th	fourth
5th	fifth
6th	sixth
7th	seventh
8th	eighth
9th	ninth
10th	tenth

2 🌑 1.53

- Play the recording. Students listen and underline the word they hear. They can compare their answers with a partner before you check with the whole class.
- Students practise saying the words in their pairs.

See tapescript below for answers.

🌑 **1.53**

1	1st
2	3
3	7th
4	9
5	10th
6	5th
7	3rd
8	5th

Language notes

- The problem with ordinal numbers is the pronunciation. The consonant clusters at the end are difficult to say. In fact, *fifth* /fɪfθ/ and *sixth* /sɪksθ/ are not easy for native speakers!
- After doing the matching task in exercise 1, take time to focus on the production of the unvoiced consonants /f/ and /θ/. Write 1st, 4th and 5th on the board. Point to 1st and bite your bottom lip. Say 'first' while releasing your bottom lip. Get students to copy and repeat. Then say and practise the /f/ sounds in 4th and 5th. Write 3rd on the board. Point to it and push your tongue out so it slightly protrudes from your mouth and presses against your top teeth. Get students to copy you. Say 'third', showing how the tip of your tongue starts beyond your teeth and goes back. Get students to repeat. Then get students to practise saying the /θ/ sound in 4th and the tricky combination of /f/ and /θ/ in 5th.

3

- Tell students to look at the diagram of Tate Modern. Ask students to listen and repeat after you the names of the different places. Then model the task. Say: *What floor is the café on? It's on the second floor.* Get students to listen and repeat.
- Put students in pairs to take it in turns to ask and answer using the prompts.
- At the end, ask students to write two or three questions and answers in their exercise books.

Extra practice

- Extend this practice by making an information gap activity.
- Draw four lines on the board with space between them, labelled 1st to 4th, and ask students to copy. Like this:

  1st _____
  2nd _____
  3rd _____
  4th _____

- Then write two lists on the board, like this:

A	B
bar	shop
Exhibition A	toilets
restaurant	education centre
telephone	Exhibition B

- Put students in pairs. Ask Student A to decide on which floor the places in their list go. They must write them on their map. Student B must write words from his/her list on the map.
- Ask students to take it in turns to ask and answer, using the question from exercise 3. They must complete their map with the places their partner tells them.

LISTENING

In this episode of the listening story (exercise 3), the Explore London tour group is visiting Tate Modern. Valerie, Dave, Sam and another woman, who is not from the tour group, each want to find a different place in the gallery and go up to the information desk to ask for directions.

1 & 2 **1.54**

- Students can work in pairs to match the words to the symbols on the map.
- Play the recording. Students listen and check their answers. Ask students to listen and repeat the words.

See answers in tapescript below.

1.54

A	public men's toilets
B	public women's toilets
C	public baby changing room
D	public telephone
E	public café
F	public information
G	public lift

3 **1.55**

▸ *Key Methodology 24: A few guidelines for listening, page 98*

- You could predict the language used in this task by asking: *You are at the Tate Modern information desk. You want some information. What do you say?* Elicit, for example, *Where are the toilets? What floor is the café on?* At this level, 'predicting what you are going to hear' is a useful, confidence-building thing to do.
- Play the recording. Students listen and tick the words from exercise 1 they hear.
- They can compare their answers with a partner before you check with the whole class.

The following words should be ticked:
men's toilets; women's toilets; baby changing room; telephone; café; lift;

1.55

I = information desk V = Valerie D = Dave S = Sam
W = woman
I: Can I help you:
V: Yes. Where is the café?
I: It's on the second floor. Go up the stairs and turn right.
V: Is there a lift?
I: Yes, there is. It's behind you.
V: Oh, yes. Thank you.

D: Excuse me. Where are the toilets?
I: Sorry?
D: The men's toilets.
I: The toilets? They're over there. They're on the left, next to the lift.
D: Where?
I: Look, the brown doors.
D: Great.

S: Is there a public telephone here?
I: Yes, there is. It's next to the stairs. It's on the right.
S: Thank you.
I: You need a card.
S: What?
I: You need a card. It doesn't accept coins.

W: Is there a baby changing room?
I: Sorry?
W: A baby changing room. I need to change the baby.
I: Yes, go down these stairs here. Then turn left and go along the hall. It's next to the women's toilets.
W: Thank you. Shhhhh.

4 🔘 **1.55**

- Read out the sentences. Play the recording again. Students listen and match each sentence to a place in exercise 1.

1	public telephone
2	public telephone
3	men's toilets
4	baby changing room
5	lift
6	café

FUNCTIONAL LANGUAGE: directions

❯ *Language reference, Student's Book page 40*

1

- Students complete the directions with a word from the box. They can compare their answers with a partner before you check with the whole class.

A	turn	left
B	go	up
C	on the	right
F	go	down
G	go	along

2 & 3 🔘 **1.56**

- Ask students to read the six sentences first. Then play the recording for students to complete the directions.
- Students look at the tapescript on page 141 in the Student's Book to check their answers.

See answers in tapescript below.

🔘 **1.56**

> 1 Where <u>is</u> the café?
> 2 It's on the second floor. Go <u>up</u> the stairs and <u>turn</u> right.
> 3 Where <u>are</u> the men's toilets?
> 4 They're over there. They're on the <u>left</u>, next to the lift.
> 5 It's next to the stairs. It's on the <u>right</u>.
> 6 Go <u>down</u> these stairs here. Then turn <u>left</u> and go <u>along</u> the hall.

4

❯ *Key Methodology 6: Dialogues 2, page 17*

- Pairwork. Put students in pairs. Tell them to take it in turns to read the dialogues in the tapescript.

Roleplay

5 & 6

❯ *Key Methodology 9: Spoken errors – fluency tasks 2, page 34*

- Pairwork. Put students into A and B pairs. Ask them to look at the map of the Modern Art Museum. Ask some simple questions to familiarize the students with the map, e.g. *What floor are the toilets on? Where is the Film and radio exhibition?*
- Read through the instructions carefully, then briefly model the activity with a strong student.
- Ask students to take it in turns to roleplay the situation.
- Monitor and carefully, prompt, and note errors.
- At the end of the activity, write a few errors on the board for the students to correct as a class.

IF YOU WANT SOMETHING EXTRA ...

❯ *Photocopiable activity, page 204*
❯ *Teaching notes, page 175*

Answer key

3 REVIEW

❯ *Student's Book page 149*

1

1 third
2 fourth
3 first
4 fifth
5 second

2

3 How many chairs are there? There is one chair.
4 Is there a desk? Yes, there is.
5 Is there a computer? No, there isn't.
6 How many lamps are there? There is one lamp.
7 Are there any plants? Yes, there are.
8 Is there a television? Yes, there is.
9 Are there any curtains? No, there aren't.

3

The MoMA (Museum of Modern Art) is in New York near
~~from~~ Madison Avenue, between Fifth and Sixth Avenue.
There are lots of ~~differents~~ <u>different</u> types of art in the
MoMA. There ~~is~~ <u>are</u> paintings, sculptures, drawings and
~~any~~ <u>some</u> photographs. There is an education centre on
the ~~one~~ <u>first</u> floor of the museum.

4

1 big: small
2 ugly: beautiful
3 horrible: lovely
4 noisy: quiet
5 new: old

5

1 any
2 some
3 a
4 are
5 a
6 Is
7 is

6

1 Yes, can I help you?
2 The toilets. OK, go along the hall here and turn left.
3 Turn left …
4 Then go down the stairs.
5 No, down the stairs.
6 opposite the information desk.

3 WRITING

❯ *Workbook page 69*

Model answer
Dear Jack
I don't live far from the school. From the school go out
and turn right. Turn right again on the second street
opposite the cinema. Turn left at the first street and walk
along this street. There is a shop on the right. My house is
next to the shop.

4A | MetroNaps

WHAT THE LESSON IS ABOUT

Theme	MetroNaps: times & routines
Speaking	Pairwork: talking about daily routines
Reading	*MetroNaps*: a magazine article about a company providing a service for busy office workers where they can go to have a nap during the day
Vocabulary	Collocations *have*, *go* & *get*
Pronunciation	Vowels 1
Functional language	Telling the time

IF YOU WANT A LEAD-IN ...

Discussion starters

> *Methodology guidelines: Discussion starters, page xii*

- Write some times on the board: *8 am*; *10 am*; *12 o'clock*; *2 pm*; *5 pm*; *8 pm*; *11 pm*. Tell students that it's a typical day and ask: What do you do at *8/10/12*, etc?
- Put students into pairs to ask each other.
- Say: *It's Sunday*. Ask the same questions.

Introducing the theme: routines

- Students write down three facts and one lie about their routine, e.g. *I get up at eight. I go to bed at nine. I eat fruit for lunch*. Put students in groups. They must read out their sentences to each other. The other students must guess which sentences are true, and which are false.

READING

In this magazine article, Will Cotton, a New York office worker, describes how he copes with his busy life by going to MetroNaps. This is a company that has a special machine, called a Metropod, which office workers can come in and use. It allows them a twenty-minute sleep during the day. Will says the break relaxes him and helps him with his work and in meetings.

1 & 2

- Students look at the picture of a MetroNaps pod and ask: *Which activity do you think people do at MetroNaps?*
- Students then read the article and check their answer.

Go to sleep.

Extra task: adjectives

- There are a set of adjectives in the text which students may not know: *busy*; *tired*; *quiet*; *relaxing*; *relaxed*; *stressed*. You could check these words with mime, e.g. yawning to show tired; biting your nails to show stressed, etc.
- Alternatively, put students in pairs to find the words in the text, and say which words they describe, *busy day*; *tired workers*.

Language notes

- A *nap* is a short sleep during the day, often taken after lunch.
- A good way of checking the meaning of *stressed* is to bite your nails, look at your watch, and mime how people feel when they are too busy at work. Then mime smiling, sitting down, etc. to show the opposite, *relaxed*.

Cultural notes

- **Downtown** means city centre in American English.
- When first built, in 1931, the **Empire State Building** was the tallest building in New York. It is 381 metres tall and has 102 floors.

3

- Students read the article again, and answer the questions. They can compare their answers with a partner before you check with the whole class.

1. He works in an office in New York.
2. He starts work at 8:15.
3. He finishes work at 6:00.
4. A *nap* is a short sleep during the day.
5. MetroNaps' offices are in the Empire State Building in New York.
6. Will likes MetroNaps because he gets his best ideas in bed, and he feels relaxed and not stressed in meetings after a nap.
7. Metronaps opens at 10:00 and closes at 6:00.
8. It is open for eight hours a day.

4

- Students put the events in the correct order. They can compare their answers with a partner before you check with the whole class.

7, 2, 5, 1, 3, 6, 4

5

- Pairwork. Students discuss the questions in pairs.
- Have a brief class feedback, and find out who has a nap during the day.

Web research task

> *Methodology guidelines: Web research tasks, page xiii*

- You could ask students to go to www.metronaps.com and find more information about MetroNaps, e.g. *How much is it? Is it open at weekends? On which floor is it?*

FUNCTIONAL LANGUAGE: telling the time

> *Language reference, Student's Book page 50*

1

- Ask students to listen to and say the times for the clocks. You could draw the clocks on the board and point to each one as you say the time.

1. It's ten o'clock.
2. It's two fifteen/a quarter past two.
3. It's six thirty/half past six.
4. It's seven forty-five/a quarter to eight.
5. It's eight fifty-five/five to nine.

Alternative procedure

- Bring in a clock. It is easy to make one. You need a large circular card – write numbers and attach hands. Or draw a big clock on the board, and use two cardboard hands, stuck on with blu tack.
- Move the hands to different positions, and ask: *What time is it?* Elicit, *It's five o'clock, It's a quarter past five, It's half past five*, etc. Model and drill each time chorally and individually.
- Once students have got the hang of saying the times, get students to ask and answer across the class. Move the hands on the clock. Then Student A says: *What time is it?* And Student B says, *It's ten past six*, etc.
- It's a good idea to model and drill times like this before doing exercises 1 to 3 in the Student's Book.

Language notes

- Every language seems to have its own unique way of expressing time, and English is no exception. Expect plenty of errors where students attempt to translate from L1.
- Note the following:

3:00	*It's three o'clock.*	
4:05	*It's five past four.*	*It's four oh five.*
7:15	*It's a quarter past seven.*	
	(or, *It's quarter past seven.*)	*It's seven fifteen.*
9:30	*It's half past nine.*	*It's nine thirty.*
6:45	*It's a quarter to seven.*	
	(or, *It's quarter to seven.*)	*It's six forty-five.*

  N.B. *o'clock* is an abbreviation of 'on the clock'.
  Some languages tend to say *half before* instead of *half past*, so be aware that this could be confusing.
  American English differs from British English here. Americans are likely to say *five of four* (rather than *five to four*), and *five after four* (rather than *five past four*).
- In English-speaking countries, the 24-hour clock tends to be used less often than in some European countries, so *it's a quarter past six* or *six fifteen in the evening* is more acceptable than *it's 18:15*.
- The students most pressing problem, however, is probably going to be manipulating the difficult consonant sounds in the numbers.
- Notice the prevalence of the schwa /ə/ sound when saying times:

  /ə/
  It's six o̲'clock.
  /ə/   /ə/ /ə/
  It's a̲ quarte̲r to̲ five.

- *Rather than saying a generalized* pay attention, *try drawing attention to the specific things you really want your students to hear, see or notice. By this I mean that it's important to avoid giving instructions, pronouncing model sentences, etc. into a noisy void – or a room where other things are currently occupying the students' minds – whether it be an electronic dictionary, a mobile phone text message, the last exercise or someone outside the window.*
- *When you want to say something important, e.g. to model a target sentence that students will repeat in a drill, try to surround it in silence rather than embedding it amidst lots of other chatter. One good way to do this is to say* listen *and then pause for up to 10 seconds, i.e. longer than feels normal, while you calmly and unthreateningly look at the students, and the students look at you and wait, before you say the sentence the first time. This has the effect of focusing attention on what you will say. Then pause again for another longer-than-expected gap before you repeat it. Say the sentence perhaps three times in total – and each time you say it, make sure you first get attention.*
- *Avoid giving multiple attention-less repetitions. I've seen some teachers model sentences fifteen or more times – and the students didn't pay any real attention to any of them.*
- *If the first (or any other) pause doesn't gather attention, then try saying* listen *again a little louder and a little more firmly – or extend the silence as long as you can bear it.*

2 & 3 💿 1.57

- Play the recording. Students listen to Will's conversations and complete the clocks. Point out that number 2 doesn't mention a time. They should leave the clock blank.
- Students turn to page 141 in the Student's Book and read the tapescript to check their answers.
- Put students in pairs to practise the conversations, with different times.

💿 1.57

> W = Will M = man   Wo = woman
>
> **1**
> **W:** Excuse me, what time is it, please?
> **M:** It's <u>five past twelve</u>.
> **W:** Thanks.
>
> **2**
> **Wo:** Excuse me, hello? What's the time, please?
> **W:** I'm sorry, I don't know. I don't have a watch.
> **Wo:** Oh, OK.
>
> **3**
> **W:** What time is your class?
> **M:** It's at <u>eight thirty</u> pm.
> **W:** That's late.
>
> **4**
> **W:** I'm tired. What's the time?
> **Wo:** It's <u>half past one</u>.
> **W:** Half past one? Time for bed!

VOCABULARY: collocations *have, go & get*

❯ *Language reference, Student's Book page 51*
❯ *Key Methodology 20, Vocabulary records, page 80*

1

* Students find the words from the box in the article on page 42. They then match them to the correct diagram.

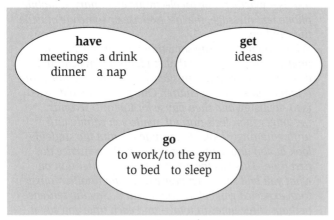

Extra lead-in task

* You could lead in here by putting *have*, *get* and *go* in circles on the board. Then put students in pairs, and tell them to write down as many words as they can think of that go with the verbs.

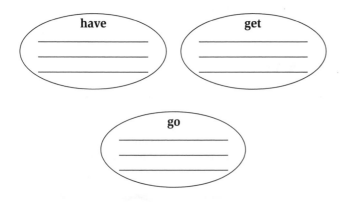

* Elicit suggestions and write them up on the board in feedback.

2

* Students could work in pairs to put the words from the box in the circles in exercise 1.

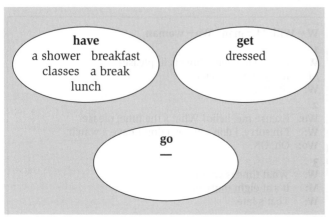

3

* Students discuss the differences between the underlined phrases as a class.
* It is a good idea to draw small diagrams on the board to show the difference.

Language note

* *Go* describes the process of moving, whereas *get* describes arriving. So, **go home** means on the way, and **get home** means arriving.
* N.B. in exercise 1, the *go* and *get* uses are interchangeable depending on the context. So, *go to sleep* describes the process, but *get to sleep* describes finally falling asleep.
* **Wake up** means stop sleeping. **Get up** means leave the bed. These are phrasal verbs. N.B. in many languages this idea would be expressed reflexively.

PRONUNCIATION: vowels 1

1 💿 1.58

❯ *Key Methodology 28: Pronunciation – phonemes, page 124*

* Play the recording. Students listen and repeat the sounds and the words.
* One thing you could do to help here, particularly if you are a native speaker, is model the shape of your mouth when producing these sounds: /æ/, /e/ and /eɪ/ all involve the lips being apart and the mouth wide. But /əʊ/ requires the lips to be circled.

💿 1.58

2 & 3 💿 1.59

* Students put the words in the correct column in exercise 1. They can then compare their answers with a partner.
* Play the recording for students to listen and check their answers.
* Play the recording again. Students listen and repeat the words.

/æ/ *have*	/e/ *get*	/eɪ/ *wake*	/əʊ/ *go*
nap	bed	break	home
flat	desk	make	no
lamp	seven	eight	

🔘 **1.59**

> have, nap, flat, lamp
> get, bed, desk, seven, any
> wake, break, make, eight, day
> go, home, no

Language notes

- English is quite a corrupt language – there is sometimes very little logic in the way a word is spelt and pronounced. However, spelling is teachable and should play an important part in pronunciation teaching. Point out the odd spellings here: *any* /e/, *break* /breɪk/, *eight* /eɪt/.
- You could point out the rule that when you add an *e*, it changes the sound, e.g. *fat* /fæt/ – *fate* /feɪt/. This explains *make* and *wake*, but, sadly, not the exception *have*.

SPEAKING

❯ *Communication activities, Student's Book pages 133 & 136*
❯ *Key Methodology 8 & 9: Spoken errors – fluency tasks 1 & 2, pages 29 & 35*

1

- Pairwork. Put students into A and B pairs. Student A turns to page 133 in the Student's Book, and Student B turns to page 136. Give each student time to prepare their questions, then let them ask and answer in pairs.
- Monitor and help if necessary. Note down errors for a correction feedback at the end.
- In feedback, ask individuals to summarize what they found out about their partner.

Alternative procedure

- It is a good idea to model the question and answer here, open class, in a sort of drill, before students practise in pairs.
- Write the following on the board: *get up, have breakfast, have a coffee, go to work, have lunch, get home.* Model the question, *What time do you get up?* Ask students to repeat chorally and individually. Go through all the questions in this way.
- Point to a question prompt and nominate a student to ask you the question. Answer truthfully. Elicit more questions from students, and get them to ask and answer across class.

2

- Pairwork. Students ask and answer questions about what they do at these times.

Extra task

- Play *Find someone who?* Write the following in a list on the board:
  wake up before 8; get up after 8.30; have coffee at 11; have lunch at 12; have a nap in the afternoon; study after 8; go to bed after 12.
  Add to or change this depending on the known habits of your class.
- Tell students to copy the list on a piece of paper. They must then walk round the class and ask *Do you ...?* questions until one student finds someone who says yes to each question.

IF YOU WANT SOMETHING EXTRA ...

❯ *Photocopiable activity, page 205*
❯ *Teacher's notes, page 175*

4B | A day off

WHAT THE LESSON IS ABOUT

Theme	Special days & dates
Speaking	Groupwork: presentations about adding an extra national holiday to the calendar
Listening	People talking about special days
Reading & listening	A radio interview about introducing a new special day – Nothing Day
Vocabulary	Months
Grammar	Prepositions of time: *in, at, on*
Functional language	Saying the date

IF YOU WANT A LEAD-IN ...

Discussion starters

❯ *Methodology guidelines: Discussion starters, page xii*

- Write *a day off* on the board. Tell students to write down five things they do on a day off. You could give them a couple of examples about what you do on your day off to give them ideas.
- Write these questions on the board:
  What do you do on a day off?
  Where do you go?
  Who do you go with?
  How do you feel?
- Students talk about days off with their partner then tell the class.

VOCABULARY: months

❯ *Language reference, Student's Book page 51*

1 1.60

- Play the recording. Students listen to the pronunciation of the months.

🔘 1.60

| January |
| March |
| April |
| July |
| September |

2 & 3 🔘 1.61

- Students write the months in the correct column in exercise 1.
- Play the recording for students to listen and check their answers.
- Play the recording again. Students listen and repeat.

☐ ◦◦◦	☐	☐ ◦	◦☐	◦ ☐ ◦
February	May June	August	– .	October November December

🔘 1.61

| February |
| May |
| June |
| August |
| October |
| November |
| December |

Language notes

❯ *Key Methodology 28: Pronunciation – phonemes, page 124*

- February /ˈfebrʊərɪ/ and August /ɔːgʌst/ have difficult vowel sounds to pronounce.
- Make sure students are putting a schwa /ə/ at the end of October /ɒktəʊbə/, etc.
- N.B. Months always start with a capital letter.

4

- Pairwork. Students work in pairs to discuss the questions.

LISTENING

Four people talk about a special day that happens every year in their country which they particularly like. They describe what they do on that day.

1 🔘 1.62

- Tell students to look at the photos. Ask: *What special day is it? What do people do on that day? Do you have this day in your country?*
- Play the recording. Students listen and match the speakers to the pictures.

1 B	2 C	3 D	4 A

🔘 1.62

1 This day is on <u>May</u> 15th. We don't have this day in Britain, but I live in Mexico and it's great. That's because I'm a teacher. All the teacher's take the day off and have a nice lunch together. On the next day, my students give me things: a bottle of wine, a book. I love it.

2 May Day. I don't work on this day, nobody works. It's a day to celebrate workers. My friends and I play a big game of football in the park. We have a drink together after the game too, of course. I go to the May Fair with my family.

3 While everybody is at a party or a restaurant or disco, I spend <u>December</u> 31st in my taxi. It's a very busy night, but I get a lot of money. There are lots of taxi drivers on the streets, and they all have customers. I get home early in the morning on January 1st and I go to bed. In the afternoon, my family and I go to a good restaurant for lunch.

4 This is a very important day, I think. It is a day for us to remember some of the important things that have happened for women in the past. It's on <u>March</u> 8th, which is in winter for me. It's not an official bank holiday, so I go to work. But I go on the Women's Day march every year, and then have a hot cup of tea with friends and talk.

2 🔊 1.62

- Play the recording again. Students listen and say what months the special days are in.

1	Teacher's Day – May	
2	May Day – May	
3	New Year's Eve – December	
4	International Women's Day – March	

3

- Pairwork. Students work in pairs to discuss the questions.

Extra task

- If you have a class with a variety of nationalities, get students to tell each other about a unique special day in their country or region. Tell them to explain why the day is special and what they do on that day.

Cultural notes

Here are some special days specific to Britain:
- **Bonfire Night** (November 5th). This celebrates the unsuccessful attempt to blow up (with gunpowder) the Houses of Parliament and the Protestant king James I in 1605. The 'Gunpowder Plot' was planned by a group of Catholics and led by Guy Fawkes, who were unhappy with the strict laws preventing them from practising their religion and wanted the return of a Catholic monarch in Britain. All over Britain, people light bonfires, watch firework displays, and burn effigies (models) of Guy Fawkes.
- **Pancake** (or *Shrove*) **Tuesday** (the last Tuesday before Lent – the Christian season of fasting). In Britain, people make and eat pancakes, (from flour, eggs and milk). They also have pancake races, in which people race each other while carrying and tossing a pancake in a pan!
- Public holidays in Britain are called *Bank Holidays*.

Web research task

❯ *Methodology guidelines: Web Research tasks, page xiii*

- Students find out about the special days in English-speaking countries below. They must find out when they take place and what people do on the days:
Bonfire Night; Pancake Tuesday; Mardi Gras; Halloween; Hogmanay; Burns' Night; Thanksgiving; Martin Luther King Day; American Independence Day; Australia Day; Boxing Day; St Patrick's Day.
Web search key words
- holiday/country

FUNCTIONAL LANGUAGE: the date

❯ *Language reference, Student's Book page 50*

1

- You could read the dates out to the students, so that they listen and repeat them.

Alternative procedure

❯ *Key Methodology 14: Drilling 1 – basics, page 55*

- Before doing exercise 1, drill dates around the class to practise form and pronunciation. Here's how:
1 Make a set of simple flashcards. Write the months on twelve cards. Write the numbers 1–31 on cards.
2 Hold up a month card and a number card, e.g. 'November' card, '11' card, and say the date: *the eleventh of November*. Students repeat. Model this for a number of dates.

3 Then just hold up the numbers and months cards, and get students to produce sentences from the visual prompts alone.

Extra task: date dictation

- Dictate five or six dates. Students must write them down in the correct number form, e.g. say: *the twelfth October two thousand and seven*. Students write: *12/10/07*.

Language notes

- N.B. 1st May, 2007 is the 'traditional' way of handwriting the date, whereas 1 May 2007 has become more acceptable with the onset of typing and computers. (May 1st, 2007 is also acceptable.) It can also be written 1/5/07.
- In American English, months are always written first, e.g. May 1st, 2007 is represented as 5/1/07 not 1/5/07.
- Notice the schwa /ə/ sounds in *the first of May*.

▪ Key Methodology 14
▪ Drilling 1: basics

- *Flashcards can provide great easy-to-use cues for drilling. Lesson 2A Grammar, Extra tasks, has some ideas for drilling using them. Other cues can be used and these are looked at in Key Methodology 15.*
- *The basic plan for a successful basic drill usually includes the following steps:*
  (a) *Show the cue (e.g. a flashcard picture). Hold it so that everyone in class can clearly see it. If necessary, walk a little around the room to allow different parts of the room a closer view.*
  (b) *Gather attention (see Key Methodology 13) and model the example sentence, speaking naturally and not over-slowly or artificially decontracting words.*
  (c) *Gesture or ask students to repeat it together three or more times. Many teachers hold out both hands, palms up, as a gesture to indicate* all *repeat. When the whole class speaks at once, it gives students an important chance to get more confident at getting their mouths around the words – and for the teacher to get a general idea if the class can say the items or not (though it's also very hard for a teacher to hear if there are significant individual problems, misunderstandings, wrong sounds, etc.). At this stage, some students may realize that they don't quite know how to say something. If you notice obvious problems you can repeat the model again – but as before – get attention before you do it.*
  (d) *Individual repetitions allow you to help individual students to get it right. Give clear feedback on errors and use techniques to help students improve. Many teachers I have observed avoid individual repetition, perhaps feeling that it unfairly puts students* in the spotlight *and draws attention to their problems. However, usually individual work is immensely fruitful and can help the whole class to improve. By helping one student to get it better, the class notices similar problems they might have and gives them feedback they can also use.*
  (e) *Now repeat the procedure for the other cues/flashcards – but as far as possible, don't model the sentences yourself. Better to allow students to try and create the new sentences themselves.*

❯ *Key Methodology: Spoken errors – fluency tasks 1 & 2, pages 29 & 35*

2

- Model this first by writing three dates on the board, and getting students to ask you why they are important.
- Students work in pairs. They write five important dates on a piece of paper, (birthday, wedding, graduation, first day at school, etc.). They then ask their partner about his or her important dates.

READING & LISTENING

The Reading text (which is also recorded) is a radio interview with Christina East, a British mental health specialist, who thinks that a new special day, called *Nothing Day* should be introduced in Britain where people do absolutely nothing but relax. This day was introduced in the USA in 1973.

1 & 2 🔘 1.63

- Lead in by writing, *Nothing Day*, on the board. Ask: *What do you think people do on Nothing Day?* Elicit some ideas. If students are unsure what to say, mime some actions to get them started, e.g. mime sleeping, reading a book, staring out of the window.
- Students read the interview with Christina East, and match the questions to the answers.
- Play the recording. Students listen to the interview and check their answers.

1	What is Nothing Day?
2	When is Nothing Day?
3	Why Nothing Day?
4	What do people do on Nothing Day?

🔘 **1.63**

CE = Christina East I = interviewer
I: What is Nothing Day?
CE: The idea comes from Harold Coffin, an American journalist. It's a day for nothing. No parties, no gifts, no cards. It's a time to have a break, to sit and do nothing.
I: When is Nothing Day?
CE: It's on January 16th. The first Nothing Day was in 1973.
I: Why Nothing Day?
CE: Because there are special days for everything. In March, we have Mother's Day, and in June we have Father's Day. In October, there's United Nations Day and Halloween, and in April, there's Earth Day.
I: What do people do on Nothing Day?
CE: Ideally, people do nothing. But that's very difficult. Here are some suggestions.
In the morning, wake up when you like. Have a relaxing breakfast. Do nothing.
In the afternoon, go for a walk. Sit in a park. Do nothing. At night, telephone an old friend and talk. Read a book, or go to bed. Do nothing.

3 🔘 1.63

- Play the recording again. Students read and listen, then mark the sentences are true or false.

1	T
2	F (It's on 16th January.)
3	F (It's in October.)
4	T

Extra task

- Elicit other things people might do on Nothing Day.
- Then get students to plan a timetable for Nothing Day. They write down their plan in pairs and present it to the class.
12 o'clock	get up
2 o'clock	look out of the window ...
3 o'clock	sit in a park

GRAMMAR: prepositions of time *in*, *at*, *on*

> *Language reference, Student's Book page 50*
> *Methodology guidelines: Grammar boxes, page xiii*

1

- Students complete the sentences with a preposition and a time word so that they are true for themselves. Do the first couple as examples.
- Tell students to make a list of time words and phrases in three columns in their exercise books, under the headings *in*, *on* and *at*.

Language notes

- The basic rules here are straightforward.
  - *at* for the time of day (*at five o'clock, at midnight*)
  - *on* for days and dates (*on Friday, on the 1st of March*)
  - *in* for parts of longer periods (*in January, in 1998*)
- Note the following that might confuse:
  - *at Christmas* but *on Christmas Day*
  - *at night* but *in the evening/morning/afternoon* and *on Friday evening/morning*, etc.
- N.B. some phrases require the: *in the evening; at the weekend; at the moment; in the twentieth century; in the past. In winter* and *in the winter* are both correct.

2

- Pairwork. Put students in pairs to read out their sentences from exercise 1 to each other.

Extra task

- Write the following on the board:
  - *at seven o'clock in the evening*
  - *on Sunday afternoon*
  - *in June*
  - *at Chritmas*
- Students must write three things they do at these times, and then tell their partner about them.

SPEAKING

1

- Groupwork. Divide students into groups of four. Each group must decide on new holidays, and make a list of what people do on the days.
- It is a good idea to brainstorm a few possible days to the board first to get student started: *Student's Day*; *Help your Parents Day*; *Be Nice Day*; *Work Longer Day*.
- You could get students to write their Special days on an A3 sheet of paper, with the things people do bulleted under each day. Students can refer to the paper when presenting.

2

- Students present their ideas for new holidays to the class.
- Have a class vote to decide which are the most interesting.

IF YOU WANT SOMETHING EXTRA ...

> *Photocopiable activity, page 206*
> *Teacher's notes, page 176*

4c Do the housework!

WHAT THE LESSON IS ABOUT

Theme	Housework
Speaking	Groupwork survey: writing & comparing a *Life at work and home* survey
Listening	A radio phone-in programme about British men & housework
Vocabulary	Verb collocations (housework)
Grammar	Frequency adverbs & phrases: *How often*; time expressions (*once a month*, etc.)
Pronunciation	Vowels 2: /aɪ/, /aʊ/, /uː/, /v/

IF YOU WANT A LEAD-IN ...

Pre-teach key words: housework

• Draw a simple house on the board:

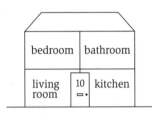

• Tell students that it's the weekend and they must do some housework. In groups of four, they must think of three jobs to do in each room, and decide which person in their group will do which job.
• At the end, they tell the class their decisions, e.g. *Manuel cleans the floor in the kitchen and washes the dishes. Julia makes the bed.*

VOCABULARY: verb collocations (housework)

❯ *Language reference, Student's Book page 51*

1
• Students match the phrases to the pictures.
• In feedback, model the words. Students listen and repeat. N.B. Students will do more work on *make* and *do* collocations in lesson 11C.

A	do the shopping	D	wash the clothes
B	clean the bathroom	E	do the dishes
C	make the bed	F	take out the rubbish

Extra task

• In groups of four, students take it in turns to mime using one of the household things. The others must guess which word is being mimed.

Language notes

• *Collocation* means words that go together. Some words have very specific collocations, e.g. *delicious food*.

2
• Pairwork. Students discuss the questions with a partner.

LISTENING

This is a radio phone-in programme, discussing a recent newspaper survey suggesting that most men don't do any housework. Two men phone up the programme to tell them what housework they do. Then the wife of the second caller phones up to contradict what her husband just said.

1
• Tell students that they are going to listen to a radio phone-in programme where the public phone the radio show and talk about a particular topic. Ask students to look at the headline and tell you what today's show is about.

Suggested answer:
It's about the results of a newspaper survey on how most British men don't do any housework.

2 **1.64**
• Tell students to look at the pictures. Play the recording for students to tick the phrases in the box in Vocabulary exercise 1 that they hear.

The following phrases should be ticked:
do the shopping; wash the clothes; make the bed

 1.64

H = host   R = Ralph   T = Tom   A = Anne

H: Hello, and welcome to our morning phone in. A survey in the newspaper, the *Daily Post*, says that 75 per cent of British men never do the housework. That's the topic for our phone in today. Is that true for you? Please ring 0800 607607. Are you a man who does the housework? Who does the housework in your house? We have several callers on the line. Let's go to the first one. What's your name?
R: Ralph.
H: Where are you from, Ralph?
R: I'm from Scotland.
H: How often do you do the housework, Ralph?
R: I sometimes <u>do the shopping</u>.
H: What does 'sometimes' mean for you, Ralph?
R: Well, every Saturday.
H: Alright, that's normal. What other housework do you do?
R: Nothing.
H: Nothing?
R: My mother always does all the housework.
H: Lucky you. Do you want to say something to your mother on the radio?
R: Yeah, thanks, Mum!
H: That's nice. OK, who's the next caller?
T: Tom, from Liverpool.
H: Good morning, Tom. How are you?
T: Fine, thanks.
H: That's good. Here's our question of the day: how often do you do the housework?
T: Every day.
H: That's interesting. What housework do you do?
T: I <u>make the bed</u> every morning.
H: Excellent Tom!
T: And I <u>wash the clothes</u>.
H: Great.
T: Thank you very much.
H: Next caller. Who is this?

> A: I'm Anne, from Liverpool. I'm Tom's wife.
> H: Hello, Anne. You have a very nice husband.
> A: But it isn't true. Tom hardly ever does the housework. I do it!
> H: Oh dear.
> A: He never makes the bed. And the clothes? Ha! He washes them once a year.
> H: What does he do?
> A: He works in an office. He's always on the phone to silly radio shows!
> H: Thank you very much for your call.

3 🔘 1.64

- Students listen to the recording again to find out which person does each of the jobs, and tick the correct column.

Name	Ralph	Ralph's mother	Tom	Tom's wife
Does the shopping once a week.	✓			
Is always on the phone.			✓	
Always does all the housework.		✓		✓

Extra task

- In pairs, students put the housework in order from best job to worst job.

Language notes

- **do** and **make** are difficult for many students to distinguish between. Use *do* to describe work: *do the housework, do the ironing, do the shopping.* Use *make* when there is creativity or construction: *make a cake, make dinner.* N.B. *Make the bed*, meaning put the sheets in order, is an exception.

GRAMMAR: frequency adverbs & phrases

❯ *Language reference, Student's Book page 50*
❯ *Methodology guidelines: Grammar boxes, page xiii*

1 🔘 1.65

❯ *Key Methodology 15: Drilling 2 – substitution, page 58*

- Tell students to read through the statements and think about (but not write) their responses.
- Play the recording. Students read and listen to the sentences, then complete the answers using the words in brackets.

See underlined answers in the tapescript below.

🔘 **1.65**

> 1 You never do the dishes.
>   That's not true. <u>I often do the dishes!</u>
> 2 You don't clean the bathroom.
>   That's not true. <u>I always clean the bathroom.</u>
> 3 You're always in front of the television.
>   That's not true. <u>I'm hardly ever in front of the television.</u>
> 4 I always wash your clothes.
>   That's not true. <u>You often wash my clothes.</u>
> 5 This flat's always dirty.
>   That's not true. <u>This flat's rarely dirty.</u>
> 6 You're usually on the telephone.
>   That's not true. <u>I'm sometimes on the telephone.</u>

Alternative procedure for stronger & weaker classes

- With stronger classes, get students to say their answers first before listening to check.
- With weaker classes, get them to write answers first, then listen again, and say the answer.

Extra task

- Put students in pairs to practise the sentences. Student A, book open, reads out each statement. Student B, book closed, must respond. When they have finished change pairs.

Language notes

- Frequency adverbs are used to talk about how often we do things. They usually go between the subject and verb, (I **often** wash the dishes). However, they *go after* the verb *to be*, (He's **always** on the phone). N.B. when an auxiliary verb is used, the frequency adverb goes between auxiliary and main verb, (I don't **usually** eat eggs, You can sometimes see Ireland from here).

**Key Methodology 15
Drilling 2: substitution**

- *Much basic classroom drilling involves simple repetition. For example:*
  T (Teacher): You never do the dishes.
  Sts (Students together): You never do the dishes.
  St: (Individual student): You never do the dishes.
- *This is useful for letting students hear example sentences and for giving them safe and unthreatening ways to practise. However, it can also be a little dull and under-challenging if over-used. More demanding drills involve the use of substitution, i.e. replacing one or more words with other words. The teacher usually gives cues, e.g. shows flashcards or says words, that tell the students what new sentence to make. For example:*
  T: I go to bed before 10 p.m.
  Sts: I go to bed before 10 p.m.
  St: I go to bed before 10 p.m.
  T: 11 (or shows flashcard of clock)
  Sts: I go to bed before 11 p.m.
  St: I go to bed before 11 p.m.
  etc.
- *In an example like the one above, the substitution is relatively easy to make as it just involves slotting in one or two words to replace others. However, some substitutions can be quite challenging when (a) the substituted word is varied, and (b) a word change causes other changes in a sentence, e.g. a verb form:*
  T: You never do the dishes.
  Sts: You never do the dishes.
  St: You never do the dishes.
  T: She (or shows flashcard of woman)
  Sts: She never does the dishes.
  St: She never does the dishes.
  T: Always (or shows flashcard of word 'always')
  Sts: She always does the dishes.
  St: She always does the dishes.
  etc.
- *A drill like this provides valuable practice in manipulation of the grammar as well as in pronunciation.*

2

- Students add an adverb of frequency to each sentence so that the sentences are true for themselves.
- Students then write four more similar sentences.
- In feedback, ask students to read out some sentences for the class. Ask the rest of the class if they *really* think it's true.

Extra task

- Students write two true sentences and one false sentence about themselves, using adverbs of frequency. They read out the sentences in groups. The rest of the group must decide which sentence is not true.

3

- Students rewrite the sentences with one of the phrases from the box. They can compare their answers with a partner before you check with the whole class.

> 1 I read the newspaper every day.
> 2 I go on holiday once a year.
> 3 Twice a week I have a nap in the afternoon.
> 4 I see my grandparents three times a year.
> 5 I do the shopping once a week.

4 & 5

- Show students how to make *How often* questions. Write: *I watch English movies* on the board. Elicit the question, *How often do you watch English films?* from students.
- Students choose two sentences from exercise 2 and two sentences from exercise 3, and make questions with *How often*.
- Pairwork. Put students in pairs to ask and answer the questions.

Alternative procedure

- You could elicit and practise *How often* questions from the board, and do a drill.
- Write in a list on the board:
    Watch English films?
    Work on Saturdays?
    Drink coffee?
    Read the newspaper?
    Have a nap?
    See your grandparents?
    Do the shopping?
- Elicit and model the *How often* question with *watch English films*. Pay attention to model clearly the weak stress in *do you* /dəjə/. Students repeat chorally and individually. Model and repeat other examples of *How often* questions from the prompts on the board.
- Point to prompts and get individual students to produce *How often* questions from them.
- Get students to ask and answer *How often* questions across the class. Finally, put them in closed pairs to practise.

PRONUNCIATION: vowels 2

> *Key Methodology 28: Pronunciation – phonemes, page 124*

1 🌐 **1.66**

- Play the recording. Students listen and repeat the sounds and the words.

🌐 **1.66**

/aɪ/	hi
/aʊ/	house
/uː/	room
/ʌ/	up

Language notes

- Diphthongs and long sounds are always difficult for students to pronounce. Try to model the mouth position for each of these sounds:
    /aɪ/ (lips are spread wide)
    /aʊ/ (lips start wide and narrow to an 'o')
    /uː/ (lips are pushed together in a pout)
    /ʌ/   (lips are relaxed, neither wide nor pouting)
- In English, spelling and pronunciation are often at odds, (*son* /sʌn/, *bus* /bʌs/).
    N.B. the /ʌ/ sound is not used in some varieties of English, e.g. where *bus* is pronounced /bʊs/. This is the case in Scotland, Northern Ireland and northern England among other places.

2 & 3 🌐 **1.67**

- Students decide which word sounds different and underline it. They can then compare their answers with a partner.
- Play the recording for students to listen and check their answers.
- Play the recording again. Students listen and repeat.

| 1 drink | 3 bread |
| 2 aunt | 4 good |

🌐 **1.67**

1	time	hi	drink	wife
2	house	aunt	brown	now
3	son	bread	bus	some
4	blue	new	June	good

SPEAKING

1

- Groupwork. Divide students into groups of three or four. Give them five minutes to make questions with *How often …?* from the prompts in the picture.
- Students take it in turns to ask and answer the questions. They must make notes of the answers for the discussion in exercise 2.

2

- Give students a few minutes to think of ways of summarizing their results.
- Ask one student from each group to stand up and tell the class their results.
- At the end, find out which group does most housework.

IF YOU WANT SOMETHING EXTRA …

> *Photocopiable activity, page 207*
> *Teacher's notes, page 176*

4D | I'm on the phone

WHAT THE LESSON IS ABOUT

Theme	Phone conversations
Speaking	Pairwork survey: a survey about phones and making phone calls
Listening	Five phone conversations
Functional language	Talking on the phone – common phone expressions; roleplaying a phone conversation
Pronunciation	Phone numbers
Did you know?	Phone facts: North America

IF YOU WANT A LEAD-IN ...

Test before you teach: quick phone calls

❯ *Methodology guidelines: Test before you teach, page xiii*

- Write the following on the board:
  1 *Is Jim at home?*
  2 *What time is it?*
  3 *Where do you live?*
  4 *How do you spell your name?*
  5 *When is your birthday?*
  6 *Would you like to go to the cinema?*
- Put students in A and B pairs. Student A phones Student B who answers.
- Student A asks question 1 and Student B improvises a reply. Then Student B phones Student A and asks question 2. And so on.
- You could model the question briefly to give students the idea:
  B: *Hello. 776694.*
  A: *Hi. This is Juan. Is Jim there.*
  B: *I'm sorry. He's on holiday.*
- However, the idea is that students improvise conversations. It doesn't matter if they are not very accurate.
- You could add to the list of questions. Use the activity to revise questions and other language from previous lessons.

SPEAKING

1

- Pairwork. Students work in pairs to ask and answer and do the phone survey.
- You could ask two or three questions open class to get students started.

PRONUNCIATION: phone numbers

1 & 2 🔘 1.68

- Play the recording. Students listen to the two phone numbers, and answer the questions.
- Play the recording again. Students listen and repeat.

> *0* is pronounced 'oh' /eu/.
> When two numbers are together, e.g. *77*, you say *double* then the number 7: *double 7.*

🔘 **1.68**

> Oh eight oh two   seven double eight   seven four three four one six   nine two eight   double two one two

Cultural note

- In Britain, phone numbers are made up of the city or area code, followed by the personal number. So, an Oxford phone number might be: 01865 794723. An inner London number might be 0207 794723.
- In the USA, numbers are made up of a three-digit city or area code, followed by the personal number in two blocks. So, a Houston number might be: 281 618 5889.
- Incidentally, when three digits come in succession, e.g. 456777, you say: four-five-six-seven-double-seven.

3 🔘 1.69

- Play the recording. Students listen and underline the phone number they hear.
- Put students in pairs to practise saying the phone numbers.

1	1 455 635 0403	3	0802 728 743
2	639 099 098	4	011 513 992 0732

🔘 **1.69**

> **1**
> A: Do you have a pen?
> B: Yes.
> A: OK, my phone number is <u>1 455 635 0403</u>.
> B: Can you repeat it?
> A: Yes, 1 455 635 0403.
>
> **2**
> A: What's your phone number?
> B: It's <u>639 099 098</u>.
> A: 639 099 098. OK. I'll call you.
> B: Great.
>
> **3**
> For any other questions, please call <u>0802 728 743</u>. That's 0802 728 743.
>
> **4**
> A: Here's my phone number: <u>011 513 992 0732</u>.
> B: Wait a minute, 011 513 992 0732?
> A: Yes, that's right.
> B: OK, thanks.

4

- Model the question by asking: *What's your phone number?* around the class. Put students in groups of four to ask the question, or get students to mingle and ask.
- In feedback, ask students to remember and tell you numbers of classmates that they heard.

Extra task

- Play the mobile phone whispering game.
- Divide the class into groups of eight. Get each group to sit in a row or a circle. Tell one student to whisper his/her mobile phone number to the person next to him/her. That person must then whisper it to the next person, and so on until it gets to the end of the row or circle. That person must then go to the board and write it up. They then ask the class if it is correct.

• A variation includes writing up five phone numbers on the board. Each group must turn its back on the board with the exception of one student. That student must relay the numbers to the next in line. The idea is to relay all the numbers along the chain before any other group does. The person at the end of the line must write the numbers down.

LISTENING

There are five short phone calls in this episode of the listening story, divided into two parts.

In the first part, Dave is speaking to Valerie (the tour guide) when his phone rings – it's his ex-girlfriend who wants to talk to him, but he doesn't want to speak to her. Then Sam tries to phone Mr Green at his office, but he isn't there, so he leaves a message. Finally, someone phones up Valerie, but he has the wrong number.

Then in the second part, Rob phones up Sharon. She gives him the name and telephone number of a woman who left a message for him. Finally, Herb phones up an airline company to confirm his flight back to Texis.

1 💿 1.70

• Ask students to read the three sentences. Tell them that *make a call* means 'do the ringing' and *get a call* means 'receive the call'. You can easily show these meanings with mimes.

• Remind students about the characters: Dave, Valerie, Sam and Herb. Ask: *Who is Valerie? Who does Dave work for? Who is Sam? Where is Herb from?*

• Play the recording. Students listen to three phone conversations, and underline the correct word, in the sentences. They can compare their answers with a partner before you check with the whole class.

> 1 gets
> 2 makes
> 3 gets

💿 1.70

> **V = Valerie D = Dave A = Angie W = woman S = Sam**
> **M = man**
> **1**
> **V:** Anyway, so this is my first job.
> **D:** Really? … I'm sorry, that's my phone. Just a minute … Hello?
> **A:** Dave, it's Angie.
> **D:** Oh, hi. How did you get this number?
> **A:** Oh, Dave … where are you? Why did you go?
> **D:** Now's not a good time. Can I call you back?
> **A:** No, I want to talk now!
> **D:** Sorry, that was my girlfriend. … Well, ex-girlfriend.
> **V:** I understand.
>
> **2**
> **W:** Hello?
> **S:** Hello, I'd like to speak to Mr Green, please.
> **W:** Sorry, he isn't here at the moment.
> **S:** Oh. Where is he?
> **W:** He's at the airport. Who's calling, please?
> **S:** It's Sam Moore.
> **W:** Would you like to leave a message?
> **S:** Yes. Please tell him to call me.
>
> **3**
> **V:** Hello?
> **M:** Is Simon there, please?
> **V:** Sorry, you have the wrong number.
> **M:** Oh, sorry. Goodbye.
> **V:** Bye.

2 💿 1.70

• Allow students a minute to read through the statements.

• Play the recording again. Students listen to the first three conversations again and say if the sentences are true or false. They can compare their answers with a partner before you check with the whole class.

> **1** 1 T
>   2 F (Dave says it isn't a good time.)
> **2** 1 F (Sam calls Mr Green, who isn't there. He's at the airport.)
>   2 F (He isn't there.)
> **3** 1 T
>   2 T

3 💿 1.71

• Allow students a minute to read through the notes.

• Play the recording. Students listen and complete the notes. They can compare their answers with a partner before you check with the whole class.

> Message for Rob
> Call Ms Colleen Kerr.
> Phone number: 0865 455 901
>
> Flight confirmation details for Mr and Mrs Curtis
> Flight number BAW 288 to Dallas USA.
> Terminal: 2
> Date: Thursday, June 20th
> Time: 8:45am

💿 1.71

> **Sh = Sharon R = Rob He = Herb TA = travel agent**
> **1**
> **Sh:** Hello, National History Society. Can I help you?
> **R:** Sharon, hi. It's Rob.
> **Sh:** Hello, Rob. How's the tour?
> **R:** Fine, fine. The museum was very interesting. Are there any messages for me?
> **Sh:** Yes, a woman called. Colleen Kerr.
> **R:** OK. Meg, give me a pen. How do you spell that?
> **Sh:** C-O-L-L-E-E-N Kerr K-E-R-R.
> **R:** Yes. And what's her phone number?
> **Sh:** 0865 455 901.
> **R:** 0865 455 901. OK. Thanks, Sharon.
> **Sh:** No problem. Bye.
> **R:** Goodbye.
>
> **2**
> **He:** Come on, pick up the phone.
> **TA:** Hello, Basic Airways?
> **He:** Hello, I'd like to confirm a flight, please.
> **TA:** Of course. Where to.
> **He:** It's to Dallas, Texas.
> **TA:** Flight number?
> **He:** Just a minute … Um, here it is – BAW 288.
> **TA:** Date?
> **He:** June 20th.
> **TA:** And your name?
> **He:** Herb Curtis.
> **TA:** Just a minute, please.
> **He:** OK. …
> **TA:** Mr Curtis?
> **He:** Yes?
> **TA:** Your flight is confirmed. Flight BAW 288 to Dallas on Thursday June 20th at 8:45 am. Terminal 2.
> **He:** Thank you very much.
> **TA:** Thank you for calling. Have a nice day.

- Play the recording again. Ask students to listen out for phone phrases, e.g. *Can I call you back*.
- At the end, get students to write the phrases they remember down. Let them check in pairs, then elicit phrases and write them on the board.
- This activity previews the *Functional language* presentation that follows in the next section neatly.

FUNCTIONAL LANGUAGE: on the phone

❯ *Language reference, Student's Book page 51*

1 & 2

- If you didn't do the extra task in the last section, you could lead in here by eliciting phone phrases from students and writing them on the board. Find out how much they know.
- Students correct the mistakes in the phrases. They can compare their answers with a partner.
- Students look at tapescripts 1.70 and 1.71 on page 142 to check their answers.

1 Just ~~a~~ minute.
2 Can I call you back?
3 I'd like to ~~say~~ speak to Mr Green.
4 Would you like to leave ~~a~~ message?
5 Please tell him to call ~~I~~ me.
6 Is Simon ~~here~~ there, please?
7 Sorry, you have the ~~number wrong~~ wrong number.
8 Hi, ~~I'm~~ it's Rob.

Language notes: phone expressions

- Phone conversations involve a lot of fairly fixed expressions. So, for example, we say, *You have the wrong number* but not (usually) *You have the number wrong*, even though it is grammatically correct. Students need to learn and remember phrases here, not improvise!
- When answering the phone, we say, *This is ...* not ✗ *I am ... .* When asking who is speaking, we say, *Is that ...?*, not ✗ *Are you ...?*

3 & 4 🔘 1.72

- Students read and complete the four telephone dialogues with the correct sentence from the box. They can then compare their answers with a partner.
- Play the recording for students listen and check their answers.
- You could play the recordings again and pause it for students to repeat.

1 Hi, Sarah. How are you?
2 Good morning, Acme Company.
3 No, he isn't. Can I take a message?
4 Is that 1823 556 0211?

🔘 **1.72**

1
A: Hello.
B: Hello, it's Sarah.
A: Hi, Sarah. How are you?

2
A: Good morning, Acme Company. Can I help you?
B: Good morning, can I speak to Mr James?
A: Yes. Just a minute.

3
A: Hello, is David there?
B: No, he isn't. Can I take a message?
A: Please tell him to call me.
B: What's your phone number?
A: It's 662 4043.

4
A: Hello, is that Michelle?
B: I'm sorry, you have the wrong number.
A: Is that 1823 556 0211?
B: No, it isn't.
A: Oh, sorry.

5

❯ *Key Methodology 6: Dialogues 2, page 16*

- Pairwork. Put students in pairs to roleplay the dialogues from exercise 3, using information about themselves.

DID YOU KNOW?

1 & 2

- Pairwork. Put students into pairs. They read the facts about phones and phone numbers in North America and discuss the questions.

Web research task

❯ *Methodology guidelines: Web research tasks, page xiii*

- Students find out the same information for other English-speaking countries, (Britain, Ireland, Australia, New Zealand).
- They could write up this information and present it to the class.

Web search key words
- telephone codes/dialling codes

IF YOU WANT SOMETHING EXTRA ...

❯ *Photocopiable activity, page 208*
❯ *Teacher's notes, page 176*

Answer key

4 REVIEW

❯ Student's Book page 150

1

1 eats/has
2 drinks/has
3 goes
4 gets
5 eats/has
6 goes

2

1 She eats/has breakfast with Will.
2 She drinks/has a coffee.
3 She goes to bed.
4 She gets up at four o'clock
5 She eats/has dinner alone.
6 She goes to work at 11 pm.

3

1 On
2 on
3 at
4 in
5 in
6 at
7 in
8 at

4

2 13/05/2007
3 04/07/2007
4 14/06/2007
5 04/09/2007
6 22/11/2007

5

1 How often do you do the dishes?
2 What do you usually do on Saturdays?
3 I never work on Saturdays.
4 I always make the bed in the morning.
5 Do you often get up early in the morning?
6 I rarely take out the rubbish.
7 Do you sometimes do the shopping on Saturday morning?

4

1 b 2 a 3 a 4 a 5 a

Model answer
Message 1
For: Sue Smith
From: Mr Brown
Day / Date: Tuesday 20th April
Time: 9:30
Phone number: 070 766901
Message: Please call (me) back

Message 2
For: Alex
From: Sally
Day / Date: Saturday
Time: 5 o'clock this afternoon
Phone number: –
Message: Please phone tonight

5A | Languages made easy!

WHAT THE LESSON IS ABOUT

Theme	Abilities; Language machines & dictionaries
Speaking	Talking about languages and using dictionaries; dialogue: asking for clarification
Reading	*Languages made easy*: a magazine article about translation machines
Grammar	*Can/can't*
Pronunciation	*Can/can't*

IF YOU WANT A LEAD-IN …

Introducing the theme: dictionaries

❯ *Key Methodology 30: Dictionaries 1 – using dictionaries effectively, page 130*

- Write four or five words on the board. For example: *broom magazine celebrate frequently*
- Tell students to find each word in the dictionary they usually use in class, whether a book or an electronic dictionary. They must find the following information about each word: meaning; pronunciation; part of speech and an example.
- Let students check their answers in pairs or groups.
- In feedback, if they are using different types of dictionaries, find out which dictionary gave most information. Find out which ones weren't up to the task.
- If you use class sets of dictionaries, this activity could be used as a 'getting to know your dictionary' task.

SPEAKING

1
- Pairwork. Students work in pairs to discuss the questions. They could also work in small groups if you wish.
- Have a brief class feedback, and find out about dictionary use in your class.

READING

In this magazine article, two types of machines are being described. They can both translate languages, but with the first one, you use a keyboard and type in the word to be translated, whereas the second one has a microphone in which you say the word you want translated, and then the machine translates it and says the translated phrase back to you.

1
- Tell students to look at the photos. Ask: *What are they? What do they do?* Use mime to check the new words in the box, e.g. *type, microphone, calculator,* etc.
- Point to the pictures, and say one or two example sentences to describe the machines to get the students started.
- Then, you could either elicit descriptions as a class using the words from the box, or put students in pairs to describe the machines to each other. Don't confirm answers yet.

2
- Students read the article to check their answers.

> The Lingo Global 29: You type a word. It knows lots of languages. It has a calculator and a clock.
> The Phraselator: It has a microphone. You hear the translation.

3
- Students read the article again, and match the sentences to the products. They can compare their answers with a partner before you check with the whole class.

> 1 LG   2 LG   3 LG   4 P   5 P   6 P   7 LG   8 P

4
- Discuss the questions with the whole class.

Web research task

❯ *Methodology guidelines: Web research tasks, page xiii*

- You could ask students to research and find out about some of the latest electronic dictionaries on sale.

Web search key words
- electronic dictionaries

GRAMMAR: *can/can't*

❯ *Language reference, Student's Book page 60*
❯ *Methodology guidelines: Grammar boxes, page xiii*

1
- Students complete the English Language Ability Survey with *can/can't*. Do the first couple of sentences as examples to get students started.
- Pairwork. Put students into pairs to compare their answers.
- In feedback, elicit sentences round the class.

Extra tasks for stronger classes
- Once students have completed the survey, they must interview their partner to find out their answers. Model it first: *Can you spell your first name? Yes, I can.*
- You could test your students' answers. In pairs, they must prove that they can answer the questions they said *yes* to, e.g. *Can you spell your first name? Yes, I can. It's M-A-R-I-A.*

Language notes
- ***Can*** and ***can't*** are modal auxiliary verbs with many uses. Here, they are used to talk about ability. However, note that students have previously come across *can* for permission in lesson 4D: *Can I take a message?*
- Like most modal auxiliary verbs, *can* transposes to form the question (*Can you …?*), and is not followed by *to*.
- Watch out for these typical errors: ✗ *Do you can swim?* ✗ *I can't to swim.*
- Pronunciation is difficult. In questions and short answers, *can* has its full value: *Can /kæn/ you draw? Yes, I can. /kæn/.*
- In the affirmative, *can* is unstressed. The main stress is on the main verb. So, here *can* is pronounced with a schwa, *I can /kən/ type.*
- *Can't* has a long /ɑː/ vowel sound. Students may simplify it to /æ/.

2

⊙ *Communication activities, Student's Book pages 134 & 136*

- Pairwork. Put students in A and B pairs. Ask Student A to turn to page 134 and Student B to turn to page 136.
- Ask students to read the example and make sure that they understand what to do.
- Students work in pairs to interview their partner, using the picture prompts, and phrases from the *Useful language* box.

Alternative procedure

⊙ *Key Methodology 14: Drilling 1 – basics, page 55*

- This task could be done as a drill from flashcards. Before the lesson, prepare eight flashcards with simple drawings of the eight activities shown in exercise 2.
- Hold up each card and elicit the verbs. Hold them up again, and elicit and model the *Can you ...?* question. Drill the question chorally and individually.
- Ask individuals and elicit *Yes, I can* and *No, I can't*. Ask: *How well?*, and elicit: *very well, quite well* and *not very well*. Get students to ask and answer across the class. Then put them in pairs to practise.

Extension task

- You could turn this into a class survey. In pairs, students prepare a survey form. They must write a list of six activities on the left of a piece of paper. They can choose their own ideas, e.g. *play golf; ride a motorbike; play the piano*.
- When they are ready, they must walk round the class and ask different students the questions. They must write the initials of each student they interview next to each activity, then put a cross (for *no*), a tick (for *yes*) and an asterisk * (for *very well*) next to each person's initials.
- In feedback, students must report their findings using *can* and *can't*.

■ Key Methodology 16
■ Helping students say it better

- *When students speak and you want to focus on accuracy rather than fluency, e.g. when you are drilling a new sentence, it's important to have techniques to help students get better at what they are saying. There is no point in doing some activities, such as drilling, unless students get clear and useful feedback, and can improve, otherwise they may think you are confirming that their errors are actually correct. The more students think about an error for themselves, the more likely they are to learn how to do it correctly. Students need your help so that they can (a) notice what they are getting wrong, and (b) start to think about how to improve. After students know the correct answer, they will need further practice opportunities to try the language out again.*

Help students to notice errors

- *You can indicate that an error has occurred by giving a cue such as:*
  1 *making a 'that's wrong' face, e.g. a slight frown, raised eyebrows, a puzzled expression, etc.*
  2 *make a gesture, e.g. a waist-height raised hand, crossed fingers or arms, etc.*
  3 *make a noise, e.g. tapping the table, saying uh-uh, making a beep sound, etc.*
  4 *showing something, e.g. holding up a flashcard with an ✗, picking up a prop such as a red pen, etc.*

- *With all of these ideas, students need to learn to associate the cue you give with the meaning that there has been an error. You can do this by saying what it means the first few times you do it, e.g. you clearly and visibly hold up a red pen and say 'there was a mistake'. After you have done this a few times, students will associate the red pen with an error and you won't need to repeat the instruction.*

Help students to improve

- *It's usually helpful to give students a chance to self-correct rather than just hearing the correct answer from elsewhere. Perhaps the best way to do this is simply to indicate that an error has occurred (see previous section), and then pause for a while to allow the student thinking time and a chance to correct it themselves.*
- *If the student tries a correction, but it's not correct yet, you can give clues and information to help them towards a right version. One good way to do this is* Finger feedback. *(See Key Methodology 17.)*
- *If the student can't self-correct, you can ask other students' ideas on how to correct the error. N.B. If possible they should tell the student who made the mistake rather than you.*
- *It may take a while before the correct version emerges. Make sure that students do not become confused between wrong guesses, and attempts, and the final right version. It is important to set the correct answer 'in concrete', i.e. focus attention on it, get students to say it, etc., so that no one is in any doubt that this is the right answer.*

PRONUNCIATION: *can/can't*

1 💿 1.73

- Play the recording. Students listen to how the words *can/can't* are pronounced in the sentences.
- Read through the language note as a class.

💿 **1.73**

It can translate.
It can't translate.

2 💿 1.74

- Students listen and underline the word they hear. They can then compare their answers with a partner before you check with the class.
- Play the recording again for students to listen and repeat the sentences.

See underlined answers in the tapescript below.

💿 **1.74**

1	It <u>can</u> translate phrases.
2	It <u>can</u> hear an English phrase.
3	You <u>can</u> read it.
4	It <u>can't</u> translate other languages.
5	It <u>can</u> tell the time.

Speaking

1 & 2 1.75

- Tell students to look at the pictures. Ask: *What can you see? What do you think they say?*
- Play the recording. Students listen to the dialogues, and match them to the pictures A and B. They can then compare their answers with a partner.
- Students look at tapescript 1.75 on page 142 to check their answers.
- Pairwork. Put students into pairs and ask them to practise the dialogues with their partner.
- You could get students to listen and repeat the dialogues from the recording.

Dialogue 1	B
Dialogue 2	A

1.75

W = woman   M = man
1
W: Travellers from Europe go to desk A, travellers from outside Europe go to desk B.
M: Excuse me, can you repeat that, please?
W: Yes, if you're from Europe, go to desk A.
2
W: So, today in class we're going to do some vocabulary, vocabulary of tourism. You know, tourism? Hotels, airports, visits to other countries … tourism. Open your books on page 80.
M: Excuse me, can you speak more slowly, please?
W: Of course. I'm sorry. Open your books on page 80, please.

Stronger classes

- Put students into pairs. They choose one of the pictures in exercise 1 and improvise the dialogue without looking at the tapescript. Give them time to practise. Then ask a few pairs to act out their dialogue for the class.

Language notes

- Note that **can** here is not being used for ability. It is used to make a request. Functionally, it expresses willingness. *Can* in requests will be looked at again in lesson 5D

3

❯ *Key Methodology 5: Dialogues 1, page 11*

- Pairwork. Put students into pairs. They must prepare a similar dialogue for the other picture on the page. Remind students to look at the *Useful language* box to help them.
- Give students five or six minutes to write their dialogue and practise it. If students agree, they can perform their dialogue in front of the class.

Extension task

❯ *Key Methodology 8: Spoken errors – fluency tasks 1, page 29*

- Before class, go through a pile of old magazines, and cut out any pictures you can find of two people talking which could be used to practise dialogues using *can* for ability. Collect a large pile. Hand out the pictures at random to students in the class. Tell them to invent a three-line conversation with at least one *can* or *can't* in it. They shouldn't write – just speak. Once they have had the conversation, they pass the picture to the next pair.
- This activity can last a while, with students improvising, say, ten or fifteen conversations, depending on the size of your class. Monitor for errors involving *can* and *can't*, and note them down for feedback at the end.

IF YOU WANT SOMETHING EXTRA …

❯ *Photocopiable activity, page 209*
❯ *Teacher's notes, page 177*

5B | Cross Canada trip

WHAT THE LESSON IS ABOUT

Theme	Canada: holidays & weather
Speaking	Pairwork. Talking about holiday photos
Listening	A conversation: people talking about a holiday in Canada and their photos
Grammar	Past simple *was/were*
Vocabulary	The weather
Did you know	*Top destinations for Canadian tourists*

IF YOU WANT A LEAD-IN …

Introducing the theme: Canada

- Find out what students know about Canada. In pairs or groups of three, students must write:
  - a) the names of three Canadian cities.
  - b) the names of three Canadian sports.
  - c) the names of three Canadian people.
  - d) the names of three things Canada is famous for.

  (Possible answers:

  Cities: Toronto, Montreal, Ottawa, Edmonton, Vancouver, Quebec City, Victoria.

  Sports: (Ice) hockey, Canadian football, baseball, lacrosse.

  People: Jim Carrey, Mike Myers, Margaret Atwood (novelist), Wayne Gretsky (ice hockey player).

  Things: forests, moose, fur, maple syrup.)

VOCABULARY: the weather

1 & 2 1.76

> *Language reference, Student's Book page 61*

- Ask students to look at the weather map of Canada. Hold up your copy of the Student's Book. Point to the cities, say them, and ask students to repeat for pronunciation. Then point to the weather symbols, and elicit, model and repeat them: *It's cloudy, It's warm*, etc.
- Students look at the weather map, and complete the sentences with the names of the cities. They can then compare their answers with a partner.
- Play the recording for students to listen and check their answers.
- Then read through the *Language note* as a class.

1	Montreal
2	Whitehorse
3	Toronto
4	Vancouver

🔊 1.76

> Good afternoon, and here is the weather report for Canada. In Montreal today, it's cloudy and windy, but warm. It's cold and snowy in Whitehorse, with temperatures of minus 12. In Toronto, it's sunny and cold, five degrees. You need your umbrellas in Vancouver today it's rainy and cool.

Alternative procedure

- As a lead in, just before the lesson starts, copy the map of Canada onto the board (or an OHT) with the symbols marked. Alternatively, you could draw the map with the students there, asking questions as you draw, e.g. *What country is this? What's the weather like?*
- Once you have established the country, and the weather symbols, model and drill the question and response, e.g. say: *What's the weather like in Toronto?*, and ask students to repeat. Then elicit, and repeat: *It's sunny*.
- Get students to ask and answer *What … like?* questions and their responses, using the map as a prompt, across the class.

Extra task

- Write the following sentences on the board:
  1 *It's very cold and snowy here.*
  2 *It's always warm and sunny here.*
  3 *It's often cold and rainy here.*
  4 *It's very hot here.*
- Students think of a country or city for each of the sentences. They write it on a piece of paper, e.g. *Morocco* or *Cape Town* for *It's always warm and sunny here.*
- Their partner must match the city or country to the description.
- Once they have matched their cities/countries, get students to ask and answer in pairs, e.g. *What's the weather like in the Arctic? It's very cold and snowy.*

Language notes

- *It* is used as an 'empty' subject in expressions referring to time, weather and temperature, e.g. *It's five o'clock.* It has no real meaning.
- Similar to *What … look like?* (introduced in unit 2), *What … like?* is an unusual expression to most students. In most languages, a literal translation of *How* or *What is the weather?* is common. Here, *like* is a preposition. Make sure students aren't responding with, e.g., ✗ *It is like cold.*

3

- Model the activity to the class by asking a few students the questions.
- Pairwork. Students work in pairs to ask and answer the questions.

Cultural notes

- Contrary to popular opinion, Canada is not always cold, at least not in the south near the US border where its major cities are. Toronto has hot, muggy summers with temperatures approaching 30˚C. In winter, however, –10˚C is common. Vancouver, on the Pacific coast, is very mild, with the temperature rarely below zero. It's famous for its rain, though. Whitehorse, however, in the Yukon territory of the far north, is seriously cold!

LISTENING

In this listening, Lara and Tom have just received their photos from their holiday in Canada. They are looking through the photos and telling a friend about where they are and what is happening.

1 **1.77**

- Tell students that they are going to listen to two people talking about their holiday photos. Point to each photo and ask: *Where are they? What can you see?*
- Play the recording. Students listen to the people talking about their holiday in Canada, and put the photos in the order they hear them. They can compare their answers with a partner before you check with the whole class.

E, C, B, A

 1.77

> **L = Lara   T = Tom**
> **L:** Our holiday in Canada was lovely. It was a cross Canada trip. This is a photo of our train. We were on the train for ten days. The scenery in Canada is beautiful. This photo … oh, where was this one, Tom?
> **T:** This photo was in <u>Halifax</u>. I remember it. Too bad about the weather, it wasn't very good.
> **L:** That's right, it wasn't. <u>It was rainy all the time there.</u> <u>The houses were lovely</u> though, and the people were very nice. …
> **T:** Look at this one. This was amazing.
> **L:** Yeah, yeah. Where was this? Was it in Quebec?
> **T:** No, it wasn't. It was <u>Montreal</u>. We were there for <u>two days</u>. <u>This city has great jazz concerts.</u>
> **L:** Who was this musician?
> **T:** I don't know. I can't remember his name. He was good though. …
> **T:** I remember this photo.
> **L:** This is <u>Toronto</u>. You can see the CN Tower there. The <u>shops weren't open</u> that day. So we were in the park … doing nothing. I wasn't very happy.
> **T:** No, you weren't. You were miserable.
> **L:** <u>It was cold!</u>
> **T:** Alright. Next photo?
> **L:** Hmm. …
> **L:** I love this hotel.
> **T:** This was in a big natural park. The park is called <u>Banff</u>. It was a <u>perfect place to go skiing</u>. Unfortunately, I can't ski. But Lara's right, the hotel was very good.
> **L:** There was a <u>Jacuzzi in our room</u>!
> **T:** Yep, good hotel. How many days were we in this park?
> **L:** Three days, I think.

2 **1.77**

- Play the recording again. Students listen and tick the words and expressions they hear.

Students should tick the following sentences:
1, 3, 5, 6, 7, 9, 10 and 11.

3

- Model the activity briefly by pointing at and describing photos.
- Pairwork. Put students in pairs to describe their Cross Canada trip, using the words in exercise 2 to talk about the photos.

4

- Discuss the questions with the whole class.

Extra task: imaginary photos

- Tell students to think of a city that they have visited, and know well. Tell them to imagine they have five photos of places in the city. Give them two to three minutes to think about how they are going to describe their imaginary photos. Allow them to make brief notes if they want.
- Then put students in pairs. They must 'show' their partner their imaginary photos, and describe them as if they are real.
- Once they have described all their photos, their partner must guess which city they described.

> **■ Key Methodology 17**
> **■ Finger feedback**
>
> - *Teachers of lower level students often want to give useful feedback to students, for example to tell them where they made a mistake in a sentence. However, with students who don't yet have much English, there is a danger that the teacher's instruction or guidance will itself be complicated and only add to the students' confusion. For this reason, it can be very useful to have feedback methods that require minimal teacher speaking. My favourite technique is to use your fingers.*
> - *Hold up your left hand in front of you (or right hand if you are left-handed) at about chest-height. Your palm should face you. The fingers can now show words in a sentence. The little finger represents the first word, the next finger is the second word, and so on. Thus, the thumb is the fifth word. If you need a longer sentence, hold up your other hand and start with the thumb as the sixth word. This gives you a clear and simple way of referring to words in a sentence up to ten words long.*
>
>
>
> - *Remember that from your viewpoint the sentence goes in the opposite direction to normal. But from a student's position, looking at your hand from the other side, the sentence goes normally from left to right. Practise in the mirror – this takes a little getting used to.*
> - *Of course, students won't immediately know that fingers mean words – so train them the first times that you use this technique.*
> - *If a student makes a mistake, e.g. ✗ Yesterday I go to London, hold up your fingers (as above) and ask them to say their sentence word by word. As they say the first word, use your right hand to hold your little finger. If students speak too quickly, slow them down and emphasize that you only want the first word. Now hold the next finger and say second word, and so on. When you come to a word that has a mistake, e.g. go instead of went, indicate it by pointing at it and frowning or shaking your head.*

- *Students should now realize that there is a problem with that word – and hopefully try to self-correct or think again.*
- *After you have used this training mode a few times, students will learn that you use fingers to mean words in a sentence. After this, you will no longer need to explicitly say what they mean each time. The fingers now become a really handy way of quickly showing that there is a mistake and pinpointing exactly where the mistake is in a sentence.*
- *When you become comfortable with that basic technique, you can soon explore other feedback messages that can be conveyed by using the fingers to show sentence structure, e.g. the words are in the wrong order, one word isn't needed, you need an extra word, etc.*
- *Similarly, when working on spelling, fingers can show letters in a word as well as words in a sentence. When working on pronunciation, fingers can show syllables in a word, e.g. when students say the word information with the stress wrongly on the first syllable, you could use your fingers to elicit the word, syllable by syllable, and then to focus on how many syllables there are; the sound of each syllable, and what the word sounds like if you stress different syllables.*

GRAMMAR: past simple *was/were*

❯ *Language reference, Student's Book, page 60*
❯ *Methodology guidelines: Grammar boxes, page xiii*

1

- Do the first couple of sentences as examples to get students started.
- Students then write answers with the words in brackets. They can compare their answers with a partner before you check with the whole class.

2	No, it wasn't. It was cheap.
3	No, it wasn't. It was a quiet part of town.
4	No, it wasn't. It was rainy and cold.
5	No, he wasn't. He was a Scottish man.
6	No, we weren't. We were there for ten days.

Extra task

- Once students have written answers, tell them to close their books, and use the prompts in exercise 1 to do a drill. Say: *The hotel was expensive.* Students respond, *No, it wasn't. It was cheap.*
- Drill the students chorally and individually.

2

- Students complete the dialogue with *was/wasn't, were/weren't*. They can compare their answers with a partner before you check with the whole class.

1	weren't
2	were
3	wasn't
4	weren't
5	were
6	was
7	were
8	were

Language notes

- ***Was(n't)*** and ***were(n't)*** are the irregular past forms of the verb *to be*. We say: *I/he/she was(n't)*, and *you/we/they were(n't)*. Remember that English, unlike most languages, does not differentiate between *you* (singular) and *you* (plural), so some students may make the error of saying, ✗ *you was*, when *you* refers to one person, thinking that they should use the singular form.
- Saying, ✗ *He was not …*, etc. is incorrect. The long version of the negative is only used in formal written English, and when strongly emphasizing the word *not*.

3

❯ *Key Methodology 5: Dialogues 1, page 11*

- Pairwork. Put students in pairs to practise reading the dialogue. Make sure they attempt the weak stress of *was* in 6.

Language notes

- ***Was*** is pronounced with a schwa in affirmative sentences when it is unstressed, *It was /wəz/ sunny*. It is given its full value in questions and negative sentences when it is stressed, *Was /wɒz/ it cold, It wasn't /wɒznt/ cold*, and in short answers, *Yes, it was /wɒz/*. Similarly, *They were /wər/ tired*, but *Were /wɜː/ they tired?, They weren't /wɜːnt/ tired* and *Yes, they were /wɜː/*. The *r* in *were* is not pronounced unless the next word begins with a vowel, *We were in Canada, /wər_ɪn/*.

DID YOU KNOW?

1 & 2

- Students read the information about Canadian tourist destinations and discuss the questions in pairs or small groups.

Web research task

❯ *Methodology guidelines: Web research tasks, page xiii*

- Students find out the top tourist destinations for people from their country, or from other English-speaking countries, write down the information and present it to the class.

Web search key words
- Country/statistics/tourism/holidays

IF YOU WANT SOMETHING EXTRA …

❯ *Photocopiable activity, page 210*
❯ *Teacher's notes, page 177*

5c | Travel essentials

WHAT THE LESSON IS ABOUT

Theme	Going on holiday
Speaking	Pairwork: deciding on things to take on holiday; asking & answering questions about what you did last year
Reading & listening	A conversation: a couple talk about their holiday preparations – what they packed in their bag & what they didn't
Grammar:	Past simple regular verbs
Pronunciation	Past simple regular verbs: /ɪd/ endings

IF YOU WANT A LEAD-IN ...

Introducing the theme: going on holiday

- Draw a rectangle on the board, and say: *I'm going on holiday and this is my suitcase.* Draw objects in it, e.g. a T-shirt, a camera, a book. As you draw, elicit the names of the things from students.
- Tell students to draw their own rectangle on a piece of paper. Tell them to draw in what they usually take on holiday. Give them four or five minutes to draw.
- When they have finished, tell them to describe what they have in their bag to other students. You will have to walk round and help with vocabulary.
- An alternative is to collect in the 'suitcases' once they have been filled in, divide students into groups of four, and give each group four random 'suitcases'. They must talk together, say what is in each suitcase, and guess whose suitcase it is.

SPEAKING

1

- Tell students to look at the picture of the bag. Ask: *What can you see? How many things can you say in English?* Elicit, model and ask students to repeat as many words as you can.

A	a dictionary	H	sunglasses
B	a camera	I	a pack of cards
C	a discman	J	a (British) passport
D	an airplane ticket (from a travel agent's)	K	a credit card
		L	an alarm clock
E	a mobile phone	M	a guide book
F	some money		(to Washington, DC)
G	a torch	N	a bag

2

- Model the activity briefly by pretending to pack your bag, saying, for example, *I think the camera is a good idea. Mmm, I agree …*, etc.
- Pairwork. Put students in pairs. They must choose five things to take.
- At the end, ask a few pairs to say what they want to take.

Extra task

- Do this as a pyramid discussion. Put students in pairs to make a list of five things. Then put pairs into groups of four. They must renegotiate and come up with a new list of five things. Finally, build up a class list on the board.

READING & LISTENING

This listening is a conversation between a husband and wife who are about to set off on holiday. There are two parts to the listening. In the first part, Walter, the husband, is very anxious and asks his wife Thelma lots of questions to check that she has packed everything. Thelma gets a little frustrated with him. In the second part, Walter and Thelma have arrived at the airport only to discover that Walter, whose job was to bring the passports, has forgotten them.

1 ● 1.78

- Tell students to look at the picture. Ask: *Where are they? Where are they going? What can you see in the picture?* Tell students that they are going on holiday. Ask: *What do you do before you go on holiday?* Try to elicit: *pack a bag, turn off the lights/electricity/computer, close the doors/windows.* Use mime to check these phrases.
- Students read and listen to their conversation to find out who packed the bags – Walter or Thelma.

Thelma Thomson

● 1.78

> **W = Walter T = Thelma**
> **W:** Come on!
> **T:** I'm here. I'm here.
> **W:** Did you turn off the lights?
> **T:** Yes, I did. <u>I turned off</u> the lights and <u>your computer</u>.
> **W:** Good. <u>Did you pack my digital camera?</u>
> **T:** <u>Yes, I did.</u> It's in the black bag <u>with your mobile phone and book</u>.
> **W:** Which book?
> **T:** The book that was on the table next to your bed.
> **W:** Oh. I didn't want a book. I wanted the ipod.
> **T:** Well, I didn't know!
> **W:** <u>We don't have the ipod then</u>.
> **T:** No, we don't.
>
> **W:** Do you have the guide book?
> **T:** Just a minute.
> **W:** Oh no, <u>you didn't remember the guide book</u>.
> **T:** <u>Yes, I did. Here it is!</u>
> **W:** <u>Plane tickets?</u>
> **T:** <u>I remembered. They're here</u>.
> **W:** Good. Good. Well, darling, we're on holiday.
> **T:** We can finally relax.

- *Add more pictures and elicit items that come into the conversation, e.g.* a coffee *and maybe ask students to predict what the conversation will be about.*
- *When students finally listen to the actual dialogue, they will be better prepared and more able to hear specific things in it. (Studies have shown that we are better able to hear things when we are already expecting to hear them.)*

Setting an extra listening task

- *Find some pictures of things that are referred to during a dialogue. Also select one or two pictures of things that are not in the dialogue. Use tape or sticky-tack to put all these cards on the board so that everyone can see them. When students listen the first time, before you use any of the Student's Book exercises, ask them to decide which of the pictures are in the recording and which not.*
- *After listening, let students compare in pairs before you hear their ideas. Don't confirm or reject anything yourself yet.*
- *On the second listening, ask students to check if they were right, and to decide which order the pictures come in, i.e. which is first, second, etc.*

2

- Students read the text again, and tick the things Walter and Thelma have in the car.

They had the following things in the car:
digital camera; mobile phone; book; guide book; plane tickets

Alternative procedure for stronger classes

- You could do this as a listening. Students must listen only (not read) and tick the words the couple have in their car. Students then read to check their answers.

3

- Pairwork. Students work in pairs, and practise reading the dialogue.

4 🔘 **1.79**

- Play the recording. Students listen to Walter and Thelma at the airport. Ask: *What is the problem?*

Walter forgot the passports.

🔘 **1.79**

Wo = woman W = Walter T = Thelma
Wo: Good morning, tickets and passports, please.
W: Here you are, tickets and … oh, wait a minute, where did you put the passports?
T: The passports? That was your job.
W: Was it?
T: Yes, it was. Do you have them?
W: Wait a minute.
T: Did you look in the black bag?
W: Yes, I did. Oh, no …
T: Oh, Walter!

GRAMMAR: past simple regular verbs

❯ *Language reference, Student's Book page 60*
❯ *Methodology guidelines: Grammar boxes, page xiii*

1

- Students complete the sentences using the past simple of the verbs in brackets. They can compare their answers with a partner before you check with the whole class.

1 remembered; didn't remember
2 wanted; didn't want
3 visited; didn't visit
4 enjoyed; didn't enjoy
5 liked; didn't like

Language notes

- To make the past tense of a regular verb, you add *ed* to the end. However, there are plenty of confusing form variations on this that you need to check and correct with students at this level. Compare:
  open + ed = opened   *close + d = closed*
  play + ed = played   *marry + ied = married*
  (vowel + *y* = don't change *y*; but consonant + *y* = change *y* to i)
- N.B. if a verb is made up of consonant + vowel + consonant, it tends to double the final consonant, e.g. *stop + p + ed = stopped*. However, two or three syllable words don't generally follow this rule, (*visited, opened, remembered*). There are surprisingly few common regular verbs made up of consonant + vowel + consonant, so this is not something to worry about too much here.
- In the negative and question forms, *do* becomes *did*, and the main verb loses its *-ed* ending. Watch out for errors involving over-applying rules, ✗ *She didn't remembered*, and of errors arising from translating from L1, ✗ *She no remembered …*, ✗ *Remembered you the book?*
- See Language notes in the pronunciation section below for pronunciation problems.

2

- It is a good idea to model this activity carefully, teacher to student, then in open pairs, before putting students in pairs to practise.
- Tell students to write five things from *Speaking* exercise 1 on a piece of paper. Model the *Did you pack …?* question by asking a few questions round the class. Then ask students to ask you the same questions. Reply with *Yes, I did* or *No, I didn't*. Then ask students to ask and answer across the class.
- Pairwork. Once the students have got the hang of this, put them in A and B pairs, to practise asking and answering the questions.

3

- Again, it is a good idea to introduce and model this activity by asking the students some *Did you …?* questions about last night.
- Students then make questions from the prompts.

2 Did you use the internet?
3 Did you cook dinner?
4 Did you study English?
5 Did you take out the rubbish?
6 Did you play football?

4

❯ *Key Methodology 7: Accurate speaking & fluent speaking, page 20*

- Pairwork. Put students in pairs to ask and answer the questions in exercise 3 about last night.
- Monitor and correct errors. Make sure that students are answering the questions by saying either *Yes, I did.* or *No I didn't.*

PRONUNCIATION: past simple regular verbs

1 🔘 **1.80**

- Play the recording. Students listen to the verbs and the past tense forms and try to explain what the difference is between group A and group B.

> In group A, the past tense forms are pronounced as one syllable.
> In group B, they are pronounced as two syllables, ending with /ɪd/.

🔘 **1.80**

> pack   packed   open   opened   watch   watched
> want   wanted   end   ended

2

- Students complete the rule with the correct ending, a or b.

> a) pronounce the *-ed* as an extra syllable /ɪd/.

Language notes

- If a verb ends with a voiced consonant or vowel sound, then *-ed* is pronounced /d/, e.g. *opened* /əʊpənd/, *played* /pleɪd/.
- If a verb ends with an unvoiced consonant, then *-ed* is pronounced /t/, e.g. *watched* /wɒtʃt/, *cooked* /kʊkt/.
- Only when a verb ends with *t* or *d*, is *-ed* pronounced /ɪd/. A major error at this level is that students want to pronounce every verb as two syllables: *watched* as ✗/wɒtʃɪd/, *opened* as ✗/əʊpəned/, etc. Be sure to correct this error, which results largely from students seeing the word written and trying to spell it out phonetically.

3 & 4 🔘 **1.81**

- Put students in pairs to decide how to pronounce the verbs.
- Play the recording. Students listen and check their answers.
- Then play the recording again for students to listen and repeat.

> 1   liked /laɪkt/ – no extra syllable; /t/ ending
> 2   closed /kləʊzd/ – no extra syllable; /d/ ending
> 3   remembered /rɪmembəd/ – no extra syllable; /d/ ending
> 4   visited /vɪzɪtɪd/ – extra syllable; /ɪd/ ending
> 5   cooked /kʊkt/ – no extra syllable; /t/ ending
> 6   started /stɑːtɪd/ – extra syllable, /ɪd/ ending

🔘 **1.81**

> 1   I liked it.
> 2   He closed the door.
> 3   They remembered it.
> 4   We visited her.
> 5   You cooked dinner.
> 6   English class started in September.

Extra task

- Play noughts and crosses. Draw the following noughts and crosses table on the board:

/ɪd/	/d/	/t/
/d/	/t/	/ɪd/
/t/	/ɪd/	/d/

- Divide the class down the middle into group X, and group O. Group X must choose a square. If they give you a past tense verb, correctly pronounced, that fits that square, you write X in it, e.g. they choose the top right square and say, liked /laɪkt/.
- Then it's Group O's turn.
- If a group gets one wrong, that square goes to the other group. The idea is to win by putting three Xs or Os in a line, horizontally, vertically or diagonally.
- Alternatively, play the game in threes. Student X plays against Student O, and the third student is the referee.

SPEAKING

1

- Students should work on their own to make questions in the past simple from the prompts. Monitor and help if necessary.

2 & 3

- Pairwork. Put students in A and B pairs. Tell students to think about their answers to the questions in 1. Tell them that one of their answers must be a lie.
- Students then take it in turns to interview each other, and guess the lie.

Alternative task

- Play *Find someone who?* Write the prompts in *Speaking* exercise 1 on the board, then tell students to stand up, walk round, and ask different people. They must try to find at least one person who says *yes* to each question.

IF YOU WANT SOMETHING EXTRA ...

❯ *Photocopiable activity, page 211*
❯ *Teacher's notes, page 178*

5D | Bed & breakfast

WHAT THE LESSON IS ABOUT

Theme	Staying at a guest house or hotel
Speaking	Talking about past holidays & staying at hotels
	Roleplay: asking for permission at a hotel
Reading	Two advertisements for hotels in Stratford-upon-Avon
Listening	Four conversations: asking for permission at a hotel
Functional language	Asking for permission

IF YOU WANT A LEAD-IN ...

Introducing the theme: staying at a hotel

- At this level, listening to the teacher is fun and motivating, so long as the teacher speaks simply and clearly. Draw the diagram below on the board, then tell a story, like the one written below. You could easily embellish this story with your own ideas and experiences.

Hotel Royal			
			My bedroom
	Dining room		
		reception	

I stayed at the Hotel Royal. It was a terrible hotel. The receptionist was very unfriendly, and the reception area wasn't clean. The dining room was terrible. The chairs were uncomfortable. The food wasn't cooked very well. My bedroom was very small and noisy. There was a bed and a table, but there wasn't any other furniture. It was terrible …

- Put students in pairs to look at the picture on the board, and retell the story.
- Students could tell the class about their own bad hotel experiences.

SPEAKING

1
- Model this task briefly by telling students about your hotel experiences, using the prompts given.
- Students then complete the sentences for themselves.

2
- Pairwork. Put students in pairs to say their sentences to each other and to compare them.
- After they have finished, ask some students to tell the class about their partner.

READING

The reading texts are two advertisements describing two very different hotels for people who want to visit Stratford-upon-Avon. The first hotel is very traditional and the second is modern. They give details about their location; when they are open; the types of rooms they have; what facilities there are, and meals available for their guests.

1
- Lead in by asking students to look at the two photos of hotels, and asking them to describe them.
- Students read the advertisements for the two hotels in Stratford, and say which hotel they would like to stay in. Let them discuss their answer in pairs before discussing as a class.

Cultural notes
- **Stratford-upon-Avon**, or *Stratford* as it is often called, is a small town on the river Avon in Warwickshire in the English midlands. It is famous as the birthplace of William Shakespeare (1564–1616), England's greatest playwright. You can visit the house where he was born, the school he attended, the church where he is buried, and watch one of his plays performed by the world famous Royal Shakespeare Company in one of Stratford's theatres. Unsurprisingly, Stratford and its many hotels are full of tourists all year round.
- A **guest house** is a small hotel, often family-run, which is often friendlier and cheaper than a hotel, but lacks its amenities.
- In Britain, a **traditional English breakfast**, or *full* or *cooked English breakfast*, comprises bacon, eggs, toast, and usually tea rather than coffee. It may also include cooked tomatoes, mushrooms and sausages. It is very popular – but most British people only have a full breakfast like this at weekends. *A continental breakfast* comprises bread and butter or a French croissant with coffee.

2
- Students read the advertisements again and say *S* for the Shakespeare Guest House, *C* for the Stratford Central Hotel or *SC* if the sentence is true for both hotels. They can compare their answers with a partner before you check with the whole class.

1 S	2 C	3 SC	4 C	5 SC	6 S	7 C

3
- Students complete the definitions with a word from the advertisements. They can compare their answers with a partner before you check with the whole class.

1	friendly
2	warm
3	complimentary
4	meal
5	available

Language notes
You may wish to extend the vocabulary search to check the following:
- **famous** is when everybody knows this place or person.
- a **barbeque area** is a place outside where you cook meat.
- a **rural location** is a place in the country.
- a **business traveller** is a person who goes from town to town on business.

Web research task

> *Methodology guidelines: Web research tasks, page xiii*

- Get students to research hotels in Stratford-upon-Avon, (or other British tourist towns), and find one they like. They must find: the price, location, type of rooms, meals, when it is open and other facilities.

Web search key words

- Stratford-upon-Avon/hotel/tourist information
- town/hotel/tourist information

LISTENING

In the first part of this episode of the listening story, the Explore London tour have arrived at a guesthouse in Stratford-upon-Avon.

Herb and Hannah (the tourists from Texas) at first love the guesthouse, as it's so old and traditionally English. They are pleased that their guidebook describes it as being friendly. However, Hannah soon meets the owner of the guesthouse and finds out that he and his dog are not so friendly. Herb too discovers that the owner isn't particularly friendly when he refuses to let him use the phone at the guesthouse, telling him that it's not for guests. He gets more upset when he discovers that he can't use his American Express credit card to pay for his bill. And finally, Herb gets very angry when he is told that he will be charged £2 for leaving their bags at reception for fifteen minutes, and concludes that the guidebook description is completely wrong.

1 🔘 1.82

- Remind students about the characters Valerie, Herb and Hannah. Ask: *Who is Valerie.* (Answer: a tour guide.) *Where are Herb and Hannah from?* (Answer: Texas, USA.)
- Students listen to the recording and then say which hotel from page 58 the Explore London tour visit.

The Shakespeare Guest House

🔘 1.82

Ha = Hannah He = Herb V = Valerie
Ha: Oh Herb, is this our hotel?
He: I think so, dear. Isn't it beautiful?
Ha: Yes. What does the book say?
He: 'A happy, friendly eighteenth century guest house, with gardens and barbeque …'. This is good, darling.
Ha: So English! I love it.
V: Is this your first time in an English bed and breakfast?
Ha: Yes, it is. We don't have things like this in Texas. Did Shakespeare live here?
V: Umm, this guest house is only 200 years old, so no, I don't think so.
He: Too bad. Maybe he lived close to here.

2 🔘 1.83

- Play the recording. Students listen to the four conversations and match each one to a sign.

Conversation 1 – B
Conversation 2 – A
Conversation 3 – C
Conversation 4 – D

🔘 1.83

Ha = Hannah O = owner He = Herb V = Valerie
1
Ha: Darling, look. A dog.
O: Oi! Excuse me! You can't go there!
Ha: I'm <u>sorry</u>. I was only looking. What's his name?
O: Rex.
Ha: Can I touch him?
O: I'm afraid you can't. He's very <u>dangerous</u>.
2
O: Hello.
He: Hi. Excuse me, but could I use your phone? My <u>mobile phone</u> doesn't work here.
O: I'm afraid we don't have a phone for the public.
He: What do you mean, no phone? What about that <u>phone</u>?
O: Sorry, it's <u>private</u>.
V: Hi, is there a problem?
He: Yes, my phone doesn't work. He says this phone is not for guests. May I use your phone, please?
V: Of course. Here you are.
He: Thank you.
3
He: I'd like to pay the bill. Can I pay by <u>credit card</u>?
O: Of course. Visa? Mastercard?
He: American Express.
O: Oh no, I'm sorry, but we don't <u>take</u> American Express.
He: Fine. Visa then.
4
He: Oh, one more thing. Our bus leaves at a quarter past <u>four</u>. Is it OK to leave our bags here, please?
O: Certainly. It's £2 an hour.
He: But it's only for <u>fifteen</u> minutes!
O: I'm sorry, it's £2 minimum to keep <u>bags</u>.
He: I can't believe this.
Ha: Herb, what's wrong?
He: Happy, friendly hotel? I don't think so.

3 & 4 🔘 1.83

- Play the recording again. Students read and listen and complete the dialogues with the correct word from the box. They can then compare their answers with a partner.
- Ask students to look at tapescript 1.83 on page 142 of the Student's Book to check their answers.

1	sorry	6	credit card
2	dangerous	7	take
3	mobile phone	8	four
4	public	9	fifteen
5	private	10	bags

Extra task

- Write *The worst hotel* and *The best hotel* on the board and give students a few minutes to think about either the best or worst hotel they stayed in. Write the following useful language on the board to help them with ideas:
  The hotel was(n't) …
  There were(n't) …
  The room was(n't) …
  The people were(n't) …
  I liked/didn't like it because …
- Students then describe the hotel to a partner.
- At the end, ask a few students to tell the class about their experiences.

FUNCTIONAL LANGUAGE: asking for permission

❯ *Language reference, Student's Book page 61*

1
- Students put the words in the correct order to make questions.
- Then nominate students to ask you the questions. Respond naturally, (humorously!), using the responses in the table.

1   May I use your phone, please?
2   Can I go to the toilet, please?
3   Is it alright if I go now?
4   Can I use your pen, please?

Alternative procedure

- Lead in by drawing the following pictures on the board, (or, better, prepare flashcards of these which you can fix to the board): a mobile phone; a cigarette with smoke coming from it; a pen; a credit card. Model the new language by pointing to the picture and saying, *Can I use your mobile phone, please? Can I smoke, please?* If students say *yes*, take the mobile and pretend to ring, or pretend to light a cigarette. If they say *no*, look disappointed.
- Once students have got the meaning here, model the form with *Can*, *May* and *Could*, and ask students to repeat. Then point to pictures, and get individual students to produce requests from the picture prompts. Make sure they are attempting a good intonation pattern. Respond to their requests by saying, *Yes, of course, Yes, go ahead, No, I'm afraid not*, etc.
- Get students to ask and answer across the class, then ask and answer in closed pairs. They are then ready to complete the table in exercise 1.

Language notes

- There is very little difference in meaning and use between ***Can I …?, Could I …?*** *and* ***May I …?*** The latter two are perhaps slightly more tentative and polite.
- The intonation pattern is very important here, as flat intonation can be rude. Make sure students start high in their intonation, and that their intonation rises at the end:

Can I use your phone, please?

2
- Nominate students to ask you the questions from exercise 1. Respond naturally, (humorously!), using the responses in the table.
- Pairwork. Put students into pairs. They take turns to ask and respond to the questions in exercise 1.
- When they have finished, you could ask students to think of three more requests in their pairs to ask you.

Roleplay

❯ *Communication activities, pages 132 & 138*

3 & 4
- A good way to do this activity is to have preparation pairs and roleplay pairs. Divide the class into equal numbers of A pairs and B pairs.
- Student A pairs read their role and look at the information on page 132 of the Student's Book. They discuss in their pairs ways of asking permission.
- Student B pairs read their role and look at the information on page 138 of the Student's Book and prepare responses.
- When students are ready, mix the pairs so that every Student A is with a Student B. Students then roleplay the situation.
- Then they change partners and repeat the roleplay with a new partner.

IF YOU WANT SOMETHING EXTRA …

❯ *Photocopiable activity, page 212*
❯ *Teacher's notes, page 178*

Answer key

5 REVIEW

❯ Student's Book page 151

1

1 When were you on holiday?
2 Where were you?
3 How many days were you there?
4 Who were you with?
5 What was the weather like?
6 Were the people nice?
7 What was the food like?
8 Was it a good holiday?

2

1 g   2 c   3 a   4 e   5 f   6 d   7 h   8 b

3

Students own answers.

4

1 was
2 was
3 were
4 was
5 was
6 was
7 was
8 was
9 were

5

1 What's your favourite weather to like?
2 The Lingo Global 29 can to translate lots of languages.
3 I can't not speak English very well.
4 The weather was lovely and was sunny.
5 Yes, I no agree. We can take lots of money.
6 I did remembered. Look! It's here.
7 Can I use your phone, please me?
8 Of course you can use.

6

2 I didn't watch television.
3 I listened to music and studied English for a couple of hours.
4 I used the internet to practise my English.
5 I looked at English websites.
6 I didn't go to bed late, around 11 o'clock.

7

Students own answers.

8

Possible answers:
1 A: Can I smoke here?
   B: Yes you can. / No, sorry you can't.
2 A: Can I pay by credit card?
   B: Yes, you can. / No, sorry you can't.
3 A: Can I use your computer, please?
   B: Yes, you can. / No, sorry you can't.
4 A: Can I use your mobile phone, please?
   B: Yes, you can. / No, sorry you can't.
5 A: Can I turn on the television, please?
   B: Yes, you can. / No, sorry you can't.
6 A: Can I ask you a question?
   B: Yes, you can. / No, sorry you can't.

5 WRITING

❯ Workbook page 73

Model answer
Dear Mario,
Last month I was on holiday in London. I was with Carlos and Fernando. The weather was terrible, but the holiday was OK. The people were friendly and we were there for two weeks.

6A | Celebrations

WHAT THE LESSON IS ABOUT

Theme	Celebrations
Speaking	Pairwork discussion: talking about celebrations
	Pairwork: telling a story about a celebration
Reading	Blogs about celebrations
Vocabulary	Celebrations
Grammar	Past simple irregular verbs

IF YOU WANT A LEAD-IN …

Introducing the theme: celebrations

- Write on the board: *Congratulations!* and say: *Congratulations!* Get students to repeat for pronunciation.
- Put students in pairs to think of five situations where people say *Congratulations!* to you. Elicit their ideas and write them on the board, e.g. *on your birthday*; *at your wedding*; *when you get a new job*; *when you pass an exam*; *when you pass your driving test*; *when you have a baby*; *when you win a competition.*
- Tell students to think of something that has happened to them recently, and write it down, e.g. *I had my 21st birthday in June. I got married in July. I won £100 on the lottery in May.* Tell students to stand up, walk round, and announce their special event. Respond with *Congratulations!*

Discussion starters

❯ *Methodology guidelines: Discussion starters, page xii*

- Write these questions on the board for students to discuss in pairs or small groups.
  What was the last celebration you went to?
  What was it for? Who was it for?
  When was it? Where was it?
  What did you do there?

VOCABULARY & SPEAKING: celebrations

1
- Students match each card on the page to a different celebration.

A	a new baby
B	a birthday
C	a wedding
D	a retirement party

2
- Pairwork. Put students in pairs to discuss the questions.

Cultural notes
- In Britain, when somebody has a new baby, friends and family send cards and buy presents for the baby, such as clothes and soft toys. Some people wet the baby's head, which means having a drink to say congratulations to the parents.

- On someone's birthday, people are given presents and sent birthday cards by friends and family. They often have a birthday cake with candles placed on it and lit. People then sing *Happy Birthday* to the person whose birthday it is, who has to blow the candles out and make a wish. The number of candles on the cake add up to the person's age. For children, there is often a birthday party with games and a birthday cake.
- At a retirement party, there is often a big dinner in which the person retiring is given a present. Traditionally, the present is a clock or gold watch to mark the time spent working. But nowadays, the present tends to be more personal. The boss and the person retiring often make a speech.
- At a church wedding in Britain, the bride wears a white dress and carries flowers. The groom traditionally wears a morning suit with long tails and a top hat. The bride always arrives after the groom. After the wedding ceremony, there is a reception for all the guests which is generally a big dinner with speeches and toasts.

READING

The reading text are three blogs from the internet in the form of a personal diary. The writers describe a celebration party they have recently been to.

1
- Ask students to look at the blogs. Ask: *What is a blog?* (Answer: *a blog is the short form of web log. Many people have a diary on their blog, which other people can read.*) Ask: *Do you write a blog? Do you write a diary?*
- Students read the blogs, and match each blog to a card from *Speaking* exercise 1.

1	The Office Blog	– card D
2	Marisa's Daily Blog	– card C
3	Our Life	– card B

Extra vocabulary task
- There are a number of difficult words in the texts. Here is a way of dealing with them:
  1 Write the following simple collocations from the texts on the board:
     A wonderful dinner
     A big surprise
     A big wedding
  2 Tell students to find the phrases in the text. Then ask check questions:
     Was the dinner very good or very bad?
     Did Richard know there were 60 people at the party?
     How did he feel?
     Are there a lot of people at a big wedding?

Cultural note
- ***For He's a Jolly Good Fellow*** was originally an American folk song and is one of the most popular songs in the English language. It is a song of celebration, sometimes sung to congratulate someone for achieving a sporting victory, or when someone retires.

> ■ **Key Methodology 19**
> ■■ **Using vocabulary check questions**

- *When you have taught a new vocabulary item, it's useful to be able to check if students have really understood the meaning. Bald questions such as Do you understand? are often not very useful because students may give the answer they think you want to hear – or they may believe that they do understand something when, in fact, they don't. It's more effective to ask questions whose answers reveal if students really do understand.*

- *Many teachers ask students to make a sentence using the new word. This can sometimes be useful, but it also a fairly unfocused task. Firstly, it is quite demanding for a student to make a whole sentence – and when you just need a quick check this can take time and waste energy. In making a new sentence, they will probably also make other mistakes which you have to decide whether to deal with or not. More importantly, students could make sentences about any subject at all, and many of their sentences will fail to clarify if they have really understood a meaning, e.g. if you have just taught blog and a student says 'I like my blog very much.' although it is superficially a correct sentence, it doesn't tell you if the student thinks blog means web log, girlfriend, tomato sauce or pet hamster.*

- *A more useful way than these two strategies is to ask questions that (a) directly focus on the meaning, and (b) don't require a long answer from students. These questions are known as concept questions or check questions.*

- *Check questions for blog (with answers in brackets) might be: Is a blog in a book? (no); Is it on the internet? (yes); Do people use a blog to write about their everyday life? (yes); Is it like a diary? (yes, usually).*

- *Questions like this are useful for asking quick-fire checks around the class. Ask one question, then name one student to answer (if you name the student before you say the question, everyone else might stop paying attention!). As soon as they answer, ask 'Is he/she right?' to another student across the room. When they have answered, ask your next question to a new student, and so on. After asking a few of these you'll have a pretty good idea if most students have got the meaning.*

2
- Students read the blogs again and put the sentences a–c in the gaps 1–3.

> 1 c   2 a   3 b

3
- Students read the sentences and mark them true or false. They can compare their answers with a partner before you check with the whole class.

> 1   F (Richard got a watch at the party)
> 2   T
> 3   T
> 4   F (They got married in the town hall, they had a party in an Indian restaurant in the evening.)
> 5   T
> 6   T

Extra task
- Ask students which of the three celebrations they would like to go to and why.

GRAMMAR: past simple irregular verbs

> ❯ *Language reference, Student's Book page 70*
> ❯ *Irregular verb list, Student's Book page 159*
> ❯ *Methodology guidelines: Grammar boxes, page xiii*

1
- Students look back at the texts in *Reading* exercise 1 on page 62, and find and underline 12 irregular past simple verbs. Tell them not to include *was*. They can then compare their answers with a partner.
- Students can then work in pairs and write down the past form of each verb they found, together with its infinitive.

> came – come
> sang – sing
> had – have
> gave – give
> could – can
> said – say
> took – take
> met – meet
> sat – sit
> ate – eat
> drank – drink
> woke – wake

Language notes
- Irregular verbs are, of course, very common in English. In fact, the majority of commonly used, basic, Anglo-Saxon verbs are irregular. Students simply have to learn and memorize them – there is no logic as to why they change as they do.
- Watch out for the common error of over-applying rules when forming negatives and questions, 7 <u>Did you went …?</u> <u>I didn't went …</u>, etc.

2

- Tell students to read the whole text quickly and then ask them where Scott was at midnight 2000. (Answer: *On a train travelling from Switzerland to Spain.*)
- Students complete the text with the past simple of the verbs in brackets. They can compare their answers with a partner before you check with the whole class.

```
 1  were
 2  had
 3  wanted
 4  didn't stop
 5  stopped
 6  drank
 7  looked
 8  didn't sleep
 9  sat
10  talked
11  got
12  was
```

3

- Students make questions in the past using the prompts. Do an example with the class to begin with.

```
1   Where did you go?
2   What did you do?
3   Who were you with?
4   What did you eat?
5   What did you drink?
6   What time did you go to bed?
```

Extra practice

- Provide some intensive spoken practice of these questions before doing exercise 4. Put the prompts on the board, model the full question, and get students to repeat.

4

- Tell students to choose a celebration, and think about their answers to the questions in exercise 3.
- Pairwork. Students work in pairs to interview their partner about their celebration.

SPEAKING

1

- Pairwork. Put students in A and B pairs. Ask students to take it in turns to complete each line of the story with an idea of their own.

2

- Students continue telling the story in turns using the phrases from the list below to give them ideas.

3

❯ *Key Methodology 8: Spoken errors – fluency tasks 1, page 28*

- Students finish the story in any way they like.
- At the end, ask one or two pairs to tell the class their story. Make a note of any errors for feedback.

IF YOU WANT SOMETHING EXTRA ...

❯ *Photocopiable activity, page 213*
❯ *Teacher's notes, page 178*

6B | Actor! Author!

What the lesson is about

Theme	Actors & authors
Speaking	Pairwork discussion: talking about books and films
	Groupwork game: playing *Actor! Author!*
Listening	*Actor! Author!*: a television quiz show – contestants guess the famous actor or author
Vocabulary	Films & books
Grammar	Past simple irregular verbs; past time expressions
Pronunciation	Past simple irregular verbs: sounds /əʊ/, /ʊ/, /ɔː/, /e/, /eɪ/ and /æ/
Did you know	*The Big Read*: Britain's ten favourite books

If you want a lead-in ...

Introducing the theme: actors

- Draw a circle on the board, and write the name of a very well-known actor in the circle. Brainstorm facts and opinions about that person from students and write them on the board, joining each fact/opinion to the circle with a line. If you're not sure about a fact given, just write a question mark next to it. Take no more than two minutes, but build up a detailed 'portrait' of the person on the board.
- Put students in pairs. They must think of a very famous actor, put that person's name in a circle on a piece of paper, then write facts and opinions (in note form – just one or two words). After one minute, get students to pass the piece of paper clockwise to the next pair. They have one minute to add facts and opinions. Pass it on again. And so on.
- Once the students have their original piece of paper back, give them a minute or two to look at the information they now have. Ask a few pairs to summarize their facts and opinions for the class.

Vocabulary & speaking: films & books

❯ *Language reference, Student's Book page 71*

1
- Students match the words to the pictures. They can compare their answers with a partner before you check with the whole class.
- Say the words, and ask students to repeat to practise the pronunciation.

A	horror
B	thriller
C	science fiction
D	comedy
E	cartoon
F	western
G	love story/romance

Language notes

- Notice the stress on the second syllable in *cartoon*, /kɑːˈtuːn/.
- There is a weak /ə/ sound at the end of *horror* /ˈhɒrə/, *thriller* /ˈθrɪlə/, and *western* /ˈwestən/.
- *Science fiction* is often abbreviated to *sci-fi* /ˈsaɪ faɪ/.

■ Key Methodology 20
■ Vocabulary records

- *The average student keeps very poor records of new vocabulary they have learnt. In many cases, the words (usually with a translation) go into long mixed-up lists that they will probably never look at again. Part of teaching a student English also involves teaching them how to study and learn more effectively. Better vocabulary records (and intelligent review and recycling of the contents) can make an important difference to a student's progress. It's worth taking some class time to focus on this.*
- *Ask students to open an exercise book or file page where they have recorded vocabulary in an earlier lesson. Write these discussion questions on the board:* Is it clear? Is it useful? How could it be better? *Make pairs or small groups, and ask students to compare briefly how they have recorded vocabulary.*
- *After a minute or two of discussion time, elicit ideas from students about current problems with their lists (e.g. hard to read, not useful information, no organization, etc.), and suggestions for improvement. Go on to offer some ideas yourself (see below).*

Some ideas for better vocabulary records
- *Give a topic name to a whole page and group only words connected with that subject, e.g. feelings, things in the house, sports, etc.*
- *Make* mind-maps *(also called* word-webs, spider-grams, *etc.) to group words in a visual way rather than just listing things linearly down the page.*
- *Use coloured pens to decorate, make lines, write words in colour, add sketches, etc. All these things help to make each page individual and more memorable.*
- *Encourage students to record more than word and translation. Other useful data includes: example sentences, typical words that collocate (i.e. go together with the word), stress marks, phonemic transcription.*
- *Design and photocopy your own blank grid, i.e. with headings for word, definition, pronunciation, example sentence, translation, etc. for students to use.*
- *Help students to make pages like this by taking vocabulary recording seriously in lesson time. When you write up words on the board, don't just write the word, but write it in a sentence, mark the stress(es), write the pronunciation, etc. Allow time for students to record them properly. Walk round to advise and cajole students into doing this better.*
- *Add in-classroom activities that explicitly make use of recycling vocabulary and using these records, e.g. have a once-a-week five-minute quiz on vocabulary from previous lessons. Start by saying a specific topic for the quiz, e.g. furniture, and allowing two minutes revision time. Students with organized pages should have a distinct advantage.*

2

- Pairwork. Elicit one or two examples to get students started. Then put students in pairs to make a list of films or books.

> *Possible list (students are more likely to think of very recent films)*
> Horror: *the Shining; The Silence of the Lambs; Halloween; Psycho; Nightmare on Elm Street; Scream 1, 2 & 3*
> Thriller: *Double Indemnity; Pulp Fiction; Silence of the Lambs; The Usual Suspects; Mission Impossible*; and any *James Bond* films, e.g. *Goldfinger*
> Science fiction: *Star Wars; E.T. Close Encounters of the Third Kind; Independence Day; The Matrix; The War of the Worlds*
> Comedy: *Four Weddings and a Funeral; Some Like it Hot; Austin Powers – International Man of Mystery; Bridget Jones – the Edge of Reason; The Nutty Professor*
> Cartoon: *Snow White and the Seven Dwarves; Beauty and the Beast; Shrek; Monsters Inc; Toy Story*
> Western: *High Noon; the Searchers; the Unforgiven; the Good, the Bad, and the Ugly; Butch Cassidy and the Sundance Kid*
> Love story/romance: *Casablanca; Doctor Zhivago; It's a Wonderful Life; Gone with the Wind; Titanic; Shakespeare in Love*

3

- Groupwork. Put pairs into groups of four. One pair reads out their names of films or books. The other pair must say what the category is in.

Monolingual or multilingual classes

- With a monolingual class, students could use L1 to make their list of films and books. But, as you monitor, if possible, try to tell them what the English name for the films or books is. In a multilingual class, students will have to use English, and may need a bit of support to translate here.
- With a monolingual class, an interesting activity is to write the names of four or five film titles in the students' L1, and ask them to translate into English. Then give the actual English film title.

4

> ⏵ *Communication activities, Student's Book pages 138 & 135*

- Pairwork. Put students in A and B pairs. Ask Student A to turn to page 138, and Student B to turn to page 135. They take it in turns to ask each other questions.
- At the end, ask a few students to summarize what their partner said.

LISTENING

This listening is in the form of a TV quiz show. Two contestants compete against each other to guess the correct name of the author or actor. They are given four clues to help them, and they have a time limit in which to make the correct guess.

1 💿 2.1

- Students listen to the beginning of the television show *Actor! Author!* Elicit what the rules are for the television show.

> Each person takes a turn and chooses a category: Actor or Author. The presenter gives them four clues about the person, and they guess who it is.

💿 **2.1**

> **J = Jim M = Mike S = Steph**
> **J:** Hello everybody, and welcome to a new episode of *Actor! Author!* My name's Jim and today we have two new contestants: Mike from London.
> **M:** Hello, Jim.
> **J:** And Steph, from Birmingham.
> **S:** Hi!
> **J:** Now remember the rules. <u>Each person takes a turn and chooses a category: Actor or Author. I give you four clues about the person, and you guess who it is. OK?</u>
> **M & S:** Yes.

2 💿 2.2

- Tell students to listen to the recording and try to guess the famous actor or author before Mike or Steph.
- In feedback, ask students what information helped them to guess.

> 1 Christopher Reeve   3 JK Rowling
> 2 Dan Brown   4 Nicole Kidman

💿 **2.2**

> **J = Jim M = Mike S = Steph**
> **J:** Mike, we'll start with you. When was the last time you saw a film?
> **M:** Well, Jim, I saw *Gladiator* last night.
> **J:** Great film. Now, what category would you like?
> **M:** Actor.
> **J:** Alright, here we go.
> He was born in Manhattan <u>in 1952</u>. He <u>fell</u> off <u>a horse</u> 12 years ago and was paralysed. His most famous movies were *Superman*, *Superman II* and *Superman III*. He <u>died in 2004</u>.
> **M:** <u>Christopher Reeve!</u>
> **J:** Yes!
>
> **J:** OK Steph, now it's your turn. What category would you like?
> **S:** Author, please.
> **J:** Do you read a lot, Steph?
> **S:** Yes, I do.
> **J:** What was the last book you <u>read</u>?
> **S:** Umm. I finished a book two weeks ago, but I can't remember the name. I'm a bit nervous.
> **J:** That's alright. Right then, here we go.
> <u>He is American</u>. His books are translated into more than <u>40 languages</u>. He <u>wrote a very famous thriller</u>. The book is set in Paris. It starts in the Louvre Museum. The main character is an art professor called Robert Langdon. It's about symbols in the art of <u>a famous Italian painter</u>, Leonardo da Vinci.
> **S:** Oh, wait … I <u>read</u> that book last year. Oh no. …
> **J:** Almost time …
> **S:** David … Dan …
> **J:** Yes?
> **S:** Dan Brown.
> **J:** Well done!
>
> **J:** Back to you Mike. What category would you like?
> **M:** Author this time, please.
> **J:** She's <u>from England</u> and she <u>taught English</u> in Portugal more than ten years ago. She is now very, very rich. Her books are also movies. She <u>wrote</u> about a boy called Harry Potter. There are <u>more than six books</u> in the series.
> **M:** I know *Harry Potter*, but the author …?
> **J:** Time, Mike.
> **M:** I don't know!

> **J:** Steph?
> **S:** JK Rowling!
> **J:** Correct!
>
> **J:** Right, Steph you can win this. What category would you like?
> **S:** Actor.
> **J:** OK, this time it's an *actress*.
> **S:** That's fine.
> **J:** She was born in 1967. She's from Australia. She won an Oscar for the film *The Hours*. She was married to Tom Cruise and made several films with him.
> **S:** Nicole Kidman! Nicole Kidman!
> **J:** Correct! Steph, you're the winner.

3 2.2

- Give students a minute to read through the information, and check vocabulary.
- Play the recording again. Students listen and underline the correct word(s).

1	1952	3	England
	a horse		English
	2004		six
2	American	4	1967
	40		Australia
	thriller		*The Hours*
	Italian		

GRAMMAR: past simple irregular verbs; past time expressions

> ❯ *Language reference, Student's Book page 70*
> ❯ *Methodology guidelines: Grammar boxes, page xiii*

1

- Ask students to look at tapescript 2.1 on page 143 of the Student's Book and underline the past tense of the verbs. They can then compare the verbs they found with a partner.
- In feedback, model these words, and ask students to repeat to practise pronunciation.

1	wrote	4	fell
2	taught	5	read
3	won	6	made

Language note

- Point out that read /riːd/ and read /red/ have the same spelling but different pronunciation. (N.B. the pronunciation of these past forms is dealt with in detail in the following *Pronunciation* section.)

2

- Students put the words in the correct order to make sentences.

1	I watched a DVD last weekend.
2	I didn't watch television last night.
3	I bought a book two months ago.
4	I didn't watch the Oscars last year.
5	I read the newspaper this morning.
6	I didn't use the internet or email yesterday.

Language notes

- This section introduces a small set of time expressions used with the past simple. These expressions generally go at the end of the sentence, but could be put at the start when emphasizing the time.
- As pointed out in the *Grammar* box, the two major problems both result from L1 interference: adding *the* when inappropriate: ✗ *the last week*, and misplacing *ago*: ✗ *ago two days*.

3

- Students change the sentences in exercise 2 so that they are true for themselves.
- You can then put students in pairs to tell each other their sentences.

Extra task for stronger classes

- Write *When did you last …?* on the board. Ask a few questions round the class: *When did you last read a book? When did you last use the internet?* Elicit answers from students, e.g. *I read a book last week. I used the internet yesterday.*
- Put students in pairs to interview their partner, using *When did you last …?*

PRONUNCIATION: past simple irregular verbs

1 & 2 2.3

- Play the recording. Students listen to the verbs and their irregular past form.
- Play the recording again for students to listen and repeat.

2.3

think	thought	understand	understood	say	said
speak	spoke	swim	swam	make	made

3 & 4 2.4

> ❯ *Key Methodology 31: Dictionaries 2 – pronunciation, page 136*

- Students complete the table with the verbs from the box in exercise 1 in the irregular past simple. They can compare their answers with a partner.
- Play the recording. Students listen and check their answers.
- Play the recording again for students to listen and repeat the verbs.

/əʊ/	/ ʊ/	/ɔː/	/e/	/eɪ/	/æ/
spoke	underst**oo**d	th**ou**ght	s**ai**d	m**a**de	sw**a**m

2.4

spoke
understood
thought
said
made
swam

Language notes

- The major problem here is that English spelling and pronunciation often don't match. Students often mispronounce because they are guessing from spelling, e.g. pronouncing *said* as /saɪd/. It is important, therefore, to get students to hear and repeat sounds without reading.
- The long /ɔː/ sound is particularly difficult to pronounce, so give students practice in making it. They need to form their lips into an 'o', their tongue low and back in the mouth, and make a long sound.

SPEAKING

1 & 2

- Groupwork. Put students into groups of three to play this speaking game. Each student must write down the names of two famous actors and two famous authors. Make sure they keep the names a secret from the other groups. They must then prepare clues to describe their actors and authors, using the prompts.

3 & 4

- Each group plays *Actor! Author!* One person in the group gives clues, the others guess. Then they change roles with someone else giving the clue.

DID YOU KNOW?

1 & 2

- Students read the text about a survey carried out by the BBC to find out what are the British people's favourite books.
- Pairwork: Work in pairs. Students discuss the questions.

Cultural notes

Below is some information about the books listed:

1 **The Lord of the Rings** trilogy was written by JRR Tolkein in the 1950s. It is a fantasy story about an imaginary land and the creatures that live there. One of which is a hobbit, Frodo Baggins, who goes on a long journey in an attempt to stop an evil lord taking possession of a powerful ring which would enable him to dominate the world.

2 **Pride and Prejudice** is Jane Austen's most popular novel. Published in 1813, it is about the Bennet family who live in a provincial English town and live off a small income. Jane Austen pokes fun at Mrs Bennet's desperate attempts to marry off her five daughters to wealthy men from the upper class, resulting in a lot of misunderstandings between her daughters and their prospective husbands.

3 Philip Pullman's **His Dark Materials** is a complex fantasy story, published in three volumes, about a parallel world where mysterious creatures mix with humans. It is a book that can be read by both children and adults and explores philosophical themes of existence, childhood innocence, love and death.

4 **The Hitchhiker's Guide to the Galaxy** was first written as a BBC radio series in 1978. It was incredibly popular in Britain at the time, and soon became a media phenomenon with five books and a TV series. In 2005, it was made into a film. It is a sort of sci-fi comedy in which the central character, Arthur Dent, a very ordinary British man, is rescued from the planet Earth just before it is destroyed, and then travels (hitchhikes) across the universe looking for the meaning of life.

5 **Harry Potter and the Goblet of Fire** is the fourth book in the series of world famous children's books, which tell the story of how Harry and his friends learn how to master the magical powers they have been born with at Hogwarts school for wizards.

6 **To Kill a Mockingbird**, Harper Lee's only published novel, was written in the 1950s. It is set in the American Deep South in the 1930s, a time of racial segregation. It is the story of a white lawyer defending a black man falsely accused of rape. The story is narrated by a nine-year-old girl and is based on an event that Harper Lee witnessed as a child growing up in Alabama. It was made into a film, starring Gregory Peck, in 1962.

7 **Winnie the Pooh**, published in 1926, is a children's book featuring the toys of Christopher Robin, the actual name of AA Milne's son. The central characters are Pooh bear, his friend Piglet, Eeyore (a donkey), and Tigger (a tiger). AA Milne died in 1956. *Winnie the Pooh* is translated into almost every language and in 1966, the first Walt Disney Pooh film was produced.

8 **Nineteen Eighty-Four** was written by left-wing journalist and author, George Orwell, in 1948. It warned of how genetics, technology and despotic government could control the lives of citizens.

9 **The Lion, the Witch and the Wardrobe** is the first book in CS Lewis's classic children's series *The Chronicles of Narnia*. It is set during the Second World War. Four children go through the back of a wardrobe and enter the magical kingdom of Narnia where it is permanently winter. The lion, Aslan, represents good who goes on to defend Narnia against an evil witch.

10 **Jane Eyre**, written by Charlotte Brontë, is the story of a poor orphan girl, who takes a job as a governess of the daughter of a wealthy man, Mr Rochester, at a large country house. At first Mr Rochester appears very sullen and mysterious. However, he and Jane gradually fall in love. But on their wedding day, Jane discovers a terrible secret about Mr Rochester – that he is already married.

Extra task

- Take this opportunity to suggest to students that they can start to read books in English. You could ask at your local publishers' office for a list of *Readers* that are suitable for this level, and suggest some of these to the students to read.

Web research tasks

❯ *Methodology guidelines: Web research tasks, page xiii*

- Students research one of the authors in the favourite books list. They must find out biographical details and other novels written.

Web search key words
- name of author/biography/books

IF YOU WANT SOMETHING EXTRA …

❯ *Photocopiable activity, page 214*
❯ *Teacher's notes, page 179*

6c | They cry easily

WHAT THE LESSON IS ABOUT

Theme	Expressing feelings & crying
Speaking	Groupwork game: playing the *Dialogue Game*
Reading	*Crying – good for your health*: a magazine article about men & crying
Vocabulary	Feelings
Grammar	Adverbs of manner
Pronunciation	Word stress 2, intonation 1

IF YOU WANT A LEAD-IN ...

Introducing the theme: crying

- Before the lesson, find a magazine picture of a person crying. Show the picture to students and ask them why they think the person is crying and what they think happened to this person. Elicit ideas, e.g. (s)he lost his/her job, her boyfriend/his girlfriend left, her cat died, etc.
- Put students in pairs to complete the sentence, *I cry when …*

Discussion starters

⊙ *Methodology guidelines: Discussion starters, page xii*

- *Do you cry easily?*
- *When did you last cry and why?*
- *In what situations do you cry?*
- *Do you think crying is good for you? Why?*

VOCABULARY: feelings

⊙ *Language reference, Student's Book page 71*

1
- Students match the sentences to the people.
- After checking the answers, read out the sentences, and ask students to listen and repeat. Consolidate the meaning of the adjectives by using an appropriate facial expression for each phrase when you say it.

1 D	2 A	3 E	4 C	5 B

▪ Key Methodology 21
▪ Recycling vocabulary

- *In order to learn a word or phrase to the point where they can use it themselves, students will often need to review them a number of times. So it's worth building in a cycle of revisiting and reviewing of vocabulary from previous lessons. Here are some ideas:*
  - *1 Once a week, look back through the previous few lessons and devise a short revision quiz on vocabulary. Include questions on meaning, spelling, word stress, etc. In class, run this as a light-hearted team quiz rather than as a serious test. Get students into the habit of a regular vocabulary revision activity.*

  - *2 Many teachers keep a word box at the front of the class. This is simply a small cardboard box or tin with a label on the front (e.g. WORDS) to show its purpose. Next to it are a pile of scraps of paper (about 8 cm by 6 cm). Whenever new words come up in class, either the teacher, or students, appointed by the teacher – write the items on the scraps, one word per scrap (no need to record definitions or other information), which are then posted into the box. In this way, the box will lesson by lesson contain more items, which can then be used in future classes. You might choose to keep separate boxes for different categories of words, e.g. verbs, nouns, phrases, etc. When you have a spare minute or two in the lesson, pick out words from the word box and use them in simple instant games or exercises. (See below.)*
- *Instead of a word box, you could collect sets or groups of words on posters around the walls. This has the advantage of encouraging learners to keep looking at them and testing themselves during quiet moments.*

Ideas for using your word box

<u>Guessing from definitions</u>
- *Pick out a word, e.g. pack, from the box. Tell the class a bit of the definition, e.g. You do this when you go on holiday. Let students guess in pairs, or teams if you like, (you could limit groups to one guess for each clue). If no one gets the right answer, give a second, third, fourth, etc. clue. Give points for correct answers.*

<u>Instant gap-fill</u>
- *Pick about five words. Write up sentences on the board with gaps where the words could go. (Don't worry too much about your sentences – use the first ones that come to mind; it's OK if there is more than one possible answer.) Tell groups that they must guess what the five words on your cards are. Allow some talking/thinking time. The winning team is the one that guesses most of the original five words.*

<u>Group check</u>
- *Make small groups. Collect a small pile of words for each group. Students should go through their set of items and test each other, seeing if they remember each word, can pronounce it, use it, etc. You can decide precise instructions to suit your students' needs. When students have discussed their group's words, they can swap them with another group and look at a new set.*

<u>Twenty questions</u>
- *Pick out a noun from the box. Students must try to guess the word by asking a maximum of 20 questions (or guesses), or else you win.*

<u>Students set questions</u>
- *Distribute three words to each student. Ask them to prepare a question for each of their words. When finished, they meet up with others and test them with their questions.*

<u>Quiet review</u>
- *Encourage students who arrive early to class (or who finish tasks early) simply to browse through some words in the box.*

2 🔵 2.5
- Play the recording. Students listen to the people at an important sports event, and put the sentences from exercise 1 in the correct order.
- Then ask students what they think the important sports event is. (Possible answer: *UEFA/European/World Cup Football Final.*)

1	She is bored.
2	He is nervous.
3	She is happy.
4	He is angry.
5	He is sad.

🔵 2.5

> **1** I don't know why we always come here. I don't care who wins. This is so stupid.
>
> **2** Oh no, is that a penalty? Oh, it is, it is. Oh, I can't watch. Oh, no ... please, please, please ...
>
> **3** I can't believe it! I can't believe it! Yeah. We won! We won!
>
> **4** Move, come on, move! Run a bit! This is terrible, terrible! You're old and pathetic! Come on ... what the?!? What was that? You can't play football, you idiots! Come on!
>
> **D = Dad S = Son**
> **5** **D:** Oh, I don't believe it .... we were so close ... this isn't right! No!
> **S:** Are you OK, Dad?
> **D:** No, son, I'm not OK.

3
- Pairwork. Put students into pairs to describe how they feel in each of the situations.
- Give one or two examples about yourself to get students started. Then students tell their partner how they feel for each situation.
- When they have finished, ask students what other situations make them happy, sad, angry, etc.

READING

This magazine article is about men and crying, and why it is more acceptable for men to cry today than it was in the past. It gives examples of US presidents and famous male sporting stars who have been seen crying on TV, and goes on to discuss the differences between why men cry and why women cry. The writer of the article concludes that it is good to cry.

1
- Tell students to look at the photos. Students discuss how they think these people feel.

Alternative procedures
- Lead in to the reading text by asking other questions, e.g. *In what situations do people cry? Do men cry more now than in the past? Do you think crying is a good thing?*
- You could make this a prediction task, and write their predictions on the board, so when students read, they can find out whether the text shares their ideas and opinions.

Cultural notes
- The photos are of:
  A **Matthew Pinsent**, the British Olympic rower who has won four successive gold medals at the Olympics (his last one in Athens in 2004).
  B **George W Bush**, the current American president.
  C **David Beckham**, English footballer who currently plays for Real Madrid. He is the captain of the English football team.
  D **Denzil Washington**, American actor.

2
- Students read the article, and choose the best title.

Crying – Good for your health

3
- Students read the sentences and mark them true or false. They can compare their answers with a partner and discuss why the false ones are incorrect, before you check with the whole class.

1	F (British psychologists and researchers say that men cry easily.)
2	T
3	T
4	F (He cried when he took his children to school for the first time.)
5	F (Men said they often cry when they are sad, when they feel bad or when they feel happy. They said they don't cry when they are angry.)
6	T

4
- Pairwork. Students work in pairs and discuss the questions.
- Then you could have a brief class discussion.

GRAMMAR: adverbs of manner
- *Language reference, Student's Book page 70*
- *Methodology guidelines: Grammar boxes, page xiii*

1
- Tell students to find and underline the adverbs of manner in the article in the *Reading* section. They can compare their answers with a partner before you check with the whole class.

easily (line 2)
quietly (line 9)
well (line 19)

Language notes
- Adverbs of manner are usually formed by adding *ly* to the adjective, (*bad* ➜ *badly*). They go after the verb, (*He plays badly*). With transitive verbs, they go after the object, (*He plays tennis badly*). Watch out for errors of omission, ✗ *He plays bad*, and word order, ✗ *He plays badly tennis*.
- Note the following exceptions to the form rules:
  easy ➜ *y* ➜ + *ily* ➜ *easily*
  good ➜ *well*
  fast ➜ *fast*   *hard* ➜ *hard*

2

- Students complete the sentences with the correct form of the word in brackets. They can compare their answers with a partner before you check with the whole class.

1 carefully
2 beautifully
3 angrily
4 fast
5 well

3

- Students underline the correct word. Remind them that adjectives go before nouns, and adverbs go after verbs.

1 quietly
2 sad
3 easily
4 good
5 hard
6 noisily

4

- Pairwork. Put students in pairs to think of a famous sports person who does the activities listed.

Extra task

- Write *I can …* on the board. Ask students to write five *I can* sentences, using adverbs from the lesson, e.g. *I can play tennis well, I can drive fast*.
- Put students in pairs to tell each other their sentences.
- Write *Can you …?* on the board. Tell students to change their statements to questions. Then, change pairs, and get students to interview their new partner. Remind them to answer *Yes, I can* or *No, I can't*.

PRONUNCIATION: word stress 2, intonation 1

1 🔘 **2.6**

- Play the recording. Students listen and repeat the adverbs of manner.
- Then tell students to underline the stressed syllable in the adverbs.

See tapescript below for answers.

🔘 **2.6**

an<u>gr</u>ily
<u>ha</u>ppily
<u>ner</u>vously
<u>slow</u>ly
<u>care</u>fully
<u>quiet</u>ly
<u>noi</u>sily

2 🔘 **2.7**

- Play the recording. Students listen to four dialogues, and say which adverb describes each dialogue.

1 quietly
2 nervously
3 carefully
4 angrily

🔘 **2.7**

1
M = man   W = woman
M: Come here, I want to tell you something.
W: What is it?
M: I love you.

2
W1 = woman 1   W2 = woman 2
W1: What's that?
W2: Where?
W1: I think there's a man at the window.

3
W = woman   C = child
W: Now, listen to me, because I don't want to repeat this.
C: OK.

4
M = man   W = woman
M: Did you remember my book?
W: No, I didn't.
M: Doh!

SPEAKING

1

- Pairwork. Put students in pairs and ask them to choose one of the dialogues from *Pronunciation* exercise 2.
- Tell students to practise reading the dialogue to each other for a few minutes and try to memorize it. Then give each pair a card with an adverb on it. They must read the dialogue out loud to the class in the manner of that adverb, and the rest of the class guesses the adverb.

Extra task

- Play the mime game. Write lots of adjectives on the board: *quiet, noisy, careful, slow, bad, good, fast, happy, nervous, angry, sad*.
- Ask a student to come up to the front of the class, and whisper an activity into his/her ear, e.g. *clean the windows, open the door, write your name on the board*. The students must then choose an adjective from the board, and mime the activity given in the manner of the adjective. The class must guess what the student did, and announce their answer in the past, using an adverb, e.g. *I think Juan cleaned the window carefully*.
- You could make this a competition by dividing the class into two halves. A student from one half mimes, and the other half gets a point if and when they produce an accurate sentence.

IF YOU WANT SOMETHING EXTRA …

❯ *Photocopiable activity, page 215*
❯ *Teacher's notes, page 179*

6D | I'm not crazy about it

WHAT THE LESSON IS ABOUT

Theme	Opinions about London and other things
Speaking	Pairwork discussion: choosing what to do in London for the day
	Groupwork discussion: talking about people & things that you like & don't like
Listening	Three conversations expressing likes & dislikes
Vocabulary	Giving opinions
Functional language	Talking about likes & dislikes

IF YOU WANT A LEAD-IN ...

Introducing the theme: opinions ·

- Ask students about the town or city where you are teaching. Elicit six or seven well-known places in the city, whether they are historical monuments, a shopping centre or a club. Tell students to choose three of the places and write down their honest opinion of each one.
- Ask students to tell the class what they think of a place. Ask others if they agree, and have a class discussion.

Test before you teach: likes & dislikes

❯ *Methodology guidelines: Test before you teach, page xiii*

- Tell students to think, for one minute, of things they like a lot, and the things they don't like. ·
- Put students in pairs. Tell them that they must tell each other about their likes and dislikes, and find four things that they have in common.
- In feedback, pairs tell the class about what they have in common.

SPEAKING

1

- Tell students to look at the photos on the page and ask them what they can see. (The photos are of: a football match, The Tower of London, Big Ben, the world's largest greenhouse – at Kew Gardens, the Temperate House)
- Ask students to look at the places recommended and decide which things they would like to do.
- Pairwork. Put students in pairs to agree on three things that they would both like to do.

2

- Pair pairs. Students compare their answers.

Cultural notes

- **Oxford Street** is London's busiest shopping street. Most major High Street stores have a branch on this street.
- **Chelsea**, in west London, and **Arsenal**, in north London, are two of England's major football clubs. In 2005, they finished first and second in England's Premier League.
- **Kew** /kjuː/ **Gardens** also known as the Royal Botanic Gardens, is in south-west London on the Thames. It has a unique collection of plants from all over the world and in 2003 became a world heritage site.

- **St Paul's Cathedral** was built by Sir Christopher Wren in the seventeenth century. It has a famous dome.
- **The London Aquarium** is on the banks of the Thames in central London and has hundreds of varieties of fish and sea life from around the world.
- One of London's oldest buildings, the **Tower of London** was begun in the eleventh century. For centuries, it was a prison. Today, it is the place where the monarch's crown jewels are kept.
- N.B. The poster hanging on the lamp post in front of Big Ben in the photo is a promotional poster for the London Olympics 2012.

Web research tasks

❯ *Methodology guidelines: Web research tasks, page xiii*

- Students find out more about the tours on offer at one of the following: Chelsea or Arsenal football club; Kew Gardens; The Tower of London, or the London Aquarium. They can find out about opening and closing times; number of tours a day; what they can see, etc.

Web search key words
- London/information

VOCABULARY: adjectives of opinion

❯ *Language reference, Student's Book page 71*

1 2.8

- Give students a minute to read through the sentences. Then play the recording. Students listen and underline the word they hear.
- Play the recording again. Students listen and repeat the sentences.

> See underlined answers in the tapescript below.

🌑 2.8

1	It was an <u>awful</u> film.
2	The shopping is <u>bad</u> here.
3	The boat ride was <u>great</u>.
4	The gardens are <u>nice</u>.
5	The football match was <u>terrible</u>.

Language notes

- *awful* /ˈɔːfəl/ is tricky to say.
- Notice the stress and schwa /ə/ sounds in these words: *excellent* /ˈeksələnt/, *terrible* /ˈtərəbl/, *horrible* /ˈhɒrəbl/.

2

❯ *Key Methodology 20: Vocabulary records, page 80*

- Students put the adjectives into the correct column. They can compare their answers with a partner before you check with the whole class.

Positive adjectives	Negative adjectives
nice	awful
lovely	terrible
great	horrible
excellent	

3

- Pairwork. Allow students time to read the list and give one or two examples to get students started. Then put students in pairs to think of examples for each category.
- Have a brief feedback to find out what ideas the students have.

LISTENING

In this episode of the listening story, various people in the Explore London tour group are talking about what they did on their free day yesterday. Dave tells Valarie about a football match he went to and admits that he doesn't really like football. He said he then went shopping afterwards. Herb and Hannah discuss a film they both saw. Herb hated it, but Hannah liked it. In the last part of the recording, we find out a little more about who Sam really is. Someone phones him up and Sam tells them that he has a man under observation in the hotel, inferring that he must be a detective. He tells the caller that he went shopping yesterday because he was following this person and that he hates shopping.

1 **2.9**

- Ask students who the following characters are in the *Listening* story: Valerie, Dave, Herb and Hannah, and Sam. Then ask students to listen to the conversations and decide which places these people on the Explore London tour are talking about.

1   go to a Chelsea football match
2   go to see a film at one of London's many cinemas
3   go shopping in London's most famous shopping districts

2.9

> **V = Valerie D = Dave He = Herb Ha = Hannah Vo = voice S = Sam**
> **V:** So, what did you do yesterday?
> **D:** I went to a football match.
> **V:** Oh really? What did you think of it?
> **D:** It was OK.
> **V:** I love football. Chelsea are my favourite team.
> **D:** Oh.
> **V:** What? You don't like football?
> **D:** I'm not crazy about it.
> **V:** Why did you go then?
> **D:** I don't know. I went shopping yesterday, too. That was good.
>
> **He:** Wasn't that awful?
> **Ha:** Sorry?
> **He:** It was awful.
> **Ha:** I liked it.
> **He:** I'm sorry, did we see the same movie? It was terrible. The actors were bad, the music was bad, everything was bad. I can't say a good word about that film.
>
> **Vo:** So, where is he now?
> **S:** He's at the hotel. I have my eye on him.
> **Vo:** How's London? Do you like the tour?
> **S:** It's alright. I went shopping yesterday.
> **Vo:** Shopping?
> **S:** Well, he went shopping, so I went shopping!
> **Vo:** What do you think of the shopping in London?
> **S:** I can't stand it. I hate shopping in general.
> **Vo:** Poor you. Did you buy anything?
> **S:** No, I didn't. Look. I'll call you back, OK?
> **Vo:** Fine then. Buy me a souvenir, will you? A lovely little London bus.

Language notes

- *I have my eye on him* means I'm watching him very carefully.

2 **2.9**

- Play the recording again. Students listen and tick the phrases they hear in the conversations.

All the phrases should be ticked.
1   I can't stand it. (Conversation 3)
2   I love football. (Conversation 1)
3   I'm not crazy about it. (Conversation 1)
4   It was OK. (Conversation 1)
5   It was awful. (Conversation 2)

FUNCTIONAL LANGUAGE: talking about likes & dislikes

> *Language reference, Student's Book page 70*

1

- Students complete the table with phrases from *Listening* exercise 2.

1	love	3	crazy about …
2	OK	4	can't stand …

Extra drill task

- Prepare simple flashcards, showing, e.g. tennis, football, cats, dogs, etc. Or just write words on pieces of paper or card, e.g. French films, pop music, politicians, etc. Hold up a picture or word flashcard, and model, e.g. *I can't stand pop music. I'm not crazy about cats.*, etc. Then hold up cards, and elicit responses from students. Correct form and pronunciation carefully.
- You could introduce *What do you think of …?* and get students asking and answering questions across the class.

2

- Students put the words in the correct order to make questions. They can compare their answers with a partner before you check with the whole class.

1   What do you think of rock music?
2   What films do you like?
3   Do you like football?
4   What do you think of your English class?

3

- Model the activity by asking a few students the questions in exercise 2.
- Pairwork. Then put students in pairs to discuss the questions.

Extra task

- You could do this as a mingle. Tell students to think of their own *What do you think of …?* or *How do you feel about …?* question, e.g. *What do you think of politics? How do you feel about golf?*
- Students then walk round class, and ask their question. Students respond with a like/dislike phrase.

SPEAKING

1

- Ask students to look at the categories. Give them one or two examples of what they could write to get them started.
- Students write the names of real people or things they like for each category into their exercise book, or on to a piece of paper. Tell them that they should choose people or things that they think students in their group will know.

2

- Groupwork. Put students in small groups of four or five.
- Model the activity with a strong student, using the example.
- Students take it in turns to ask other people in their group about the people and things they wrote in exercise 1.
- Monitor and prompt where necessary. Make sure students are using a variety of the new expressions.

3

- Ask each group to report back to the rest of the class two people or two things all the students in their group liked.

IF YOU WANT SOMETHING EXTRA ...

❯ *Photocopiable activity, page 216*
❯ *Teacher's notes, page 180*

Answer key

Student's Book page 152

6 REVIEW

1

Our new baby blog

Marcos is now one week old! We ~~goed~~ <u>went</u> for a walk in the park with him yesterday. He opened his eyes and looked at his mother for five minutes! It was beautiful. I ~~not go~~ <u>didn't go</u> to work last week. I stayed at home and ~~doed~~ <u>did</u> the housework. My parents saw Marcos on Saturday. They ~~was~~ <u>were</u> very happy. My father ~~sayed~~ <u>said</u> Marcos looks exactly like me! Here is a photo of Marcos with his grandparents.

2

1 was
2 studied
3 started
4 worked
5 was
6 made
7 won
8 became
9 changed
10 was
11 died

3

1 died
2 won
3 made
4 wrote
5 won
6 wrote
7 made, won

4

1 Can you read this very <u>carefully</u>, please?
2 He cried really <u>quietly</u> and we couldn't hear him.
3 She speaks English <u>well</u>.
4 You sing very <u>beautifully</u>. Can you sing again, please?
5 Can you speak <u>slowly</u>? I can't understand you.

5

1 ☺   5 ☹
2 ☹   6 ☺
3 ☺   7 ☺
4 ☹

6

Students' own answers.

6 WRITING

Model answer
Dear James,

Sorry to hear you are ill.
Hope you feel better soon.

Anna

7A | Miracle diets?

WHAT THE LESSON IS ABOUT

Theme	Diets
Speaking	Inventing your own 'miracle' diet
Listening	*Exposed*: a television programme dicussing three diets
Vocabulary	Food 1
Grammar	Countable & uncountable nouns *Some, any*

IF YOU WANT A LEAD-IN ...

Test before you teach: food vocabulary

❯ *Methodology guidelines: Test before you teach, page xiii*
❯ *Key Methodology 11: Flashcards 2 – presenting vocabulary, page 40*

- Use flashcards to introduce the food words in this lesson.
- Draw simple symbols on pieces of card to show the different foods you want to introduce, e.g. *oranges, bananas, bread, chicken*, etc.
- In class, hold up each card and elicit the word. Model it and drill it round the class. Once you have introduced all the words, hold up two cards at once, and ask individual students to say, for example, *tomatoes* and *bananas*.
- You can then go on to use the *Vocabulary* section in the Student's Book to check and consolidate.

Discussion starters

❯ *Methodology guidelines: Discussion starters, page xii*

- *What food is good for you?*
- *What food is bad for you?*
- *What do you like eating?*

■ **Key Methodology 22**
■ **Making a language-rich classroom**

- *A good way to encourage learners to use English more is to fill your classroom with English language things. The atmosphere of the room may encourage students (just a little bit) to see English as interesting and enjoyable.*
- **Posters** *help to brighten up a room and create a more attractive workspace. You could ask local businesses, travel agents, etc., if they have any free marketing posters. You might also be able to get some at conferences or from your coursebook publisher's local office..*
- **Students' own work.** *Put students' writing and tasks around the room. As the course progresses, the walls will be filled with more and more stuff. In some classroom tasks, ask students to prepare work specifically for display on the wall, e.g. a poster summarizing a grammar point or an advertisement for their great new product.*
- **Tourist leaflets** *are a great noticeboard or wall decoration. If you or your friends visit an English-speaking country, make sure you spend some time in a tourist information centre. Leaflets are usually free – and filled with great pictures of famous places, along with interesting text.*

- **A Browse Box** *is a box filled with things just asking to be read. Not your dusty old thrown-out classic texts. But up-to-date things that students will be keen to look at. Again, many things can be found free: shop catalogues, colour magazines, advertising leaflets, etc. Include a few Readers, i.e. books specially simplified to help students to understand. Encourage students to look through whenever they have free time. Set up a simple borrowing system. Add to the stock whenever you can.*
- **Music.** *Have English language songs playing when students arrive in class and at the end of the lesson. Keep a small selection of music in class. Allow students to select a song to enjoy as a reward for doing good work or behaving well!*

VOCABULARY: food 1

❯ *Language reference, page 81*

1
- Students match the words to the pictures. They can compare their answers with a partner before you check with the whole class.

A	eggs	G	bread
B	apples	H	lettuce
C	fish	I	milk
D	ice cream	J	chicken
E	cake	K	potatoes
F	bananas		

2 & 3 🔘 **2.10**
- Students complete the information for the *Nutrition Reference Guide*. They can compare their answers with a partner before you check with the whole class.
- Play the recording. Students listen and check their answers.
- Play the recording again. Students listen and repeat the words.

1	bread	6/7	apples/bananas
2/3	fish/chicken	8	eggs
4/5	lettuce/potatoes	9/10	ice cream/cake

🔘 **2.10**

> **A:** bread, pasta
> **B:** steak, fish, chicken
> **A:** carrots, lettuce, tomatoes, potatoes
> **B:** apples, oranges, bananas, lemons
> **A:** eggs, cheese, milk
> **B:** chocolate, ice cream, cake

Language notes

- Pay attention to the stress and weak-stressed schwa /ə/ sounds in some of these words. Notably: *'cereals* /siriːeːls/, *'vegetables* /vedztebels/, *to'matoes* /temaːteuz/, *po'tatoes* /peteiteuz/, *ba'nanas* /benaːnez/, *'chocolate* /tʃok(e)let/.

4

- Model the activity briefly by asking a few *Do you like …?* questions round the class.
- Pairwork. Students ask and answer questions in pairs.

LISTENING

This listening is a TV interview with two dieticians, who talk about the Two Fs diet and the Low C diet. They tell the listeners what they have to do to follow the diets and the results they can achieve from doing so. The interviewer then goes on to talk briefly about a third diet: the Soup diet.

1

- Ask students to read the extract from a TV magazine. Ask: *What's the name of the show? What sort of show is it?* (Answer: *a chat show.*) *What is the show about? Would you like to watch it?*

> The show is about miracle diets and asks the question: do they work?

Language notes

- *Exposed* means that something is made known publicly because you think it is wrong, e.g. journalists 'expose' corrupt politicians or environmental scandals.

2 ● 2.11

- Play the recording. Students listen to part of the programme, and underline the name of each diet mentioned.

> Diet 1: The Two Fs diet
> Diet 2: The Low C diet
> Diet 3: The Soup diet

 2.11

> **D = Daniel Barber M = Martha Jones A = Alex Willis**
> **D:** Good evening. I'm speaking to Martha Jones, famous for the Two Fs diet: Fruit and Fish. Martha, tell me about your diet.
> **M:** Sure. It's simple. On our diet you can only eat fruit and fish. For example, have some fruit for breakfast. Don't eat any bread or drink any coffee in the morning. For lunch, eat fish and some tomatoes.
> **D:** Tomatoes?
> **M:** Yes, tomatoes are a fruit.
> **D:** OK. What can I drink?
> **M:** Water and fruit juice. You can't drink any wine, or beer or anything like that.
> **D:** And what does this diet do for me?
> **M:** You can see results very fast. Two or three kilos in a week. You feel good, too. Fish and fruit are a very good combination.
> **D:** Thank you.
>
> **D:** Our second diet is a Low C diet – that's C for carbohydrates. I asked Alex Willis about this diet. Alex, what can I eat on the Low C diet?
> **A:** First, let me say it's a variation of the No C diet. So, eat lots of meat, chicken and fish.
> **D:** Meat and chicken and fish?
> **A:** Well, not at the same time. Eggs are good, too.
> **D:** So, if I have eggs for breakfast, with some bread …
> **A:** No, no, no, no, no! Bread, no.
> **D:** No bread?
> **A:** Bread is a carbohydrate. Don't eat any bread or pasta. And don't eat any fruit either. This is the key to this diet.

> **D:** What about vegetables?
> **A:** You can eat some lettuce, for example, but don't eat any potatoes or carrots.
> **D:** And what does this diet do for me?
> **A:** Amazing results, fast! Many famous people follow this diet and it works, I guarantee you. Here, look at our list of celebrities …
> **D:** Thank you.
>
> **D:** Our third diet was the Soup diet. I couldn't speak to a representative of the Soup diet, but this is what their website says: 'In our amazing Soup diet, you can eat anything you want, but it has to be in soup form. This is because the human body digests soups very easily.' They have a list of soups you can buy from their website: fish soup, pasta soup and my favourite, banana and chocolate soup. Their website says that you can lose five kilos in a week with their diet.

Language notes

- *Carbohydrates* are foods that supply the body with heat and energy, e.g. sugar, bread and potatoes.
- When the stomach *digests* food, it changes it into substances the body needs.
- With stronger students, you may wish to point out one or two common collocations with vocabulary in the text: *go on a diet; lose weight/five kilos.*

3 ● 2.11

- Give students a couple of minutes to read through Daniel Barber's notes. Play the recording again. Students listen and underline the correct word in the notes.

> **Diet 1**
> 1 fruit
> 2 bread
> 3 tomatoes
> 4 2 or 3
>
> **Diet 2**
> 5 chicken
> 6 fruit
> 7 potatoes
>
> **Diet 3**
> 8 pasta soup
> 9 chocolate
> 10 5

Stronger classes

- Give students a couple of minutes to read through Daniel Barber's notes, and see if they can remember or guess the correct answer before you play the recording again.

4

- Give students a minute to discuss the questions in pairs. Then ask them for their opinions in open class and have a short class discussion.

Web research tasks

❯ *Methodology guidelines: Web research tasks, page xiii*

- Brainstorm a few popular diets from students, e.g. the F-plan diet, the Atkins diet. Then ask students to research one or two diets on the web, and say what sort of food you can eat on the diets, and why they work.

Web search key words

- diets

GRAMMAR: countable & uncountable nouns

⊙ *Language reference, Student's Book page 80*
⊙ *Methodology guidelines: Grammar boxes, page xiii*

1
• Ask students to look back at the foods listed on page 72, and mark them countable (C) or uncountable (U). Do the first two as examples. They can compare their answers with a partner before you check with the whole class.
• In feedback, you could build up a countable list and an uncountable list on the board. Ask students to add other foods they know to the lists.

> Countable: potatoes; bananas; apples; eggs; cake; carrots; tomatoes; oranges; lemons; chocolate
> Uncountable: fish; chicken; lettuce; ice cream; bread; milk; cake; pasta; steak; cheese; chocolate (a piece)

Language notes

• Countability and uncountability can be more confusing than you'd expect. Although this concept exists in European languages, a word that is uncountable in English, e.g. *fruit*, may be countable in another language. Naturally, mistakes occur whenever this is the case.
• English differentiates between **some** (affirmative) and **any** (negative/questions). In many languages the same word is used, regardless of whether it is affirmative or negative. Watch out for errors like, ✗ *I haven't got some apples*.
• Be aware that many food words can be both countable (*a chocolate* – a small one in a box), and uncountable (*some chocolate* – part of a large block). Note also that *cake* and *bread* are uncountable when you have a piece or slice of them.

2 & 3 ⊙ 2.12
• Students underline the correct word in the sentences. They can then compare their answers with a partner.
• Play the recording. Students listen carefully and check their answers.
• Play the recording again. Students repeat the sentences, but only the ones that are true for them personally.

> | 1 | coffee | 4 | an |
> |---|---|---|---|
> | 2 | any | 5 | pasta |
> | 3 | French bread | | |

⊙ **2.12**

> 1 I had some <u>coffee</u> for breakfast.
> 2 I don't have <u>any</u> beer at home.
> 3 I like <u>French bread</u>.
> 4 I have <u>an</u> orange in my bag.
> 5 I ate some <u>pasta</u> yesterday.

Extra tasks for stronger classes

1
Tell students to change the statements in exercise 2 to questions, e.g. *Did you have any coffee for breakfast?* Ask students to interview each other.

2
Write five words on the board, e.g. *fish, cake, lemons, lettuce, ice cream*. Tell students to write five true sentences about the words, e.g. *I don't have any lemons at home.* Students read out their sentences in pairs.

4
• Students complete the dialogue with *some* or *any*. They can compare their answers with a partner before you check with the whole class.

> | 1 | some | 6 | some |
> |---|---|---|---|
> | 2 | any | 7 | some |
> | 3 | any | 8 | any |
> | 4 | any | 9 | some |
> | 5 | some | 10 | any |

5
• Pairwork. Put students in pairs to read the dialogue. Monitor and correct errors.

Extension task

⊙ *Key Methodology 25: Giving extra practice – instant roleplays, page 105*

• Write the following lists on the board

  ✓ *apples; bananas; water; fish; tomato salad; tomatoes*

  ✗ *bread; coffee; tea; meat; vegetables*

• With books closed, ask students to improvise the dialogue in exercise 4, using the prompts on the board.

SPEAKING

1
• Pairwork. Students work in pairs to invent their own 'miracle diet'. They must make a list of foods people can eat and a list of foods people can't eat, and give a name to their diet. Monitor and help with ideas.

2
• Give pairs a minute or two to think about how they are going to describe their diet, using the phrases in the *Useful language* box.
• Groupwork. Put pairs in groups of four to talk about their diets.
• In feedback, ask students to tell the class about the diets they discussed.

Alternative procedure

• Alternatively, you could do this activity as a mingle.
• First, students prepare their 'miracle diet' in pairs.
• Then, one person in each pair (Student A) walks round the class, ready to describe the diet.
• The other person in each pair (Student B) must walk round asking questions to find out about other diets. Student Bs must find the diet they like the best.
• At the end, ask Student Bs to tell the class whose diet they thought was the best.

IF YOU WANT SOMETHING EXTRA ...

⊙ *Photocopiable activity, page 217*
⊙ *Teacher's notes, page 180*

7B | Rice

WHAT THE LESSON IS ABOUT

Theme	Rice
Speaking	Pairwork discussion: talking about rice
	Pairwork communication: describing differences in pictures of food
Reading	Rice: a magazine article about the importance of rice
Vocabulary	Food 2
Grammar	*How much /How many*
	A lot, not much, not many, none
Pronunciation	Word stress 3: counting syllables

IF YOU WANT A LEAD-IN ...

Introducing the theme: rice

- Write *Rice dishes* on the board. Ask students to tell you as many different rice dishes as they can think of, e.g. *paella* (Spain), *rice and beans* (Mexico), *risotto* (Italy), *pilau rice* (India), *dirty rice* (Louisiana, USA).
- Naturally, this works well in a country where there are many rice dishes, or in a class where there are students from many countries.
- In a multinational class, ask students what ingredients there are in the rice dishes they mention.

Discussion starters

⊙ *Methodology guidelines: Discussion starters, page xii*

- Write these questions on the board.
  What is the national food of these countries?
     Italy (pasta)   Mexico (rice)   Algeria (couscous)
     UK (potatoes)   Thailand (rice)
  What popular dishes from these countries do you know which include this food?
- Put students in pairs to discuss the questions, then discuss as a class.
  (Possible answers:
  Italy (pasta – lasagne, spaghetti carbonara, etc.)
  Mexico (rice – chili con carne/rice and beans)
  Algeria (couscous – tajine (a chicken or lamb dish) or shakshuka (a vegetable dish))
  UK (potatoes – fish and chips, shepherd's pie)
  Thailand (rice – red/green curry))

SPEAKING

1
- Pairwork. Students discuss the questions in pairs.

Cultural notes

- *Rice*, of course, can be eaten with just about any implement: fork, spoon or fingers. In China and Japan, they use *chopsticks*.

READING

⊙ *Key Methodology 23: Reading skills & strategies, page 94*

The reading text is a magazine article about the importance of rice as the staple diet for half the world's population. It discusses where it grows; what other uses it has, and talks

about special programmes set up to protect the production and distribution of rice in poor countries where there are environment problems, pollution and wars.

1
- Get students to predict the content of the text by asking them to look at the headings, e.g. *Rice in danger*, and ask them why they think it is in danger. Elicit one or two ideas.
- Students skim read the magazine article about rice, and match the paragraphs 1–3 to three of the headings a–d.

> 1 b   2 d   3 a

Extra task

- Write the following words from the text on the board: *Myanmar; Columbia; rain forests; toothpaste; survive.*
- Ask students to look at the text, then write a sentence about the words on the board, e.g. *A lot of people eat rice in Myanmar.*

Language note

- **Combination** means a mixture of things.
- A **desert** is a large hot area of land, usually of sand, that has very little water or plant life. The stress on this word is on the first syllable. N.B. De'sert with the stress on the second syllable means to leave someone or something and to never come back.
- **cosmetics** is something you put on your face to make you look more attractive.
- **production** (verb = *produce*) means to make something or grow something in large quantities.
- **distribution** means when something is transported to a large number of people.

Cultural notes

- **Myanmar** is a country in south-east Asia, bordered by India, China and Thailand. It was called Burma until 1989.
- A metric tonne is 1,000 kilos.

> ### ▣ Key Methodology 23
> ### ▪ Reading skills & strategies
>
> - *Reading texts can be used as a vehicle to introduce grammar or vocabulary items. But texts can also be used in skills training; to help students become better readers. Coursebook tasks linked to a text can often address both aims to some degree. As a teacher, it's important to remember that a text isn't only there to serve the first aim. Don't approach reading work solely with the intention of using it to extract language items for study. You can also help students to become more skilful, capable readers.*
> - *Many students approach reading texts in a word-by-word manner, moving slowly across and down the page, stopping at any unknown word – or constantly checking a dictionary for every problem. This kind of slow, very careful intensive reading is sometimes useful, but it isn't appropriate for most real-world documents. It's possible to understand every word in a text and still have no idea what it's about! Students usually benefit from training in more effective ways of reading.*

- *Much real-world reading is done quite fast. Although the eye does move backwards and forwards to compensate for things misread or misunderstood, the general progress is consistently forwards. If things are not understood, we tend to make a guess or ignore them and keep moving on, until there is any substantial comprehension failure or difficulty, at which point we might consciously go back and try to repair the problem.*
- *Many students might benefit from classroom work that required them to work quickly on texts without recourse to the usual stop-start-dictionary strategy. One useful teaching idea for this is to (a) ask students to cover up or turn over texts, only looking at them when you say go, and stopping when you say stop, and then (b) set tight (and I mean really tight) time limits, e.g. '10 seconds', '30 seconds', etc. Students are usually initially shocked by tight time limits – but they seem to soon realize that it is possible to get answers even in a short time, after which they often enjoy the challenge of finding answers with such a restriction. In this way, students learn to read in a different way.*
- *With a lot of real-life reading, we don't need to understand every word, e.g. if I want to find out when a certain film is on at the cinema, it wouldn't make much sense to start reading a newspaper from the top left word on the front cover – and then read all the text, page by page, till I find the section I want. Better to search rapidly till I spot the piece I want. This strategy of moving one's eyes rapidly through a text to find particular things, is called 'scanning'. Practise scanning by asking students to find certain information on a page.*
- *Sometimes when reading, we only need to get a general meaning from a text, perhaps to decide if we have limited time, if we want to be able to get an overview of a subject, or perhaps, if we want to decide if we will read the text more carefully afterwards. The strategy of fast reading to get a general overview of the contents is called 'skimming'. Practise skimming by asking gist questions about the general content of a text, e.g. what's it about, what kind of text genre (advertisement, newspaper article, letter, etc.) it is.*

2
- Students scan the article and find the information to answer the questions. They can compare their answers with a partner before you check with the whole class.

1	Three kilograms.
2	Half a kilogram.
3	More than 500 million tonnes.
4	Almost everywhere – wet land; dry land; tropical rainforests; deserts.
5	more than 140,000.
6	Paper; wine; bread; beer; sweets; cosmetics; toothpaste.
7	They need rice to survive.

3
- Students underline two facts in the text they didn't know before reading the article, and then compare with a partner.
- They can then have a brief class discussion.

GRAMMAR: *how much / how many*

> *Language reference, Student's Book page 80*
> *Methodology guidelines: Grammar boxes, page xiii*

1
- Students make questions using the words in the table. Tell them that there is often more than one possible sentence.
- In feedback, ask different individuals to give you sentences. You could model a good pronunciation pattern (note the strong stresses on the key noun in column 2, and the key verb in column 3), and get students to repeat.

How many people are there in your English class?
How much water do you buy every week? / do you drink every day?
How much coffee do you buy every week? / do you drink every day?
How much rice/bread do you buy every week? / did you eat yesterday?
How many eggs do you buy every week? / did you eat yesterday?
How many hours did you sleep last night?

Language notes
- In many languages the equivalents of **How much** and **How many** change according to gender as well as countability. Moreover, countable nouns in English may well be uncountable in the students' L1. So, it is important that students are made aware that they must apply *English* rules here – translating does not work!
- Pay attention to pronunciation here: *much* /mʌtʃ/ and *many* /menɪː/, and the rising intonation in the short question.

2
- Pairwork. Students ask and answer the questions from exercise 1.
- Model the activity with a strong student.

Language notes
- A simple rule to get across to students is that we use **some** and **a lot of** in the affirmative (*I have a lot of rice*), and *any*, *much* or *many* in the negative and interrogative, (*I haven't got much rice*). N.B. *many* (but not *much*) tends to be used in the affirmative to mean *a large number of*.
- **Lots of** is less formal than *a lot of*.

VOCABULARY: food 2

> *Language reference, Student's Book page 81*

1 🔵 **2.13**
- Ask students to look at the photos of the two dishes. Ask: *What are these dishes? What foods are in these dishes?* Do not confirm answers yet.
- Play the recording. Students read and listen to the descriptions of the rice dishes and check their guesses.
- Ask students to underline all the food and drink words. They then translate these words into their language, with dictionaries if they have them. In monolingual classes, students can check each other's answers.

Photo 1: Rice and beans.
Photo 2: Paella.
See underlined food and drink words in the tapescript on page 96.

2.13

> **1**
> This is a dish I learnt in Mexico. It's called <u>rice</u> and <u>beans</u>. It's simple – it has rice, beans and <u>corn</u>. I like it for breakfast, with <u>eggs</u> and a large cup of <u>coffee</u> with lots of <u>sugar</u>. Delicious!
>
> **2**
> There are lots of different kinds of paella in Spain. For this paella you need rice, different kinds of <u>shellfish</u>, Spanish <u>sausages</u>, an <u>onion</u>, some <u>garlic</u>, <u>tomatoes</u>, <u>salt</u>, <u>pepper</u> and a <u>lemon</u>. It's wonderful with red <u>wine</u> on a hot summer day.

2
- You could ask students to work in pairs to decide which words are countable and which are uncountable.
- Then say the words for the students to repeat after you.

> Countable: eggs; sausages; onion; tomatoes; lemon
> Uncountable: rice; beans; corn; coffee; sugar; shellfish; garlic; salt; pepper; wine

Extra tasks

1
- Do a class survey. Write a simple table on the board, with the food types taught in the lesson in a column on the left, and the words *a lot, not much, not many,* and *none* across the top.
- Students copy the table, then walk round the class asking the question, *How much/many _____ did you eat/drink last weekend?* Students must ask as many people as they can in five minutes.
- Then ask students to sit down, compare their answers with a partner, and tell the class their results.

2
- Using the texts here as a model, students write a short description of a rice dish popular in their country.

Web research tasks

❯ *Methodology guidelines: Web research tasks, page xiii*

- Ask students to research rice dishes from around the world, e.g. paella, risotto. They must find the names and ingredients of one or two dishes, then present their findings to the class.

Web search key words
- recipe /cooking / ingredients / name of food

PRONUNCIATION: word stress 3

1 **2.14**
- Play the recording. Students listen and read the three shopping lists. Ask them how many syllables each of the words in each list have.

> Will's shopping list: one syllable
> Jenny's shopping list: two syllables
> Samantha's shopping list: three syllables

 2.14

> Will's shopping list:
> cheese
> bread
> milk

> Jenny's shopping list:
> sugar
> sausage
> onion
>
> Samantha's shopping list:
> banana
> oranges
> tomatoes

2 & 3 **2.15**
- Students could work in pairs to put the words into the correct shopping lists in exercise 1.
- Play the recording. Students listen and check their answers.
- Students then work on their own to add more words to each list.

> *See tapescript below for answers.*
> *Possible additional words:*
> Will's shopping list: eggs; wine; beans; corn; salt
> Jenny's shopping list: water; garlic; lemon; shellfish; pepper
> Samantha's shopping list: cucumber; broccoli

 2.15

> Will's shopping list:
> cheese
> bread
> milk
> rice
> cake
>
> Jenny's shopping list:
> sugar
> sausage
> onion
> ice cream
> lettuce
>
> Samantha's shopping list:
> banana
> oranges
> tomatoes
> sausages
> potatoes

4
- Pairwork. Students take it in turns to read the lists to their partner, who can add any new words to their list.

Language notes
- **Onion** is pronounced /ˈʌnjən/.
- Notice the difficult /dʒɪz/ sound at the end of **oranges** and **sausages**.

SPEAKING

❯ *Communication activites, Student's Book pages 134 & 135*

1
- Pairwork. Put students in A and B pairs. Student A turns to page 133 and Student B turns to page 134. Give them two minutes to make sure that they know all the words.
- Model the activity with a student. Ask: *Do you have any bananas? How many bananas do you have?* Elicit a response. Then ask students to work in pairs to ask and answer questions, and find six differences between the photos.

IF YOU WANT SOMETHING EXTRA ...

❯ *Photocopiable activity, page 218*
❯ *Teacher's notes, page 180*

7c | Fussy eaters

WHAT THE LESSON IS ABOUT

Theme	Fussy eaters
Speaking	Pairwork discussion: talking about food
	Pairwork: dialogues complaining about food & drink
Listening	Conversations about eating habits
Vocabulary	Describing food
Grammar	*Too*

IF YOU WANT A LEAD-IN ...

Introducing the theme: fussy eaters

- Write the following sentences on the board. (Or dictate them.)

    Sam doesn't eat meat.
    Jill doesn't like spicy food.
    Jerry can't eat cold food.
    Bill doesn't drink alcohol.
    Mary doesn't like food that is green.

- Put students in groups of four. Tell them that all these people are coming to their house for dinner. They have four minutes to think of a starter, main course, dessert and drink to suit all their guests.
- Students present their dinner menus. Decide which is best.

SPEAKING & VOCABULARY: describing food

> *Language reference, Student's Book page 81*

1

- Model the activity by pointing to a picture and asking the question. Elicit responses from individuals.
- Pairwork. Put students in pairs to discuss the different dishes.

2 2.16

- Play the recording. Students listen and match the adjectives in the box to the dishes in exercise 1.
- Play the recording again. Students listen and repeat the words.
- Then get students to translate the words into their language, with the help of a dictionary.

1	sushi: raw; old
2	chips: salty
3	curry: spicy
4	spinach: cooked
5	brownies à la mode: hot; sweet

2.16

1
A: What's this?
B: Sushi.
A: Sushi?
B: Yes, it's Japanese. It's raw fish. It's cold.

2
A: Would you like any salt with your chips?
B: No, thanks. These chips are very salty already.
A: Oh, I always put extra salt on.

3
A: How's your curry?
B: Excellent. It's very spicy. Can you give me some water, please?

4
A: Oh no. I can't stand spinach.
B: You can't?
A: No, not cooked spinach anyway. Horrible.

5
A: Brownies à la mode.
B: What does brownies 'à la mode' mean?
A: Well, the brownies are like a nice hot chocolate cake, and then you add a spoonful of cold ice cream. That's à la mode.
B: It looks very sweet to me.
A: I know.

Cultural notes

- **Sushi** is a Japanese food that consists of small cakes of cold rice with raw fish, egg, or vegetables on top or inside.
- **Curry** is an Indian (or Thai) dish consisting of meat or vegetables cooked in a sauce with a hot flavour, often eaten with rice. Curry is a very popular dish in Britain.
- **Brownies** are a type of flat chocolate cake, served in squares.

Language notes

- You could double-check the words by asking students to complete sentence prompts like the ones below.
    Chocolate is ...
    Curry is ...
    Sushi is ...

3

- Give students a couple of minutes to think about how to ask the questions, e.g. *Do you like spicy food?*, but tell them not to write anything.
- Groupwork. Divide students into groups of six to eight. They could sit in a circle, or stand together in a group. Students ask each other the questions, and write down the names of any person who says *yes*. In feedback, students tell the class who, in their group, likes or eats what.

LISTENING

These four short conversations relate to people who are fussy about what they eat or drink.

1

- Read the definition of fussy eater as a class. Ask students to tell you about any fussy eaters they know.

2 2.17

- Play the recording. Students listen to the four conversations, and put the food words in the order they hear them.

1	hamburgers
2	wine
3	cake
4	rice

🔵 **2.17**

M = man W = woman

1
W: I'm not a fussy eater. But my brother is. He's a very fussy eater. It's terrible. He only eats <u>hamburgers</u>, and he drinks lots of cola.
M: How old is your brother?
W: He's twenty-six years old! That's why it's terrible!

2
M: This <u>red wine</u> is very good.
W: I don't know. I think it's too young.
M: What year is it?
W: Just a minute. 2004. Yes, definitely too young.
M: I think it's good.

3
W: How can you eat that?
M: What?
W: That <u>cake</u>!
M: Do you want some?
W: Good Lord, no. It's too sweet.
M: You're too fussy. Relax a little.

4
W: And so we didn't eat it. Is there a fussy eater in your family?
M: Oh, yes. We invited my daughter and her boyfriend for dinner. It was awful. My wife made a delicious steak, and my daughter's boyfriend didn't eat anything. He said it was too salty. He was on a special diet. He's a swimmer and he can only eat <u>rice</u>.
W: What did you do?
M: My wife made him a very big plate of rice.

---

3 🔵 **2.17**

- Play the recording again. Students listen and mark the sentences true or false.

1	T
2	T
3	T
4	F (He said the food was too salty and he was on a special diet.)

■ Key Methodology 24
■ **A few guidelines for listening**

- *Some teachers use coursebook recordings as if they were a test rather than a way of helping students to get better at listening. The following is an example of this kind of 'test approach' for Lesson 7C, exercise 2:*
  Teacher: Listen and put the food words in order.
  (Teacher plays recording). OK, what's the order?
  Emese (a student): hamburgers, red wine, onions, cake, rice, chicken
  Teacher: Very good. Right. Now look at exercise 3.
- *This is like a test because it is purely finding out if one student (probably one of the strongest, fastest students) can do the task. This student passed the test – but what about the others? Did some of them have problems? Did they have different answers? Did the teacher's approach help them to learn to listen better?*
- *Even if you now went on to ask other students, you'd be unlikely to hear any different response. If Gabor originally thought that the answer was different, he has just heard you say that Emese's answer was correct. So if you now ask Gabor he will simply parrot her answer. Students aren't stupid!*

- *In order to teach listening, rather than just test it, teachers need to be clear that getting the right answer isn't an indicator that students are learning to listen better. Think of Emese's answer above. It seems quite likely that even she didn't learn to listen better in this task. She could already do it. The listening task didn't significantly help her. The fact that she had a correct answer doesn't indicate that she became more skilful.*
- *Here are a few teacher strategies that may help make listening work more useful:*
  1 Before you check answers, put students into pairs to tell their answers to each other. This gets everyone thinking and, perhaps, giving reasons why they thought their answer was right.
  2 When you check answers in the whole class, don't immediately say 'Yes, that's right', when you hear the right answer(s). Maintain a blank face, i.e. don't show whether you think an answer is correct or not. Similarly, don't immediately tell anyone that their answer is wrong. This technique is surprisingly hard to do! It seems to be a natural inclination to immediately smile and say 'good' when you hear a right answer! But work on this. It's an incredibly useful technique! Just acknowledge that the student has said something, e.g. So you think that the answer is 'London' or just Thank you, and then ask a few more students.
- *If you get all correct answers, you have found that students could do the task and you can state clearly that they are right and then move on. But if you hear different answers, it is an indication that at least some students need more chances to listen in order to catch the information. This is a cue to play the recording again. Summarize the answers students said to you orally or on the board, and ask them to listen again to check which (if any) are correct. Because you haven't told anyone what the right answer is, everyone will be interested to listen and check their ideas. This focused re-listening is where you start teaching rather than testing listening. Repeat the blank-face questioning afterwards and decide if students need to hear the recording again.*
- *Remember – telling students the answer isn't teaching listening – the only person who got practice listening was the teacher.*

4
- Pairwork. Students discuss the questions in pairs.

Extra task

- Play the chain game. Tell students to write down one thing they don't eat and one thing they don't drink. Student A then says, for example, *I'm fussy, I don't eat curry and I don't drink milk.* The next student says: *Juan is fussy. He doesn't eat curry and he doesn't drink milk. I don't eat pasta and I don't drink beer.* The next student must remember and say what both the previous people said, and add their own sentence. This 'chain' continues until students can't remember what was said anymore.

GRAMMAR: *too*

❯ *Language reference, Student's Book page 80*
❯ *Methodology guidelines: Grammar boxes, page xiii*

1

- Students match the sentences in column A with the sentences in column B. They can compare their answers with a partner before you check with the whole class.

1 e   2 d   3 c   4 f   5 b   6 a

Language notes

- ***Too*** has a negative meaning. It means more than is needed or wanted. Be aware that in some languages *too* and *very* are expressed by the same word. Students often think that *too* is just a strong way of saying *very*, leading to errors like, ✗ *My girlfriend is beautiful and too tall!*
- When speaking, make sure students strongly stress *too*.

2 & 3 2.18

- Students put the words in the correct order to make sentences. They can compare their answers with a partner before you check with the whole class.
- Play the recording. Students listen and check their answers.
- Play the recording again. Students repeat if the sentence is true for them.

See tapescript below for answers.

🔘 2.18

1   It's too hot in here.
2   I'm not very tired.
3   This class is too easy.
4   Food is very expensive in my country.
5   Chocolate is too sweet for me.
6   It's very cloudy today.

Prompt drill for too

- You could do a simple prompt drill for *too* using some of the language in the lesson. For example:
  Teacher says: *I don't like Indian food.*
  Class says: *It's too spicy.*
  Teacher says: *I want to eat breakfast.*
  Class says: *It's too late.*
- Use these other ideas (and add your own):
  I don't like chocolate. / I can't eat hamburgers.
  My flat is ten metres long.
  I can't speak Japanese.
  Try to encourage students to keep to a fast pace.

SPEAKING

1 🔘 2.19

- Play the recording. Ask students to read and listen to the dialogue.

🔘 2.19

M = man   W = waiter
M: Excuse me, waiter?
W: Yes, sir.
M: <u>I can't eat this soup. It's too cold.</u>
W: I'm sorry, sir.
M: I hate cold soup!

2

- Ask students to look at the three pictures and match one of them to the dialogue. Then ask them what the problem is. (Answer: *The soup is too cold.*)

Picture B

3 & 4

- Ask students to look at the two other pictures and ask: *Where are they? What's the problem?*
- Pairwork. Put students in pairs to choose either picture A or C and write a dialogue. Monitor and help if necessary. Make sure they are using *too* correctly.
- Ask pairs to act out their dialogue to another pair.

Extension task

❯ *Key Methodology 25: Giving extra practice – instant roleplays, page 105*

- You could extend this into a roleplay. Divide the class into groups of five. Try to group students who worked on the same dialogue in *Speaking* exercises 3 and 4 together. Sit each group round a table, and tell them they are in a restaurant. One student must stand up – they are the waiter. The other students must complain about their food. The waiter must be polite and apologize.

IF YOU WANT SOMETHING EXTRA ...

❯ *Photocopiable activity, page 219*
❯ *Teacher's notes, page 181*

7D | Eat out

WHAT THE LESSON IS ABOUT

Theme	Eating out
Speaking	Pairwork: completing an eating out survey
	Pairwork guided conversation: at a restaurant
Listening	A conversation in a restaurant
Vocabulary	Eating out
Functional language	In a restaurant
Pronunciation	Word linking 1
Did you know?	Eating out in America

IF YOU WANT A LEAD-IN ...

Test before you teach: restaurant vocabulary

❯ *Methodology guidelines: Test before you teach, page xiii*

- Tell the students that they are sitting at a table in a restaurant. Tell them to close their eyes and picture the scene. Ask students: *What did you see?* Elicit as much restaurant vocabulary as you can, e.g. *table, chairs, menu, bill, tip, waiter/waitress, salt, pepper, knife, fork*. Build up words on the board.
- Alternatively, put a large picture of a restaurant scene on the board, and use that to elicit words.

Introducing the theme: eating out

❯ *Key Methodology 25: Giving extra practice – instant roleplays, page 105*

- Put students in pairs, a waiter and a customer. Tell students that they are in a fast food restaurant. They have 30 seconds to roleplay the situation.
- Then tell them to roleplay the following situations:
  a) an expensive restaurant; b) a factory cafeteria;
  c) a coffee shop, d) a pizzeria, e) a bar.
- Don't worry about how simple or inaccurate the roleplays are. It's just practice in improvising in English.

Discussion starters

❯ *Methodology guidelines: Discussion starters, page xii*

- If your students are reasonably mature, and live in the same town, you could get them to tell you about eating out there. Write the following questions on the board, ask students to discuss them in pairs, then tell you what they think.
  1 *What's the best restaurant in town?*
  2 *What's the best place to get food at lunchtime?*
  3 *Where do you go most often?*

SPEAKING & READING

The reading text is a short survey on eating habits.

1
- Students read the sentences and number them 1 to 3 according to how often they do these things. Do the first one yourself as an example.

2
- Pairwork. Students compare their results in pairs and calculate their points.
- Have a brief feedback to find out which student in the class eats out the most.

VOCABULARY: eating out

❯ *Language reference, Student's Book page 81*

1 & 2 2.20
- Students match the words in column A with the words in column B to make sentences. They can compare their answers with a partner before you check with the whole class.
- Play the recording. Students listen and check their answers.
- Play the recording again. Students listen and repeat the sentences.

1 b	2 e	3 a	4 d	5 f	6 g	7 c

🔘 2.20

1	We asked for a table for two in the non smoking section.
2	We looked at the menu.
3	The waiter asked us what we wanted to eat.
4	We had fish for the main course.
5	We ate some chocolate cake for dessert.
6	When we finished the meal, we asked for the bill.
7	We left a tip for the waiter.

Culture notes

- It is common in Britain and North America to leave a ***tip*** at the end of the meal for the waiter or waitress. The tip is usually ten to fifteen per cent of the cost of the meal. Be careful – sometimes it is already included in the bill, so make sure you don't pay twice!

Language notes

- You may wish to point out the verb + preposition collocations here: *ask for* and *look at*.
- Point out the restaurant expressions: *ask for the bill; look at the menu; a table for two; leave a tip*. Add others: *pay the bill, order food*.

LISTENING

In this episode of the listening story, Herb and Hannah (the American couple from Texas) have gone to a pizza restaurant for a meal. Herb orders a beer and a Mexican spicy pizza, and Hannah orders a sparkling mineral water and a mushroom risotto.

In the part 2 of this episode, Herb and Hannah discover that someone has stolen their money and they are unable to pay for their meal.

1 🔘 2.21
- Ask students to look at the menu. Set the scene and check vocabulary by asking questions, e.g. *Is there any meat in the lasagne? What is in the Mexican spicy pizza?*

- Play the recording. Students listen and tick the food Herb and Hannah order on the menu.

> Mushroom risotto.
> Mexican spicy pizza.
> Sparkling mineral water.
> Beer.

2.21

> **He = Herb Ha = Hannah Wr = waiter**
> **Wr:** Can I help you?
> **He:** Table for two, please.
> **Wr:** Smoking or non smoking?
> **He:** Non smoking, please.
> **Wr:** This way, please.
>
> **Wr:** Anything to drink?
> **He:** Yes, <u>a beer, please</u>.
> **Ha:** And a <u>mineral water</u> for me, please.
> **Wr:** Sparkling or still?
> **Ha:** <u>Sparkling</u>, please.
> **He:** Could we have the menu too, please?
> **Wr:** Of course.
>
> **Wr:** Here you are. A beer and a sparkling mineral water.
> **He:/Ha:** Thank you.
> **Wr:** Are you ready to order?
> **He:** Yes, we are. Hannah?
> **Ha:** <u>Can I have the mushroom risotto?</u>
> **Wr:** Yes. OK.
> **He:** <u>And can I have the Mexican spicy pizza?</u>
> **Wr:** Thank you.
>
> **He:** Well, that was delicious! Not too spicy.
> **Ha:** I loved my risotto.
> **He:** Waiter!
> **Wr:** Yes?
> **He:** Can we have the bill, please?
> **Wr:** Would you like a dessert? Coffee?
> **He:** No, thanks. You?
> **Ha:** No coffee for me, thank you. Just the bill.
> **Wr:** Of course. Here you are.

2 2.21

> Key Methodology 5: Dialogues 1, page 11

- Play the recording again. Students listen and complete the dialogue. They can compare their answers with a partner before you check with the whole class.

> 1 two; Non smoking
> 2 drink
> 3 menu
> 4 ready
> 5 bill

Alternative procedures

- Before doing exercise 2, play each dialogue and ask students to listen and write down what they hear – like a dictation. So, play dialogue 1. On first hearing, students might catch, *table … please … non smoke … please*. Let them check in pairs. Play the dialogue again, and again, until students have heard and written the whole dialogue.
- Once they have written all the dialogues, ask students to practise saying the dialogues as they listen. Then move on to exercise 2 so that they can check what they heard and wrote.

Stronger classes

- With stronger classes, you could ask students to work in pairs, look at the gapped dialogues and remember or guess the missing words. Then play the recording for students to check their answers.

3 2.22

- Play the recording. Students listen to the end of the meal. Then ask them what happens in the recording.

> Somebody took their money. They can't pay.

2.22

> **He = Herb Ha = Hannah Wr = waiter**
> **He:** Can I pay by credit card?
> **Wr:** Of course.
> **He:** Fine … wait a minute. I don't have my money here. Hannah, do you have my wallet?
> **Ha:** I don't think so, Herb. No, I don't. I can pay with my credit card. Oh no.
> **He:** What is it?
> **Ha:** My money isn't here!
> **He:** What do you mean?
> **Ha:** I think someone took our money, Herb.
> **He:** I can't believe this.
> **Ha:** Oh no …

FUNCTIONAL LANGUAGE: in a restaurant

> Language reference, Student's Book, page 80

1

- Students correct the mistake in the sentences. Do the first as an example. They can compare their answers with a partner before you check with the whole class.

> 2 Here ~~are you~~ <u>you are</u>.
> 3 That ~~are~~ <u>is</u> £15, please.
> 4 Could I ~~has~~ <u>have</u> the fish, please?
> 5 Can I pay by ~~the~~ credit card?
> 6 Anything ~~for~~ <u>to</u> drink?
> 7 Can we have ~~a~~ <u>the</u> bill, please?

Language notes

- *Can I …?* and *Could I …?* are more or less synonymous in this situation. *Could* is a little more tentative and polite.

PRONUNCIATION: word linking 1

1 & 2 2.23

- Play the recording. Students listen and say how many words they hear. Remind them that contractions count as two words.
- Play the recording more than once. They can compare their answers with a partner before you check with the whole class.
- Students look at tapescript 2.23 on page 144 to check their answers.

> 1 4 words   4 6 words
> 2 5 words   5 5 words
> 3 6 words   6 5 words

🔘 **2.23**

1	Can I help you?
2	Are you ready to order?
3	Could we have the menu, please?
4	I'd like a pizza, please.
5	Would you like a drink?
6	Can I have the bill?

Language notes

- The two main areas of word linking to worry about here are, linking from consonant to vowel, (*Can I* … /kae‿nai/), and the use of contractions, (*I'd*).
- It's important to get students to say *please* with a rising intonation when practising this language.

3 🔘 2.23

❯ *Key Methodology 29: pronunciation – don't avoid intonation, page 126*

- Play the recording again. Students listen and repeat.

Extra task

- Students choose and write two sentences from the lesson. They say them to their partner, as naturally as they can, and their partner must say how many words.

SPEAKING

1 & 2

❯ *Key Methodology 8: Spoken errors – fluency tasks 1, page 29*

- Pairwork. Put students in A and B pairs. Tell them to look at the directions silently, and think what they might say. They can look up phrases in the *Language reference* section on page 80, but they can't write anything.
- When they are ready, ask students to roleplay the interview, following the directions, and using phrases from the lesson.
- Then tell students to change roles and repeat.
- You could ask them to change partners, and repeat again.
- Monitor carefully, and note down errors for a class feedback at the end.

Alternative procedure

- Play a mime game. Let students read through the directions for the roleplay, and prepare as before. Then mime the roleplay. At the front of the class, pretend to be the waiter taking people to the table. Then (silently) ask about drink and food, bring the food, then bring the bill.
- Do the mime again. This time students must provide the soundtrack. They shout out what waiter and customer are saying during the mime. Use 'thumbs up' signs when students use the correct expression.
- Finally, with a strong class, you could ask two students to come to the front of the class and mime the roleplay. Two students, sitting behind, have to provide the soundtrack.

DID YOU KNOW?

1 & 2

- Pairwork. Students read the text and discuss the questions.

Extra task

- Ask students to write a short description of eating out in their country.

Web research tasks

❯ *Methodology guidelines: Web research tasks, page xiii*

- Ask students to go on the internet and find out other facts about eating out in the USA.

Web search key words

- eating out USA / family diner

IF YOU WANT SOMETHING EXTRA …

❯ *Photocopiable activity, page 220*
❯ *Teacher's notes, page 181*

Answer key

● Student's Book page 153

7 REVIEW

1

1 fish
2 carrots
3 rice
4 eggs
5 chicken

2

How much … ?	*How many …?*
chocolate	apples
milk	oranges
sugar	eggs
juice	tomatoes
chicken	

3

2 How much chocolate do you have?
3 How much milk do you want?
4 How many oranges do you need?
5 How many eggs do you have?
6 How many tomatoes do you need?

4

The following pictures should be ticked:
A; B; C; D; E; F; G

5

1 How much rice do you eat every week?
2 Can I have some wine, please?
3 I'd like a table for two, please.
4 Excuse me. This soup is too salty!
5 Do you have any German beer?
6 I don't eat raw vegetables.

6

1 b   2 a   3 b   4 a   5 b

7

1 non-smoking
2 main course
3 dessert
4 bill
5 tip

7 WRITING

● Workbook page 77

Model answer
In the summer, I like to eat greek Salad. To make it you need four tomatoes, a cucumber, some olives and some Greek (Feta) cheese. You also need a little olive oil and lemon juice. It's easy to make and tastes delicious.

8A | I hate flying

WHAT THE LESSON IS ABOUT

Theme	Flying; transport
Speaking	Pairwork discussion: talking about travel Class mingle: completing a questionnaire about travel
Reading	*Fear of flying*: a magazine article about the fear of flying
Vocabulary	Transport
Grammar	Verb + *-ing*
Pronunciation	The sound /ŋ/

IF YOU WANT A LEAD-IN ...

Test before you teach: verb + -ing

⊙ *Methodology guidelines: Test before you teach, page xiii*

- Draw a line on the board like the one in *Grammar* exercise 1 in this lesson:

- Write the following words on the board: *flying; travelling; working; studying English; getting up; going out; being alone; going to parties*, etc.
- Ask students to copy the line and write the words on the line to show their true feelings.
- In pairs or small groups, students ask each other about their line, e.g. *Do you like travelling? Why?*

Discussion starters

⊙ *Methodology guidelines: Discussion starters, page xii*

- *How did you get to school today?*
- *Do you like travelling by bus/car/train/plane, etc.*
- *Which ways of travelling do you think are the most dangerous.*

SPEAKING

1
- Pairwork. Students ask and answer the questions in pairs.

READING
This magazine article is about the common phobia: fear of flying. The writer talks about how she overcame this fear by taking a special day course at an airport. She describes what happened on the course and how it helped her.

1
- Students read the magazine article and put the events in the correct order.

> 3, 4, 1, 2

Language notes

- **Psychology** is the study of the mind and how it affects behaviour.
- **A phobia** is a fear of something, e.g flying, spiders, the outdoors, etc.
- **A pilot** is a person who flies a plane.
- **To survive** means to stay alive in a difficult situation.

2
- Students read the article again and answer the questions. They can compare their answers with a partner before you check with the whole class.

> 1 More than 25 million.
> 2 Probably yes because she says she hated flying, so she must have experienced it.
> 3 She loved travelling.
> 4 A psychologist.
> 5 They held hands. Some cried.
> 6 She booked a flight to Hong Kong.

3
- Pairwork. Students discuss the questions in pairs.

Extra reading task

- There are a number of adjectives used in the text that may be new. You could check students know them by writing the following words on the board:

    safe happy afraid nervous tired relaxed

- Students check the words in their dictionaries.
- You could double-check them by using mime. Then ask: *Which of the words describe how you feel when you are on a plane?*

GRAMMAR: verb + *-ing*

⊙ *Language reference, Student's Book page 90*
⊙ *Methodology guidelines: Grammar boxes, page xiii*

1
- Students put the words in the correct order on the line. They can compare their answers with a partner before you check with the whole class.

love	like	don't mind	don't like	hate
☺☺	☺	☺	☹	☹☹

Language notes

- Both *I like flying* and *I like to fly* are grammatically correct. The difference is very subtle. *I like flying* means I like the activity in general. *I like to fly* means I like to do the specific action. British English speakers will interchange both forms, but tend to use the *-ing* form most of the time. For this reason, it is best to just stick with the *-ing* use here. In US English, *like* + infinitive is generally used.
  N.B. in many languages verbs are generally followed by infinitives, so the idea that, in English, some verbs are followed by *-ing* may be novel.
- Forming *-ing* from the infinitive is straightforward. However, note the slight exceptions:

    arrive – 'e' = arriving; sit + 't' = sitting.

2

- Students could work in pairs to find and underline examples of the verbs in exercise 1 in the article, and the verbs that go with them.

> don't like flying … (line 1)
> hate or hated flying … (line 5)
> hated flying. (line 8)
> loved travelling …, love travelling … (line 13)
> hate flying … (line 14)
> don't mind flying … (line 31)
> don't like eating … (line 32)

3

- Students complete the sentences with a word from the box, using the -*ing* form. They can compare their answers with a partner before you check with the whole class.

1	going	4	waiting
2	sitting	5	eating
3	talking		

4

> ❷ *Communication activites, Student's Book pages 134 & 136*

- Pairwork. Put students in A and B pairs. Student A turns to page 134 and Student B turns to page 136. Ask students to say what they can see in their pictures and elicit the vocabulary.
- Students then ask and answer questions about what their partner likes doing, using the pictures.

VOCABULARY: transport

> ❷ *Language reference, Student's Book page 91*

1 & 2 ◉ **2.24**

- Students put the words into two groups. They can then compare their answers with a partner.
- Play the recording. Students listen and check their answers.
- Play the recording again. Students listen and repeat.

See answers in tapescript below.

◉ **2.24**

> A airport, car park, railway station, bus stop, port
> B car, plane, boat, motorbike, train, bicycle, bus, underground, on foot

Language notes

- You may wish to introduce the word *by* here, which will help students produce whole sentences in exercise 3. Note that we say, **by** *bus/train/car*, etc., but **on** *foot*.
- N.B. American English differs from British English:
  Car park (*British English*) = *parking lot* (*US English*)
  Underground (*British English*) = *subway* (*US English*)

3

> ❷ *Key Methodology 25: Giving extra practice – instant roleplays, page 105*

- Model the activity by asking students the questions in open class. Decide whether you want your students to produce short answers or whole sentences. Elicit a response, e.g. *bus*, *by bus*, or *I go by bus*.
- Pairwork. Students ask and answer the questions.

Alternative procedure

> ❷ *Key Methodology 29: Pronunciation – don't avoid intonation!, page 126*

- You could use this activity to practise the question form.
- Write the question below on the board, and show the intonation arrow above it. Ask students to listen and repeat. They should start their intonation high, fall on *home*, then rise on *city centre*.
- Model and drill the other questions before letting students talk in pairs.

How do you get from your home to the city centre?

> ■ **Key Methodology 25**
> ■ **Giving extra practice: instant roleplays**
>
> - *A quick and useful way to provide students with more practice in a language area is to set up an instant roleplay. Teachers sometimes avoid roleplay because they think it involves lots of preparation of roleplay cards or because they think students won't like it, finding it too 'silly'.*
> - *Both of these objections can be made to evaporate. Don't make a big thing out of roleplay. Don't announce it as something special or unusual. Just drop it into the lesson along with all the other practice. You don't need complicated cards – a simple instruction will do. And very often, it's possible to add a roleplay into a lesson when you realize that students need more practice, even if you haven't planned anything in advance. With a little practice, they are not very hard to invent spontaneously on the spot.*
> - *To make a simple roleplay, you need to tell the students (a) where they are; (b) who they are, and (c) what they should talk about. It's often possible to say this in just one or two short sentences. If you want to give more instructions, you can also mention any further information that might help, e.g. some things that should happen during the conversation – or perhaps remind students of useful language. But often the simple (a), (b), (c) instruction is sufficient.*
>   *For example, in Lesson 8A, imagine that you want to give students more practice in the grammar verbs + ing. To make an extra roleplay practice, first make sure you have the language aim clearly in mind. Whatever task you devise, it needs to get students using that language. In Lesson 8A, an obvious task would be to give students a chance to use the language they worked on in exercise 3. When they have finished doing the questions, say 'In pairs. You are both sitting on a plane. Talk to the passenger next to you. Tell them what you think about flying'. If you want to add more colour to the situation, you could add 'It's a terrible journey. The plane keeps bumping. You feel sick!'.*
> - *Sometimes you can use an instant roleplay to extend or add a little more context to a coursebook exercise, e.g. in Lesson 8A, Vocabulary exercise 4, turn the task into a roleplay by saying 'In pairs. One of you lives in the town. The other person is a tourist. The tourist must ask the local person how to go somewhere'.*

- *You can also use roleplay as a way of repeating a task when students need more practice without it seeming too dull, e.g. if you wanted to repeat Lesson 8A, Speaking exercise 1, you could say 'OK. Now think of a famous person (e.g. President of America, a famous pop star/actor, etc.). Now – you ARE that person! Meet other people and ask them your questions. But remember to answer as the famous person, not as you!*
- *Simple props, e.g. a mobile phone, a train ticket, a wallet and some coins, etc., can often help to make roleplays more fun.*

PRONUNCIATION: /ŋ/

1 **2.25**
- Play the recording. Students listen and repeat the words.
- In feedback, ask what sound the words have in common. (Answer: /ŋ/.) Model the sound.

🔘 **2.25**

| waiting |
| young |
| flying |
| eating |
| think |
| English |

Language notes

- /ŋ/ is a sound peculiar to English, which many students may find difficult to reproduce. It starts nasal like /n/ and ends with a slight stop at the back of the throat. The important thing is not to pronounce a hard /g/ at the end.

2 🔘 **2.26**
- Play the recording. Students listen and complete the sentences. They can compare their answers with a partner before you check with the whole class.

See underlined answers in tapescript below.

🔘 **2.26**

1	I <u>like</u> flying.
2	I <u>love</u> speaking English.
3	I <u>don't like</u> watching horror films.
4	I <u>hate</u> writing exams.

3
- Ask students to complete the sentences with *like/don't like/hate*, etc. so they are true for themselves.
- Then put them in small groups to say the sentences to each other. Monitor and make sure students are pronouncing /ŋ/ correctly.

SPEAKING

❯ *Key Methodology 25: giving extra practice – instant roleplays, page 105*

1
- Read through the instructions as a class. Then give students a minute or two to prepare questions from the prompts.
- Model the activity by asking a confident student one or two questions, and pretending to write their name when they answer *yes*.
- Ask students to mingle and ask questions. Give a time limit, say ten minutes. They must ask *Did you …?* and *Wh-* questions. The aim is to get a 'yes' answer to each question and write the name of the person who said *yes* next to the question.
- In feedback, ask students *Who?* questions and elicit responses.

Web research tasks

❯ *Methodology guidelines: Web research tasks, page xiii*

- Find a good course in the UK for people who have a fear of flying. What do you do on the course?
Web search key words
- 'fear of flying' courses, UK

IF YOU WANT SOMETHING EXTRA …

❯ *Photocopiable activity, page 221*
❯ *Teacher's notes, page 181*

8B | Traffic jam

WHAT THE LESSON IS ABOUT

Theme	Traffic problems
Speaking	Class mingle – game: *In Traffic*
Listening	A traffic report on the radio
Vocabulary	Action verbs
Grammar	Present continuous
Did you know?	*London's traffic law*

IF YOU WANT A LEAD-IN ...

Test before you teach: present continuous

❯ *Methodology guidelines: Test before you teach, page xiii*

- If you have access to a video or DVD player, you could do this activity with a strong class. Find a sequence from a feature film or TV program with quite a lot of action on it.
- Put students in pairs and make them sit back to back so that one student can see the screen, and the other can't. Play the sequence (it should last no more than five minutes). The student who can see the screen must describe what's happening in as much detail as they can (using the present continuous, hopefully). Their partner must listen and take notes.
- At the end, students discuss the notes, then watch the sequence again together.

Discussion starters

❯ *Methodology guidelines: Discussion starters, page xii*

Write these questions on the board, check the underlined words, then have a class discussion.
- *Are you often in a <u>traffic</u> jam?*
- *When is <u>rush hour</u> in your city?*
- *How often is there an <u>accident</u> in this area?*
- *What can you do to improve roads?*

Language note

- **A traffic jam** is a line of vehicles not moving or moving slowly on a busy or blocked road.
- **The rush hour** is a time of day when the roads are very busy, (often eight to nine in the morning, and five to six in the evening in the UK).
- **An accident** here means a crash involving one or more vehicles.

LISTENING

1

- Tell students to look at the photo and ask them what they can see.
- Say: *Imagine you are in the situation in the photo. How do you feel?*

2 💿 2.27

- Play the recording. Students listen and say what the problem is in each picture. Let them discuss their ideas with a partner before discussing as a class.

A	A large group of people are standing in the middle of Oxford Street. The traffic isn't moving.
B	There is an escaped lion in the middle of the road.
C	There is a bus on fire.
D	Someone is driving on the wrong side of the road.

💿 2.27

K = Kate J = John

K: Yes, that was Aretha Franklin, another classic tune. Coming up we have lots more music and news, but first here's the traffic news. And it's a busy day out on the roads, isn't it, John?

J: Yes, it is Kate. Good morning. We have an accident in Regent Street. <u>There's a bus on fire</u>. Everybody is OK, but traffic is moving very slowly.
<u>A large group of people are standing in the middle of Oxford Street</u>. I can't hear them, but I think they are standing in front of the cars and singing! So, <u>traffic isn't moving</u>. The police are talking to them at the moment.

K: Can you tell us anything about the incident on Euston Road?

J: Yes, Kate. <u>There's a lion</u> – yes, I said a lion – on Euston Road. I'm looking at the camera now. A lot of cars are moving slowly around it. It's sitting <u>in the middle of the road</u> and looking at the cars ...

K: Where did it come from? Do you have any more news?

J: Well, the police say that they think it escaped from the zoo. I'm waiting for more information on that. We have a report coming in now from East London. There's a big traffic problem. <u>Someone is driving on the wrong side of the road.</u>

K: It's another crazy day for drivers, then. Next traffic update at half past ten. Thanks, John.

3 💿 2.27

- Play the recording again. Students listen and mark the sentences true or false. They can compare their answers with a partner before you check with the whole class.

1	T
2	F (It's moving very slowly.)
3	T
4	F (They're standing in front of the cars.)
5	F (The police are talking to the people standing in the middle of Oxford Street.)
6	T

Cultural notes

- **Oxford Street**, **Regent Street** and **Euston** /juːsten/ **Road** are busy roads in Central London.
- **The M25** is the motorway that orbits London – it's regularly blocked by traffic jams.
- In the UK, cars (usually) drive on the left.

4

- Students can discuss the question in pairs or small groups.

Extra discussion

- *Are you often in a traffic jam? Where? When?*
- *When were you last in a traffic jam? How did you feel? What did you do?*

Web research tasks

❯ *Methodology guidelines: Web research tasks, page xiii*

- Ask students to find out facts and figures about traffic jams and accidents in their city or country.

Web search key words
- traffic/statistics/accidents/name of city or country

GRAMMAR: present continuous

◎ *Language reference, Student's Book page 90*
◎ *Methodology guidelines: Grammar boxes, page xiii*

1

- Ask students in pairs to look at tapescript 2.27 on page 144, and find and underline examples of the present continuous.

2

◎ *Key Methodology 26: Giving extra practice – repeating exercises, page 108*

- Students write questions and answers in the present continuous. They can then compare their answers with a partner before discussing as a class.
- Put students in pairs to practise asking and answering. They must work from the prompts in the Student's Book, not from the questions and answers that they have written out in full.

1	What are the people doing? The people are standing in the street.
2	Where are they going? They're going to the city centre.
3	Who are the police talking to? They're talking to the demonstrators.
4	What is the lion doing? It's sitting in the road.
5	What is the car doing? It's driving on the wrong side of the road.
6	What is the woman doing? She's talking on her mobile phone.

Language notes

- English uses the present continuous to talk about events happening now or around now. As such, it is used with active not stative verbs.
- In terms of form, students need to manipulate the verb *to be* correctly. They need to be aware that *am*, *is* and *are* contract to *I'm*, *he's*, *we're*, etc. They must also remember the form rules when changing infinitive to the *-ing* form, (*drive* – 'e' = *driving*; *run* + 'n' = *running*, etc.).
- Be aware that in some other languages the present simple form is used in this context. If you have a monolingual class, it is useful to think about how similar the use of present continuous in students' L1 is to the use in English. If it's the same, this tense will be straightforward. If not, students will need lots of contextualized practice to get the hang of it.

> ### Key Methodology 26
> ### Giving extra practice: repeating exercises
>
> - *Sometimes once isn't enough. You may feel that students need to tackle an exercise again before they have really learnt something. But you don't want it to feel boring or hear 'But we did this already'. Here are a few ideas, using Lesson 8B, Grammar, exercise 2 as an example.*

Books closed – orally

- *After students have finished and checked the exercise, tell them to work in A and B pairs. Student A keeps their book open. Student B closes their book.*
- *Students now do the exercise again orally with Student A reading the question and Student B answering, e.g. Student A says what / they / do and Student B must make the sentence. Then Student A says the reply, e.g. They / move / a car to the side of the road, and Student B gives the sentence.*
- *When Student B has answered both parts, Student A now says the complete question, e.g. 'What are they doing', and Student B replies with the answer (without any further prompt!).*
- *After the pair have done all seven questions, they swap roles and do it again.*

Team game

- *Similar to the idea above, you could repeat the exercise as a team game.*
- *Tell the class to close their books. Divide the class into teams and set questions in turns to different teams. If they get the answer completely correct, the team gets a point. If there is a mistake, the next team can get a bonus point if they get it right.*

Teacher does the exercise

- *Tell students to keep their coursebooks open, but close any books where they wrote answers. Ask the students to read you the questions, one by one. Tell the students to spot if you make any mistakes. Answer them, mostly correctly, but with occasional small (or big) errors. If the students spot a mistake, congratulate them. If they don't, ask them to repeat the question and listen again to your answer to try and spot the error.*

3

- Model the activity by saying two or three sentences about people you know, e.g. *mmm, what's Jo doing? Oh yes, she's working in her office.*
- Students write sentences about people they know. Monitor and help if necessary, and correct errors.

4

- Pairwork. Put students in pairs. Tell them to write the names of the people in exercise 3 on a different piece of paper. They exchange pieces of paper with their partner, then students ask questions about the people on their partner's paper.

Extra task

◎ *Key Methodology 10: Flashcards 1 – the essentials, page 37*

- Prepare flashcards with stick figures doing the actions in the lesson.
- Hold up the cards and ask, *What's he/she doing?* or *What are they doing?* Students answer. Then get students to ask and answer from the flashcard prompts across the class.

VOCABULARY: action verbs

❯ *Language reference, Student's Book page 91*

1

- Students write the missing letters in the infinitive verbs. They can compare their answers with a partner before you check with the whole class.
- In feedback, check the meanings of the verbs with simple mimes.

sing	kiss
walk	smoke
drive	sleep
run	

2

- Students look at the pictures and make sentences, using the verbs from exercise 1 in the present continuous. They can compare their answers with a partner before you check with the whole class.

A   She's walking.
B   He's smoking (a pipe).
C   He's sleeping.
D   He's singing.
E   She's driving (a sports car).
F   They're kissing.
G   They're running.

SPEAKING

1

- Before the lesson prepare lots of small pieces of paper with the following actions written on them.
  You are eating sandwiches.
  You are drinking tea.
  You are listening to rock music.
  You are smoking.
  You are studying.
  You are listening to a football match.
  You are talking on the phone.
  You are taking photos with your mobile phones.
  You are angry. Some of you are crying.
  You are singing a song.
  You are sleeping.
- Model the activity first by pretending to be in a car stuck in a traffic jam. Mime the following actions for the students to guess what you are doing:
  You are listening to the radio.
  You are sleeping.
  You are opening the window.
  You are looking at your watch (and getting angry!).
- Tell students to read the instructions for the *In Traffic Game*, then discuss them with a partner to check they understand.

2

- Put students in groups of four or five, and make sure they sit in a circle. Hand out a piece of paper to each person in the group. They must take it in turns to mime their action while the rest of the group guess what they are doing.

DID YOU KNOW?

1 & 2

- Students read the text about London's traffic law and discuss the questions in pairs.

IF YOU WANT SOMETHING EXTRA ...

❯ *Photocopiable activity, page 222*
❯ *Teacher's notes, page 182*

8c | Follow that car!

WHAT THE LESSON IS ABOUT

Theme	A TV detective show
Speaking	Pairwork communication: describing a normal day & a special day
Reading & listening	Dialogue from a TV detective show: Tracy Dick P.I. – a private investigator reports back to a client on the person she is following
Vocabulary	Collocations: (transport)
Grammar	Present simple vs present continuous

IF YOU WANT A LEAD-IN ...

Discussion starters

> *Methodology guidelines: Discussion starters, page xii*

- *What TV detective shows do you know?*
- *What is the name of the detective in the show?*
- *What usually happens in the show?*
- *What do you like about it?*

Pre-teach key words: transport vocabulary

> *Key Methodology 12: Flashcards 3 – more ways of presenting vocabulary, page 43*

- Revise key transport vocabulary: *car, taxi, motorbike, bus, coach*. You could do this by using flashcards to elicit the words, or by miming the words, e.g. by miming standing on a bus or starting up a motorbike.

READING & LISTENING

This listening story is from an invented television show. Tracy Dick, is a private detective who follows people she has been instructed to investigate on her motorbike. Her client, Mrs Lunan, wants Tracy to follow her husband as she thinks he is having an affair. Tracy reports back to Mrs Lunan where her husband is and what he is doing. Mrs Lunan is distraught to find out that her husband has gone to a restaurant and is waiting for someone with a bunch of flowers.

In the second part of the story, Mr Lunan phones his wife to say that he has booked a table for them at their favourite restaurant as a surprise, and he's waiting for her to come and join him.

1

- Ask students to look at the pictures and get them to describe what is happening in each picture.
- Ask students to tell you what they think the show is about.

> It's about Tracy Dick who is a private investigator. She's following a man whose wife thinks he is having a relationship with another woman.

Language & cultural notes

- **PI** = Private Investigator (US English). Also called a Private Detective or Private Eye.
- Tracy's name is a play on Dick Tracy. Dick Tracy was a popular comic book detective hero in the 1930s and 1940s.

Extra tasks

1

- Preview the language taught in the lesson (the present continuous) by asking *What's happening?* and *What's she/he doing?* Whilst pointing to each picture, try to elicit detailed descriptions. Write up new words on the board.

2

- Pre-teach some key phrases from the story by writing the following on the board:
  Motorcycle detective   Follow that car!   Where's my husband?   He never buys flowers!
  Check the meaning of the phrases by asking students to predict what the story could be about.

2 ● 2.28

- Play the recording. Students read and listen to the show. They number the pictures in the correct order. They can compare their answers with a partner before you check with the whole class.

1 middle night	3 bottom right	5 middle left
2 top left	4 bottom left	

● 2.28

A = announcer T = Tracy ML = Mrs Lunan	
A:	Tracy Dick P.I. Motorbike Detectives
T:	Mrs Lunan, it's Tracy Dick here.
ML:	Yes?
T:	You asked me to call you. I'm outside your husband's office now.
ML:	Oh, thank you. He doesn't leave work before six o'clock. And it's now only half past five.
T:	Well, Mrs Lunan, your husband is leaving work now.
ML:	What's he doing.
T:	He's taking a taxi.
ML:	But my husband hardly ever takes taxis! He says they're too expensive! He usually goes by bus.
T:	Do you want me to follow him?
ML:	Yes, yes! Follow that car!
T:	Mrs Lunan? I'm in the centre of the city.
ML:	Where's my husband?
T:	Mr Lunan is paying the taxi driver ... He's getting out of the taxi.
ML:	Where is he exactly?
T:	He's in front of a restaurant, the Green Leaf.
ML:	He always goes to that restaurant. We went there together in the past ...
T:	He's not going in the restaurant. He's going into a flower shop.
ML:	What?! He never buys flowers!
T:	I'm parking my motorbike now.
ML:	Phone me back, please.
ML:	Hello?
T:	I'm in the restaurant. Mr Lunan is at another table.
ML:	What is he doing now?
T:	He's looking for something ... his mobile phone.
ML:	Yes?
T:	He's making a phone call.
ML:	Can you hear? Who's he phoning? This is terrible!

Alternative procedure

- With stronger classes, play the recording with the reading text covered. Students must put the pictures in order, then check by reading the text.

3

- Students read the story again, and choose the correct words to complete the sentences. They can compare their answers with a partner before you check with the whole class.

1 a   2 b   3 a   4 a   5 a   6 a   7 b

Extra task

- It is a good idea to practise question forms in the present simple and present continuous in feedback. Ask, for example, *What time does Mr Lunan usually leave work?* and encourage a whole sentence answer. You could get students to ask and answer across class in a class feedback.

4

❯ *Key Methodology 24: A few guidelines for listening, page 98*

- Pairwork. Put students in pairs to ask the questions, and guess the end of the story.
- In feedback, encourage lots of speculative answers to create a prediction task for the listening in exercise 5.

5 💿 **2.29**

- Play the recording. Students listen to the end of the story, and check their predictions.

Mr Lunan is phoning Mrs Lunan. He secretly arranged a surprise romantic dinner for them at their favourite restaurant.

💿 **2.29**

> **T = Tracy ML = Mrs Lunan MRL = Mr Lunan**
> **ML:** Can you hear? Who is he phoning? This is terrible! Just a minute, it's my mobile phone. Hello?
> **MRL:** Hello, darling.
> **ML:** John?
> **MRL:** Yes, it's me. I have a surprise for you.
> **ML:** Oh, John …
> **MRL:** Do you remember the Green Leaf restaurant?
> **ML:** Yes …
> **MRL:** I'm waiting for you. I have a table for two.
> **ML:** Oh, John …
> **MRL:** Darling, take a taxi.
> **ML:** Yes, I … yes.
> **MRL:** Come quickly darling. I love you.
> **ML:** I love you, too.
>
> **ML:** Sorry, Ms Dick?
> **T:** That's alright, Mrs Lunan. I heard. I'm happy everything is OK.
> **ML:** Yes, I …
> **T:** Don't worry. You can pay me by cheque or credit card.

Extra task for stronger classes

❯ *Key Methodology 25: Giving extra practice – instant roleplays, page 105*

- Divide students into pairs. They must improvise the dialogue between Tracy and Mrs Lunan, using the pictures as prompts, with the text covered.

VOCABULARY: collocations (transport)

❯ *Language reference, Student's Book page 91*

1 & 2 💿 **2.30**

- Students choose the correct verb that collocates with the transport noun. They can then compare their answers with a partner.
- Students then listen to the recording to check their answers.

See underlined answers in the tapescript below.

💿 **2.30**

> 1 Can you <u>ride</u> a motorbike?
> 2 Can you <u>drive</u> a car?
> 3 How often do you <u>take</u> a taxi?
> 4 Do you <u>take</u> the train to work?

3

- Pairwork. Put students in pairs. They ask and answer the questions with a partner.

GRAMMAR: present simple vs present continuous

❯ *Language reference, Student's Book page 90*
❯ *Methodology guidelines: Grammar boxes, page xiii*

1

- Students decide if these sentences are present simple (PS) or present continuous (PC). They can compare their answers with a partner before you check with the whole class.

1 PC   2 PC   3 PC   4 PS   5 PC   6 PS

Language notes

- The difference in use is quite straightforward to explain: present simple is what we do every day, whereas present continuous is what we are doing now. Be aware, however, that in many languages the present simple is used for both uses.
- See *Language notes* in Units 2D and 8A for form and pronunciation problems.

2

- Students complete the conversation with the present simple or the present continuous of the verbs in brackets. Do the first as an example. They can then compare their answers with a partner.

1 do
2 do
3 Are
4 working
5 'm following
6 's talking
7 drink
8 's waiting
9 'm working

3 **2.31**

● *Key Methodology 6: Dialogues 2, page 16*

- Play the recording. Students listen to the recording and check their answers.
- Put students in pairs to practise reading the dialogue.

1	do
2	do
3	Are
4	working
5	'm following
6	's talking
7	drink
8	's waiting
9	'm working

 2.31

P = Pete   T = Tracy
P: So, what <u>do</u> you <u>do</u>?
T: I'm a private detective.
P: That's interesting. <u>Are</u> you <u>working</u> now?
T: Yes, I am. At the moment I<u>'m following</u> a man.
P: How exciting! Is he in this bar?
T: Yes, he is. Right now he<u>'s talking</u> to another woman.
P: Would you like a glass of wine?
T: No, thank you. I never <u>drink</u> at work.
P: So … who asked you to follow this man?
T: His wife. She<u>'s waiting</u> for me to call her now.
P: Is she? When you finish, why don't you come with me?
T: I don't think so, Mr Hunt. You see, at the moment, I<u>'m working</u> for your wife.

Extra task

- Write the following statements on the board:
  I'm a teacher   Here at the school   At eight o'clock
  She's working in the city   I watch TV   I'm talking to you!
- Put students in pairs. Tell them that you have written some answers to some questions on the board. The students must think what the correct questions are, e.g. *What do you do? What is your sister doing now?* When the pairs have prepared their questions, ask them to ask you a question. If it is correct, give them the answer from the board.

SPEAKING

1

● *Communication activites, Student's Book pages 137 & 133*

- Pairwork. Put students in A and B pairs. Student A must read about Phil and Sarah on page 137 of the Student's Book. Student B must read about Phil and Sarah on page 133.
- Tell students to take it in turns to ask questions and tell each other their information.

> ■ **Key Methodology 27**
> ■ **Turning the pages**
>
> - *This isn't a new technique or a bright idea for a different way of doing things. It's just a reminder. But it is quite an important reminder.*
> - *When you teach, don't get so concerned with the syllabus or the requirements that you get too obsessed with simply moving through the book, and lose touch with the reason that you are using the book in the first place. Try to go at the speed of the learning. If necessary, slow down. If appropriate, speed up. You are aiming for the students to learn English well. Getting through the book is purely incidental to this. Teach the students, not the book. Use the book to help you help the students to learn.*

IF YOU WANT SOMETHING EXTRA …

● *Photocopiable activity, page 223*
● *Teacher's notes, page 182*

8D | Let's take the bus

WHAT THE LESSON IS ABOUT

Theme	Travelling
Speaking	Describing what is happening in a picture
	Groupwork dialogue: making suggestions about things to do
Listening	Conversations about crossing London
Vocabulary	*Take*
Functional language	Suggestions
Pronunciation	Intonation 2

IF YOU WANT A LEAD-IN ...

Introducing the theme: travelling

- Write the names of five or six well-known places in or around the city where you are teaching. Ask: *What's the best way to get there?* and point to one of the places. Elicit or model the best way, e.g. *Take the number 41 bus to the centre, then go on foot.*
- Put students in groups of three or four to decide on the best route to each place, then tell the class.

SPEAKING

1

- Ask students to look at the picture and tell you who the people are (Rob, Meg (the Australian couple) and Delilah (the tourist from New Zealand Brian picked up from the airport in Lesson 2D) from the listening story). Ask them to tell you what the people are doing and where they think they are going. Try to elicit lots of suggestions.

> They are looking at the underground map of London.
> They want to travel across London by underground.

LISTENING

In this episode of the listening story, Rob, Meg and Delilah are going to a concert at the Royal Albert Hall. They need to find there way there on their own as Valerie (the tour guide) is taking Herb and Hannah (the couple from Texas) to the police station to report that their money and passports have been stolen. (See Lesson 7D.) The journey to the Albert Hall is problematic for Rob, Meg and Delilah: first they catch the wrong underground train, then, after taking three buses, Rob decides that they should walk the last 15 minutes, but it starts raining. Delilah is fed up and calls for a taxi.

1 🔘 **2.32**

- Play the recording. Students listen and answer the questions. They can compare their answers with a partner before you check with the whole class.

> They are going to a concert at the Royal Albert Hall.
> They take three different forms of transport (underground, bus, taxi).

🔘 **2.32**

R = Rob M = Meg D = Delilah Ma = man	
D:	Hi, guys.
R/M:	Hi, Hello.
D:	I'm ready for the concert. Where's Valerie?
R:	She's <u>taking Herb and Hannah to the police station</u>.
D:	Really? Why? Are they alright?
R:	Someone <u>took their money and passports</u>.
D:	That's terrible.
M:	So, what do we do now?
R:	We could go to the concert. Just the three of us.
D:	OK. Where is it?
R:	At the ... <u>Royal Albert Hall</u>.
D:	I know. Let's <u>take a taxi</u>.
R:	A taxi? No, no, no. Taxis here are too expensive. We can <u>take the underground</u>.
D:	Where are we?
R:	We're here. Camden Town.
M:	Camden Town or Camden Road?
R:	Camden Town. So, we can <u>take the black line</u> here ...
D:	<u>Let's ask the man over there</u>.
R:	No, no, no. It's OK. Look, the black line to Euston, then change to the ...Victoria line ... wait a minute, where am I?
D:	Excuse me, we're going to the Royal Albert Hall, and er ...?
Ma:	That's easy, love. <u>Take the Northern Line </u>to Euston, change at Euston onto the Victoria Line, then get off at Victoria station. Get on the District line, the green line, and go to South Kensington. It <u>takes around 40 minutes</u>.
D:	Thank you. .... Did you understand that?
R/M:	No.
D:	Why don't we <u>take that taxi</u> now?
R:	Wait. He said the Northern Line! Let's go on that.
M:	I think we <u>took the wrong train</u>. This is Kings Cross.
D:	What do we do now?
R:	Let's go up to the street and <u>take a bus</u>. At least we can see London that way. And we can <u>take photographs</u>.
M:	That's a good idea.
D:	We could also see London in a nice taxi.
M:	That was the third bus! I'm tired of buses.
R:	We're nearly there. We can walk now. It <u>takes 15 minutes</u> to the concert hall.
M:	I don't think that's a good idea. I don't want to walk.
D:	It's raining. I didn't <u>take an umbrella</u>!
R:	Wait ... It's not far.
D:	<u>Taxi! Taxi!</u>

2 🔘 **2.32**

- Play the recording again. Students listen and complete the sentences with a word from the box. They can compare their answers with a partner before you check with the whole class.

1	the police station	5	the wrong train
2	the Royal Albert Hall	6	by bus
3	a man	7	an umbrella
4	the directions	8	a taxi

Cultural notes

- **The London Underground** or *Tube* is made up of more than ten different lines, which interconnect at many different points. It can be very confusing for tourists. Camden Town, Euston and King's Cross are all stations on the Northern line, (which is always marked in black on the map of the underground).
- **The Royal Albert Hall** is a concert hall in Kensington. It was built in the late nineteenth century and named after Queen Victoria's husband Prince Albert. It is famous for hosting the annual Proms concerts.

FUNCTIONAL LANGUAGE: suggestions

⟩ *Language reference, Student's Book page 90*

1

- Students put the words in order to make suggestions. They can compare their answers with a partner before you check with the whole class.

1 We could go to the concert.
2 We can take the underground.
3 Let's ask the man over there.
4 We could see a nice London taxi.
5 Why don't we take that taxi now?
6 Let's go up the street.

Language notes

- Although grammatically very different, these forms express the same idea. They need to be taught and learnt as fixed expressions.
  N.B. *Let's* is an abbreviation of *Let us*. However, the longer form is almost never used.
- These forms are followed by the base verb. Watch out for students trying to slip in an unnecessary *to*: ✗ *We could to go … Let's to go …*

PRONUNCIATION: intonation 2

1 & 2 🔘 **2.33**

⟩ *Key Methodology 29: Pronunciation – don't avoid intonation!, page 126*

- Play the recording. Students listen and underline the correct answer.
- Play the recording again. Students listen and repeat.

a) 1   b) 2

🔘 **2.33**

1 We can take the underground.
2 We can take the underground.

1 Let's take a bus.
2 Let's take a bus.

Language notes

- English uses a wide intonation range. It is important for students to approximate this in order to sound friendly, polite or tentative. Get students to start their intonation high, and make sure it is rising at the end.

  Let's take a bus. ↗

- Refer to this when students are doing exercises 2 and 4.

3 🔘 **2.34**

- Play the recording. Students listen to the suggestions, and tick them if they are friendly and put a cross if they are not. They can compare their answers with a partner before you check with the whole class.
- Play the recording again if students are unsure.

1 ✓   2 ✗   3 ✗   4 ✓

🔘 **2.34**

1 Why don't we wait for the bus?
2 We can go on foot.
3 We could take a taxi.
4 Let's go by train.

4

- Model the activity with a student. Point to the first picture, and say, *Let's go by bus*. Shake your head, and encourage the student to give a *No* answer.
- Pairwork. Put students in pairs to make and respond to suggestions, using the pictures.

Extra lead-in task

⟩ *Key Methodology 11: Flashcards: 2 – presenting vocabulary, page 40*

- Flashcards work well here. Draw simple pictures of the means of transport on cards. Hold up a card, model a suggestion and get students to repeat. Do this with all the cards. Then hold them up and get students to make suggestions to you. Respond with a response phrase. Then get students to ask and answer across the class.
- Once students have had lots of practice at producing the form and intonation accurately, put them in pairs to do exercise 4.

VOCABULARY: *take*

1

- Read through the examples as a class.

Language notes

- *Take* is a very common verb in English with a wide range of uses.
- If you have a monolingual class, use translation here. Ask students to translate the use of *take* in each example.
- Find out whether the Students' L1 is the same or different to English

2

- In pairs, students look at tapescript 2.32 on page 144 of the Student's Book. They must find and underline all the examples of *take* + noun(s).

… taking Herb and Hannah to the police station.
… took their money and passports.
… take a taxi
… take the underground
… take the black line …
Take the Northern Line …
… takes around 40 minutes.
… take that taxi …
… took the wrong train.
… take a bus.
… take photographs.
… takes 15 minutes …
… take an umbrella!

3
- Students complete Rob's diary with words from the box. Let students check their answers in pairs.

> 1   a taxi
> 2   a photograph
> 3   twenty minutes
> 4   a sandwich
> 5   her camera

4
- Pairwork. Tell students to close their eyes and think of the last journey they went on. Ask the questions in open class, while the students imagine the journey. Tell students not to speak – they just listen to you asking the questions.
- Put students in pairs to ask and answer the questions and describe their journey. Monitor and help if necessary.

SPEAKING

1

❯ *Key Methodology 8: Spoken errors – fluency tasks 1, page 28*

- Groupwork. Divide students into two groups, Group A and Group B. Give each group a minute or so to talk together and think of things to do during their free week.
- Students from Group A then make suggestions, and students from Group B respond.
- Listen and note errors. In feedback, write errors on the board for students to correct as a class.

Extra task for stronger classes

- It is a good idea to collect a pile of leaflets advertising local museums, attractions and events from the tourist information office in your city. Or perhaps there are some in your school.
- Divide students into groups of four to six. Hand out a pile of leaflets to each group. Tell them they must look at the leaflets, and decide where they would like to go this weekend.
- Once students have decided individually where they would like to go, tell them to make suggestions to their group. They must discuss and ask questions and decide where they are all going to go together at the weekend.

Web research tasks

❯ *Methodology guidelines: Web research tasks, page xiii*

- Tell students in pairs or groups to plan a weekend in London. They must find a museum, a theatre show, and a historic monument that they want to visit.
- Students tell the rest of the class what their plans are.

Web search key words
- what's on/time out/theatre listings/London

IF YOU WANT SOMETHING EXTRA ...

❯ *Photocopiable activity, page 224*
❯ *Teacher's notes, page 182*

Answer key

8 REVIEW

❯ Student's Book page 154

1

1 airports
2 cars
3 motorbikes
4 railway stations
5 planes

2

1 take
2 travelling
3 drive
4 waiting
5 standing

3

1 b   2 a   3 a   4 a   5 a   6 b

4

1, 9, 6, 2, 4, 5, 7, 3, 8

5

1 loves watching
2 loves eating
3 hates flying
4 loves playing

6

Possible answers:
1 A girl is running.
2 A man and woman are kissing.
3 A dog and cat are running.
4 A man and a woman are driving sports cars.
5 A boy is eating a hot dog.
6 A cook is waiting for some customers.

8 WRITING

❯ Workbook page 79

Model answer
Hi Harry,

Let's go out tonight. We could go to a football match at the stadium. It starts at 8 o'clock. Why don't we meet for a drink in the bar opposite the stadium at 7 o'clock?

Call me.

John

9A | A good impression

WHAT THE LESSON IS ABOUT

Theme	Making a good impression
Speaking	Pairwork discussion: talking about what you notice when you meet someone for the first time
	Pairwork discussion: giving advice on making a good impressions
Reading	*www.a good impression.com*: a website about first impressions
Vocabulary	Clothes
Grammar	*Should/shouldn't*
Pronunciation	Final *-e*

IF YOU WANT A LEAD-IN ...

Introducing the theme: making a good impression

- Put students into pairs and give each pairs three pictures of different people. Tell them that they must describe the people and decide which person they will employ in their family company and why. Tell them to discuss their physical appearance and clothes.

Discussion starters

❯ *Methodology guidelines: Discussion starters, page xii*

- *When is it important to make a good impression?*
- *What do you do to make a good impression:*
  a) at a job interview?
  b) on a date?

SPEAKING

1
- Model the activity first by saying what you notice first about a person. Then give students a minute to put the qualities in order.

2
- Pairwork. Put students in pairs to compare and discuss their lists.

Alternative procedure

- You could put students in groups to discuss and agree on a group order. Elicit the list and write it on the board.

VOCABULARY: clothes

❯ *Language reference, Student's Book page 101*

1 & 2 💿 2.35
- Students match the pictures A–M with the words in the box.
- Students then listen to the recording and check their answers. Then pause the recording after each word for students to repeat.

See tapescript below for answers.

💿 **2.35**

A	T-shirt
B	jeans
C	shoes
D	jumper
E	shirt
F	boots
G	trousers
H	dress
I	trainers
J	tie
K	sock
L	jacket
M	skirt

Language notes

- You may want to introduce the word 'top', used as a generic term to describe anything from a T-shirt to a pullover worn on the upper part of the body.
- A **blouse** is a buttoned up shirt worn by women.
  A **jersey** is also called a *pullover* or a *jumper*.
- There are some difficult vowel sounds to focus on here, notably the long /ɜː/ in *skirt* and *shirt*, the long /ɔː/ in *shorts*, the /uː/ in *suit*, and the /au/ in *blouse* /blauz/.

3
- Students complete the sentences so that they are true for themselves. Monitor and help if necessary.
- You could then put students in pairs to tell each other their sentences.
- Then, in feedback, ask individual students to tell the class what their partner told them.

Extra tasks

1
- Play a guessing game. Divide the class into groups of four. Each student must describe the clothes of somebody in the class, i.e. not in their group.
- The other students in the group must guess who they are describing.

2
- Have a class fashion show. Divide the class into groups of four. They must write a script which describes what each person in their group is wearing.
- They choose one person to read the script. The other students take it in turns to walk up and down the class as if they are on a catwalk, e.g. Juan walks on the catwalk, whilst his group mate says, *Juan is wearing a green jersey and black trousers ...*

READING

> *Methodology 23: Reading skills & strategies, page 94*

This reading text is a webpage giving people advice on what you need to do to make a good impression the first time you meet someone. It advises people on the importance of eye contact; clothes; body language and cultural awareness.

1
- Ask students to look at the web address and ask them what they think the webpage is about.
- Students read the webpage and check their predictions.

It is about how to make a good impression when meeting someone for the first time.

2
- Students read the text again and answer the questions. They can compare their answers with a partner before you check with the whole class.

1 Visual; vocal; verbal.
2 Visual.
3 David Hill; Gill Launders; Peter Cranford.
4 Emma Lowry; Jennifer Dawson.
5 Michael Dobbs; Jennifer Dawson.

Extra task
- Divide students into groups of four. Tell them to design and write an advice leaflet for people going for their first job interview. They must choose six dos and don'ts and then write them, bulleted, in leaflet form.
- You could then stick the leaflets around the classroom walls for students to read.
  Useful language:
  Always …
  Never …
  The worst thing you can do is …

3
- Students first work on their own to tick the sentences in the webpage that they agree with.
- Pairwork. Students work in pairs to compare their sentences.

PRONUNCIATION: final -*e*

> *Key Methodology 28: pronunciation – phonemes, page 124*

1 🔘 **2.36**
- Play the recording. Students listen to the pronunciation of the words.
- Then read the rule as a class.

🔘 **2.36**

/eɪ/: make
/aɪ/: rice
/eɪ/: ate
/əʊ/: phone

2 & 3 🔘 **2.37**
- Ask students to pronounce the underlined letter in each word.
- Play the recording. Students listen and check their answers.
- Play the recording again. Students listen and repeat the words.

smile /aɪ/
clothes /əʊ/
face /eɪ/
time /aɪ/
smoke /əʊ/
take /eɪ/
fine /aɪ/
phrase /eɪ/
arrive /aɪ/
wine /aɪ/
cake /eɪ/
nice /aɪ/

🔘 **2.37**

smile
clothes
face
time
smoke
take
fine
phrase
arrive
wine
cake
nice

Extra task
- You could get students to categorize the words under phonetic symbol headings. Then add other words to each category. For example:

/eɪ/	/aɪ/	/əʊ/
face	wine	clothes
take	nice	smoke
phrase	smile	
cake	time	
	fine	
	arrive	

- In English, we don't pronounce the letter *-e* at the end of words. However, by adding an *-e* after a word that ends consonant-vowel-consonant, it changes the sound of the vowel. For example:
  - *Tim* /tim/ ➡ *time* /taɪm/
  - *rat* /ræt/ ➡ *rate* /reɪt/
- As always, there are plenty of exceptions to this rule: *some*, *have*, etc.

GRAMMAR: *should/shouldn't*

◉ *Language reference, Student's Book page 100*
◉ *Methodology guidelines: Grammar boxes, page xiii*

1
- Students rewrite the sentences using the word in brackets.

> 2 They shouldn't talk loudly.
> 3 Should I listen to the other person?
> 4 Should he do something?
> 5 She shouldn't wear smart clothes.
> 6 You shouldn't ask the teacher.
> 7 You should talk in English.

Language notes
- We use the modal verb ***should/shouldn't*** + verb to give advice about something.
- In terms of form, watch out for students inserting an unnecessary *to*: ✗ *You should to wear ...*
  N.B. *shouldn't* is almost always used in its abbreviated form.
- In terms of pronunciation, you may need to drill the difficult /ʊ/ and /e/ sounds in these words: /ʃʊd/, /ʃʊdənt/.

2

◉ *Key Methodology 25: Giving extra practice – instant roleplays, page 105*
- Students match the questions and answers. They can compare their answers with a partner before you check with the whole class.
- You could then put students in pairs to ask and answer the questions.

> 1 b   2 a   3 e   4 d   5 c

SPEAKING

1
- Give students a minute or two to read the instructions and think what their answers to the questions in *Grammar* exercise 2 might be.

2
- Pairwork. Put students in pairs to tell each other what they would say.
- You could put students in male/female pairs to roleplay the interview. Student A asks the questions in exercise 2. Student B responds with their own ideas.
- For more mature students, they could talk about husband/wife's parents or a new boss instead of parents.

IF YOU WANT SOMETHING EXTRA ...

◉ *Photocopiable activity, page 225*
◉ *Teacher's notes, page 183*

9B | Body moving

WHAT THE LESSON IS ABOUT

Theme	Exercising the body at work
Speaking	Pairwork discussion: answering a health survey about exercising the body Pairwork: giving instructions for a stretching exercise
Reading	*Health – Are you sitting comfortably?*: a magazine article about health and giving advice for people who have to sit for a long time at work
Listening	Exercise instructions
Vocabulary	Body
Grammar	Imperatives

IF YOU WANT A LEAD-IN …

Introducing the theme: exercising the body

- Tell students to stand up. Then give them a series of instructions. Every time you give one of the instructions, mime it, and give students time to do the action.

  Stretch your arms above your head.
  Shake your left leg.
  Shake your right leg.
  Move your left shoulder.
  Move your right shoulder.
  Walk round in a small circle.
  Move your neck to the left – now to the right.
  Now sit down.

- Ask students: *Do you feel good now? Is it a good idea to move about when you are working or studying?*

SPEAKING & READING

1

- Pairwork. Model the activity by asking three or four of the questions at random to students in the class. Then put students in pairs to ask and answer the questions.
- Have a class feedback. Get students to tell the class about their partners. Find out how many students said *yes* to more than two questions.

2

- You could put students in pairs to predict what the article is about.

Extra task

- You could pre-teach key vocabulary by writing the following phrases on the board, and asking students which ones they expect to find in the article.

  a comfortable chair   keep your back straight
  go on holiday   stretch your arms
  take frequent breaks   eat chocolate

3

- Students read the rest of the article and check their predictions in exercise 2.

  3   Problems and advice for people who sit for a long time.

4

- Students read the article again and put the phrases in the correct place. They can compare their answers with a partner before you check with the whole class.

  1 d   2 a   3 b   4 c

5

- You could put students in pairs or small groups to discuss the things in exercise 4.

VOCABULARY: body

> *Language reference, Student's Book page 101*

1

- Students find and underline seven words in the article connected to the body. They can compare their answers with a partner before you check with the whole class.

  back; arms; neck (line 5)
  wrists (line 6)
  back (line 14)
  feet (line 15)
  arms; hands (line 34)
  shoulders (line 35)

2

- Students match the body parts with the words in the box. They can compare their answers with a partner before you check with the whole class.

  A   eyes
  B   chest
  C   fingers
  D   knee
  E   hand
  F   wrist
  G   arm
  H   elbow
  I   leg
  J   head
  K   neck
  L   shoulder
  M   back
  N   stomach
  O   foot/feet

3 🌐 2.38

- Play the recording. Students listen and tick the words they hear.
- Play the recording again. Students listen and repeat the body parts.

  The following words should be ticked:
  foot; stomach; leg; wrist; knee; back; hand; elbow; fingers; shoulders; head; eyes

🔴 **2.38**

---
1 My foot!
2 My stomach!
3 My leg!
4 I think, I think it's my wrist.
5 My knee!
6 My back!
7 Take my hand!
8 That's my elbow.
9 My fingers, so cold, my fingers.
10 That's right. On the shoulders.
11 Use your head!
12 Look at her eyes.

Language notes

- Interestingly, body parts are an area where English spelling bears little resemblance to its pronunciation. Point out the silent letters in *knee* and *wrist*, and the difficult pronunciations of *shoulder* /ʃəʊldə/, *elbow* /elbəʊ/, and *stomach* /stʊmæk/.

4

- In this game, you give instructions to the students prefixed with *Simon says*. Students must immediately obey the instruction. However, if you give an instruction without saying *Simon says*, students must disobey it. Any student who obeys an instruction without the prefix *Simon says* is *out*. Keep playing until there is only one student left – the winner!
- Here is an example game.
    Teacher: *Simon says stand up.* (all students stand)
    Teacher: *Simon says stretch your arms.* (all students stretch)
    Teacher: *Now sit down.* (two students sit down – they are out)
- Continue the game with the rest of the class.
- You could use the opportunity here to review prepositions (*behind*, *above*, etc.). You could also pre-teach some useful verbs: *stretch*, *hold* and *bend*, for example.

GRAMMAR: imperatives

❯ *Language reference, Student's Book page 100*
❯ *Methodology guidelines: Grammar boxes, page xiii*

1

- Students find and underline all the verbs in the imperative in the text on page 94.

---
(1) <u>Sit</u> correctly; <u>Keep</u> your back straight …
(2) <u>Take</u> breaks often; <u>Don't sit</u> …; <u>Stand</u> up and <u>walk</u> around.
(3) <u>Drink</u> water; <u>Don't drink</u> lots of coffee or tea.
(4) <u>Move</u> your body; <u>Stretch</u> your arms …; <u>Don't stretch</u> …

2

- You could put students in pairs to make sentences for each picture, using the verbs and phrases in the box in the imperative.
- In feedback, ask a student from one pair to read out an instruction. The rest of the class must point to the correct picture.

A Don't smoke.
B Don't take photos
C Don't walk
D Don't speak
E Walk
F Turn right
G Drive slowly

Alternative procedure for weaker classes

- This works well with flashcards. Copy road signs onto flashcards then show them in class, eliciting accurate sentences from students round the class.

Language notes

- As the imperative form of the verb in English is the same as the infinitive, it is quite a straightforward thing for students to grasp. Be aware, however, that in most languages the imperative is a different form to the infinitive, which may cause some confusion.

SPEAKING

1 **2.39**

- Ask students to look at the picture and listen to the instructions on the recording for the exercise.

🔴 **2.39**

Stand up. Move your fingers. At the same time you're moving your fingers, move your arms. Now move your shoulders and arms. Stop moving your arms. Move one leg and then the other leg. Sit down again.
---

2 🔴 **2.39**

- Students listen again, follow the instructions, and do the stretches in class.
- Alternatively, get students to read out instructions from tapescript 2.39 on page 144 to their partner, who must listen and act on the instructions.

3

❯ *Communication activites, Student's Book pages 133 & 135*

- Put students in A and B pairs. Student A looks at page 133 and Student B looks at page 135. Give students three or four minutes to think about and write instructions. Monitor and help with ideas and vocabulary.
- Tell students to sit face to face and take it in turns to instruct each other in how to do their exercise.
- They then describe other exercises they know to their partner.

Extra task

- Put students in pairs to think up and write a short exercise routine, using language from the lesson. Ask a pair to come to the front of the class. They must read out their instructions. The rest of the class must do the routine.

IF YOU WANT SOMETHING EXTRA ...

❯ *Photocopiable activity, page 226*
❯ *Teacher's notes, page 183*

9c | Never forget a face

WHAT THE LESSON IS ABOUT

Theme	Describing faces
Speaking	Pairwork discussion: talking about what you can & what you can't remember
	Pairwork – game: doing a memory test
Listening	A radio interview about how people remember faces
Vocabulary	Face
Grammar	*Whose* & possessive pronouns
Pronunciation	The sound /h/
Did you know?	*Faces on coins*: information about coins

IF YOU WANT A LEAD-IN …

Introducing the theme: describing faces

- Draw a large oval on the board. Ask students to copy it onto a piece of paper. Tell them to draw it as large as they can. Tell the class that someone broke into the school yesterday, and the police are looking for him/her. Then give a detailed description. For example:
  He has big, blue eyes, and long, dark hair. He has a big mouth and bad teeth. He has an earring in his right ear. He has a wide nose and a long chin. He's wearing glasses and he has a beard.
- Students listen to the description and draw the person's face on their piece of paper.
- At the end, they compare their drawing with those of other students in the class.

Test before you teach: whose

❯ *Methodology guidelines: Test before you teach, page xiii*

- Find two magazine pictures of interesting-looking people. Put them on the board. Give the people names, and write them on the board. Then ask a few questions, e.g. *Who's got glasses? Whose eyes are green? Whose face is long?*
- Take the pictures off the board. Students in pairs must describe one of the pictures. Their partner must guess which one.

SPEAKING

1

- Pre-teach *remember, forget* and *memory*. You could do this by eliciting the words. Say: *What's the opposite of remember?* (forget) *What's the noun from remember?* (memory).
- Ask students to read the sentences and tick the ones that are true for themselves.

2

- Students change the sentences in exercise 1 so that they are true for themselves. Do the first as an example.
- You could then put students in pairs to compare their opinions.
- This is an opportunity to revise language from earlier in the Student's Book. Students should be changing *can* to *can't* and using a range of frequency adverbs, *rarely, sometimes,* etc.

VOCABULARY: face

❯ *Language reference, Student's Book page 101*

1

- Students match the words to the parts of the picture. They can compare their answers with a partner before you check with the whole class.

A	hair
B	nose
C	ear
D	mouth
E	chin
F	tooth (plural teeth)
G	cheek
H	eye

2 🔘 2.40

- Play the recording. Students listen and touch the parts of the face that they hear.
- Play the recording again. Students listen and repeat the words.

🔘 2.40

1	Touch your nose.
2	Touch your hair.
3	Touch your chin.
4	Touch your eyes.
5	Touch your ears.
6	Touch your teeth.
7	Touch your cheeks.
8	Touch your mouth.

Extra task

- Students play *Simon says…* again, (see 9B *Vocabulary* exercise 4). This time they do it in groups of five. One person is Simon. The rest must follow instructions until there is a winner.
- Useful language: possible instructions
  Open/close your eyes/mouth.
  Touch your chin/mouth/hair.
  Touch your left/right cheek/ear.
  Brush your teeth.
  Hold your nose.
  Pull your hair.

Language notes

- These body parts have difficult pronunciations. Notably the consonant cluster /tʃ/ in *chin* and *cheeks*. And the unvoiced /θ/ sound at the end of *mouth* and *tooth*. *Ear* is pronounced as a diphthong, /ɪə/, and the *r* is silent.
- The plural of *tooth* is *teeth*.
- *Hair* is uncountable: *I have some hair on my head*, not *a hair*; *My hair is …*, not *My hairs are …*

LISTENING

This listening is a radio interview with an expert on the human memory, who talks specifically about how we remember faces.

1 & 2 2.41

- Pre-teach key vocabulary before listening. Teach 'top part of the face' and 'bottom part of the face' by pointing to them on your face.
- Pairwork. Put students in pairs to describe the pictures to each other.
- In feedback, ask what was strange about the photos but don't confirm answers yet.
- Play the recording. Students listen and say what is wrong with the pictures.

> All the boys have the same face but different hair styles. The Mona Lisa has an Elvis hair.

 2.41

> **I = interviewer D = David**
> **I:** Good afternoon. In the studio with us today we have David Barker. David works for the Exploratorium Museum in San Francisco, and is going to talk to us about memory and the human face. Hello, David.
> **D:** Hello.
> **I:** Now, my memory isn't very good. How's yours?
> **D:** It's OK.
> **I:** There's an expression in English, 'I never forget a face.' Is that true for you?
> **D:** Well, it depends really. I'm interested in how we remember a human face. Many experts now believe that the top part of the face is more important than the bottom part.
> **I:** What do you mean?
> **D:** OK. For example, look at this picture.
> **I:** This one here, with all the boys?
> **D:** Yes. What do you notice about it?
> **I:** I think this is an old picture. They're young, on a sports team. That's all.
> **D:** Interesting. Because in this picture, if you look closely, all the boys have exactly the same face.
> **I:** Really?! Oh, yes, you're right!
> **D:** Hair is very important for memory. In fact, hair is the most important factor, then the eyes, then the nose.
> **I:** This is the top part of the face.
> **D:** Yes, the bottom part of the face, the mouth and err … chin are not so important. Look at this photo.
> **I:** It looks very funny!
> **D:** Yes. It's a combination of two faces, but with different hair again. Whose face is it, do you think?
> **I:** Hmmm … very difficult. Is that … is that the Mona Lisa's face?
> **D:** Yes, it's hers.
> **I:** Why is this difficult?
> **D:** Because we've put Elvis' hair on her face.
> **I:** Whose hair is it?
> **D:** Elvis. The King of Rock and Roll.
> **W:** Oh, yes. Now I can see it.
> **D:** Yes. So you see how the hair makes it difficult. This is why famous people wear hats when they don't want people to know who they are.
> **W:** They also wear sunglasses.
> **D:** Yes, that's right.

● Key Methodology 28: Pronunciation – phonemes, page 124

Cultural notes

- The **Mona Lisa** (also called *La Gioconda*) was painted by Leonardo da Vinci in 1503–1506 and hangs in the Louvre Museum in Paris. People throughout the centuries have been fascinated by her image, and there have been many copies and adaptations of the painting, one of the most notable being when Marcel Duchamp added a small beard and moustache to his version of the Mona Lisa in 1919.

3 & 4 ● 2.41

- Play the recording again. Students listen and answer the questions. They then check their answers with tapescript 2.41 on page 1.45 of the Student's Book.

> 1   The woman.
> 2   The top of the face.
> 3   All the boys have exactly the same face.
> 4   The Mona Lisa.
> 5   Elvis Presley's.
> 6   They wear hats and sunglasses when they don't want people to know who they are.

PRONUNCIATION: /h/

1 ● 2.42

- Give students a minute to look at the words in the box. Ask them to think how they might be pronounced.
- Play the recording. Students listen and tick the words that begin with a /h/ sound.
- Play the recording again. Students listen and repeat.

> *All words all begin with a /h/ sound:*
> All the words begin with a /h/ sound apart from *what*

● **2.42**

> house
> hot
> hospital
> what
> whose
> hair
> happy
> have
> his
> has
> hamburgers
> who
> her
> hour

Extra task

- If /h/ is a difficult sound for your students to articulate, then show them how to make it, and give them some practice. Tell them, and show them, that the aspirated /h/ in English is not a hard sound but a breathy sound, like a dog panting! Get them to hold their hand or a piece of paper in front of their mouth, and make the breathy /h/ sound. The paper should move, but only slightly.

Language notes

- Confusingly, with *what* and *where*, the *h* is silent and the *w* is pronounced. But with *who* and *whose*, the *w* is silent and the *h* is pronounced. It is a good idea to drill these words from the spoken prompt, and get students familiar with using them without reading them.
- A minority of words in English have a silent *h*, e.g. *hour, honour, heir*. They tend to be words imported from French.
  N.B. *hotel* may be pronounced with a silent *h*, following the French, but this is an old-fashioned use nowadays.

2 & 3 **2.43**

- Students complete the sentences with words from exercise 1. They can then compare their answers with a partner.
- Play the recording. Students listen and check their answers.

See underlined answers in the tapescript below.

🔘 **2.43**

1	Helen and Harry work in a <u>hospital</u>.
2	They <u>have</u> lunch together every day.
3	He has <u>hamburgers</u> and she has <u>hot</u> soup.
4	Helen's <u>happy</u> with Harry.
5	But Helen <u>has</u> a problem.
6	She hardly ever remembers <u>his</u> name.

4 🔘 **2.43**

- Play the recording again for students to listen and repeat.

> ▣ **Key Methodology 28**
> ▣ **Pronunciation – phonemes**
>
> - *Individual sounds are called phonemes. Learners with the same mother tongue will tend to have similar successes or difficulties in pronouncing certain phonemes. Depending on the phonemes present in the mother tongue, an English sound such as /h/ may seem either very simple to your class, or rather strange and difficult. The phoneme may be virtually identical to one they use, or be different but similar enough that they can get by with using their own phoneme, or it may have no close equivalent in the mother tongue, in which case it will require some careful work. When using this coursebook, you will need to decide which sounds deserve more attention from your class, and which ones you can safely study and then move on.*
> - *Popular ways to help students make phonemes well include: clearly modelling and showing the lip shape and tongue position. Another way is to use a stretching gesture to show that a vowel sound is long; or a knife-chop gesture (i.e. cutting the air quickly with your hand) to show that it is short. You could get students to notice the difference between voiced and unvoiced consonants by getting them to place a finger at their throats and feel the difference between buzz and no buzz.*

- *Many teachers find that a phonemic chart on the classroom wall is an invaluable tool for work on pronunciation. This is a poster showing all the phonemes used in a particular accent of a language, e.g. South-east UK English (so-called RP). You could make one yourself on A3 paper. Lesson by lesson, introduce new phonemes to the students using the chart as a visual aid. Use it to show the pronunciation of new words (by tapping on the sounds one by one). Use it to indicate or correct problems (by tapping on the wrong sound – or its correction). Play games by getting students to point at words (or sentences) which others must interpret.*
- *Don't be worried if there are few instant breakthroughs in work on sounds. Remember that with most pronunciation work, recognition and awareness will precede production – often by a fairly long time. This means that students won't necessarily be able to produce new sounds the first times they hear them. They first need some time to recognize that there is a sound that needs working on. They will probably need many chances to hear it, and to be helped in noticing what features it has and how it is produced.*
- *Most usefully, if you aren't comfortable with phonemic transcription yourself, it's really worth investing a little time and energy into learning it. It's just so useful in teaching!*

> ❯ *For more work on phonemes see Key Methodology 31: Dictionaries 2, page oo.*

GRAMMAR: *whose* & possessive pronouns

❯ *Language reference, Student's Book page 100*
❯ *Methodology guidelines: Grammar boxes, page xiii*

1

- Students rewrite the sentences using possessive pronouns. They can compare their answers with a partner before you check with the whole class.

2	They're hers.
3	It's mine.
4	Here's yours.
5	Is this ours?
6	It isn't theirs.
7	Where's yours?
8	That's his

Extra task

- You could easily turn exercise 1 into a prompt drill. Feedback on the exercise by reading out each sentence, and getting students to say: *It's his, They're hers*, etc. Then improvise more sentences, or use the ones below. Ask individuals to respond with the appropriate pronoun.
- Possible prompts:
  It's her house.
  Where are their pens?
  It's our party.
  There's my dog.
  It's your T-shirt.

2
- Students underline the correct word. They can compare their answers with a partner before you check with the whole class.

1	hers
2	theirs
3	her
4	Who's
5	Whose
6	yours

Language notes

- **Whose** is used to ask about possession. It means *Who does it belong to?* It can be used as a determiner followed by a noun, e.g. *Whose book is that?* or as a question pronoun without the noun, *Whose is that?*
- Problems include confusing *whose* with *who* or *who's*, and pronouncing the long /uː/ sound, /huːz/.
- It is easy for students to start confusing possessive adjectives and possessive pronouns, as the forms are only subtly different, e.g. ✗ *It's mine house*, and ✗ *They're yours books*, where students start to think that *yours* must be a plural form. Students need plenty of practice with transformation exercises.

SPEAKING

> *Communication activites, Student's Book page 134*

1
- Ask students to tell you what the objects are in the pictures. Model and repeat words for pronunciation.
- Give students one minute to memorize the people and which objects belong to them.
- Put students in A and B pairs. Model the dialogue below with a good student, while pointing to the objects then the people.

  Whose dog is this?
  It's theirs.
  Whose sunglasses are these?
  They're his.

- Tell students to turn to page 134. They ask and answer questions with their partner to say which objects belong to which person, pointing to the objects and their owners as they do so.
- In feedback, find out who has the better memory in each pair.

DID YOU KNOW?

1 & 2
- Students read the information about coins.
- Students then discuss the questions in pairs.

Cultural notes

- Although independent countries, Australia, Belize, Canada, Fiji, and New Zealand are members of the British Commonwealth and recognize Queen Elizabeth II as their ceremonial head of state, (even though she rarely visits).
- Although self-governing, **Bermuda** is still a colony. It is an island in the North Atlantic.
- **Belize** is in central America, near Guatemala.
- **Fiji** consists of two islands in the south-west Pacific.
- **Hong Kong**, on the south-east coast of China, was a British colony from 1842 until 1997.

Web research tasks

> *Methodology guidelines: Web research tasks, page xiii*

1
- Students could research other members of the British Commonwealth on the web.

Web search key words
- Britain/commonwealth/members

2
- Students could find out what is on the 'tails' side of euros, US coins, or coins of other countries.

Web search key words
- US coins/euros

IF YOU WANT SOMETHING EXTRA ...

> *Photocopiable activity, page 227*
> *Teacher's notes, page 183*

9D | Not feeling well

WHAT THE LESSON IS ABOUT

Theme	Feeling ill
Speaking	Pairwork roleplays: not feeling well. Roleplay between (1) employee/boss; (2) parent/child
Listening	Five conversations about feeling ill
Vocabulary	Health problems
Functional language	Asking & saying how you feel

IF YOU WANT A LEAD-IN ...

Introducing the theme: feeling ill

- Pretend you are ill. Cough, groan, hold your head and stomach. Try to get students to say something: *How are you? Are you OK? Are you ill?* It doesn't matter what. Respond by describing your ailments.
- Then ask students in the class how they are and get them to respond.
- Put them in pairs to ask each other how they feel.

VOCABULARY: health problems

❯ *Language reference, Student's Book page 101*

1

- Students match the pictures to the sentences. They can compare their answers with a partner before you check with the whole class.

1 B	2 C	3 D	4 A

2

❯ *Key Methodology 29: Pronunciation – don't avoid intonation!, page 126*

- Students complete the sentences with the words in the box. They can compare their answers with a partner before you check with the whole class.
- In feedback, if you have a monolingual class, ask students to say what the words mean in their language.
- Model and drill the words for pronunciation.

1	tired
2	sick
3	stomach
4	head
5	arm
6	toothache
7	a stomachache

Language notes

- **hurt** = verb; **pain** = noun; **ache** = a slight but repetitive pain
- Point out, *I'm/I feel* + adjective, and *I've got* + noun.
- Point out the pronunciation of **ache** /eik/, and particularly, *stomachache* /'stʌməkeik/.

■ Key Methodology 29
■ Pronunciation – don't avoid intonation!

- *Teachers often say that they are nervous about working on intonation. They feel under-informed and can't see any structured way of working on it. I think that intonation doesn't really deserve this fierce and mysterious reputation.*
- *As a basic teaching technique for intonation, all that you need to do is model a normal pronunciation yourself and ask students to copy it.*
- *When teachers model sentences for students, they often, in trying to be helpful, offer a very artificial model of how something is said, e.g. they slow things down, say each word separately, without linking or contractions, say many syllables with equal stress and use a much flatter-than-normal intonation. This is done through good motives, but actually achieves the opposite outcome as it doesn't help train students to hear or say real sentences in the real world.*
- *Don't read out sentences as dry, feelingless examples of dead language! When you plan to model a sentence for your class, think about how you'd actually say it in a real-life exchange, e.g. imagine a specific situation you might be in, rather than just saying a contextless sentence. So, for example, if I was modelling a sentence from Vocabulary 2 in lesson 9D: I'm ill, I've got a headache, etc., I might imagine telling these comments to my best friend just after I've arrived at work in the morning.*
- *Try as far as possible to say the sentence normally. Keep the natural intonation – or even exaggerate it a little. Make it sound like you are really feeling ill, or really have a headache.*
- *Use gestures and facial expressions to emphasize the meaning.*
- *When you ask students to repeat a sentence, don't allow them to say it in a flat way. Give them clear feedback that getting the words in the right order isn't enough. I often mimic a dull bah-bah-bah sound back to the class to show how they sound. Make students try it again (and again) until the music sounds good.*
- *Remember that grammar is not the only important thing in a student's sentences when they speak. In fact, getting the intonation right (or wrong) is a vital part of communicating (or not communicating) successfully. Your students need help and feedback on this.*

3

- Pairwork. Put students in pairs to discuss the questions.

LISTENING

In this episode of the listening story, it's the day after the Explore London tour visited the Bella Pizza restaurant (see Lesson 8D), and Valerie doesn't feel well. She has an upset stomach and a doctor calls to see how she is. He asks her what she ate for dinner last night and she tells him she had a spicy Mexican pizza at the restaurant. Herb realizes that he had the same pizza as her and suddenly feels ill.

1 **2.44**

- Ask students to look at the picture and tell you who the people are and say what they think they are talking about.
- Give students a minute to read through the statements.
- Play the recording. Students listen and tick the phrases they hear. They can compare their answers with a partner before you check with the whole class.

1	Are you alright?
2	I don't feel well.
3	I'm fine; is there a doctor here?
4	How's your stomach?
5	Are you OK?

2.44

D = Dave V = Valerie Ha = Hannah He = Herb
Dr = doctor

1
D:	Valerie, <u>are you alright</u>?
V:	Hi, Dave. I don't know, <u>I don't feel well</u>.
D:	Here, sit down. Sit down.
V:	Oh, OK.
D:	What's wrong?
V:	<u>I've got a headache.</u> I feel cold. Oh, and my stomach.
D:	Here, put on my jacket.
V:	Thank you.

2
Ha:	<u>What's the matter</u>, sweetie?
V:	I don't feel well.
Ha:	Oh, no.
V:	It's alright. <u>I'm fine</u>, really.
Ha:	Was it something you ate last night?
V:	I don't know. Maybe …
Ha:	Here, take off that jacket.
V:	OK.

3
V:	Oh, no.
He/Ha:	<u>What's wrong?</u>
V:	I think … I think I'm going to be sick.
Ha:	Do you want to go to the toilet?
V:	Yes, sorry.
He:	<u>What's wrong</u> with Valerie? Did she drink too much wine?
Ha:	<u>Is there a doctor here</u>? Somebody call a doctor!

4
V:	Hello. Are you a doctor?
Dr:	Yes, I am. How do you feel?
V:	I feel alright now, thanks.
Dr:	Good, good. Stand up. <u>How's your stomach?</u>
V:	Not very good, but better now.
Dr:	What did you eat for dinner last night?
V:	I had a pizza. A Mexican spicy pizza at Bella Pizza restaurant. Was that the problem?
Dr:	I'm sorry, but it probably was. Here, take two aspirin and lie down. You should sleep.
V:	Thank you, doctor.

5
Dr:	Is she alright, doctor?
Dr:	She'll be fine. … Did anyone else eat the Mexican spicy pizza yesterday?
He/Ha:/D:	No.
Ha:	Herb, didn't you …?
He:	Wait a minute. You're right. Oh …
D:	<u>Are you OK</u>, Herb?
He:	Oh, no. I don't think so. <u>I feel sick</u> …

Language notes

- **Put on** is the opposite of **take off**.
- **I feel ill** (British English) = **I feel sick** (US English). In British English, *I feel sick* means that you want to physically vomit.

2 **2.44**

- Play the recording again. Students listen and put the events in the correct order. They can compare their answers with a partner before you check with the whole class.

4, 5, 1, 6, 3, 2

3

- Students match the words in A to the words in B to make phrases. They can compare their answers with a partner before you check with the whole class.

1 d 2 e 3 a 4 c 5 b

FUNCTIONAL LANGUAGE: asking/saying how you feel

> *Language reference, Student's Book page 101*

1

- Students look at tapescript 2.44 on page 145 of the Student's Book, and find examples of the phrases in the box. They can then compare with a partner.

See phrases underlined in the tapescript on this page.

2

> *Key Methodology 29: Pronunciation – don't avoid intonation, page 126*

- Give students a moment to look at the pictures. Then model the activity briefly for the class. Ask: *What's the matter?* Make sure you use an exaggeratedly 'caring' intonation pattern, rising at the end. Then mime a problem, and respond, e.g. *I don't feel well. I've got a cold.*
- Pairwork. Put students in pairs to ask and answer from the picture prompts.

Extra task

- Put students in threes. Student A mimes a problem. Student B says, *What's the matter?* Student C says *He/she's got a headache*; *Her/His back hurts*, etc. Students change roles, and do it again.

3 & 4 **2.45**

> *Key Methodology 6: Dialogues 2, page 16*

- Students complete the dialogues using the words in the box. They can then compare their answers with a partner.
- Play the recording. Students listen and check their answers.
- Students then practise the dialogues with the whole class and then in pairs.

1
(1) are; (2) well; (3) matter; (4) got
2
(1) wrong ; (2) fine; (3) home; (4) I'm
3
(1) cold; (2) fine; (3) head

2.45

1
A: Hi, how <u>are</u> you?
B: Oh, I don't feel very <u>well</u>.
A: What's the <u>matter</u>?
B: I've <u>got</u> a headache.
A: You should lie down.
2
A: Are you alright? What's <u>wrong</u>?
B: I'm <u>fine</u>, thanks. I'm a little tired.
A: Do you want to go <u>home</u>?
B: No, <u>I'm</u> fine. Really.
3
A: Can I go out now?
B: No, you can't. You've got a <u>cold</u>.
A: I feel <u>fine</u>. My <u>head</u> doesn't hurt now.
B: You should stay in bed.

Roleplay

❯ *Key Methodology 8: Spoken errors – fluency tasks 1, page 28*

5
- Pairwork. Put students in A and B pairs. Ask them to read their roles in roleplay 1. Give them two or three minutes to think what they are going to say. Then ask them to act out the conversation. Monitor and make a note of any errors.
- Repeat the procedure with roleplay 2.
- In feedback, write any errors on the board, and ask students to correct them as a class.

Weaker classes

- With weaker classes, get the pairs to write their dialogues.
- You could then ask a few pairs to act out their dialogues for the class.

IF YOU WANT SOMETHING EXTRA …

❯ *Photocopiable activity, page 228*
❯ *Teacher's notes, page 184*

Answer key

9 REVIEW

❯ *Student's Book page 155*

1

| 1 A | 2 A | 3 B | 4 B | 5 B | 6 A | 7 A | 8 AB | 9 B | 10 B |

2

1 should say
2 shouldn't wear
3 should find out
4 should answer
5 shouldn't be
6 shouldn't smoke

3

Students' own answers.

4

1	A: yours	B: mine	
2	A: his	B: theirs	A: hers; his
3	B: mine	A: yours	
4	A: yours	B: mine; his	

5

1 What's <u>the</u> matter?
2 Thank you <u>very</u> much.
3 I've got <u>a</u> stomach ache. And I'm cold.
4 Here, put <u>on</u> my jacket.
5 Are <u>you</u> alright?
6 I don't know. I don't <u>feel</u> very well.

6

5, 6, 1, 3, 4, 2

9 WRITING

❯ *Workbook page 81*

Model answer
Dear Jason,

You should think about this carefully because first impressions are important. You shouldn't wear casual clothes like jeans or a T-shirt. You should wear smart clothes, maybe a suit and a tie.

Ashley

10A It's illegal

WHAT THE LESSON IS ABOUT

Theme	Laws
Speaking	Pairwork & groupwork discussion: inventing classroom laws
Reading	*Strange laws in American cities*: a magazine article about strange laws in the USA
Vocabulary	Places in a city
Grammar	*Must/mustn't/needn't*
Did you know?	*No Smoking*: an article about banning smoking in public places in Ireland

IF YOU WANT A LEAD-IN ...

Introducing the theme: laws

- Write three 'personal' laws on the board:

  My laws

  It's illegal to work on Monday morning.
  It's against the law to shout at cats.
  You mustn't wear T-shirts with 'messages' on them.

- Naturally, adapt the laws to make them personal. And check the vocabulary.
- Tell students to think of and write two or three personal laws. Let them tell their partner then the class.

Discussion starters

❯ *Methodology guidelines: Discussion starters, page xii*

- *What rules do you have at work/in college?*
- *Which rules do you like?*
- *Which are bad rules?*

VOCABULARY: places in a city

❯ *Language reference, Student's Book page 111*

1

- Students complete the sentences with a word from the box. They can compare their answers with a partner before you check with the whole class.

1	town hall
2	bank
3	shop
4	stadium
5	library

2

❯ *Key Methodology 30: Dictionaries 1 – using dictionaries effectively, page 130*

- Students write similar sentences for the places. They can then compare their sentences in pairs.
- In feedback, ask students to give you different sentences.

Extra task

- Students prepare their own sentences to describe the places in 1 and 2, replacing the name of the place with *It*. In pairs, students take it in turns to read out a description, e.g. *It is a place where you find books.* Their partner must guess the place.

▪ Key Methodology 30
▪ Dictionaries 1: using dicionaries effectively

- *For years, teachers have harangued their poor students to stop using small bilingual dictionaries and to buy a monolingual dictionary. Teachers prefer the latter because they contain a great deal of useful information about language items beyond a simple definition, e.g. pronunciation, collocations, example sentences, etc. Teachers are also aware that the simplicity of a direct translation can't convey the breadth of meaning and uses an item may have in the other language. Students, however, have often been reluctant to dump their bilingual dictionaries, finding the instant comfort of a translation into their own language quick and helpful.*
- *To some extent this argument may be sinking as the years move on, and more and better quality electronic dictionaries appear. The new handheld machines can often provide features from both translation and monolingual dictionaries, and even add new features such as audible pronunciation (admittedly often still in rather robotic voices) and instant thesauruses. Currently, they also seem to have surprising errors and oddities, e.g. archaic language given equal weight as current usage. These problems though, are likely to diminish as the years pass.*
- *Whichever dictionary students have, they need to be able to use it as effectively as possible. To do this students usually need some training including both introductory teaching and practice exercises.*
- *Some important areas to work on:*
  1 *Understanding abbreviations and entry conventions, e.g. [C] for countable noun [+ of] to show typical prepositional collocation pattern.*
  2 *Reading phonemic symbols to find out how a word is said, rather than just how it's spelt.*
  3 *Selecting the right meaning when there is a choice of different ones.*
  4 *Using grammar information to find plurals, past participles, etc.*
  5 *Using example sentences as a guide to create other new sentences.*
- *Students using printed dictionaries will also need to understand alphabetical order, especially finding items where the second or third letter determines the order, e.g. hole / home / hope.*

  N.B. the alphabet may be difficult not only for learners who use different script, e.g. Arabic speakers, Japanese, Russians, etc., but also for users of a Roman script that has a different set of letters or different sequence of letters, e.g. Hungarian, Czech, etc.

❯ *Key Methodology: Dictionaries 2: pronunciation, page 136.*

3

• Put students in pairs to discuss the signs.

> Possible answers:
> A shop; library; bank; town hall; school; hotel; hospital
> B bank
> C library; school; hospital
> D shop; hotel; hospital

READING

This magazine article is about a collection of some rather strange laws from different parts of the United States which two American students have researched and put on the internet.

1

❯ *Key Methodology 23: Reading skills & strategies, page 94*

• Students read the magazine article quickly and choose the best title.
• Remind students that they are reading for gist. They should not worry about words they don't know.

> 3 Strange laws in American cities.

2

• Students read the article again, and answer the questions. Let them discuss their answers in pairs.

> Possible answers:
> 1 Destin, Florida; Baldwin Park, California
> 2 Destin, Florida; Milford, Massachusetts; Baldwin Park, California; the state of Virginia
> 3 Destin, Florida; the state of Virginia; Walnut, California
> 4 Miami Beach, Florida; Cathedral City, California; Toledo, Ohio

Language notes

• **To get dressed** means to put clothes on.
• **To shout** is to say something in a loud voice.
• **Rude** is the opposite of polite.

3

• Pairwork. Put students in pairs to discuss the questions.

Extra task

• Give students three minutes to look back at the article, and memorize which law goes with which place.
• Divide students into groups of five. Student A is the quizmaster. Student B and C are team 1. Student D and E are team 2.
• The quizmaster asks team 1, e.g. *What's the law in Canton, Ohio?* The pair get a point if they can remember. If not, the other pair get a chance to answer.
• The quizmaster takes it in turns to ask each pair a question. The winner is the team with most points.

Web research task

❯ *Methodology guidelines: Web research tasks, page xiii*

• Get students to find more 'dumb laws' and make a note of the ones they like best.

Web search key words

• dumb/stupid/laws

GRAMMAR: *must / mustn't / needn't*

❯ *Language reference, Student's Book page 110*
❯ *Methodology guidelines: Grammar boxes, page xiii*

1

• Students rewrite the sentences using the words in brackets. They can compare their answers with a partner before you check with the whole class.

> 2 You must wear a tie.
> 3 You needn't have a permit to buy a dog.
> 4 He mustn't go now.
> 5 You must call the police.
> 6 The students needn't prepare the lesson.

Language notes

• **Must** is an obligation. **Mustn't** is a prohibition. **Needn't** expresses a lack of necessity. Be aware that *mustn't*, in some languages, may look like a form that expresses lack of obligation.
• As modal verbs, these forms are followed by a base form of the verb without *to*, (so watch out for errors like ✗, *You must to speak …*, etc.).
• *Must, mustn't* and *needn't* are rarely used in the question form, and as a result this is not taught here. However, be aware that the question is made by transposing, e.g. *Must I …? / Need I …?*, not by using *do*. So, watch out for errors like, ✗ *Do you must …?*
• The *t* in *must* is silent when it is followed by a verb that starts with a consonant: *You must go* /mʌsgeu/. The *t* in *mustn't* is always silent: /mʌsent/.
• Although it is too difficult for students to deal with here, note that *have to* has a similar meaning to *must*. In fact, they are often interchangeable. The rule is that we use *must* for personal obligations (*I must work harder at school*) and *have to* for obligations imposed from outside (*you have to complete this form*). So, if you say, *I must go*, it implies that the decision is yours, whereas *I have to go* implies that there is an 'outside' obligation. N.B. *mustn't* means not allowed, whereas *don't have to* means no obligation, and has a similar meaning to *needn't*. This can cause problems for students of some languages.

2

• Students complete the sentences with *must* or *mustn't* and a verb to make typical laws for each situation. They can compare their answers with a partner before you check with the whole class.

> **A library**
> 2 must have
> 3 must bring
> **A bus**
> 4 must pay
> 5 must buy
> 6 mustn't smoke

SPEAKING

1
- Pairwork. Put students in pairs. Ask them to read through the phrases. Deal with any vocabulary problems.
- Ask pairs to categorize the words. Have a class feedback.

> *Probable answers:*
> **For the students:** do the homework every day; speak in English all the time
> **For the teacher:** explain again if the students don't understand; speak quickly; correct the homework
> **For the teacher and students:** come to class late; turn off mobile phones in class; use the book in every lesson

2
- Ask pairs to take it in turns to make sentences with the phrases in exercise 1.
- Get students to say the phrases first to each other, then ask them to write three or four down, and add one of their own.

3
- Groupwork. Put pairs into groups of four to compare their classroom laws. Get them to write their five most important classroom laws.
- You could elicit lists and build up a class list on the board. Or you could collect the lists that students put together, pass them to other groups, and get them to discuss and adapt the rules.

Extra task

> ❯ *Key Methodology 22: Making a language-rich classroom, page 91*

- Once you have got a definitive class list of laws, copy them on to a large sheet of paper or card, and pin them to the class noticeboard. From now on there is no excuse for being late or answering a mobile!

DID YOU KNOW?

1 & 2
- Students read the article about smoking.
- Students then discuss the questions in pairs.

> ## Language notes
> - *quit* = stop
> - *To pass* a law means to officially approve of and make something a law.

IF YOU WANT SOMETHING EXTRA ...

> ❯ *Photocopiable activity, page 229*
> ❯ *Teacher's notes, page 184*

10B | Life in the capital

WHAT THE LESSON IS ABOUT

Theme	Capital cities
Speaking	Pairwork discussion: talking about living in the capital city
	Groupwork roleplay: advising people about moving to another city
Listening	Two people talking about life in the capital city of their country
Vocabulary	Describing a city
Grammar	Comparatives
Pronunciation	Word stress 4

IF YOU WANT A LEAD-IN ...

Introducing the theme: capital cities

- Write the names of ten countries on the board. Choose ten countries that students in your class are likely to know the capital of. If you have a multinational class from all over the world, choose countries to reflect this mix. Below is a mix, reflecting places mentioned in the unit:
  Spain Peru Greece Russia USA Germany China Japan Brazil Sweden
- Put students in groups of three. They have one minute to write down the capital city of each country. Have a class feedback, and find out who got most answers right.
  (Answers – capitals (in order): *Madrid; Lima; Athens; Moscow; Washington DC; Berlin; Beijing; Tokyo; Rio de Janeiro; Stockholm.*)
- Ask each group to write two sentences to describe one of the cities, e.g. *It is very hot in summer. The Acropolis is a famous monument in this city.* (Answer: *Greece.*)
- When they are ready, ask groups to read out their sentences without saying the name of the city. The rest of the class must guess which one is being described.
- If you have a mature, knowledgeable class, make it more challenging by having them guess the capitals of English-speaking countries:
  Canada (Ottawa); *Australia* (Canberra); *South Africa* (Pretoria); *Wales* (Cardiff); *Scotland* (Edinburgh); *New Zealand* (Wellington); *Ireland* (Dublin).

Test before you teach: comparisons

> *Methodology guidelines: Test before you teach, page xiii*

- Write the names of two well-known capitals on the board, e.g. *Paris* and *Mexico City*.
- Put students in pairs to think of five differences between the cities. Students tell the class what they thought of.
- Hopefully, this is an opportunity for students to use comparatives: *Paris is older, Mexico City is bigger*, etc.

SPEAKING

> *Key Methodology 7: Accurate speaking & fluent speaking, page 20*

1
- Model the activity briefly by asking the questions round the class.
- Pairwork. Put students in pairs to ask and answer the questions.

VOCABULARY: adjectives

> *Language reference, Student's Book page 111*

1

> *Key Methodology 30: Dictionaries 1 – using dictionaries effectively, page 130*

- Ask students what country is Rome the capital of and what they can see there, e.g. the Colosseum, the Roman Forum, the Pantheon, the Vatican museum, St Peter's Cathedral, etc.
- Ask students to read the questionnaire, and check the meaning of any words they don't understand in a dictionary.

Extra task
- Use mime to check the words, e.g. say: *Which word am I doing?* Then mime each word in turn:
  1 Mime *friendly* by smiling and pretending to meet and hug lots of people.
  2 Mime *dangerous* by creeping along looking worried.
  3 Mime *noisy* by covering your ears.
  4 Mime *polluted* by holding your nose.

2 🔊 2.46
- Play the recording. Students listen to a non-native speaker Giovanni, talking about living in his country's capital city Rome, and tick the answers *yes* or *no* in exercise 1. They can compare their answers with a partner before you check with the whole class.

1	Yes
2	Yes
3	Yes (in some areas)
4	Yes
5	Yes
6	Yes
7	Yes

🔊 2.46

> I = interviewer G = Giovanni
> I: So, tell me about Rome. Are the people friendly?
> G: Yes, they are. They're very friendly.
> I: Is it an expensive place?
> G: Yes, it is. That's the problem with life in the capital.
> I: Is it dangerous to walk on the streets at night?
> G: It depends where you are. In some areas yes, it can be dangerous.
> I: Can you visit interesting things in your city?
> G: Yes, you can. Of course! There are lots of museums, art galleries, monuments ...
> I: Is it very noisy?
> G: Yes, it is. Very noisy. Rome is famous for noise.
> I: Are there any beautiful or historical buildings?
> G: Of course. It has the most beautiful buildings in Europe. The Colosseum, for example. There's also the Vatican.
> I: Is the air polluted?
> G: Yes, it is. Unfortunately.

Culture notes

- **Rome** is the capital city of Italy. Its most famous building is the Colosseum, a huge amphitheatre that is 2,000 years old.
- **The Vatican City** is a state within Rome, and is dominated by the dome of St Peter's Cathedral. The Vatican includes the papal apartments where the Pope, the leader of the Roman Catholic Church, lives, and a museum which houses a huge collection of sculptures and paintings, as well as the Sistine Chapel, with its famous ceiling decorated with frescoes by Michelangelo.
- As a major city, Rome has some problems with crime (mostly from pickpockets and bag snatchers) – but no more than other comparable European cities.

3 & 4 2.47

- Students match the words in the box to their opposites in exercise 1. Play the recording again for students to check their answers.
- Play the recording again for students to repeat the words

See answers in the tapescript below.

2.47

```
safe – dangerous
boring – interesting
quiet – noisy
ugly – beautiful
clean – polluted
unfriendly – friendly
cheap – expensive
modern – historical
```

5

- Pairwork. Put students in pairs. Give students a few minutes to think about a city, town or village that they know well. They then interview each other about the place using the questions in the questionnaire in exercise 1.
- Students note answers then report their findings to the class in feedback.

Multilingual classes

- If you have a variety of languages and nationalities in your class, students could interview each other about the capital cities in their countries. They could do this as a mingle.
- In feedback, they could compare the cities they found out about.

LISTENING

In this listening, two people talk about their capital cities. The first speaker lives in Alicante and compares it with life in Madrid, and says that life in Alicante is much better. The second speaker comes from Athens and talks about the positive and negative things about living there compared with other cities in Greece.

1

> *Key Methodology 24: A few guidelines for listening, page 98*

- Put students in pairs to look at the pictures of different capital cities. Ask them how many capital cities can they recognize and what they can tell the class about the cities.
- In feedback, get students to tell each other about each of the cities.

```
Photo 1: Mexico city
Photo 2: Athens (Acropolis)
Photo 3: Madrid (Plaza del Sol)
Photo 4: Washington DC (the Capitol building)
Photo 5: Rome (Colosseum)
Photo 6: Paris (the river Seine and the Eiffel Tower)
```

Culture notes

- **The Palacio de Comunicaciones** (the Communications Palace) is the most impressive building in the Plaza de Cibeles, Madrid. It was built between 1905 and 1917 in the Neoclassical style and is often compared to a wedding cake. It is the main post office in Madrid. In the centre of the square is the fountain of Cibeles, one of the most important symbols of Madrid and a gathering point for local football fans to celebrate winning a match.
- **The Plaza del la Constitución** is the main square in the historic centre of Mexico City. It is the site of important national events and festivals. The church overlooking the square is the **Catedral Metropolitana**, which is one of the largest cathedrals in Latin America. It was begun in the 16th century and wasn't completed until 1813.
- **The Colosseum** was built between 70–82 AD. It is the greatest amphitheatre of the antiquity. After the fall of the Roman Empire, it was abandoned. It then became a source of building materials and an inspiration for artist in the Renaissance period. Today, it is a great tourist attraction, excavation site for archaeologists, and often used as a backdrop for events and shows.
- **The Eiffel Tower** was built by Gustave Eiffel for the International Exhibition of Paris in 1889, held to commemorate the centenary of the French Revolution. It is 300 metres high and was the tallest building in the world until 1930.
- **The Acropolis** ('high city') is 150 metres above sea level and the city of Athens. The most important temples were built between 460-430 BC. They are the Parthenon, the Erechtheion, and the Temple of Nike.
- In 1790, Washington was chosen as the permanent seat of government, as it was midway between the northern and southern states of America. Construction of **the Capitol** began in 1793, but there were delays, and it was set fire to by the British during the War of Independence. It was rebuilt in 1846.

2 🔊 2.48

- Play the recording. Students listen to Sofia and Nick talking about what living in their capital city is like. Ask students which capital cities they are talking about.

```
1   Sofia – Madrid, Spain
2   Nick – Athens, Greece
```

🔊 2.48

---
1 Sofia

Oh no, I don't live in the capital, Madrid. I live in Alicante with my husband and two sons. It's in the south of Spain, on the coast of the Mediterranean Sea. It's smaller than Madrid, but life is much better. Madrid is too big. In the summer, it's too hot, and in the winter, it's too cold. That's why people from Madrid come here. And there are a lot more children here – at least you see more families with two or three children. Life is more expensive in Madrid. Too expensive for many big families.

---

2 Nick

Life in the capital city, Athens, is faster than in other cities of Greece. I was born in Athens, I live in Athens, and it's true – life is very fast! Athens is noisier and dirtier – but it has more of everything: more money, opportunities, jobs, noise, pollution, entertainment … bigger and better stadiums and sports facilities …

Many Greeks say that people in Athens aren't very friendly, they don't have time for you. This isn't true. I know lots of very friendly people here in Athens.

3 🌐 **2.48**

- Play the recording again. Students listen and mark the sentences true or false. Ask students to try and explain why the false sentences are incorrect.

1 F (Sofia doesn't live in the capital – she lives in Alicante.)
2 T
3 T
4 T
5 F (He thinks it is nosier and dirtier than the other cities.)
6 T

GRAMMAR: comparatives

❯ *Language reference, Student's Book page 110*
❯ *Methodology guidelines: Grammar boxes, page xiii*

1

❯ *Key Methodology 14: Drilling 1 – basics, page 55*

- Students make the comparative form of the adjective. They can compare their answers with a partner before you check with the whole class.

cold – colder
bad – worse
small – smaller
interesting – more interesting
big – bigger
cosmopolitan – more cosmopolitan
friendly – friendlier
good – better
happy – happier
dangerous – more dangerous
safe – safer
polluted – more polluted

Language notes

- English forms comparatives in two ways: by adding *-er* to adjectives of one syllable, or two syllables when the second syllable ends in *-y*, and by putting *more* in front of adjectives of two syllables or more. Other languages (sensibly) choose one method or the other. The fact that English has two ways of expressing this concept makes it tricky. Watch out for students saying ✗ *more small* or ✗ *more smaller*, and ✗ *interestinger*.
- Forming comparatives can cause confusion as there are lots of minor exceptions to the add *-er* rule. Notably, *friendly - y + ier; safe + r; big + g + er. Good (better), bad (worse), far (farther or further)* are common exceptions.
- Students often confuse *than* with *that*: ✗ *It is bigger that …*

- Take time to practise the pronunciation in drills. The stress is on the things being compared and on the adjective. Consequently, *-er* and *than* are weakly stressed:
/ə/ /ə/
*Alicante is **smaller** than **Madrid**.*

2

- Have a brief lead-in. Ask students to tell you what the capital of Canada is and what other Canadian cities they know. Then ask: *What do you know about Canada?* Tell them to look back at Lesson 5B if they need reminding.
- Students complete the text. They must put the adjectives in brackets into the comparative form. They can compare their answers with a partner before you check with the whole class.

1 smaller
2 colder
3 more interesting
4 bigger
5 more cosmopolitan
6 friendlier
7 worse
8 safer

Cultural notes

- ***Ottawa*** /ˈɒtəwə/ has a population of about 300,000. It became Canada's capital in 1867.
- ***Toronto*** /təˈrɒntəʊ/ has a population of about 700,000.
- Both cities are in the state of Ontario in south-east Canada.

3

- Put students in pairs. Ask them to read the information carefully. Ask a few questions, e.g. *What's the population of New York? How many crimes are there in White Plains every year?*
- Students use the information to write sentences.

2 New York City is bigger than White Plains.
3 White Plains is cheaper than New York City.
4 New York City is more polluted than White Plains.
5 White Plains is safer than New York City.
6 New York City is closer to the capital than White Plains.

Extra task

Ask students to write sentences to compare two cities in their country.

Web research tasks

❯ *Methodology guidelines: Web research tasks, page xiii*

- Ask students to research statistics about their capital or about capitals in English-speaking countries.
- You could get students to choose two cities they are interested in, and find the information provided in exercise 3. They must report this information to the class in comparative sentences.

Web search key words
- statistics/information/population, crime, etc./name of cities

PRONUNCIATION: word stress 4

1 **2.49**

❯ *Key Methodology: Dictionaries 2 – pronunciation, page 136*

- Play the recording. Students listen to the words and count the syllables. They can compare their answers with a partner before you check with the whole class.

```
1  frien/dly – 2
2  cold – 1
3  pol/lu/ted – 3
4  ex/pen/sive – 3
5  noi/sy – 2
6  clean – 1
7  beau/ti/ful – 3
```

 2.49

```
1  friendly
2  cold
3  polluted
4  expensive
5  noisy
6  clean
7  beautiful
```

2 & 3 **2.49**

- Students mark the stress and say the words.
- Play the recording again for students to listen and check.
- You could then ask students to listen and repeat.

```
1  friĕn/dly
2  cŏld
3  pol/lŭ/ted
4  ex/pĕn/sive
5  nŏi/sy
6  clĕan
7  bĕau/ti/ful
```

Language notes

- The first *e* in *interesting* is usually not pronounced: /ɪntrestɪn/.

Key Methodology 31
Dictionaries 2: pronunciation

- *Here are some practical suggestions for helping students use pronunciation features of their dictionaries better.*

Phonemic symbols

- *You will of course need to introduce your students to phonemic symbols (see Key Methodology 28: Phonemes, page 124). Beyond this foundation knowledge, your students will probably need lots of practice in recognizing and using phonemic transcriptions in the dictionary. Some ideas:*
  1 *Ask students to look up and copy out phonemic transcriptions of words recently studied. Encourage students to start recording phonemes alongside all new words learnt.*

2 *Write a vowel phoneme on the board. Students must write down (without using a dictionary) ten different words they already know and understand that have this phoneme. When they have written the list, they check the dictionary to see if they were correct.*
3 *Write the spelling of some familiar words on the board, e.g.* language, translate, *etc. Students then work in pairs to decide what they think the phonemic transcription is. When finished, they check in the dictionary to see if they are correct.*
4 *Select some one-syllable words that have one of three different vowel sounds, e.g. Set 1:* soon / new / food; *Set 2:* could / wood / put; *Set 3:* up / love / country. *In class, write the three vowel phonemes (/uː/; /ʊ/; and /ʌ/) as column headings for three columns, and in a separate list write the words – but in a mixed-up order. Pairs should now sort out the words into three columns according to their vowel sound. You could ask them to do this without a dictionary (checking afterwards) or using a dictionary to do the task.*

Word stress

- *When teaching a new word, get in the habit of asking students 'How many syllables?'. Sometimes ask students to check in the dictionary to find where the stress(es) are before you tell them. Mark stress on new words you write on the board.*
- *Write up a selection of words students already know. Ask pairs to divide them up into lists of one, two, three and four syllable words – and mark the stress(es) in each word. Students check in the dictionary afterwards.*
- *Use circles or boxes to write up some stress patterns on the board, e.g. ooO Ooo oO Oo. Write a mixed-up list of words on the board, e.g.* other, finally, company, exchange, *etc., and ask students to match each word to one of the patterns (and check in the dictionary afterwards). Then ask students to think of three more words to fit each of these patterns (and check in the dictionary).*

SPEAKING

❯ *Communication activites, Student's Book pages 133, 138 & 135*

1

❯ *Key Methodology 7: Accurate speaking & fluent speaking, page 21*

- Divide students into groups of three, A, B and C. Ask each student to turn to their respective pages and read their role carefully. Give students two or three minutes to prepare what they are going to say.
- Students act out the roleplay. Monitor each group carefully, and note errors for a class feedback at the end.
- In feedback, ask Student A whose advice they are going to take.

2

- Students discuss in their groups then as a class.

IF YOU WANT SOMETHING EXTRA …

❯ *Photocopiable activity, page 230*
❯ *Teacher's notes, page 184*

10c | Best of the best

WHAT THE LESSON IS ABOUT

Theme	Things to do in a city: Cape Town
Speaking	Pairwork & groupwork discussion: talking about the best three things to see in your home town or city
	Pairwork: giving advice about what things to do and places to go in a city
Reading	*Best of the best – Cape Town*: an extract from a guide book about what's best in Cape Town
Vocabulary	*go* + verb + *ing*
Grammar	Superlatives

IF YOU WANT A LEAD-IN ...

Introducing the theme: things to do in a city

- Put students in pairs. Ask them to talk together and decide which city is the most interesting in the world. Once they have chosen their city, ask each pair to prepare reasons why, using the *Useful language* below.
- Pairs take it in turns to present their cities. At the end, have a class vote and choose the most interesting city.
- Useful language:
  We chose ... because ...
  You can see ...
  There are ...
  It is full of ...

SPEAKING

1
- Pairwork. Put students in pairs to make their list. If students come from different towns, tell them to work together but produce two separate lists, one for each town.

2
- Groupwork. Put pairs into groups of four to compare their list and decide which one is the most interesting.

READING

The reading text is an extract from a guide book for Cape Town. It gives suggestions on the best things to see and do in the city, plus the most expensive place to stay.

1

◉ *Key Methodology 10: Flashcards 1 – the essentials, page 37*

- Pairwork. Put students in pairs to make notes about Cape Town. Let them refer to the photos for ideas.
- In feedback, build up a list of facts and opinions on the board.

Extra task

- You could use this lead-in to pre-teach key words in the text.
- Tell students to keep their books closed and write these words up on the board.
  beach mountain landmark ocean shark
  jewellery souvenirs wine dance floor cable car
  diving sightseeing prison apartheid
- Ask students if they can name the city. Help them with any words that they don't understand.

Cultural notes

Apartheid was a system that existed in South Africa from the 1940s to the 1980s. It was basically a political system that separated people in the country according to race. It effectively meant that only white people had political power and wealth.

2

◉ *Key Methodology 23: Reading skills & strategies, page 94*

- Students read the extract from a guide book for Cape Town, and match the photographs A–C to the correct paragraph.
- They can compare their answers with a partner before you check with the whole class.

A 2	B 3	C 1

3
- Students put the sentences a–g back in the gaps 1–6 in the article.
- Help students do this activity in three stages. First, ask them to read the statements and say what they think they are about. Second, ask them to look at the paragraph headings, and guess which sentence goes where. Third, ask them to look at the 'gap' in the text and check their answers.

1 b	2 a	3 f	4 e	5 c	6 d

4
- Pairwork. Put students in pairs to decide which places they would like to visit.
- Have a class feedback. Find out which places are the most popular.

Web research tasks

◉ *Methodology guidelines: Web research tasks, page xiii*

- You could ask students to find out more information about Cape Town. They could choose one of the following categories to research: 'Nelson Mandela and Robben Island'; 'Places to stay in Cape Town';'Table Mountain'; 'shopping at the Victoria & Albert waterfront'; 'Adventure holidays', and present their information to the rest of the class.

Web search key words
- Cape Town/visitor information/places to visit

VOCABULARY: *go* + verb + *-ing*

◉ *Language reference, Student's Book page 111*

1
- Use mime to check the *-ing* words in column A.
- Students match the sentence halves in column A with those in column B to make sentences. They can compare their answers with a partner before you check with the whole class.

1 f	2 b	3 d	4 a	5 c	6 e

2
- Pairwork. Put students in pairs to discuss the questions.

GRAMMAR: superlatives

⟩ *Language reference, Student's Book page 110*
⟩ *Methodology guidelines: Grammar boxes, page xiii*

1
* Students underline all the superlatives in the text on page 106 of the Student's Book. They can compare their answers with a partner before you check with the whole class.

> Best of <u>the best</u>
> ... one of South Africa's <u>most beautiful</u> cities. (line 1)
> ... <u>the best</u> Cape Town has to offer. (line 5)
> <u>The most exciting</u> thing to do (line 6)
> ... <u>the most famous</u> mountain ... (line 8)
> <u>The most frightening</u> activity (line 12)
> ... <u>the most dangerous</u> animal ... (line 15)
> <u>The best</u> shopping (line 16)
> ... <u>the best</u> and <u>most popular</u> shopping centre ... (lines 17–18)
> <u>The most expensive</u> place to stay (line 23)
> <u>The most historical</u> place (line 28)
> ... one of South Africa's <u>worst</u> prisons ... (line 30)
> <u>The wildest</u> night out (line 33)
> ... <u>the biggest</u> nightclub ... (line 34)
> ... <u>the best</u> place to go dancing ... (line 35)

Language notes
* As with comparatives, students have problems with superlatives when their first language is different, leading to errors such as, ✗ *the most biggest*.
* The main stress is on the adjective, not the word *most*.

2 **2.50**
* Tell students that they will hear twelve sentences. After each sentence there will be a pause for them to make a superlative sentence. They will then hear the superlative sentence.
* One way of doing this is to play the recording once, and get the class to make superlatives. Then play it again, and nominate individuals to make superlatives.

> *See tapescript below for answers.*

 2.50

> A safe city. – The safest city.
> A big car. – The biggest car.
> An expensive hotel. – The most expensive hotel.
> A friendly teacher. – The friendliest teacher.
> A modern house. – The most modern house.
> A cheap meal. – The cheapest meal.
> A bad day. – The worst day.
> My good friend. – My best friend.

3
* Students complete the sentences by putting the adjectives in brackets into the superlative form.
* Put students in pairs to compare answers, and say where in Cape Town the people are in each conversation.

> 1 the most expensive (at the Green Point market)
> 2 the biggest (at the Dockside)
> 3 the craziest; the most dangerous (on a shark adventure tour)
> 4 the highest (on Table Mountain)
> 5 the most important (on Robben Island)

> ▪ **Key Methodology 32:**
> ▪ **Dictionaries 3**
> **Understanding the information**

* *Many students seem never to completely understand or know how to use the grammar information given by dictionaries. Quiz tasks are a good way of introducing and practising use of this information.*

Quiz: abbreviations & symbols
* *Write these or similar items on the board or prepare a printed handout (examples are from the Macmillan dictionary):*
> *sb *** adj sth [+that] [plural] ➡*
* *Ask students to study the information or introduction pages of a dictionary and find out what they mean.*
* *Answers: sb (somebody) *** (very frequent word) adj (adjective) sth (something) [+that] (followed by that) [plural] (only used in plural) ➡ (look at another word or page).*
* *Ask students to look up the following words and find which ones use the items above:*
> *give, fast, promise, fish*

Quiz: checking grammar
* *Prepare a short quiz that forces students to look up words and make decisions based on grammatical information. You could dictate questions, write them on the board or prepare a printed handout. If you use any of the following examples, bear in mind that not all dictionaries include the same information and some answers may not be found in your students' books.*
> *1 Is success a noun or a verb or both?*
> *2 Is news countable or uncountable?*
> *3 Is draper a word often used in modern English?*
> *4 Find a good word to fill the gap in these sentences:*
> *(1) There was a long queue ... concert tickets.*
> *(2) When you arrive at the museum ... the queue for the Egyptian exhibition.*
> *5 What is the plural of sheep?*

SPEAKING

1
* Students make questions with the phrases (1–6). Do the first as an example.

> 2   What's the most interesting monument?
> 3   What's the most dangerous part of the city?
> 4   What's the nicest park?
> 5   What's the worst time of year to visit the city?
> 6   What are the most important festivals in the city?

2 & 3

⟩ *Key Methodology 7: Accurate speaking & fluent speaking, page 20*

* Pairwork. Put students in A and B pairs. Student A thinks of a city they know well. Student B then asks Student A about the city, using the questions in exercise 1. They then swap roles.
* Students then repeat the activity with a different partner.

IF YOU WANT SOMETHING EXTRA ...

⟩ *Photocopiable activity, page 231*
⟩ *Teacher's notes, page 185*

10D | City souvenirs

WHAT THE LESSON IS ABOUT

Theme	Souvenirs
Speaking	Pairwork discussion: talking about souvenirs
	Groupwork roleplay: buying & selling souvenirs in a shop
Listening	A conversation in a souvenir shop
Vocabulary	Size & colours
Functional language	In a shop
Pronunciation	Word linking 2

IF YOU WANT A LEAD-IN ...

Introducing the theme: souvenirs

- Bring into class two of your own souvenirs. (You could draw them or write what they are on the board – but bringing in the actual souvenirs is more interesting.)
- Pass the souvenirs round the class. Tell students to think of questions to ask you as they pass round the objects. Once you have the objects back, get students to ask you questions. Answer as truthfully as you can.
- Possible questions: *Where did you get it? Why did you buy it? Why is it important to you? How much was it?*

Pre-teach key words: souvenirs

- Write souvenirs on the board. Elicit the type of thing that people buy for souvenirs and write them on the board. Elicit: *postcards, T-shirts, key chains, bags, ornaments, ashtrays, badges, caps, cups and mugs,* etc.
- Students say which of these things they bought recently.

SPEAKING

1
- Pairwork. Put students in pairs to discuss the questions.
- In feedback, get students to tell the class about any interesting souvenirs their partner told them about.

VOCABULARY: size & colours

❯ *Language reference, Student's Book page 111*

1

❯ *Key Methodology 7: Accurate speaking & fluent speaking, page 20*

- Ask students to look at the pictures and ask them what they can see. (Answers: *a teddy bear; a football shirt; a taxi; a T-shirt, and a keyring.*)
- Students complete the descriptions of the souvenirs with a word from the box. They can compare their answers with a partner before you check with the whole class.

1	blue
2	silver
3	black
4	red, white
5	brown

Language notes

- In English, adjectives go before nouns. Adjectives of size usually go before adjectives of colour.

2
- Students can work in pairs to describe other things in the gift shop, using the words in the box.

1	It's a white T-shirt.
2	They're blue towels.
3	It's a small yellow pen.
4	It's a small dark brown teddy bear.
5	It's a small black taxi.
6	It's a big red football shirt
7	It's a big red mug.

LISTENING

In this episode of the listening story, Rob and Meg (the Australian couple from the Explore London tour) are in a souvenir shop in London and Meg is deciding what gifts to take home for their family.

1 **2.51**
- Play the recording. Students listen to Rob and Meg in the gift shop. Ask, *What do they buy? How much does it cost?*

Pens, mugs and books – £24.90

🔘 **2.51**

> **M = Meg R = Rob SA = shop assistant**
> **SA:** Hello, can I help you?
> **R:** No, I'm just looking, thank you.
> **M:** Excuse me, hello?
> **SA:** Yes?
> **M:** Do you have any small London mugs?
> **SA:** No, just these.
> **M:** Oh. Can I have <u>two of the red mugs</u> then, please?
> **SA:** Of course.
> **M:** Oh, these pens are pretty. How much are they?
> **SA:** <u>£1.50 each.</u>
> **M:** Can I have <u>five pens</u>, too, please?
> **SA:** Yeah, here you are.
> **M:** Thank you.
> **R:** Are we OK, now?
> **M:** Yes, look. I've got two mugs for my parents and these pens for the children.
> **R:** And I have a book on <u>London football teams</u>. Look! Only £2!
> **M:** Oh ...
> **SA:** Hello.
> **M:** Yes, these, please.
> **SA:** <u>The pens, two mugs and the books ...</u> That's <u>£24.90</u>, please.
> **M:** Here you are. Could I have <u>two bags</u>, please?
> **SA:** Bags are over there.
> **M:** Oh. Thank you.

Language & cultural note

- ***It's a bargain*** means it's very cheap at the price.

139

2 **2.51**

- Play the recording again. Students listen and answer the questions. They can compare their answers with a partner before you check with the whole class.

> 1 Two.
> 2 £1.50 each.
> 3 Five.
> 4 London football teams.
> 5 Two.

FUNCTIONAL LANGUAGE: in a shop

> ❯ *Language reference, Student's Book page 110*

1

- Students complete the dialogues with the phrases in the box. They can compare their answers with a partner.

> 1   1 can I help you?
>   2 I can't see a price.
>   3 You're welcome.
>
> 2   4 Do you have any keyrings?
>   5 No, I'm sorry we don't.
>   6 OK, thanks.
>
> 3   7 Anything else?
>   8 How much are they?
>   9 The book and these postcards then, please.
>
> 4 10 Here you are.
>   11 Would you like a bag for that?
>   12 Bye.

2 **2.52**

> ❯ *Key Methodology 5: Dialogues 1: page 11*

- Play the recordings. Students listen and check their answers.
- Put students in pairs to practise the dialogues.

2.52

> **1**
> **SA = shop assistant   C = customer**
> SA: Hello, <u>can I help you?</u>
> C: Yes, please. How much is this book? <u>I can't see a price.</u>
> SA: Just a minute. It's £7.95.
> C: Thank you.
> SA: <u>You're welcome.</u>
>
> **2**
> C: <u>Do you have any keyrings?</u>
> SA: Yes, we do. There are silver ones and these black ones.
> C: Do you have any with the cathedral on it?
> SA: <u>No, I'm sorry we don't.</u>
> C: <u>OK, thanks.</u>
>
> **3**
> SA: <u>Anything else?</u>
> C: Yes, I'd like some postcards, please.
> SA: They're over here.
> C: <u>How much are they?</u>
> SA: They're four for a pound.
> C: Fine. <u>The book and these postcards then, please.</u>
>
> **4**
> SA: That's £8.95.
> C: <u>Here you are.</u> £10.
> SA: Here's your change. <u>Would you like a bag for that?</u>
> C: No, thanks, that's alright. Goodbye.
> SA: <u>Bye.</u>

PRONUNCIATION: word linking 2

1 **2.53**

- Play the recording. Students listen and notice how some of the words are joined together.
- Play the recording again. Ask students to listen and repeat.

2.53

> Can‿I help you?
> How much‿is it?
> Just‿a minute.
> Anything‿else?
> They're‿over there.
> Would‿you like‿a bag?
> Here you‿are.

2

- You could put students in pairs to practise saying the sentences in exercise 1. Remind them to say the sentences quickly.

Language notes

- Most of the sentences feature the same form of linking. When a word ends with a consonant sound, and the next word starts with a vowel sound, the consonant effectively joins the vowel, e.g. *anything‿else* /enɪθɪn//gels/.
- Notice that *they're* normally ends with a vowel sound, /ðeə/, but an *r* intrudes when the next word starts with a vowel: /ðeərəʊvə/
- *Would you* becomes /wʊdʒə/.
- In the phrase *Here you‿are*, a *w* sound intrudes between the vowel sound at the end of *you* and the vowel sound in *are*: /hɪə juː ɑː/

SPEAKING

> ❯ *Key Methodology 7: Accurate speaking & fluent speaking, page 20*

1

- Divide students into groups of three, A, B and C.
- Give the tourists two minutes to think what souvenirs they are going to buy, and give the shop assistants two minutes to think what they are going to say.
- Students act out their roleplays in threes. Monitor, prompt, and note errors for a whole class feedback.

Extra task

- This is a way of extending the roleplay into a whole class mingle.
- Elicit (or just write up) these types of souvenirs to the board:
    books   pens and pencils   jewelery   rings   necklaces   key chains   badges   bags   teddy bears
- Get students to add to the list.
- Ask four pairs of students to be shopkeepers. If your class layout allows it, get each pair to sit in a corner of the classroom, ideally behind a desk or table. They must decide what sort of gift shop they have, and exactly what they sell. Give them four minutes. The rest of the class must choose three types of souvenir that they would like to buy, and prepare to describe them in detail.
- When the students are ready, ask them to go round the class, visiting the four shops, trying to find the perfect souvenir.

Web research tasks

❯ *Methodology guidelines: Web research tasks, page xiii*

- Students can research souvenirs from London on the internet to help provide them with ideas to use for the *Speaking* activity.

Web search key words

- London/souvenir

IF YOU WANT SOMETHING EXTRA ...

❯ *Photocopiable activity, page 232*
❯ *Teacher's notes, page 185*

Answer key

10 REVIEW

❯ *Student's Book page 156*

1

> *Possible answers:*
> 2 ... a place where you can stay when you are on holiday.
> 3 ... a place where you can put your money.
> 4 ... a place that has all the offices of the town government.
> 5 ... is a place where you can buy things.
> 6 ... is a place you go to when you are ill.
> 7 ... is a place where you can see sports events, like football matches.
> 8 ... is a place where you learn things.

2

> 1 You mustn't ~~to~~ take photographs in the airport.
> 2 Children mustn't ~~not~~ buy cigarettes.
> 3 You needn't ~~to~~ go to school after you are 16 years old.
> 4 You must ~~to~~ be 15 years old to get married.
> 5 You ~~don't~~ mustn't smoke in public buildings.
> 6 You must ~~can~~ have a licence to have a television.
> 7 You needn't ~~not~~ have a licence to buy a gun.

3

> *Students' own answers.*

4

> *Students' own answers.*

5

> 2 hotter
> 3 safer
> 4 better
> 5 uglier
> 6 more expensive

6

> 1 F (The mask is bigger than the keyring./ The keyring is smaller than the mask.)
> 2 T
> 3 F (The African mask is the most expensive souvenir.)
> 4 T
> 5 T
> 6 T

7

> *Possible answers:*
> The CD is cheaper than the mask.
> The mask is more expensive than the keyring.
> The CD is bigger than the keyring.

8

> 1 richest
> 2 bigger
> 3 colder
> 4 biggest
> 5 largest
> 6 bigger; biggest

9

> 7, 5, 2, 8, 3, 6, 1, 4, 9

10

> *Students' own answers.*

10 WRITING

❯ *Workbook page 83*

> *Model answer*
> My town is quite small and very beautiful. The town square has lots of historical buildings and is the oldest part of the town. You should see the old castle near to the centre. There are also lots of shops to buy souvenirs. The best place to stay is the Garden Hotel. It isn't very expensive. The best way to get around is on foot.

11A | Working behind the scenes

What the lesson is about

Theme	Jobs
Speaking	Pairwork discussion: talking about work
	Pairwork game: *Guess the job* – asking questions to guess the job
Listening	*Behind the scenes*: a television documentary programme about jobs in a hospital
Vocabulary	Jobs
Grammar:	Question review
Pronunciation	The sounds /w/, /v/ & /b/
Did you know?	Information about the NHS (National Health Service) in Britain

If you want a lead-in ...

Introducing the theme: jobs

- Ask students to think about someone in their family who works unusual hours. Put the them in groups of fours. They must take turns to describe their family member's typical day. The other students must guess their job.

Pre-teach key words: jobs

- Use mime to elicit some or all of the jobs introduced in the lesson. Ask students: *What's my job?* Then mime a builder putting bricks in a wall, a shop assistant using a till, an actor acting, etc. If students guess the job, model and drill the word.
- Put students in threes to mime and guess jobs.

Test before you teach: questions

❯ *Methodology guidelines: Test before you teach, page xiii*

- Write four or five jobs on the board. Tell students that they must ask questions to guess which job you are thinking of. Students must ask *Do you ...?* questions. You can only say *yes* or *no*. They have a maximum of ten questions to ask before they must guess the job.
- You could get students to play the game in threes.

Vocabulary & speaking: jobs

❯ *Language reference, Student's Book page 121*

1 & 2 ● 2.54

- Students match the words to the pictures.
- Play the recording for students to listen and check their answers.

1	I'm a doctor.	4	I'm a security guard.
2	I'm an accountant.	5	I'm a secretary.
3	I'm a waiter.	6	I'm an actor.

● 2.54

I = interviewer W = woman M = man

1
I: What do you do?
W: I'm a doctor.

2
I: What do you do?
M: I'm an accountant.

3
I: What do you do?
M: I'm a waiter.

4
I: What do you do?
W: I'm a secretary.

5
I: What do you do?
M: I'm an actor.

6
I: What do you do?
W: I'm a security guard.

■ Key Methodology 33
■ Books-closed presentations

- *Even with the best of coursebooks, a class teacher needs to vary routine approaches so as to keep the class alert and engaged. One good way is to avoid the ritual 'Open your books at page 92' start to each lesson by doing a books-closed presentation.*
- *At its simplest, do a books-closed presentation by just doing that, i.e. doing the tasks from the book, but with students' books closed! If students need examples, read them aloud or write them on the board. Such work can help to focus attention, compared with when students read books with heads down and limited person-to-person eye contact.*
- *For more adventurous book-closed work, you could devise your own way of introducing language – and then go on to use the coursebook material later in the lesson. A good idea is to do a contextualized presentation as described below.*
- *N.B. Books-closed presentations are good for grammar and vocabulary work – but avoid anything that has a lot of text (for the obvious reason that students would need to read that text!).*

A contextualized presentation

- *Think of a situation in which it would be natural to use the grammar or vocabulary you want to work on. In Lesson 11A, Vocabulary and speaking 1 (job vocabulary), you might think of a person having an interview at a job centre (i.e. a place where people go to find a new job). The situation you choose should reflect realistic real-life uses of the language – but that doesn't prevent you thinking of something that is slightly humorous. Once you have chosen your situation, think out a story or conversation that you can use in order to introduce the language. For example:*

Clerk: What job are you looking for?
Jack: I want to be an accountant.
Clerk   Are you good with numbers?
Jack: Er ... no. *(Pause)* I want to be a police officer.
Clerk: Are you fit?
Jack: Er ... no. *(Pause)* I want to be a doctor.
etc., etc.

• *In class, draw a simple picture of the scene, e.g. two stick people sitting across a desk, then introduce your story/dialogue to the class. Elicit as much as possible from students rather than telling them yourself (it's more involving and interesting), e.g. draw a word balloon above Jack's head and draw a symbol for each job there – a calculator for accountant, a stethoscope for doctor, etc. Then see if students can name each job. If they can't, you'll have to tell them yourself, of course (but at least you'll have found out that it's genuinely new for them).*

Language notes

• Point out the unusual pronunciation of *lawyer* /lɔːjə/, and the stress in *ac'countant* and *re'ceptionist*.
• *-er* and *-or* endings are pronounced as a weak schwa /ə/ sound. Also note the weak schwa /ə/ sound in *waitress* and *actress*.

3 2.55

• Play the recording. Students listen and underline the correct words.
• They can compare their answers with a partner. Ask them to discuss which job is being described in each sentence.
• In feedback, ask students what job from exercise 1 each speaker is talking about.

1	for	3	in	5	with
2	of	4	at	6	on

2.55

1 I work <u>for</u> a big company.
2 I'm in charge <u>of</u> other people.
3 I work <u>in</u> a restaurant.
4 I work <u>at</u> home.
5 I work <u>with</u> the public.
6 I often work <u>on</u> a computer.

4

• Pairwork. Put students in pairs to discuss the questions.

Cultural notes

• In the last 30 years, many jobs whose names were gender specific have changed, e.g. *policeman* to *police officer*, *fireman* to *fire fighter*, *air hostess* to *flight attendant*, *salesman* to *sales rep*. The *-ess* ending to denote feminine jobs is dying out. So, women are likely to call themselves *manager* not *manageress*.
• Jobs with low status have also undergone change. *Secretaries* are often called *PAs* (personal assistants) nowadays.

PRONUNCIATION: /w/, /v/ & /b/

1 2.56

❯ *Key Methodology 28: Pronunciation – phonemes, page 124*

• Play the recording. Students listen and say the words in the table.

2.56

/**w**/: waiter; Will; Washington; Wendy; working; whisky
/**v**/: vet; Victoria; Vincent; vegetables; vocabulary; Vienna
/**b**/: builder; Bob; Barbara; Brighton; bread; beer

2 2.57

• Play the recording. Students listen and read the text. Point out that the strong stresses are all on words that start with *w*.
• Ask students to practise saying the tongue-twister in pairs. Then ask a few individuals to say it for the class.

2.57

Will is a waiter. He lives in Washington. He likes working and whisky.

3

• You could put students in pairs to make similar texts with other words from the box.
• In feedback, ask some students to say their sentences out loud for the class.

Extra task for stronger classes

• Get students in pairs to write their own tongue-twister. It doesn't have to follow the pattern above, but it must be grammatically correct and contain as many words as possible.
• Pairs write their tongue-twister on the board. Other students must try to say it.

Language notes

• These sounds are all voiced. Where they differ is in the position of the lips and teeth when the sound is first made.
  To make a /w/ the lips need to be pushed together in a small 'o'.
  To make /v/ the teeth need to bite then release the lower lip.
  To make /b/ the lips need to be pressed together then released.
• Show students how physically to make these sounds by getting them to watch, then imitate what your mouth does while you read out some of the words in the table in exercise 1.

LISTENING

This listening is from a TV documentary show in which two people talk about their jobs working behind the scenes at a hospital. They talk about what they do; who they work with; when they started; if they like their jobs and what other people think of their job.

1 & 2 2.58

• Ask students to read the description about the television show. Tell them not to worry about the gaps.
• Then play the recording for students to complete the description. They can compare their answers with a partner before you check with the whole class.
• In feedback, ask: *Do they like their jobs?* (Answer: *Yes, both speakers like their jobs.*)

hospital; security guard; accountant

Language notes

• *Behind the scenes* is a theatrical term which means anyone who works behind the scenes, does a job that the public doesn't notice or hear about.
• An *invisible job* is, similarly, a job that nobody notices is being done.

🔲 **2.58**

> I = interviewer   J = Janet   M = Michael
>
> **I:** Tell us about yourself.
> **J:** OK, my name's Janet. I'm from Canada, and I work in the security office of a big <u>hospital</u> in London.
> **I:** What do you do?
> **J:** I'm a <u>security guard.</u> Er … most of the time I watch the security televisions. It's not a very difficult job.
> **I:** Who do you work with?
> **J:** I work with <u>two other security guards in the office.</u> They are both men.
> **I:** When did you start here?
> **J:** <u>I started at this hospital two years ago.</u>
> **I:** Do you like your job?
> **J:** <u>Yeah, yeah, I do.</u>
> **I:** Why?
> **J:** Well, I like working at night. I always like working at night. It's quiet. It's easy work. I have a nice boss.
> **I:** What do other people think of your job?
> **J:** I think my job is great, <u>but my parents don't like it.</u> My father is very traditional. He says that a security guard is a man's job. Yeah, well … what can you do?
>
> **I:** Hello, what's your name?
> **M:** Michael.
> **I:** Where do you work in the hospital?
> **M:** I work in the accounts department.
> **I:** <u>So you're an accountant?</u>
> **M:** <u>Yes, I am.</u>
> **I:** Who do you work with?
> **M:** <u>There are three people in the office.</u>
> **I:** When did you start here?
> **M:** I worked in London for ten years in a big company. <u>But I didn't like it. I started at this hospital last year.</u>
> **I:** Do you like your job?
> **M:** Yes, I do. <u>Many people say, 'Oh, accounts, that's boring'. But I like it.</u>
> **I:** <u>Why do you like your job?</u>
> **M:** <u>Because it's interesting</u>, I like working with numbers.

3 🔲 **2.58**

- Play the recording again. Students listen and underline the correct words to complete the sentences.

1	two men	4	two people
2	two	5	last year
3	doesn't like	6	isn't boring

4

- Pairwork. Put students in pairs to discuss the questions.
- In feedback, ask individuals who know someone who works in a hospital to tell the class about them.

Extra task

- Tell students that they are going to write a description of a typical day at work for a magazine article called *A day in the life*. They can describe their own job or one of the jobs described in the lesson.
- Give students five minutes to prepare notes. They must prepare to write about everything that happens on a typical day: when the start work; where they work; who they work with; what they do and when; when they have breaks and lunch; when they go home; what they like and don't like, etc.
- Get students to write their articles – five or six sentences – in class or for homework.

GRAMMAR: question review

> ◗ *Language reference, Student's Book page 120*
> ◗ *Methodology guidelines: Grammar boxes, page xiii*

1 & 2

- Students correct the mistakes in the questions. They can then compare their answers with a partner.
- Ask students look at the tapescript 2.58 on page 145 to check their answers.

> 1 What <u>do</u> you do?
> 2 When did ~~start you~~ <u>you start</u> here?
> 3 What do other people ~~thinks~~ <u>think</u> of your job?
> 4 <u>Do</u> you like your job?
> 5 Where <u>do</u> you work in the hospital?
> 6 Why ~~you do~~ <u>do you</u> like your job?

Language notes

- Students have come across question words and question word order in earlier lessons. The aim here is to give students further practice in manipulating the difficult forms of this vital area.
- It is a good idea to show forms in a table. That way you can refer to it to correct when students have problems in the exercise that follow. Copy the following on to the board:

Question word	Auxiliary verb	Subject	Infinitive
What	do	you	do?
Where	does	he	live?
What time	did	they	leave home?

3

- Students complete the questions about work with a question word from the box. They can compare their answers with a partner before you check with the whole class.

1	Where	5	What
2	What	6	Why
3	Who	7	How many
4	When		

4

- Pairwork. Students ask and answer the questions in exercise 3.

SPEAKING

1 & 2

- Students play *Guess the job*. Put them in A and B pairs. Student A must choose a job from the lesson. Student B must ask the questions in *Grammar* exercise 3.
- After asking the questions, Student B must guess Student A's job.
- Students then swap roles and repeat the activity.

Alternative procedure for stronger classes

- To avoid Student B merely reading out the questions from exercise 3, write them in abbreviated form as prompts at random on the board. For example:
  Name? From? Study? Work with? Start work? Do today? Like? Where?
- Students must remember and form the questions before asking.
- With the questions as prompts on the board, you could do this as a mingle. Students walk round the class and interview as many people as they can in five minutes.

Did you know?

1 & 2
- Students read the text about the National Health Service.
- Put students in pairs to discuss the questions.

Web research tasks

❯ *Methodology guidelines: Web research tasks, page xiii*

- Ask students to research the health service in their countries. They must find three or four interesting facts or statistics about health workers, and write a short report in English like the text in the *Did you know?* section.

Web search key words
- health service/name of country/statistics

If you want something extra …

❯ *Photocopiable activity, page 233*
❯ *Teacher's notes, page 185*

11B | The future of work

WHAT THE LESSON IS ABOUT

Theme	Work in the future
Speaking	Pairwork discussion: talking about your future working life/work Pairwork discussion: doing a quiz : *My future working life* & comparing the results
Reading	*The future won't wait ... will you?*: a magazine article about the future of work in the 21st century
Vocabulary	Describing work
Grammar	Predictions (*will*)

IF YOU WANT A LEAD-IN ...

Discussion starters

❯ *Methodology guidelines: Discussion starters, page xii*

- *Do you think you will be in the same job ten years from now?*
- *What will be your job?*
- *In the future, what will be good jobs? What will be common jobs? What jobs will disappear?*

Introducing the theme: work in the future

- Put students in pairs to think of three predictions about working life twenty years from now.
- Ask pairs to tell the class their predictions. Find out if the rest of the class agrees.

SPEAKING

1
- Students read the sentences and circle *I agree / I disagree / I don't know.*

2
- Pairwork. Put students in pairs to compare their answers and give reasons for their opinions.
- In feedback, find out the general opinion of the class.
- You could introduce some useful language on the board to help students discuss their ideas.
  Useful language:
  Personally, I think that ... because ...
  In my opinion, ...
  I'm not sure why ... but ...
  I strongly agree with the point that ...
  I don't agree that ...

READING

The reading text is a website review of a book about the future of work around the world. It is about what changes people can expect in their future working lives.

1

❯ *Key Methodology 23: Reading skills & strategies, page 94*

- Ask students to guess what the book is about from the title: *Futurework*.
- Students read the text to find out what is *Futurework*.

> 1 A book about the future of work in Britain.

2
- Students read the text again and mark the sentences true or false. They can compare their answers with a partner before you check with the whole class.
- In feedback, get students to give reasons why they have chosen true or false.

> 1 T
> 2 F (Lancaster's book is based on several years investigating and researching into jobs in Britain and around the world.)
> 3 T
> 4 T
> 5 T/F ('That is good news and bad news. If your job is at home, where will you go for a day off?')
> 6 T
> 7 T

3
- Pairwork. Put students in pairs to discuss the predictions and if they apply to their countries.
- Have a class discussion. Ask for a few opinions, and find out what the general feeling is.

Extra task

- Ask students to make their own predictions about the future of work.

Extra vocabulary task

❯ *Key Methodology 20: Vocabulary records, page 80*

- *Work* vocabulary in the text is dealt with in the *Vocabulary* section. However, there are three other sets of vocabulary in the text that you may want to deal with. They are *books, communication technology* and *places of work*.
- Write the three headings above on the board. Put students in pairs to find words in the text connected with each set.
  (Answers:
  Books: *author*; *chapter*
  Communication technology: *mobile phones*; *laptop computers*; *email*; *the internet*
  Places of work: *office*; *home*; *shops*; *hospitals*; *centres for old people*; *hotels*; *restaurants*.

Web research tasks

❯ *Methodology guidelines: Web research tasks, page xiii*

- Students can find more predictions about work in the future.

Web search key words
- future/work

VOCABULARY: describing work

❯ *Language reference, Student's Book page 121*

1
- Students find the opposites of the words in the text. They can compare their answers with a partner before you check with the whole class.

part time ≠ full-time	temporary ≠ permanent
badly paid ≠ well-paid	unemployed ≠ employed

2

- Students complete the sentences with a word from exercise 1. They can compare their answers with a partner before you check with the whole class.

1	temporary	3	badly-paid
2	part-time	4	unemployed

3

- Pairwork. Put students in pairs to discuss the questions.

Language notes

- The compound adjectives *well-'paid* and *badly-'paid* have a stronger stress on the last syllable, whereas *'full-time* and *'part-time* have stronger stresses on the first syllable.

GRAMMAR: predictions (*will*)

> *Language reference, Student's Book page 120*
> *Methodology guidelines: Grammar boxes, page xiii*

1

- Students complete the sentences with *will/will not* + verb. Do the first as an example. Tell them to use contractions. They can compare their answers with a partner before you check with the whole class.

Possible answers:			
1	won't use; 'll work	4	will be; will be
2	will control	5	won't cook; 'll buy
3	will have	6	won't live; 'll live

Language notes

- ***Will*** is a modal verb. We use it to talk about predictions in the future when the prediction is a personal opinion or a certainty.
- Students need to get used to using the abbreviated forms, (*I'll, we'll, won't*, etc.). Watch out for the unnecessary *to*: ✗ *He will to go.*
- The difficult-to-say diphthongs caused by the abbreviated forms are problematic: *I'll* /aɪəl/, *we'll* /wiːəl/. Make sure that students are saying *won't* /wəʊnt/ not *want* /wɒnt/. N.B. the abbreviated *'ll* form tends to be used with pronouns. *I will* or *he will*, etc. sound wrong in normal conversation because they emphasize *will* too strongly.
- In fast speech, it is possible to use abbreviated *'ll* with nouns, e.g. *People'll live underground.* However, *will* is more often said and always written when using nouns.
- *Will* is used here for making predictions. However, as a modal verb it has a wide variety of functional uses. Not only can it express a spontaneous intention, it can be used to express functions such as offers (*I'll help*); warnings (*You'll be hurt*); threats (*I'll kill you*); promises (*I'll marry you*); deductions (*That'll be Sam*), and habits (*He'll sit there all day doing nothing*).

2

- Students match the sentences in exercise 1 to the other books in the box. They can compare their answers with a partner before you check with the whole class.

Futurelive: 2, 6
Futuredrive: 1, 3
Futureeat: 4, 5

3 🔘 **2.59**

> *Key Methodology 14: Drilling 1 – basics, page 55*

- This is a prompt drill. Play the recording. Pause the recording after each prompt for students to respond personally, using *I'll* or *I won't*.
- Play the recording a second time. This time nominate two or three individuals to repeat after each prompt.

🔘 **2.59**

1	be rich.
2	be happy.
3	have a job.
4	be married.
5	have children.
6	live in another country.
7	be famous.

Extension task

- Write a list of 'funny' prompts on the board, and get students to make sentences from them. You could do this in pairs, then ask a student to summarize what their partner said, thus having to manipulate from *I'll* to *He'll* or *She'll*.
- Possible list of prompts:
    live in a castle
    speak perfect English
    have a pet tiger
    go on holiday every month
    get married to a film star
    be a private investigator

4 🔘 **2.59**

- Pairwork. Put students in pairs. Play the first prompt, and model to show students that you want them to ask and answer the questions.
- Play the recording. Students listen and ask and answer.

Extra task

- Have a class discussion about the statements in exercise 1. Do students think they will be true?

SPEAKING

1

- Ask a few questions open class to lead in: *in 10 years, will you be rich? Will you be here or in another country? Will you be married?* Elicit a few responses from students.
- Give students up to ten minutes to do the quiz. Monitor and help with vocabulary if necessary.

2

> *Key Methodology 7: Accurate speaking & fluent speaking, page 20*

- Pairwork. Put students in pairs to tell each other about their working lives.
- In feedback, ask pairs to say who is more optimistic about the future.

Extension task

- Get students to write three or four more predictions about the future.
- Alternatively, get students to write three or four questions about the future then ask the class.

IF YOU WANT SOMETHING EXTRA ...

> *Photocopiable activity, page 234*
> *Teacher's notes, page 186*

11c | 16 before 60

WHAT THE LESSON IS ABOUT

Theme	Having a healthy lifestyle
Speaking	Pairwork & groupwork: giving advice on how to have a long and happy life
	Giving advice on lifestyle; Talking about plans for the future
Reading	*16 things to do before you're 60 years old*: a magazine article giving suggestions about how to make your life happier & healthier
Listening	Radio programme: people talking about a magazine article: *16 things to do before you're 60 years old*, & their future plans
Vocabulary	collocations *make & do*
Grammar	*Going to* future
Pronunciation	/tə/

IF YOU WANT A LEAD-IN ...

Discussion starters

● *Methodology guidelines: Discussion starters, page xii*

- Write on the board:
  What makes me happy?
  What makes me feel stressed?
- Give students two or three minutes to think of things personal to them to put in each category.
- When students are ready, let them discuss their ideas in pairs. Then elicit suggestions for each category from the class.

Introducing the theme: having a healthy lifestyle

- Write the following on the board:
  sleep well   do exercise   eat well   be optimistic
  drink lots of water   don't worry   smile and laugh
- Ask students: *Which of these are important to you? Do you think these things are important for a happy and healthy life? What other things are important?*

SPEAKING & READING

This magazine article provides a list of 16 things the author considers you should do before you are 60 years old, in order to achieve a happy and healthy life at that age.

1
- Lead in by writing the first sentence prompt on the board, and eliciting a few suggestions from the class.
- Pairwork. Put students in pairs to complete the sentences.

2
- Groupwork. Put pairs in groups of four to compare their answers.
- Have a brief class feedback.

Language notes

- Using **you should** for advice is revision. There is no need to overtly teach it. However, make sure that students are using a base verb after *should*, and not inserting an unnecessary ✗ *to*.

3

● *Key Methodology 23: Reading skills & strategies, page 94*

- Ask students to look at the photos and tell you what the people are doing. Use the pictures to pre-teach: *laugh* /lɑːf/; *vote*; *throw away rubbish*; *do exercise*.
- Students read the magazine article and match the photos A to C with the correct paragraph. They can compare their answers with a partner before you check with the whole class.

A 14	B 3	C 8

Language notes

- An **optimist** is someone who is positive and believes that the future will be good.
- A **pessimist** is someone who is negative and believes that the future will be bad.

4
- Students read the article again, and decide which paragraphs talk about which topic. They can compare their answers with a partner before you check with the whole class.
- There may be some debate about some of the topics, e.g. item 1 is about 'school' as well as 'work'; item 14 is about 'feelings' as well as 'exercise'.

1 food and drink 11, 15
2 exercise 3, 14
3 feelings 2, 7, (14), 16
4 cigarettes 12
5 school 1
6 money 10
7 your teeth 13
8 sleep 9
9 politics 8
10 work 1, 2, 6

5
- Students match the highlighted words in the text to the definitions.

1	volunteer work
2	Take a break
3	regret
4	Quit
5	chance
6	Save money

6
- Students read the article again, and put a tick next to the things they already do, or did in the past.

7
- Pairwork. Put students in pairs to compare their lists.
- In feedback, find out which students are living life as best as they can.

Extension task

- Tell students to work in pairs and use the sentence prompts in exercise 1. They should find out about the things their partner is not doing and give them advice, e.g. *If you want to be happy at work, you should take more breaks.*

VOCABULARY: collocations *make* & *do*

> *Language reference, Student's Book page 121*

1

- Students look back at the text on page 116 and find and underline all the examples of *make* and *do* collocations. N.B. They should not underline *do* when it is used as an auxiliary. Do the first one as an example.
- Let them check their findings with a partner.

make people happier and healthier (Introduction)
do you do (things) (Introduction)
going to do (things) (Introduction)
do something different (Paragraph 1)
Make plans (Paragraph 1)
do a job (Paragraph 2)
do more exercise (Paragraph 3)
make a mistake (Paragraph 4)
Don't make the same mistake (Paragraph 4)
Make things simple (Paragraph 5)
Do some volunteer work (Paragraph 6)
makes you happier and live longer (Paragraph 6)
make friends (Paragraph 7)
Make a difference (Paragraph 8)
Make an appointment (Paragraph 13)
makes you healthier, more beautiful and more relaxed (Paragraph 15)
can't do; can do (things) (Paragraph 16)

Language notes

- In many languages ***make*** and ***do*** are either expressed by the same verb, or by two verbs but with a very different set of collocations. Consequently, this is an area ripe for errors such as ✗ *do mistakes* or ✗ *make my homework*.
- There are some often broken but useful rules:
  1 We use *do* with *work*, (*do homework, do a job*), including all the tasks around the home or office, (*do the washing, do the ironing, do the typing*). We also use *do* with *thing* or when we don't know what is being done, (*do nothing, What's he doing?*).
  2 We use *make* when there is an idea of creation or construction, either physically or mentally, (*make a cake, make a plan*).
  3 *Make*, however, is used idiomatically with lots of noun collocations when the students' L1 would probably use another verb, (*make a mistake, make friends, make time*). It is best to get students to simply learn these as fixed collocations.
- Remind students that *do* can be both a full verb and an auxiliary verb.

2

- Give students two or three minutes to use the prompts in the box to prepare true sentences.
- Put students in pairs to tell each other their sentences. In feedback, ask some students to present a report on what their partner told them to the class.

LISTENING

This listening is a radio programme in which four people are asked for their views about the magazine article *16 things to do before you're 60*. They tell the reporter what things they already do in their life and what things they think are a good idea and intend to do in the future.

1 **2.60**

- Read through the introduction as a class. Make sure students are clear that they must tick the numbered headings 1–16 in the article.
- Play the recording. Students listen and tick the things in the article that they hear.

Students should tick:
1, 3, 5, 7, 8, 9, 12, 15

2.60

> R = reporter D = David S = Sandra W = Will A = Ali
> J = Jarvis
> **R:** What about you, David?
> **D:** Well, I'm already 64 years old. Next year, I'm not going to work any more. So, <u>number 1</u> is good for me. I'm going to go and live in France. I'd like to practise my French more. Let's see, what else … <u>a good bed</u>. Yes, that makes me think. I'm going to get a good bed. The bed we have is ten years old.
> **R:** Sandra, what things are you going to do?
> **S:** Oh yes, I read all about the benefits of water in a magazine once. That's my resolution. I'm going to <u>drink more water</u>. And I'm going to tell my husband about <u>optimists</u> living longer than pessimists do. He always sees the bad side of everything!
> **R:** So, Will, is there anything here for you?
> **W:** Well, I already play football and do lots of sports, so <u>number 3</u> isn't a new thing for me. I'm not going to live in another country, or stop work, either.
> **R:** Well, are you going to do anything on the list?
> **W:** OK, OK. Ummm … <u>Number 5</u>. My desk, especially, which is terrible. I'm going to clean my desk.
> **R:** Ali, what about you?
> **A:** Every year I say I'm going to <u>stop smoking</u>, I'm going to stop smoking. But then I always find an excuse to start again. What else is on the list? <u>Exercise</u> is a good idea. Yes, I'm going to go to a gym, starting next year. And I'm going to quit smoking.
> **R:** And what about you, Jarvis?
> **J:** I only work here part time, I'm still at university. When I finish, in two years, <u>I'm going to take a long break</u>. I'm going to travel around China on a motorbike with a friend. I got the idea from a film. I'm also going to <u>vote</u> in the next election, but I always vote in elections because I think that's important.

2 **2.60**

- Play the recording again. Students listen and match the sentences to the people. They can compare their answers with a partner before you check with the whole class.

1   Jarvis
2   Ali
3   Sandra
4   David
5   Will

GRAMMAR: *going to*

> *Language reference, Student's Book page 120*
> *Methodology guidelines: Grammar boxes, page xiii*

1

- Students put the words in the correct order to make sentences. They can compare their answers with a partner before you check with the whole class.

1 David is going to buy a good bed.
2 She is going to drink more water.
3 Will is not going to live in another country.
4 I'm going to stop smoking.

Language notes

- Here, **be + going to** + infinitive is introduced to talk about plans in the future. It is introduced in a simple, restricted context with the emphasis on getting students to manipulate and be aware of this new form. Students are likely to make a range of form errors: ✗ *I going to quit smoking; When you are going to quit?; He is going ride on a motorcycle.*
- At this level, students are not really up to contrasting tenses. However, be aware that the choice of which future tense to use is subtle and depends largely on the intent and point of view of the speaker. Contrast:

   I'm going to quit smoking next week. (A plan – an intention decided earlier.)
   I'll quit smoking next week. (A spontaneous intention – decided now.)
   I'm going to go to the gym next week. (A plan – an intention decided earlier.)
   I'm going to the gym next week. (An arrangement – planned and put in your 'diary'.)

- The difference between *going to* + infinitive and present continuous is very subtle and often not worth worrying about – it depends on whether the speaker is emphasizing the intent or the arrangement, e.g. in *She's going to go to the gym next year* the speaker is emphasizing intent – she's determined. In another context, however, *She's going to the gym on Friday*, for example, the emphasis is on the arrangement, and the present continuous is preferred.
   There is no need to burden students with this – but in case they ask, well, you know now.

2
- Students complete the reporter's questions to Jarvis about the trip he is going to make. They can compare their answers with a partner before you check with the whole class.

2 Who are you going to go with?
3 When are you going to make this trip?
4 How are you going to get there?
5 What are you going to do?

3
- Tell students to close their eyes for a moment, and think of a trip they are going to make in the future, or if they haven't got one planned, to imagine a dream trip. Ask the questions in exercise 2. Ask the first question, and give students a moment to imagine but not say their answer. Pause after each question to give students time to picture their answer.
- Tell students to open their eyes. Give them one minute to make notes about their trip.

4
- Pairwork. Put students in pairs to interview their partner about their trip, using the questions in exercise 2.
- In feedback, ask students to tell the class about their partner's dream trip.

Alternative procedure

- Before doing exercise 4, write the question prompts from exercise 2 on the board: *Where/go, Who/go with*, etc.
- Drill the class from the prompts. Say: *Where are you going to go?* and ask students to repeat chorally and individually. Do this for each question. Then point to the prompts and get individuals to produce sentences from them. You could get students to ask and answer the questions across the class.
- By doing this drill, it helps students do the interview in exercise 4 without merely reading the questions out, and, hopefully with natural rhythm and pronunciation.

PRONUNCIATION: /tə/

1 **2.61**
- Play the recording. Students listen and to the pronunciation of the word to in the sentences.

 2.61

1 I'm going to drink more water.
2 I'm going to stop smoking.
3 What are you going to do?
4 Who are you going to go with?

Language notes

- Note the pronunciation of *going to* /gəʊɪntə/: *to* is unstressed, so it is pronounced with a weak schwa /ə/ sound.
- Also note the stress and the intonation in a *going to* question:

   What are you going to do?

2
- Put students in pairs to practise saying the sentences with the short pronunciation of *to* /tə/.

SPEAKING

1
- Tell students to refer to the text for ideas, then write four or five sentences about things they are or aren't going to do in the future.

2
- Pairwork. Put students in pairs to share their ideas. Then have a class feedback.

Web research tasks

❯ *Methodology guidelines: Web research tasks, page xiii*

- Find other advice on how to lead a healthy lifestyle on the web.
- You can also find pictures about the topic and make posters which can be displayed around the classroom.

Web search key words
- healthy lifestyle/health and work

IF YOU WANT SOMETHING EXTRA …

❯ *Photocopiable activity, page 235*
❯ *Teacher's notes, page 186*

11D | Love and work

WHAT THE LESSON IS ABOUT

Theme	Love in the workplace
Speaking	Pairwork discussion: talking about love in the workplace
	Pairwork dialogue: invitations
Reading	A website discussion about love in the workplace
Listening	Three conversations about invitations
Vocabulary	Phrasal verbs
Functional language	Invitations

IF YOU WANT A LEAD-IN ...

Test before you teach: invitations

❯ *Methodology guidelines: Test before you teach, page xiii*

- Write on the board: *Saturday night*. Tell students to think about what they would like to do on Saturday night. Make some suggestions: *go to the cinema*; *go to a restaurant*; *go to a disco*; *go to a party*; *stay in and watch a DVD*.
- Tell students to stand up and walk round the class, invite people to do the activity they have chosen, and find others who would like to do the same. Model the activity, by asking students, for example, *Would you like to go to a party?* Tell students that when they find somebody who wants to do the same thing, they should continue walking round the class with them. Eventually, students should find themselves in groups, according to which activity they want to do.

READING & SPEAKING

This reading text is from an internet discussion board. Six people have written about their own experiences having a relationship with someone at work, and whether they thought it was a good or bad idea.

1

- Ask students to look at the pictures and the heading of the webpage in exercise 1. Ask: *What can you see in the pictures? What do you think the webpage is about?*

It's about the problems of falling in love in the workplace.

2

- Ask students to read the comments about 'Love and Work' on the internet discussion board and answer the question. You could put students in pairs to discuss their answers.

1, 3, 4 and 5 think it's bad.
2 thinks it's good.
6 doesn't say, but probably thinks it's bad

3

- Pairwork. Put students in pairs to discuss the questions. Have a class feedback and find out general opinions.

VOCABULARY: phrasal verbs

❯ *Language reference, Student's Book page 121*

1

- Students underline the phrasal verbs in the text.

ask (me) out (comment 1)
go out (comment 3); went out with (comment 5)
broke up (comment 5)
get along (comment 4)

Language notes

- The aim here is to introduce students to the phenomenon of phrasal verbs at this level. There is no need to go into the complexities of the different types of phrasal verb. However, below is a brief summary:
  1 **ask** (someone) **out** = verb + adverb: a separable phrasal verb, meaning that the adverb can be separated from the verb by the object.
  2 **go out**, **break up**, **get along** = verb + adverb: here, used intransitively – they take no object.
  3 However, *go out*, *break up* and *get along* can be used as three part phrasal verbs by adding the preposition *with*: *go out with* (someone).

2

- Students match the phrasal verbs from exercise 1 with the definitions. They can compare their answers with a partner before you check with the whole class.

1 go out
2 get along
3 break up
4 ask out

3

- Students complete the sentences with a verb from the box. They can compare their answers with a partner before you check with the whole class.

1	go	5	break
2	go	6	break
3	asks	7	get
4	asks	8	get

4

- You could put students in pairs to discuss the sentences.
- Then have a brief class feedback.

Extra task for stronger students

- Ask students to work in pairs to make questions to ask their classmates. Monitor and help if necessary. Possible questions:
  Do you get along with your brothers and sisters?
  Who are you going out with?
  Do woman ask out men in your country?
  When did you last break up with somebody?
- Put pairs into groups of four to ask their questions.

LISTENING

In this episode of the listening story, it's the last evening of the Explore London tour and the group are at the hotel. In the first conversation the hotel manager asks Valerie out for a meal, but she refuses. He sounds a little too friendly. In the second interview, Dave asks Valerie out for a drink and she accepts. In the final conversation, Sam interrupts Dave and Valerie when he arrives with several police officers. Sam identifies himself to Dave as a police inspector and invites Dave to the police station to talk to him about Herb and Hannah's stolen money.

1 ⊙ 2.62

- Tell students to look at the photos and identify the characters. Ask them to tell you where they think they are and what they are saying.
- Play the recording. Students listen to the conversations and make a note of the person in each picture who does the inviting, and the name of the person who they invite.

> 1 The hotel manager, invites Valerie.
> 2 Dave invites Valerie.
> 3 Sam invites Dave.

⊙ 2.62

> HM = hotel manager V = Valerie D = Dave S = Sam
>
> **1**
> HM: So, you're the tour guide.
> V: Sorry, oh yes, yes, I am.
> HM: What's your name?
> V: Valerie.
> HM: My name's James. I'm the hotel manager. You can call me Jim.
> V: Nice to meet you, Jim.
> HM: So, when does the tour finish?
> V: Tomorrow.
> HM: Would you like to have dinner with me tomorrow night?
> V: No, I'm sorry. I'm busy.
> HM: Oh, well, then. Too bad.
> V: Mmm.
>
> **2**
> D: Hi, Valerie.
> V: Hello, Dave.
> D: I was thinking. The tour is going to finish tomorrow. Are you busy tomorrow night?
> V: Umm. I … no, I'm not. Why?
> D: Would you like to have a drink with me?
> V: Yes, I'd love to.
>
> **3**
> S: Excuse me, Dave?
> D: Yes.
> S: Can we speak in private for a moment?
> D: What do you want to talk about? Who are these people?
> S: I'm a police officer. These are my colleagues.
> D: What?! Why?
> V: What's the matter?
> S: We want to talk to Dave about the Curtises' money, and passports. Can you open your bag, please?
> D: I want a lawyer.
> S: Don't worry, you can make a phone call. Would you like to come with us now to the police station?

2 ⊙ 2.62

- Play the recording again. Students listen and mark the sentences true or false.

> **1**
> 1 T
> 2 F (The hotel manager wants to have dinner with Valerie.)
> **2**
> 3 T
> 4 F (Valerie says she'd love to have a drink with Dave.)
> **3**
> 5 F (Sam is a police officer.)
> 6 T

FUNCTIONAL LANGUAGE: invitations

❯ *Language reference, Student's Book page 121*

1 & 2

- Students correct the mistakes in the sentences. They can then compare their answers with a partner.
- In pairs, students look at tapescript 2.62 on page 146 to check their answers.

> 1 Would you like <u>to</u> have dinner with me tomorrow night?
> 2 No, I'm sorry. I<u>'m</u> busy.
> 3 Would you like to have a drink <u>with</u> me?
> 4 Yes, I<u>'d</u> love to.
> 5 ~~Do~~ <u>Would</u> you like to come with us now to the police station?

Extra task

❯ *Key Methodology 29: Pronunciation – don't avoid intonation!, page 126*

- Write these prompts in a list on the board: *have dinner*; *see a film*; *have a coffee*; *go shopping*; *go to a club*; *have a drink*. Alternatively, make simple drawings of each of these activities on flashcards, which you can hold up to elicit the language.
- Point to a prompt, then model the question, e.g. *Would you like to have dinner?* Make sure you use a wide, friendly intonation pattern, with your voice rising at the end. Students repeat chorally and individually. Do this with all the prompts. Then get students to ask and answer across the class, practising the invitations and responses.
- Put students in pairs to practise.

SPEAKING

1 🎧 **2.63**
- Play the recording. Students read and listen to the dialogue.

🎧 **2.63**

> **A1 = Ant 1 A2 = Ant 2**
> **A1:** Hello.
> **A2:** Hi. How are you?
> **A1:** Fine, thanks. What are you doing?
> **A2:** Oh, nothing much.
> **A1:** Would you like to have a cup of tea with me?
> **A2:** Oh, yes. That would be nice.
> **A1:** I know a very good café near here.
> **A2:** Good. Let's go.

2
- Pairwork. Put students in pairs to practise the dialogue.

3
- Pairwork. Put students in pairs to choose one of the roles in the box. Once they have chosen their role, they must prepare a dialogue.
- Students can then read their dialogue out to another pair.
- Alternatively, ask a few pairs to act out their dialogue for the class. The class must guess their roles.

Extra task

- Tell students to write *Thursday; Friday; Saturday; Sunday* in a list on a piece of paper. Tell them that they are busy on two of the evenings of these days, and free on the other two. Tell them to choose two evenings and write down what they are doing then, e.g. *having dinner; going to the cinema*. Tell students to stand up and walk round, and invite people to the things they have on. If they are free, they can say *yes* to any invitation. If they are busy, they must say *no*. After five minutes, ask students to sit down. Find out if anybody is now busy every evening.

IF YOU WANT SOMETHING EXTRA ...

❯ *Photocopiable activity, page 236*
❯ *Teacher's notes, page 186*

Answer key

11 REVIEW

❯ *Student's Book page 157*

1

1 in
2 of
3 time
4 for
5 paid

2

1 What do you do?
2 Where do you work?
3 Who do you work with?
4 When/What time do you start work?
5 When did you start here?
6 Do you like your job?

3

1 People will work from home.
2 It will be much colder than now.
3 People won't eat fresh fruit and vegetables.
4 Everyone will speak the same language.
5 Everyone will travel by electric cars.
6 People won't live in houses, they will live underground.
7 People won't live in the countryside, they will live in cities.

4

Students' own answers.

5

1 off
2 up
3 off
4 down
5 up
6 out
7 on

6

Students' own answers.

7

1 went
2 met
3 asked
4 broke
5 met
6 got

8

5, 2, 6, 3, 1, 4

11 WRITING

❯ *Workbook page 85*

Model answer
Hi Janos,

This summer I'm going to England and I'm going to get a temporary job. I'm going to work as a receptionist in a small hotel. The job isn't very well paid, but I'll be speaking English all day and I think it will be useful for the future. I don't want to work all summer. I will spend a week in London sightseeing and shopping.

Bye for now. Write soon.

Szilvia

12A | Lifetime achievements

WHAT THE LESSON IS ABOUT

Theme	Music; the Grammy Lifetime Achievement Awards
Speaking	Pairwork discussion: talking about different kinds of music
	Pairwork & groupwork discussion: choosing a singer or group to win a Lifetime Achievement Award
Reading	A magazine article about some winners of the Grammy Lifetime Achievement Awards
Vocabulary	Music
Grammar	Present perfect 1: affirmative
Pronunciation	Contractions

IF YOU WANT A LEAD-IN ...

Introducing the theme: music

- Music can be used in the classroom to relax, set the scene, create mood, or get students thinking. From your CD collection, find some music that evokes certain feelings or scenes. It could be classical music, or it could be instrumental music on pop or rock albums. Here are a few things you could do with the music.
  1 Play some music. Students listen, eyes closed if they like, then they write down how they felt while listening.
  2 Play some music. Ask: *Where are you?* Students don't speak – but they imagine where they are – a beach, castle, prison ... Ask: *Who are you with? Where are you going? What's happening? What happens in the end?* Pause between each question to give students time to imagine. At the end, get students to tell a partner or the class their story.
  3 Play some music. Tell students to imagine it is the soundtrack to a film. Ask: *What sort of film? Who is in it? Where is it set? What happens in the film?* Again, students tell their stories at the end.

Discussion starters

> *Methodology guidelines: Discussion starters, page xii*

- Write the following on the board.
  The greatest <u>band</u> *in the world.*
  The best <u>album</u> *I've ever bought.*
  The most amazing rock <u>concert</u> *I've ever been to.*
  The best <u>song</u> *I've ever heard.*
  The biggest <u>hit</u> *ever in my country.*
- Check the meaning of the words underlined. Then give students one minute to think of their own answers. Then tell their partner.
- Have a class discussion.

SPEAKING & VOCABULARY: music

> *Language reference, Student's Book page 131*

1
- Students put the words into two groups. They can compare their answers with a partner before you check with the whole class.

People who make music	Kinds of music
singer, musician, songwriter, band	rock, pop, jazz, R&B, rap, folk, classical

2
- If you have a monolingual class, ask them to translate and compare the words.

3 💿 2.64
- Play the recording. Students listen and write down what kinds of music they hear. They can compare their answers with a partner before you check with the whole class.
- In feedback, find out which types of music students like.

The music is:
rock; jazz; pop; classical; rap

4
- Pairwork. Put students in pairs to discuss the questions.

Extra task
- Ask students to think of performers and musicians who are well known in each category. They could match the people in the photos to the categories. See if any students can sing a line or verse from any pop song in English.

Cultural notes
- **R&B** = rhythm and blues
- Performers in each category:
  rock (Rolling Stones; U2; Coldplay)
  pop (Britney; Kylie; boy bands like Blue)
  jazz (Louis Armstrong; John Coltrane; Miles Davis)
  R&B (Aretha Franklin; Beyonce)
  rap (Eminem; 50 cent)
  folk (Bob Dylan; Joni Mitchell)
  classical (Mozart; Beethoven; Pavarotti).

READING

The reading text is an article about the American Grammy awards, with three short biographies of past winners: the Rolling Stones; Bob Dylan and Aretha Franklin.

1
- If you haven't already done so, ask students to look at the photos. Ask: *What do you think the Grammy Awards are?*

2
- Students read the article. Put them in pairs to match pictures to performers mentioned in the article, and decide which person is not mentioned.

C   Britney Spears is not in the article.

3
- Students read the biographies again and answer the questions. They can compare their answers with a partner before you check with the whole class.

> 1   One.
> 2   Bob Dylan: *Blowin' in the Wind* and *Mr Tambourine Man*.
>   Aretha Franklin: *Respect*; *You Make Me Feel Like a Natural Woman*; *I Never Loved a Man (The Way I Love You)*.
> 3   Britain.
> 4   On every continent in the world.
> 5   The Queen of Soul.
> 6   Bob Dylan.

4
- Pairwork. Put students in pairs to discuss the questions.

> A   Bob Dylan
> B   Aretha Franklin
> C   Britney Speers
> D   The Rolling Stones

Cultural notes

- **Grammy** is an abbreviation of *gramophone* (an old-fashioned word for record player). In Britain, a similar annual ceremony is held, called the *Brit Awards*. You could ask whether there is a similar ceremony in the students' countries.
- An **Oscar** or *Academy Award* is presented in Hollywood to the best film and film stars every year.

GRAMMAR: present perfect 1 – affirmative

❯ *Language reference, Student's Book page 130*
❯ *Methodology guidelines: Grammar boxes, page xiii*

1
- Students work in pairs underline all the examples of the present perfect in the text.

> ... have made (line 6)
> ... haven't stopped making (line 12)
> ... have made; ... have had (line 13)
> ... have given (line 14)
> ... have said (line 19)
> ... has written (line 20)
> ... has won (line 22)
> ... has changed (line 23)
> ... has made (lines 28–29)
> ... has sung (line 29)

Language notes

- The present perfect is a very commonly used tense in English. However, it is very difficult for students at this level to grasp its use. This is because it is likely that, in the students' L1, this form may well exist, but be used very differently.
- For example, in many languages, the form *have* + past participle is used to express experiences with or without a specific time marker. So watch out for errors like ✗ *He has won a Grammy last year.*

2

- Students make the past participles of the verbs. They can then compare their answers with a partner before checking them with the *Irregular verb list* on page 159 of the Student's Book.
- In feedback, point out that past participles of regular verbs are the same as past simple forms. However, the past participles of irregular verbs vary, and need to be learnt by heart. You could ask students to listen to and repeat the words after you.

> make – made
> say – said
> write – written
> stop – stopped
> change – changed
> give – given
> sing – sung
> have – had
> win – won

Language notes

- **Been** is the past participle form of both *be* and *go*.
- Notice the difficult pronunciation of the following: *said* /sed/; *written* /ritən/; *stopped* /stɒpt/.

3
- Lead in by asking students if they have heard of Joni /dʒəʊniː/ Mitchell. Ask what they know about her. (If you have a CD of her music, play a brief extract, and ask students what sort of music it is, and whether they like it.)
- Students complete the text by putting the words in brackets into the present perfect. They can compare their answers with a partner before you check with the whole class.

> 1   's made
> 2   have said
> 3   has written
> 4   has been
> 5   's won

Extra task

- Ask students in pairs to think of a famous person. They must write four sentences to describe their lifetime achievements, using the present perfect affirmative. When they are ready, each pair read out their sentences. The rest of the class must guess which person they are describing.

PRONUNCIATION: contractions

1 🎵 **2.65**
- Play the recording. Students listen to the contractions.
- You could play the recording again. Students listen and repeat.

🎵 **2.65**

I have won an award.	I've won an award.
He has not won an award.	He hasn't won an award.
They have won an award.	They've won an award.

2 & 3 **2.66**

- Put students in pairs to say the sentences with contractions.
- Play the recording. Students listen and check their answers.
- Play the recording again. Students listen and repeat the sentences.

See answers in the tapescript below.

 2.66

1	We <u>haven't</u> won an award.
2	He<u>'s</u> written a song.
3	She <u>hasn't</u> changed musical style.
4	You <u>haven't</u> won.
5	It <u>hasn't</u> been easy.
6	I <u>haven't</u> said the truth.

Language notes

- The use of diphthongs, long vowels and schwa sounds may prove tricky for students here. Notice *I've* /aɪv/, *we've* /wiːv/; *they've* /theɪv/; *haven't* /hæv(ə)nt/ and *hasn't* /hæs(ə)nt/.
- A nice idea, when listening and repeating in exercise 1, is to hold up your thumb and forefinger. Push them together to show the contractions.

SPEAKING

1 2.67

- Ask questions to find out what and how much students know about Robbie Williams.
- Students read and listen to a person talking about Robbie Williams.

 2.67

I think Robbie Williams should get a Lifetime Achievement Award. He's made some great CDs. He's written lots of songs. He's given concerts all round the world. He's been number one in many countries, and he's written a book. I think he's a great singer.

Cultural notes

- **Robbie Williams** is a British pop star whose biggest hits include *Angels* and *Let Me Entertain You*. He used to be in the successful boy band *Take That*, and went solo in 1997. He has won a lot of Brit awards.

2

- Pairwork. Put students in pairs to decide on a musician or group. Once they have decided, give them two or three minutes to brainstorm reasons why they should get a Lifetime Achievement Award for their work.
- You could write up some sentence starters on the board as prompts:

    She/he's sung …
    She/he's written …
    She/he's made …
    She/he's been …

3

- Pairwork. Put pairs into groups of four to talk about their musicians or groups.
- In feedback, ask one student from each group to summarize what was said.

Extension task

- You could roleplay this as a Grammy ceremony. Ask one student from each pair to come to the front of the class and make their presentation in support of their favourite musician or group. At the end, have a vote and choose the winner of the Lifetime Achievement Award.

Web research tasks

❯ *Methodology guidelines: Web research tasks, page xiii*

- Find out about another Grammy winner of the Lifetime Achievement Award and write a similar biography.

Web search key words
- grammy/awards/lifetime

IF YOU WANT SOMETHING EXTRA …

❯ *Photocopiable activity, page 237*
❯ *Teacher's notes, page 187*

12B | A public life

WHAT THE LESSON IS ABOUT

Theme	Appearing in public
Speaking	Pairwork discussion: talking about speaking in public
	Pairwork: answering a questionnaire about speaking in public
Listening	Three street interviews asking people if they have ever appeared in public on the television or the radio
Grammar	Present perfect 2: questions & negative
Pronunciation	Irregular past participles
Did you know?	Information about *Time* magazine's Person of the Year

IF YOU WANT A LEAD-IN ...

Introducing the theme: appearing in public

- Write on the board: *I'm famous because …*
- Tell students to ask you ten questions to find out why you are famous, e.g. *Were you on TV? Did you meet the queen? Do you have a famous brother?*
- After ten questions, tell students why you are famous. (Make something up if you're really not famous at all!)
- Divide students into groups of four. Tell students to think of a real reason why they are famous. Students ask ten questions and try to find out why they are famous.

Test before you teach: irregular past participles

- ⊙ *Methodology guidelines: Test before you teach, page xiii*

- Play past participles noughts and crosses.
- Draw the following table on the board:

Be	Give	Sing
Write	Do	Make
Have	Win	Come

- Divide the class into two teams, 'team X' and 'team O'.
- Team X goes first. They choose a square. If they produce an accurate present perfect sentence, using the participle form of the verb in the square, they win the square, and you write X in that square on the board. Then it is O's turn.
- The winner is the first team to get their symbol in a row of three, horizontally, vertically or diagonally.

SPEAKING

1
- You could lead in to this task by asking questions about the pictures, e.g. *Where are they? What are they doing? What are they talking about? How do they feel?*
- Pairwork. Put students in A and B pairs. They take it in turns to describe and guess the photos.

2
- Students could discuss the questions in pairs.
- In feedback, elicit stories from students who have been in 'public' situations.

LISTENING

This listening comes from a radio interview in which the reporter tries to find out how many ordinary members of the public have ever appeared in public on television or on the radio, after a survey had been carried out which said one in four Americans have been on television.

1
- Ask students to look at the headlines and check the vocabulary.
- Then have a class discussion on whether they think the statements are true for their country.

Language note
- **Obsessed with** means thinking about something all the time. You could also be obsessed with someone. It has negative connotations.

2 ⊙ 2.68
- Play the recording. Students listen and tick the words they hear. They can compare their answers with a partner before you check with the whole class.

The following words should be ticked:
television; radio; game show; newspaper; a letter; the evening news

⊙ **2.68**

> **J = journalist M1 = man 1 W = woman M2 = man 2**
>
> **1**
> **J:** Hi. Can I ask you some questions?
> **M1:** I'm busy, but OK.
> **J:** One survey says that one in four Americans have been on television. Have you ever been on <u>television</u>?
> **M1:** No, I haven't. I've never been on television. And I don't want to be.
> **J:** Have you ever spoken on the <u>radio</u>?
> **M1:** No, never. Sorry, I'm very busy now.
> **J:** OK, thank you.
>
> **2**
> **J:** Excuse me, have you ever been on television?
> **W:** Yes, I have! I was on a <u>game show</u> once. Have you heard of *The Big Award*?
> **J:** Yes, I have. It's on Channel 4. Did you win anything?
> **W:** No, I was in the audience.
> **J:** Great. One more question. Have you spoken on the radio?
> **W:** No, I haven't.
> **J:** Have you written <u>a letter</u> to a newspaper?
> **W:** No, I haven't.
> **J:** Thanks.
>
> **3**
> **J:** Hello.
> **M2:** Hello.
> **J:** I'm doing a survey. Can I ask you some questions?
> **M2:** Sure.
> **J:** Have you ever been on television?
> **M2:** What do you think?
> **J:** I'm sorry? I don't understand.
> **M2:** I work on television. I announce the <u>evening news</u>. Have you seen me?
> **J:** Oh, yes, I have! You're wearing a hat. I didn't recognize you.
> **M2:** That's alright.
> **J:** Well, thanks anyway.

3 🔘 **2.68**

- Play the recording again. Students listen and complete the table. They can compare their answers with a partner before you check with the whole class.

	Speaker 1	Speaker 2	Speaker 3
been on TV	✗	✓	✓
spoken on radio	✗	✗	?
written to newspaper	?	✗	?

Extra task

- To preview the grammar point, ask a few *Have you ever ...?* questions round the class. Ask: *Have you ever been on TV?/spoken on the radio?/written to a newspaper?* Ask: *When? Why?*

GRAMMAR: present perfect 2 – questions & negative

❯ *Language reference, Student's Book page 130*
❯ *Methodology guidelines: Grammar boxes, page xiii*

1

- Students complete the past participles then match them to the infinitives in the box. They can compare their answers with a partner before checking them with the *Irregular verb list* on page 159 of the Student's Book.

> been – be
> spoken – speak
> called – call
> had – have
> seen – see
> written – write
> heard – hear

2

- Students put the words in brackets into the present perfect to complete the dialogue. Remind them to use contractions where possible. They can then compare their answers with a partner.

> 1 Have you ever been
> 2 Have you ever spoken
> 3 have you called
> 4 Have you ever had
> 5 've written
> 6 Have you heard
> 7 've never heard
> 8 've never seen

Language notes

- Here, students need to manipulate question forms with **ever** and short forms. Common errors to watch out for include avoiding inversion to make questions, ✗ *You have ever been on TV?*, and getting short forms wrong, ✗ *Yes, I have ever been*, etc.

3 🔘 **2.69**

- Play the recording. Students listen and check their answers.
- Pairwork. Put students in pairs to practise the conversation.

🔘 **2.69**

> **J = journalist M = Martin**
> **J:** <u>Have you ever been</u> on television?
> **M:** No, I haven't.
> **J:** <u>Have you ever spoken</u> on the radio?
> **M:** What do you mean?
> **J:** Well, <u>have you called</u> a radio station?
> **M:** Yes, I have.
> **J:** <u>Have you ever had</u> your photo in the newspaper?
> **M:** Yes, I have. I've written several letters to the newspaper. One time my photo was next to my letter. <u>Have you heard</u> of the *Daily Star*?
> **J:** No, I haven't. I've never heard of it. I work for the *Weekly Times*.
> **M:** I've never seen your newspaper.

Extra pronunciation drill

- Do a prompt drill to practise form and pronunciation fully.
- Write a list of prompts on the board: *meet/famous person; drive/fast car; go/diving*, etc. (Alternatively, make flashcards with pictures to denote these activities.)
- Point to a prompt, (or hold up a flashcard), and model the question. Students repeat.
- Do this with all the questions. Make sure you pay attention to the linking in *Have _you_(w)_ever*. Then point to prompts, and nominate a student to ask another student across the class. Do this a number of times until most students have had a go. Correct errors of form and pronunciation.

Extra tasks

1

- Write the following list on the board:
  > *have breakfast in bed?*
  > *meet a very famous person?*
  > *read a book in English?*
  > *study all night for a test?*
  > *cook a meal for more than eight people?*
  > *drive a very fast car?*
  > *visit an English-speaking country?*
  > *give flowers to someone?*
  > *go diving in the ocean?*
- Ask students to make questions using the words in the box. They can compare their answers with a partner before you check with the whole class.
  > (Answers:
  > *Have you ever ...*   *had breakfast in bed?*
  > *met a very famous person?*
  > *read a book in English?*
  > *studied all night for a test?*
  > *cooked a meal for more than eight people?*
  > *driven a very fast car?*
  > *visited an English-speaking country?*
  > *given flowers to someone?*
  > *gone diving in the ocean?*)
- Put students in pairs. They must take it in turns to ask and answer the questions. Model the exercise with a good student first.
- Monitor the pairwork task carefully, and note errors for a whole class error feedback on the board at the end.

- In feedback, find which students have done which activities.

2

- You could easily adapt this task to play *Find someone who* … Write ten or twelve prompts on the board or on handouts: *meet/famous person; drive/fast car; go/diving,* etc. Students copy them. Then students walk round the class, asking *Have you ever …?* questions. They must find at least one person who has done each activity in order to win.

PRONUNCIATION: irregular past participles

1 💿 **2.70**

- Play the recording. Students listen to the past participles.

💿 **2.70**

/əʊ/	known, spoken
/ɪ/	given, driven
/ʌ/	won, done
/eɪ/	made, paid
/e/	read, met

2 & 3 💿 **2.71**

- Students put the words in the correct column in exercise 1. They can compare their answers with a partner.
- Play the recording. Students listen and check their answers.
- Play the recording again. Students listen and repeat the words.

/əʊ/	/ɪ/	/ʌ/	/eɪ/	/e/
broken	written	come	taken	slept

💿 **2.71**

known, spoken, broken
given, driven, written
won, done, come
made, paid, taken
read, met, slept

Language notes

- Notice that there are few clues in English spelling as to the pronunciation of past participles, (*read* and *met*, for example). Students need to be aware that English spelling is not phonetic.

SPEAKING

1

- Ask students to read the *A Public Life* questionnaire and make the questions. Note that students should only make questions from the prompts in the first column. Monitor and help with vocabulary and question-forming problems.

2

- Read through the instructions as a class and model the activity with one or two students.
- Pairwork. Put students in pairs and give them five minutes to ask and answer questions. Monitor, prompt, and note errors for a class feedback.

3

- Ask one person in each pair to report back to the rest of the class to find out who has the most public life.

Extension task

- Write on the board: *A sporting life; A fashionable life; A working life.*
- Ask groups to think of four or five questions to write their own *Have you ever* questionnaire about one of the topics. For example for the first topic, they could ask:
  Have you ever won a sporting competition? Have you ever watched a major football match?
  For the second topic: *Have you ever bought designer clothes?*
  For the third, *Have you ever worked at the weekend?*
- Once groups have prepared their questionnaires, ask one person from each group to stand up and move to the next group (in a clockwise direction) with their questions. They must then ask their new group their questions.

DID YOU KNOW?

1 & 2

- Students read the information about *Time* magazine.
- Students discuss the questions in pairs.

Cultural notes

- **Time magazine** is a monthly American magazine with articles on important political and social issues. It also has articles on science and arts subjects.

Web research tasks

❯ *Methodology guidelines: Web research tasks, page xiii*

- Students could go on the internet to find out about other people of the year.

Web search key words

- Time/person of the year

IF YOU WANT SOMETHING EXTRA …

❯ *Photocopiable activity, page 238*
❯ *Teacher's notes, page 187*

12c | English in your life

What the lesson is about

Theme	Learning English
Speaking	Pairwork discussion: talking about learning English
	Groupwork presentations: giving a short presentation
Reading	*Why learn English with us? Because we're the best*: brochure for a language school
Grammar	Verb forms (review)

If you want a lead-in ...

Discussion starters

⊘ *Methodology guidelines: Discussions starters, page xii*

- Write the following questions on the board:
  Why are you learning English?
  In what situations do you need to speak English?
  What do you enjoy about learning English? What do you dislike?
  How well are you doing at learning English?!

Speaking

1

- Lead in by asking: *When learning English, what is important?* Elicit a few suggestions open class before doing the exercise in the Student's Book.
- Pairwork. Ask students to read the sentences and decide on which three are very important and which three aren't very important to them. They then compare their ideas with a partner.

2

- Students then work with another pair and discuss what other things are important when learning English.
- In feedback, elicit other things that are important to the students in your class.

Reading

This reading text is an advertising brochure in which former students talk about their experiences studying at the International School of English.

1

⊘ *Methodology 23: Reading skills & strategies, page 94*

- Students read the text quickly for gist, and decide what kind of text it is. They can compare their answers with a partner before you check with the whole class.

An advertisement brochure for a language school

Language notes

- If you give someone your **personal attention**, then you watch, listen and think just about that person.

2

- Students read the text again and answer the questions. They can compare their answers with a partner before you check with the whole class.

1 Renata
2 Monica
3 Kanda
4 Constantine
5 Kanda
6 Monica
7 Doris
8 Constantine

3

- Pairwork. Students discuss the question with a partner.

Grammar: verb forms (review)

⊘ *Language reference, Student's Book page 130*
⊘ *Methodology guidelines: Grammar boxes, page xiii*

1

- Students find examples of the verb forms in the text.

1 ... everybody in my country <u>will speak</u> English. (Constantine); <u>I'm going to come</u> back ... (Renata)
2 <u>I'm studying now</u> ... (Kanda); <u>I'm learning</u> lots of ... (Monica); ... all the children in my country <u>are learning</u> ... (Constantine); <u>I'm studying</u> English because ... (Constantine)
3 I <u>like</u> this school ... (Kanda); the teacher <u>gives</u> us ... (Kanda); <u>I'm</u> a student ... (Monica); I <u>speak</u> a lot of English. (Monica); so I <u>come</u> here ... (Monica)
4 <u>I don't practise.</u> (Monica)
5 <u>I didn't know</u> any English ... (Doris); we <u>didn't study</u> English ... (Constantine)
6 I <u>came</u> ... (Doris); I <u>thought</u> ... (Doris); I <u>saw</u> ... (Doris); We also <u>had</u> ... (Doris); I <u>knew</u> ... (Doris); I <u>was</u> ... (Constantine); I <u>had</u> ... (Renata); I was very ... (Renata); the teachers <u>were</u> ... (Renata); they always <u>made</u> ... (Renata); we <u>could</u> ... (Renata)
7 I <u>wanted</u> ... (Doris); I <u>started</u> ... (Doris); I <u>liked</u> ... (Renata)
8 I <u>have been</u> at ... (Kanda); ... your school <u>have helped</u> me ... (Monica); I <u>haven't studied</u> English before. (Constantine)

2

- Students complete the *English in your Life* questionnaire with the correct form of the words in brackets. They can compare their answers with a partner before you check with the whole class.

2 do you have
3 do you do
4 was
5 did you start
6 Have you ever seen
7 Have you ever spoken
8 Are you going to study
9 Are you going to visit

3

- Pairwork. Put students in pairs to ask and answer the questions in exercise 2.
- In feedback, ask questions 1, 5 and 8 open class.

Extra tasks

1

- Copy the basic format of the questions in exercise 2 on to the board as prompts, e.g. *Why are you _____ing ...?; How often do you...?; When did you start ...?*, etc.
- Get students in pairs to make their own questions using the prompts. Put pairs into groups of four to ask the questions.

2

- Students work in small groups to create a brochure for their own language school. Ask them to write their own comments about their school, like the ones in the *Reading* text, and decide on the courses, and the prices, etc.

SPEAKING

1 **2.72**

- Give students a moment to read through the topics.
- Play the recording. Students listen and tick the topic the person is talking about.

Learning a language

2.72

In my country, English is an important language. It wasn't always important, but it is now. In the past, people learnt French or German at school. Now, everybody is learning English. For learning a language, I think it's important to learn new vocabulary and grammar, but it's also very important to practise speaking. For me, learning English is difficult, and I think speaking is the most difficult. I can understand English in books, and in magazines, but when I listen to English or American people, I don't understand. In my classes, we practise speaking a lot. When I started the year, it was impossible. I couldn't pronounce any sentences in English. Now it's better.

2

- Give students a couple of minutes to choose a topic for their presentation.

3

- Give students five minutes to make notes for their presentation. Monitor and help with ideas and vocabulary.
- You could brainstorm some ideas to the board about the topics if students are short of inspiration.

4 & 5

> *Key Methodology 7: Accurate speaking & fluent speaking, page 20*
> *Key Methodology 16: Helping students say it better, page 65*

- Groupwork. Put students in small groups. Tell students to read the rules carefully.
- One person presents their topic. Remind students who aren't speaking that as they listen they should think of one question to ask the speaker about their talk.
- At the end, the other students must ask their questions. Another student then presents their topic, and so on.
- Use the opportunity of one student speaking at length to do some individual error correction. Monitor each group as students speak, and note down errors made by at least one student in each group. At the end, hand the errors on a piece of paper to the group to correct together.

Extension task

- Write the list of topics in *Speaking* exercise 1 on the board, and number them.
    1 *Foods I like and don't like*
    2 *Where I live*
    3 *The capital city of my country*
    4 *A typical day*
    5 *A person that wins an award*
    6 *A favourite thing*
    7 *Learning a language*
- Divide the class into groups of four. One student must start talking about topic 1. If they run out of things to say, the student to their right must take over, and start talking.
- After a minute or so, shout out a number at random, e.g. *five*. The student who is talking must change over to topic five, and keep talking.
- Again, when that student runs out of ideas, the student to their right takes over. Keep changing topic and student until the students are tired!

IF YOU WANT SOMETHING EXTRA ...

> *Photocopiable activity, page 239*
> *Teacher's notes, page 187*

12D The end

WHAT THE LESSON IS ABOUT

Theme	The end of the course
Speaking	Pairwork discussion: proverbs about coming to the end of something & talking about how you feel at the end of something
	Groupwork game: playing *The Explore Tour* – a travel game
Listening	Four conversations at the end of the Explore London tour
Functional language	Thanking

IF YOU WANT A LEAD-IN …

Discussion starters

❯ *Methodology guidelines: Discussions starters, page xii*

* Write the following sentence starters on the board.
   On this course, I've learnt …
   On this course, I've enjoyed …
   The best thing was … The worst thing was …
   In the future, I'm going to …
* Ask students to complete the prompts for themselves, then discuss them in small groups.

Key Methodology 34
Coming to the end

* *Towards the end of a course don't just come to the last page of the book and close it! Allow your students the chance to notice what they have achieved and to celebrate this milestone. Although (as we have noted earlier) simply having 'done' a book doesn't necessarily mean that students have learnt it all, all the same, most students who have worked fairly conscientiously should find that their English is now significantly better than when they started. Here are some ideas for celebrating the achievement.*

Reflection on the course
* *Ask students to reflect individually on what they have learnt during the course. Ask them to make notes about how they felt about their English at the start of the book – and how they feel now. Students could write in their own language in order to express ideas more precisely. Allow a few minutes and then make pairs or groups for students to compare and discuss.*

Looking back at the book
* *Ask students to look back through the book and pick out lessons according to the questions you write on the board – e.g. the most interesting topic, the dullest topic, the most difficult grammar point, the funniest activity, something I didn't enjoy doing, the best picture, the most beautiful word, etc. Let students answer individually – then compare later.*

Students set the test
* *Rather than setting a big test yourself, letting students write their own test actually involves a great deal of useful review and revision. Elicit or suggest four or five different question types, e.g. multiple choice, gap-fill, etc. Show example questions. Distribute language areas to different pairs or groups, e.g. make & do. Allow sufficient time for students to write questions. You could check these yourself – or alternately allow the whole class to check together. When you have collected questions and copied them for everyone, run it as a test.*

The humane test
* *Rather than setting a secret test at the end of the course, do it openly and publicly. Show students the test paper a day or two before. Talk through some questions with them. Let students work together to agree some answers. Allow students to look up anything they want to. Let them take the paper home. In the test lesson, tell students the total marks and get students to predict how many they will get. Run the test then in the normal way. At the end, see how close students got to their prediction – and why. This way of running a test is much more than a test. It emphasises and celebrates progress – and all the preparation is a valuable revision exercise.*

Medal ceremony
* *Hand-draw some medals, one for each student. Cut them out and attach some sticking method (tape, pin etc). In class, make a big thing about awarding these to your students in a ceremonial way! Could be fun!*

SPEAKING

1
* Ask students to translate the proverbs into their own language. Ask them if there are any similar expressions in their language and what they are in English.

2

❯ *Key Methodology 7: Accurate speaking & fluent speaking, page 20*

* Pairwork. Put students in pairs to ask and answer the questions.
* You could put the following words on the board to help students answer the questions: *tired, relieved, disappointed, sad, happy, worried.*

LISTENING

This is the final episode of the listening story. There are five short conversations which revise functional language from the course. It is the end of the holiday for the Explore London tour.

In the first conversation, Valerie tells Meg that Sam is an undercover policeman who had been following Dave from the beginning of the tour, as he was suspected of stealing money from wealthy Americans.

In the second conversation, Valerie gives a short speech saying goodbye to the people on the tour.

In the third conversation, Delilah asks the hotel manager if she could leave her bags at reception.

In the fourth conversation, Meg and Rob enquire about how to get to the railway station.

In the final conversation, Hannah thanks Sam for recovering the money and invites him to her ranch in Texas.

1 🌀 **2.73**

- Students listen to the five conversations, and match the conversations 1–5 to the sentences a–e.

a 5   b 1   c 4   d 3   e 2

💿 **2.73**

**M = Meg V = Valerie D = Delilah HM = hotel manager
R = Rob Ha = Hannah S = Sam**

1
M: So, Valerie, what happened in the end with Dave?
V: Well, Sam and the police came and took him to the police station.
M: Sam?
V: Yes, I didn't know, but he's a police officer. He's followed Dave from the beginning of the tour.
M: No!
V: Yes. It seems that Dave has taken money from people, usually older, richer Americans, on several different tours. This wasn't the first time.
M: No!!
V: Yes. The police found all the Curtises' money in Dave's room, and credit cards from lots of other people.
M: That's incredible. Where's Dave now?
V: He's in jail. And I thought he was really nice.
M: Oh. You just can never tell about some people.

2
V: Well, everyone, this is the end of our tour. Brian is going to take people to the airport. He's waiting outside. I also wanted to say <u>thank you very much</u>. It was really, really nice to meet you. I mean that honestly! This was my first tour and I had a very nice time. There's a paper going round for you to put your email addresses on if you want to write to each other. My email address is at the top. You can write to me!

3
D: Hi there.
HM: Hello.
D: Are you the hotel manager?
HM: Yes, I am.
D: Look, I know this is a busy time …
HM: That's fine. I always have time for a beautiful young woman …
D: <u>Thanks</u>. Um. Can I leave my bags here for half an hour?
HM: Of course. Of course. I can keep them in my private room.
D: No, here is fine.
HM: They will be safe here.
D: <u>Thank you</u>.
HM: <u>You're welcome</u>.

4
R: Meg?
M: Yes?
R: We're going to the train station, right?
M: Yes, that's right.
R: So, how do we get there?
M: I don't know. Why don't we take a taxi?
R: No, no, no taxis this time. Excuse me, Valerie?
V: Yes?
R: How can we get to the train station?
V: Don't worry, Brian can take you later.
R: Really? Oh, <u>thanks a lot</u>!
V: <u>Don't mention it</u>.

5
Ha: Oh, there you are! Sam!
S: Hello, Mrs Curtis.
Ha: I never knew you were a policeman.
S: Well, I was undercover.
Ha: My husband and I just want to say <u>thank you very much</u> for getting our money back and catching that bad man.
S: <u>That's alright</u>. It's my job.
Ha: I know, I know. And you do a very good job, too.
S: Mm.
Ha: Would you like to come to our ranch in Texas next month? We'd love to see you.
S: I … Texas?
Ha: Don't worry, we can pay for everything for you. My husband has lots of money.
S: <u>Thank you very much</u>, but I can't. I'm sorry. I'm going to … um, Scotland.
Ha: Oh.
S: Yes, Scotland. Very important case. Um, maybe another time?

Language notes

- **_Undercover_**: to work undercover is to work secretly.
- **_A ranch_** is found in the US or Australia. It is a large farm where cows, horses, etc. are kept.
- **_A case_** is a situation or crime that involves the police or the law.

2 💿 **2.73**

- Play the recording again. Students listen and answer the questions.

Conversation 1
1   In Dave's room.
2   He's a police officer.
Conversation 2
3   He's taking them to the airport.
4   Their email addresses.
Conversation 3
5   She wants to leave her bags at reception.
Conversation 4
6   No.
7   Brian is going to take them.
Conversation 5
8   To her ranch in Texas.
9   In Scotland.

FUNCTIONAL LANGUAGE: thinking

❯ *Language reference, Student's Book page 131*

1

- Students find examples of thanking and the responses in tapescript 2.73 on page 146 of the Student's Book. They then complete the *Functional language* box.

Giving thanks
Thank you.
Thank you <u>very</u> much.
Thanks a <u>lot</u>.
That's very kind of you.

Responses
You're <u>welcome</u>.
Don't mention it.
That's <u>alright</u>.

Stronger classes

- Ask students to look at the *Functional language* box first and try complete the missing words before listening to the recording.

2 & 3 2.74

❯ *Key Methodology 29: Pronunciation – don't forget intonation!*

- Students choose the correct response. They can then compare their answers with a partner.
- Play the recording. Students listen and check their answers.
- You could play the recording again, pausing after each line. Students listen and repeat.
- Put students in pairs to practise the dialogues.

> 1 a 2 a 3 b 4 b 5 a

🔘 **2.74**

1
A: We've bought you a little gift.
B: Oh, thank you.

2
C: Thank you very much for dinner.
D: You're welcome.

3
E: Here, you can have my pen.
F: Thanks.

4
G: Thank you very much for everything you've done.
H: Don't mention it.

5
I: Excuse me. You left your wallet in the shop.
J: Oh. Thank you very much.

Language notes

- It is important to get students to attempt a lively and expressive intonation pattern when saying all these expressions in exercise 3. Flat intonation can sound rude and disinterested – even ironic. The basic intonation pattern here should start high, get higher, and be falling at the end:

  Thanks a lot.

4

- Pairwork. Put students in pairs to prepare two similar dialogues.
- You could elicit a few ideas for situations before they start.
- Students practise their dialogues with their partner. Ask a few pairs to stand up and act out a dialogue for the class. Make sure that they are using the correct intonation.

Extension task

- Write a series of situations on the board: *saying goodbye to a teacher*; *leaving a friend's house after dinner*; *returning a DVD you borrowed*; *telling someone their hair looks good*; *thanking someone who has saved your life.*
- Students must improvise dialogues for each situation. For example:

  Thanks for teaching me a lot of English.
  You're welcome.

SPEAKING

❯ *Communication activites, Student's Book page 159*

1

- The aim of this game is to revise vocabulary and functional language from the course. You will need to bring enough dice to the lesson so that each group has one to play the game. So, if you have a class of twenty, you will need five dice. You could also bring different coloured counters, (although students could always use coins or other objects).
- Pre-teach the following games vocabulary which is necessary to understand the instructions:
  dice   counter   square   throw the dice.
- Groupwork. Put students in groups of three or four. Tell them to read the instructions. Ask a few check questions to make sure everybody understands, e.g. *What do you do when you are in a green square?*
- Students play the travel game. Monitor and help. You could note errors to judge how well they have taken on board the language taught on the course. Alternatively, you could just approach this as light-hearted fun. It's the end of the course after all!

IF YOU WANT SOMETHING EXTRA ...

❯ *Photocopiable activity, page 240*
❯ *Teacher's notes, page 188*

Answer key

12 REVIEW

❯ *Student's Book page 158*

1

1 've sung
2 've written
3 've made
4 've won
5 've had
6 've been

2

Students' own answers.

3

1 Have you ever had breakfast in bed?
2 Have you ever read a book in English?
3 Have you ever cooked a meal for more than eight people?
4 Have you ever visited an English-speaking country?
5 Have you ever been diving in the sea?

4

Students' own answers.

5

Part One
1 Present simple
2 Present continuous
3 Past simple
4 Future (*will*)
5 Present simple
6 Present perfect
7 Past simple
8 Future (*going to*)

Part Two
1 Present simple
2 Present perfect
3 Past simple
4 Present continuous
5 Future (*will*)
6 Present perfect
7 Future (*going to*)

6

1
A: What a beautiful gift! Thank you very much.
B: You're welcome.

2
A: Excuse me. ~~I could~~ Could I use your phone for a minute?
B: Sure. Here you are.
A: Thank you.

3
A: Why ~~we don't~~ don't we ask the teacher?
B: Yes, that's a good idea.
A: OK, then.

4
A: What ~~does~~ is the matter?
B: Nothing. I'm fine.
A: You look tired.

5
A: What do you think of the *Star Wars* films?
B: I think they're great.
A: I don't like them.

12 WRITING

❯ *Workbook page 87*

Model answer
Dear Sam,

Thank you for a wonderful evening. I had a really good time and the food was delicious. It was very nice meeting all your friends and I hope they could understand my English. Next time you should come to my flat and have dinner.

Thank you again
Yukiko

Resource materials

Worksheet	Interaction	Activity	Focus
B1 How do you spell that?	Groupwork	Spelling game	Vocabulary: international English words.
B2 Numbers bingo	Whole class	Game	Vocabulary: numbers.
1A This is her credit card	Groupwork	Game	Possessive adjectives. Vocabulary: objects (1).
1B Worldwide dominoes	Groupwork	Game	Vocabulary: countries & nationalities.
1C What's this?	Pairwork	Board game	Demonstrative adjectives. Singular & plural nouns. *A* or *an*. Vocabulary: objects (2).
1D Would you like a cup of coffee?	Whole class	Class mingle	Introducing & making small talk. Offers & responses.
2A Expat lifestyle profiles	Pairwork	Information gap	Present simple verbs. Verbs & vocabulary for everyday activities.
2B Do you play football?	Pairwork	Questionnaire	Present simple questions & short answers.
2C Girls just wanna have fun	Pairwork	Song	Vocabulary: the family. Listening. Understanding lyrics.
2D Find your double	Whole class	Class mingle	Describing people.
3A A flat by the river	Pairwork	Information gap	Prepositions of place.
3B Is there a plant in the study?	Pairwork	Memory game	*There is/there are. How many.* Vocabulary: parts of a house.
3C There are two lamps	Pairwork	Find the differences	Vocabulary: furniture.
3D Finding the hotel shop	Pairwork	Information gap	Asking for & giving directions.
4A I say a little prayer	Pairwork	Song	Present simple verbs. Listening. Understanding lyrics.
4B I usually play football on Saturday	Groupwork	Matching sentence halves	Prepositions of time: *in, at, on.*
4C How often do you ...?	Whole class	Class mingle	Adverbs of frequency.
4D Just a minute, please.	Pairwork	Roleplay (making phone calls)	Talking on the phone & leaving messages.
5A I believe I can fly	Pairwork	Song	*Can/can't.* Listening. Understanding lyrics.
5B What was the weather like?	Pairwork	Information gap	*Was/were.* Vocabulary: the weather. Asking about holidays.
5C My ideal holiday	Pairwork & groupwork	Questionnaire	Past simple regular verbs.
5D A weekend away	Individual & groupwork	Roleplay (booking accommodation)	Asking for & giving or refusing permission.
6A What did you do last night?	Pairwork	Find the differences	Past simple irregular.
6B Who's the actor?	Pairwork	Information gap	Past simple regular & irregular verbs.
6C Do you sing badly?	Individual & pairwork	Guessing game	Adverbs of manner.
6D Can't stand coffee	Whole class	Class mingle	Present simple questions & answers. Talking about likes & dislikes.

Resource materials

Worksheet	Interaction	Activity	Focus
7A Which diet?	Pairwork	Guessing game	Questions with any. Vocabulary: food.
7B Recipes	Pairwork	Information gap	*How much & how many.*
7C Are you a fussy eater?	Pairwork	Questionnaire	Vocabulary: describing food.
7D Restaurant trip	Groupwork	Roleplay (at a restaurant)	Ordering food at a restaurant.
8A He loves playing football	Whole class	Miming game	Verbs + *-ing.*
8B Traffic report	Pairwork	Information gap	Present continuous.
8C Sailing	Pairwork	Song	Present continuous. Listening. Understanding lyrics.
8D Let's go by train	Pairwork	Roleplay (a night out)	Making arrangements. Vocabulary: transportation.
9A What should I wear/do/take with me?	Pairwork	Game	*Should/shouldn't* for giving advice.
9B Stand on one foot!	Groupwork	Action game	Responding to imperatives. Vocabulary: body parts.
9C Who is it?	Pairwork	Guessing game	Vocabulary: physical characteristics. Possessive pronouns. Describing people.
9D At the doctor's	Pairwork	Roleplay (at the doctor's)	Asking/saying how you feel. Giving advice.
10A Rules dominoes	Pairwork	Game	*Must, mustn't & needn't.*
10B Comparing capitals	Pairwork	Reading & discussion	Comparatives.
10C Which holiday?	Pairwork	Information gap & discussion	*Go + -ing.* Superlatives.
10D Shopping for souvenirs	Groupwork	Roleplay (at the shops)	Buying things in shops. Vocabulary: size and colours.
11A What do I do?	Pairwork	Guessing game	Question words. Vocabulary: jobs.
11B How organized are you?	Pairwork & groupwork	Questionnaire	*Will.*
11C Life quiz	Pairwork	Questionnaire	Adverbs of frequency.
11D Who wants to go out with me?	Whole class	Class mingle	Accepting and declining invitations. Phrasal verbs.
12A Pop careers	Pairwork	Guessing game	Present perfect & past simple to describe achievements.
12B Have you ever …?	Groupwork	Board game	Present perfect. Talking about life experiences.
12C Fields of gold	Pairwork	Song	Revision of verb forms. Listening. Understanding lyrics.
12D Goodbye!	Pairwork	Roleplay (parting)	Saying goodbye. Thanking.

Teacher's notes

BASICS 1 How do you spell that?

ACTIVITY
Groupwork. Spelling game.

FOCUS
Vocabulary: international English words.

PREPARATION
Photocopy one worksheet for each group of three or four students. Cut up the cards on section B of each worksheet.

PROCEDURE
- Explain to students that they are going to play a language game.
- Hand out one copy of the picture board and a set of letter cards to each group of students.
- Explain to students that they have to take turns to make the words that they see on the picture board, using the letter cards. Elect someone in the group to mix up the letter cards if you haven't already done so.
- Place the cards face up on the table.
- Students take it in turns to choose two cards with the aim of making one of the words from the picture boards.
- Once a player has made a word, they place the letter cards in the correct order on the appropriate picture on the board, e.g. football.
- Players continue making words until they have successfully spelt all the words on the board.
- Check the answers with the class.

EXTENSION
- Ask students to spell the words out loud to each other, taking turns to ask and answer, e.g. A: 'How do you spell photo?' B: 'P-H-O-T-O.' If you want to make it more difficult, ask them to do it by memory without using the letter cards.

BASICS 2 Numbers bingo

ACTIVITY
Whole class. Game.

FOCUS
Vocabulary: numbers.

PREPARATION
Photocopy one copy of Worksheet 1 for each group of eight students. Cut up the 'numbers cards'. Photocopy Worksheet 2, the 'caller's card', for yourself.

PROCEDURE
- Explain to students that they are going to play a game of 'numbers bingo'.

- Hand out one numbers card to each student.
- Explain that you are going to call out various numbers and, as you do so, students cross out the numbers on their card that they hear. Ask them to use a pencil, so that you can reuse the cards.
- Call out the numbers at random. Each time you call out a number, cross it off your 'caller's card', so that you can keep a record of what you have said and so do not duplicate numbers.
- When a player has crossed out all the numbers on their card, they must put up their hand and shout 'Bingo!' The first person to do this is the winner.
- To check the answers, ask the student to call out their numbers one by one. Check that you have crossed them off your card.
- Ask the students to rub out their answers and to exchange their cards with the person next to them. Repeat the game.
- With stronger classes, students can take turns to call out the numbers.

EXTENSION
- For writing practice, ask students to write down the numbers they hear as well as crossing them off the grid. Once they have called 'Bingo!' check their spelling by asking them to spell out the words to the rest of the class. Award a point for every correct spelling and deduct a point for every incorrect spelling.

1A This is her credit card

ACTIVITY
Groupwork. Game.

FOCUS
Possessive adjectives. Vocabulary: objects 1.

PREPARATION
Photocopy one worksheet for each group of four students. Cut up the cards on each worksheet.

PROCEDURE
- Explain to students that they are going to play a game.
- Divide one set of cards between each group. Each student should have four cards.
- Ask students to write their name on the writing line on each card.
- Elect one member of each group to collect the cards and mix them up. They then deal out the cards again between the group.
- The students must read the name on the card and then give it back to the owner. Before doing so, they must take turns to announce to the rest of the group who the card belongs to, e.g. 'This isn't my TV. It's his/her TV.' In some cases they will have been dealt their own card, in which case they tell the rest of the group, e.g. 'This is my credit card.' and keep it.
- Encourage students to use the possessive adjectives *his, her, your* rather than the name of the person.

1B Worldwide dominoes

ACTIVITY
Groupwork. Game.

FOCUS
Vocabulary: countries and nationalities.

PREPARATION
Photocopy one worksheet for each group of three students. Cut up the domino pieces.

PROCEDURE
- Explain to students that they are going to play a game of dominoes.
- Hand out one set of dominoes to each group.
- Ask the students to divide the dominoes evenly between them.
- Explain the rules. The first student puts down a domino. The next student must put down a domino which corresponds to either the country or the nationality on the preceding domino, e.g. France – French or Italian – Italy.
- If the student hasn't got the correct matching domino, they miss a turn. The first person to put down all their dominoes is the winner.

EXTENSION
- Students repeat the game, but this time they say aloud their country of origin and nationality according to the domino they are putting down, e.g. 'I'm French. I'm from France'. Stronger students could practise the question form as well, e.g. 'I'm Chinese. I'm from China. Where are you from?'

1C What's this?

ACTIVITY
Pairwork. Board game.

FOCUS
Demonstrative adjectives: *this, that, these, those*.
Singular and plural nouns; *a* or *an*.
Vocabulary: objects 2.

PREPARATION
Photocopy one worksheet for each pair. Each pair will also need a coin and two counters.

PROCEDURE
- Explain to students that they are going to play a board game to practise saying *this, that, these* and *those*.
- Hand out one worksheet to each pair, and distribute the coins and counters.
- Show students the board. Explain the meaning of 'miss a turn'.
- Demonstrate how to play the game, and explain the rules.
1 Place both counters on the 'START' square.
2 Toss the coin. Heads means move forward one space; tails means move forward two spaces.
3 Move the counter one space on the board.

4 Look at the artwork on the square and say the correct phrase, e.g. 'These are pens'.
5 Each student must judge their partner's response. If a player makes a grammatical mistake, they have to go back one square and it is the other student's turn.
6 If the sentence is correct, toss the coin again and say another phrase, e.g. 'This is a bottle of water'.
7 The winner is the first student to reach the 'FINISH' square.

EXTENSION
- Students can use the game to practise the question form. Players take turns to ask and answer questions when they land on a square, e.g. A: 'What's this?' B: 'It's a key.'

ANSWERS
1 These are pens.
2 This is a bottle of water.
4 That is a bus.
5 This is a mobile phone.
6 That is a camera.
7 Those are keys.
9 This is an alarm clock.
10 Those are glasses.
11 That is a taxi.
12 This is a book.
13 That is a newspaper.
14 This is an umbrella.
16 Those are buses.
17 This is a key.
18 That is a pen.
20 These are bags.

1D Would you like a cup of coffee?

ACTIVITY
Whole class. Class mingle.

FOCUS
Introducing and making small talk.
Offers and responses.

PREPARATION
Photocopy one worksheet for each group of 16 students. Cut up the role cards. You can duplicate the 'guest cards' if you have to make up class numbers, but the 'waiter cards' must remain as eight.

PROCEDURE
- Explain to students that they are going to do a roleplay that involves the whole class. They are all at a drinks party and some of them are 'guests' and some of them are 'waiters'.
- Whole class. Explain what each of the students has to do. The 'guests' must invent a name and nationality for themselves and mingle at the party, introducing themselves and talking to all the other 'guests'.

Meanwhile, the 'waiters' must circulate and offer the 'guests' drinks. Each 'waiter' has a card with a picture of the drink that they will be serving. Each 'guest' has a card with his/her name and a list of the three drinks he/she will be drinking at the party, so they must accept or refuse the 'waiter's' offer as appropriate.

- Select eight students to act as 'waiters', and divide the waiter role cards between them.
- Distribute the necessary number of guest role cards to the rest of the class. Ask 'guests' to invent names and nationalities and write them on their cards. When they have been offered all of the drinks on their list, and they have introduced themselves to all of the other 'guests' at the party, they may sit down.

2A Expat lifestyle profiles

ACTIVITY
Pairwork. Information gap.

FOCUS
Present simple verbs. Verbs and vocabulary for everyday activities.

PREPARATION
Photocopy one worksheet for each pair. Cut the worksheet in half.

PROCEDURE
- Explain to students that they are going to take turns to exchange information with their partner in order to complete a table.
- Pairwork. Hand out worksheets to students A and B, making sure that students don't show them to each other.
- Explain to students that each of the four people in the table lives and works abroad, and that students can build up a complete picture of all four people's lives by talking to their partner.
- Students look at the information on their table and take turns to read complete sentences to their partner, e.g. 'Frank works in an office'.
- Each partner listens and writes the missing information on his/her table until it is complete.
- When they have finished, students take turns to read the four complete lifestyle profiles to each other.

VARIATION/EXTENSION
- Stronger students could complete their tables by asking yes/no questions, e.g. A: 'Does Maria live in a house?' B: 'Yes, she does. She lives in a house in London.'
- At the end of the activity, students could act out a roleplay. Ask students to choose a character and roleplay a meeting. Suggest some questions they could use to start the conversation, e.g. 'Hello, my name's Frank. I live in New York. What's your name? Where do you live? What languages do you speak?'

2B Do you play football?

ACTIVITY
Pairwork. Questionnaire.

FOCUS
Present simple questions and short answers.

PREPARATION
Photocopy one questionnaire for each student.

PROCEDURE
- Explain to students that they are going to complete a questionnaire and then interview their partner.
- Pairwork. Hand out one worksheet to each student.
- Students complete the 'Me' column of the questionnaire with a tick (✔) for yes (they do or have this thing) or a cross (✗) for no (they do not do or have this thing).
- When they have finished, they interview their partner by asking questions, e.g. 'Do you talk about your feelings?' and complete the *Partner 1* column in the same way. Make sure they write their partner's name on the line at the top of the column.
- When they have finished interviewing their first partner, students find a new partner, and complete the *Partner 2* column in the same way.
- In new pairs, students take turns to ask each other questions about their previous partner, e.g. A: 'Does Mario have a dog?/Has Mario got a dog?' B: 'No, he doesn't./No, he hasn't.'

EXTENSION
- As an open class activity, students take turns to stand up and ask each other one question from the questionnaire, e.g. A: 'Who is your partner?' B: 'Leila.' A: 'Does Leila speak Turkish?' B: 'Yes, she does.'
- Students write a profile about their partner on a separate sheet of paper. Collect the papers and then choose a student to read one of the profiles aloud. The rest of the class tries to guess who it is. Repeat with all the profiles.

2C Girls just wanna have fun

ACTIVITY
Pairwork. Song.

FOCUS
Vocabulary: the family.
Listening. Understanding lyrics.

PREPARATION
Photocopy one worksheet for each pair. CD player.

 [1]

PROCEDURE
- Explain to students that they are going to listen to a song.
- Pairwork. Hand out one worksheet to each pair.
- Explain that some of the lyrics are in bold print because the students must listen and decide if these words are right or wrong.

- Play the first verse. Ask students to correct any bold words that they think are wrong.
- Check the answers with the class.
- Play the whole song. The students listen and correct the bold words they think are wrong. Check the answers with the class.
- Play the recording again and go through the song line by line.
- Go through the questions with the students, comparing different answers. Make notes on the board.
- Play the recording again if necessary, and check the answers with the class.

ANSWERS

1   2 mother   3 girls
        4 father   6 girls   8 one
        9 they   11 girls

2   1 She lives with her parents.
        2 She wants to have fun.
        3 We don't know.
        4 Yes, she does.

Note

'Girls just wanna have fun' was sung by Cyndi Lauper in 1983.

2D   Find your double

ACTIVITY
Whole class & pairwork. Class mingle.

FOCUS
Describing people.

PREPARATION
Photocopy one worksheet per group of 16 students. Cut up the cards on each worksheet.

PROCEDURE
- Explain to students that they are going to do a class mingle activity.
- Hand out one card to each student.
- Class mingle. Explain that each student has a partner with exactly the same description as that on their card. They must go around the class and ask each other questions in order to find their identical partner, e.g. A: 'What do you look like?' B: 'I'm tall and thin.' A: 'What colour eyes do you have?' B: 'I have green eyes.'
- When they have found their identical partner, they may sit down.

EXTENSION
- Pairwork. Students work with their identical partner. They have to write a more detailed profile of their character, but they must work alone. They mustn't let their partner see what they are writing. Encourage them to think of as much information as they can, e.g. profession (singer, film star), height (1 metre 50), looks (ugly, beautiful). Give them a limited amount of time, e.g. one minute. Then, with their partner, they compare differences and similarities in what they have written.

3A   A flat by the river

ACTIVITY
Pairwork. Information gap.

FOCUS
Prepositions of place.

PREPARATION
Photocopy one worksheet for each pair. Cut the worksheet in half.

PROCEDURE
- Explain to students that they are going to take turns to exchange information with their partner about a text on where someone lives.
- Hand out worksheets to students A and B.
- Demonstrate the activity.
1 Explain that some of the sentences on each worksheet are incomplete and that it is necessary to ask questions in order to find the missing information.
2 Write the first incomplete sentence from worksheet B on the board: 'Gerry Thompson lives in _____.'
3 Elicit the correct question from the class: 'Where does Gerry Thompson live?' Then ask a student with worksheet A for the answer. Write the answer in the gapped sentence.
4 Do this with two or three more examples, demonstrating how the students take it in turns to ask and answer questions.
- Pairwork. Students now do the activity, taking turns to ask their partner questions about the information on their sheet.
- Tell students that, if necessary, they should ask each other how to spell words.
- When they have finished, students check their answers with each other.
- Go through the answers with the class as an open class activity.

EXTENSION
- Students rewrite the texts by replacing some of the key nouns in the text. Demonstrate by starting off as an open class activity, and then letting the students continue in pairs, e.g. Gerry Thompson lives in **Barcelona**. He has a **big flat** in the **city centre** and a big house **by the sea**. During the week he lives in his **house by the sea**. The house is next to a small **restaurant** …
Encourage students to be as imaginative as possible. In this way, they are motivated to ask about and add new vocabulary to the existing lexis.

3B   Is there a plant in the study?

ACTIVITY
Pairwork. Memory game.

FOCUS
There is/there are.
How many.
Vocabulary: parts of a school.

PREPARATION
Photocopy one worksheet for each pair students.

PROCEDURE
- Explain to students that they are going to play a memory game.
- Hand out one worksheet to each pair.
- Explain that they are going to look at the picture for a short time and remember as many details as possible. Then they are going to test each other by asking questions.
- Give the students a short time, e.g. 30 seconds, to look at the picture. They aren't allowed to take notes.
- When the allocated time is up, ask students to turn the picture face down on the table and take turns to ask each other questions.
- Give them a short time, e.g. five minutes, to ask each other questions. Encourage them to include as much detail as possible, such as an item and a room, e.g. A: 'Is there a lift in the hall?' B: 'No, there isn't.' A: 'Are there any windows in the garage?' B: 'No, there aren't.'
- They shouldn't correct their partners if they think they are wrong. They must just make a note of their answers.
- When the allocated time is up, students turn their picture back and check their answers. The player with the most correct answers is the winner.

EXTENSION
- Still working in pairs, each student writes a short description of a place that they know well, e.g. their school, favourite café, favourite restaurant, cinema, theatre, etc. When they have finished, they read it out to their partner, who must guess what it is.

3C There are two lamps

ACTIVITY
Pairwork. Find the differences.

FOCUS
Vocabulary: furniture.

PREPARATION
Photocopy one worksheet for each pair. Cut the worksheet in half.

PROCEDURE
- Explain to students that they are going to take turns to describe their picture to their partner. In doing so, they must identify ten differences.
- Pairwork. Hand out worksheets to students A and B. Demonstrate the activity with a student in front of the class.
- Students take turns to talk about their picture to their partner. Encourage them to ask and answer questions, e.g. A: 'In my picture there are two lamps'. B: 'Where are they?'
- Students make notes of the differences.
- When they have finished, they should go through their findings with each other.
- Check the answers with the rest of the class.

3D Finding the hotel shop

ACTIVITY
Pairwork. Information gap.

FOCUS
Asking for and giving directions.

PREPARATION
Photocopy one worksheet for each pair. Cut the worksheet in half.

PROCEDURE
- Explain to students that they are going to practise asking for and giving directions inside a hotel.
- Before starting the activity, elicit some of the target language and make notes on the board, e.g. *turn left/right …, go along the corridor …, it's on the left/right …, it's next to …*
- Practise some model exchanges as an open class activity to ensure that the students know how to use ordinal numbers within this context, e.g. 'It's on the first/second floor'.
- Pairwork. Hand out worksheets to students A and B.
- Students take turns to ask for directions and find the places on their plan.

4A I say a little prayer

ACTIVITY
Pairwork. Song.

FOCUS
Present simple verbs.
Listening. Understanding lyrics.

PREPARATION
Photocopy one worksheet for each pair. CD player.

 [2]

PROCEDURE
- Explain to students that they are going to listen to a song.
- Pairwork. Hand out one worksheet to each pair.
- Ask them to fold over the worksheet so that they can't see the lyrics.
- Play the recording once. Students listen and tick the words in 1 when they hear them. Play the recording again if necessary.
- Tell the students to look at the lyrics. Play the recording again and tell the students to write the words from 1 in the gaps.
- Check the answers with the class. Play the recording again if necessary and go through the song line by line.

> ### ANSWERS
> 1 wake up   2 put   3 say   4 live   5 run   6 think
> 7 believe   8 love   9 answer

Note
'I say a little prayer' was sung by Aretha Franklin in 1968.

4B I usually play football on Saturday

ACTIVITY
Groupwork. Matching sentence halves.

FOCUS
Prepositions of time: *in, at, on.*

PREPARATION
Photocopy one worksheet for each group of four students. Cut the worksheet in half. Cut the part sentences in each section into strips. Do not mix them up. Hand out three sentences from section A and three from section B to each member of the group.

PROCEDURE
- Explain to students that they are going to play a matching game.
- Introduce the concept by writing an example of a 'sentence beginning' on the board, e.g. *I sometimes play football …* Elicit a number of suitable endings from the class, e.g. *… at the weekend, … in the evening, … on Sundays, … at 12 o'clock.*
- Explain that it is important to keep the game as oral practice, so the students must not allow the rest of the group to see their sentences.
- The aim of the game is to make complete, *logical* sentences.
- Students take turns to read out a 'sentence beginning' from their selection. They can only say it once, so they must speak very clearly.
- The first student to reply with a matching 'sentence ending' makes the match. As most 'sentence beginnings' can match with more than one 'sentence ending', the students have to be quick and listen carefully.
- Once the group has agreed that it is acceptable, the two students should put the complete sentence together on the table in front of them.
- The first player to put down all their cards is the winner.
- When everyone has finished, go through the answers with the class, comparing the different answers between each group.

EXTENSION
- Students remain working in their groups. Choose a 'sentence beginning' and read it aloud to the class. The groups then have exactly 30 seconds to write as many alternative endings as possible. At the end of 30 seconds, blow a whistle or clap your hands to indicate that the allotted time is up, and read out another 'sentence beginning'. Do this for five sentences in total. At the end, the groups go through their answers and add up the total of different endings for each sentence. Check the answers with the class. The group with the most correct endings per sentence wins a point. The group with the most points is the winner.

4C How often do you …?

ACTIVITY
Whole class. Class mingle.

FOCUS
Adverbs of frequency.

PREPARATION
Photocopy one worksheet for each student.

PROCEDURE
- Explain to students that they are going to go around the class and ask each other questions.
- Hand out one worksheet to each student.
- Explain that they need to turn each statement into a question and then go round the class asking the questions. Ask students to look at the first activity on the list, and elicit the question they need to ask: 'How often do you read in the bath?' Elicit a possible answer, e.g. 'I rarely read in the bath' and write the question and answer on the board.
- Students go around the class asking each other questions about the activities on their worksheet. They must find a person whose reply matches the prompt on their questionnaire, e.g. A: 'How often do you read in the bath?' B: 'I always read in the bath.' They write that person's name in the *Name* column on the worksheet.
- When they have written a name against every activity on the worksheet, students sit down.
- Students can either compare their answers with a partner, or you can go through the answers as an open class activity.

EXTENSION
- Play a true/false game. Divide the class into two teams. Students take turns to read out one of their results to the other team, having first decided whether or not to read out a true result or a false result. The other team must decide if it's true or false. Award a point for every correct answer. The first team to reach a score of 20 is the winner.
- Students write complete sentences based on the information in their questionnaire, e.g. 'Franco always reads in the bath.' 'Miles usually goes to work on Saturdays.'

4D Just a minute, please.

ACTIVITY
Pairwork. Roleplay (making phone calls).

FOCUS
Talking on the phone and leaving messages.

PREPARATION
Photocopy one worksheet for each pair. Cut the worksheet in half.

PROCEDURE
- Explain to students that they are going to practise talking to each other on the phone.
- Before doing the activity, elicit some of the expressions and write them on the board, e.g. 'Is Mrs Beach there, please?' 'Can I take a message?' 'I'll call you back.' 'Just a minute, please.' 'Would you like to leave a message?' 'I'd like to speak to Joe, please.'
- Choose a student and demonstrate a simple phone call with him/her to the rest of the class.
- Pairwork. Hand out worksheets to students A and B.
- Students read their cards and take turns making calls and answering the telephone.
- Go around the class, checking and helping where necessary.

5A I believe I can fly

ACTIVITY
Pairwork. Song.

FOCUS
Can/can't.
Listening. Understanding lyrics.

PREPARATION
Photocopy one worksheet for each pair. CD player.

 [3]

PROCEDURE
- Explain to students that they are going to listen to a song.
- Divide students into pairs. Hand out one worksheet to each pair.
- Explain that some of the lines are missing and appear above the lyrics.
- Play the recording once. Students listen, and working in pairs try and identify the correct lines. Play the recording again if necessary.
- Play the recording again. Students write the lines in the gaps.
- Check the answers with the class. Play the recording again and go through the song line by line.

ANSWERS
1 then I can do it
2 I believe I can fly
3 I believe I can soar
4 Sometimes silence can seem so loud
5 then I can be it
6 I believe I can touch the sky
7 If I can see it

Note
'I believe I can fly' was sung by R. Kelly in 1996.

5B What was the weather like?

ACTIVITY
Pairwork. Information gap.

FOCUS
Was/were.
Vocabulary: the weather.   Asking about holidays.

PREPARATION
Photocopy one worksheet for each pair. Cut the worksheet in half.

PROCEDURE
- Explain to students that they are going to take turns to exchange information with their partner about a holiday they have had. The information about their holiday is on their worksheet.
- Give the students time to read about their holiday.
- Pairwork. Hand out worksheets to students A and B.
- Elicit the first question they should ask, 'Where were you?' Then ask one pair to demonstrate the first question and answer 'I was in the French Alps/Sydney, Australia.' Make sure that they answer questions fully but only write notes of their partner's answers, e.g. *French Alps*.
- Students take turns to ask their partner questions about their holiday, and to make notes in the holiday profile.
- When they have finished, students check their answers by taking turns to read out their partner's holiday profile.

EXTENSION
- As a freer practice exercise, students can use the question prompts to ask each other about a recent holiday they have had. They should make notes. When they have finished, they can work in small groups and tell each other about their partner's holiday, e.g. 'Micha was in Tenerife. The weather was very hot. The tour guide was very friendly.'

ANSWERS
Student A

Where were you?	(I was in) the French Alps.
Who were you with?	(I was with) my family.
What was the weather like?	(It was) cold and snowy, about -5°
What was the hotel like?	(It was) an apartment. (It was) great.
Was it expensive?	No, (it wasn't).
How many days were you there?	(We were there for) 7 days.
Was your tour guide friendly?	Yes, (she was).
Was it a good holiday?	Yes, (it was fantastic).

Student B

Where were you?	(I was in) Sydney, Australia.
Who were you with?	(I was with) my best friend, Sam.
What was the weather like?	(It was) very hot and sunny, about 32°.
What was the hotel like?	(It was) fantastic.
Was it expensive?	Yes, (it was).
How many days were you there?	(We were there for) 5 days.
Was your tour guide friendly?	No, (he wasn't).
Was it a good holiday?	Yes, (it was great).

5C My ideal holiday

ACTIVITY
Pairwork & groupwork. Questionnaire.

FOCUS
Past simple regular verbs.

PREPARATION
Photocopy one worksheet for each student.

PROCEDURE
- Explain to students that they are going to do a questionnaire about holidays.
- Pairwork. Hand out one worksheet to each student.
- Read through the questionnaire with the class and pre-teach some of the new vocabulary, e.g. 'swimming costume', 'shorts', 'trainers', 'sunset'.
- Explain that students have to make the statements into questions. Elicit the first question, 'Did you pack a swimming costume, a guide book and a digital camera?'
- Students take turns to ask each other the questions. They circle the score at the end of their partner's chosen answer.
- When they have finished, they add up their partner's score.
- Read the score analysis to the class.
- Groupwork. Ask students to get into groups of four and tell each other about their partner, e.g. 'Keiko's ideal holiday is at the beach.' Encourage them to discuss the scores with the group, and whether they agree with the results.

ANSWERS
1–7 You love sun, sea and sand. Your ideal holiday is at the beach. Go to the Caribbean, Thailand or Australia!
8–14 You love history and culture and good food. Your ideal holiday is in a European city. Go to Lisbon, Barcelona or Rome!
15–21 You like sport, swimming and lots of activities. Your ideal holiday is at a Sports Activity Centre. Go to Scotland, Wales, the south of France or the USA!

5D A weekend away

ACTIVITY
Individual & groupwork. Roleplay (booking accommodation).

FOCUS
Asking for and giving or refusing permission.

PREPARATION
Cut the worksheet in half. Make one photocopy of the top section for each student in the class. Make one photocopy of the bottom section for each group of four students. Cut up the four 'accommodation cards' in the bottom section for each group.

PROCEDURE
- Explain to students that they are going to practise booking accommodation.
- Divide students into groups of four. Hand out a copy of the top section to each student. Explain that before they book their accommodation they have to plan what kind of accommodation they are looking for.
- Revise and pre-teach some of the vocabulary students will need, e.g. 'room service', 'shared bathroom', 'entertainment'.
- Individual. Ask students to look at the prompts and to make notes. Encourage them to think of as much additional detail as possible, e.g. Will they arrive at their destination late in the evening? Will they want breakfast in their room, or dinner in the hotel? Will they want to make important phone calls? What will they want to do in the evening? Give students two or three minutes to do this.
- When they have made their notes, hand out the 'accommodation cards' to each group so that each student has one card.
- Groupwork. Students take turns to go around the members of their group asking and answering questions. Explain that they are looking for the most suitable accommodation for themselves, and they will need to ask everyone in the group so that they can compare the different types.
- Once they have asked everyone in the group, they have to choose the most appropriate place to stay.
- Students take turns to explain their choice to the rest of the group.

6A What did you do last night?

ACTIVITY
Pairwork. Find the differences.

FOCUS
Past simple irregular.

PREPARATION
Photocopy one worksheet for each pair. Cut the worksheet in half.

PROCEDURE
- Explain to students that they are going to play a memory game.
- Hand out worksheets to students A and B. Tell students to make sure that their partner can't see their pictures.
- Explain to students that it was their birthday last night. The pictures show how they celebrated. Their partner has a slightly different picture. They must take turns to ask and answer questions to find five things that they did differently from their partner.
- Demonstrate the activity with a student at the front of the class, with you as A and the student as B.
1 Ask the first question: 'Where did you go?' The student replies and asks you the same question. When you have answered, ask the class if the information is the same or different (it's the same).
2 Continue like this, taking turns to ask the question first, until a difference is found. Write the different answers on the board: 'I was with my parents.' and 'I was with my friends'.

- Pairwork. Students now do the activity, using the question prompts provided to make questions using the past simple.
- When they have finished, students check their answers with each other.
- Go through the answers with the class.

EXTENSION

- Students stay in their pairs and tell each other how they really celebrated their last birthday. Ask some of them to tell the class about the celebrations.

ANSWERS

Student A
(Who were you with?) I was with my mum and dad.
(What did you eat?) I ate a pizza.
(What did you drink?) I drank wine.
(What did you do next?) I had a coffee.
(What time did you go to bed?) I went to bed at 1.00.

Student B
(Who were you with?) I was with my friends (Sarah and Rob).
(What did you eat?) I ate a hamburger.
(What did you drink?) I drank beer.
(What did you do next?) I had a shower.
(What time did you go to bed?) I went to bed at 11.30.

6B Who's the actor?

ACTIVITY
Pairwork. Information gap.

FOCUS
Past simple regular and irregular verbs.

PREPARATION
Photocopy one worksheet for each pair. Cut the worksheet in half.

PROCEDURE
- Pairwork. Hand out worksheets to students A and B.
- Ask students to look at the missing information. They write the questions below in full.
- Students take turns to ask their questions. They write in the missing information.
- Students discuss the biographies together. They decide who the actor is.

ANSWERS

Student A
1 (Where was she born?) England
2 (When did she act in her first film?) 1994
3 (What was her most famous film?) *Titanic*
4 (Who did she marry in 2003?) Sam Mendes
5 (What film did she act in in 2004?) *Finding Neverland*

Student B
1 (When was she born?) 1975
2 (What was her first film?) *Heavenly Creatures*
3 (When did she act in her most famous film?) 1997
4 (Who did she marry in 1998?) Jim Threapleton
5 (Who did she act with in 2004?) Johnny Depp

The actor is Kate Winslet.

6C Do you sing badly?

ACTIVITY
Individual & pairwork. Guessing game.

FOCUS
Adverbs of manner.

PREPARATION
Photocopy one worksheet for each student.

PROCEDURE
- Hand out one worksheet to each student. Divide the class into pairs.
- Individual. Ask students to think about how they do the different activities. They write down one adverb for each verb in the 'Me' column. Point out that they can use the same adverb more than once. They should make sure that their partner can't see what they are writing.
- When they have finished, ask them to guess how their partner does each of the things. They write a list of adverbs in the 'My partner' column.
- Pairwork. Students then take turns asking their partners questions to check if their guesses were right. They can use the examples on the worksheet as models.
- Students keep a record of their scores by putting ticks or crosses in the last column. The one who made the most correct guesses is the winner.

EXTENSION
- Ask students to report to the class what they learnt about their partners, e.g. 'Janine eats fast and speaks English carefully'.

6D Can't stand coffee

ACTIVITY
Whole class. Class mingle.

FOCUS
Present simple questions and answers.
Talking about likes and dislikes.

PREPARATION
Photocopy one worksheet for each student.

PROCEDURE
- Tell students that they are going to go around the class and find out about each other's likes and dislikes. Hand out one worksheet to each student.
- Ask students to read through the example questions and answers at the top. Remind students that we use 'it' for singular items and uncountable items, and 'them' for plural items.
- Students walk around the class asking different people if they like the things mentioned. They reply using the phrases given in the examples.
- Students record the names of the students who reply appropriately in the 'name' column.
- When students have written a name against every item on the worksheet, they sit down.

EXTENSION
- Ask different students to tell the class what they found out about different people, e.g. 'Sandra hates shopping, but she doesn't mind exams! Lucas loves parties!'

7A Which diet?

ACTIVITY
Pairwork. Guessing game.

FOCUS
Questions with *any*.
Vocabulary: food.

PREPARATION
Photocopy one worksheet for each pair.

PROCEDURE
- Explain to students that they are going to play a guessing game.
- Hand out one worksheet to each pair.
- Ask students to choose one of the diets. They mustn't tell their partner which one it is.
- Student A asks questions to find out what Student B's diet is. He/she can use the examples on the worksheet as models. If a certain food isn't mentioned in the diet, students should assume they can't eat it.
- When Student B has guessed the diet, students swap over and play the game again.

VARIATION
- With weaker classes, students can give clues about what they can eat instead of asking and answering questions, e.g. 'I can eat tomatoes.' 'The green diet?' 'No. I can eat cold meat.' 'The cold food diet!'

7B Recipes

ACTIVITY
Pairwork. Information gap.

FOCUS
How much & *how many*.

PREPARATION
Photocopy one worksheet for each pair. Cut the worksheet in half.

PROCEDURE
- Hand out worksheets to students A and B.
- Ask students to look at the ingredients for the recipes. Explain the meaning of the weights and measurements *grams*, *kilograms* (kg) and *spoonfuls*.
- Students take turns asking questions to find out how much/many of each ingredient they need. They use the examples as models.
- When they have completed their list of ingredients, students work together to complete the list of countable/uncountable words.

EXTENSION
- Students write a list of ingredients for a recipe that they know. Ask some of the students to read their list to the class. Encourage other students to ask how much/many of the different ingredients they need.

ANSWERS
Spanish Omelette
1 kg of potatoes
4 spoonfuls of oil
1 onion
2 tomatoes
6 eggs

Chocolate soufflé
200 grams of chocolate
3 spoonfuls of milk
100 grams of sugar
20 grams of butter
3 eggs

countable	uncountable
potatoes	oil
onions	chocolate
tomatoes	milk
eggs	sugar

7C Are you a fussy eater?

ACTIVITY
Pairwork. Questionnaire.

FOCUS
Vocabulary: describing food.

PREPARATION
Photocopy one worksheet for each pair.

PROCEDURE
- Explain to students that they are going to complete a questionnaire about attitudes to food.
- Hand out one worksheet to each pair.
- Students take turns to ask the questions with their partner. They keep a record of their partner's points for each question answered.
- When they have finished, students add up all of their partner's points to find their total score.
- Read the analysis to the class. Ask students whether they agree or disagree with what it says about them.

EXTENSION
- Ask students to tell the class what they can remember about their partner's eating habits, e.g. 'Marga never eats raw food or spicy food. She doesn't like trying new food. She's a fussy eater!'

ANSWERS
Analysis
0–5   Oh dear! You're a very fussy eater. You always eat the same food. You need a more interesting diet.
6–10   You're not usually a fussy eater, but you are fussy sometimes. Try more new food.
11–16 Well done! Nothing is too spicy, too cold or too hot for you!

7D Restaurant trip

ACTIVITY
Groupwork. Roleplay (at a restaurant).

FOCUS
Ordering food at a restaurant.

PREPARATION
Photocopy one worksheet for each group of four students. Cut the worksheet into three along the dotted lines. Cut up the 'problem cards' for each group.

PROCEDURE
- Explain to students that they are going to practise ordering food in a restaurant.
- Explain that one student is the waiter and the other three are customers. Give the 'waiter' the menu and the 'waiter card'. Place the 'problem cards' face down on the table.
- The 'waiter' must greet the 'customers' and give them the menu. Then he/she takes orders for their drinks and food. The 'waiter' has a list of items that the restaurant has run out of. If any 'customers' choose these, he/she must apologise and offer an alternative.
- At any time after the food/drinks arrive, the 'customers' can turn over a 'problem card' and tell the 'waiter' what's wrong. The 'waiter' apologises and sorts out the problem.
- When the 'customers' have finished, they ask for the bill.
- The roleplay can be repeated, with a different person playing the part of the waiter. Each customer should take a different 'problem card'.

VARIATION
- The roleplay could be done in pairs. The 'customer' takes all the 'problem cards' and calls the 'waiter' three times to make different complaints.

8A He loves playing football

ACTIVITY
Whole class. Miming game.

FOCUS
Verbs + -ing.

PREPARATION
Photocopy one worksheet per group of 16 students. Cut up the cards on each worksheet.

PROCEDURE
- Give one card to each student. Tell them to make sure that no one else can see it. Ask them to complete the sentence with an appropriate verb (love, like, don't mind, don't like or hate).
- Explain that students have to mime their sentence to the rest of the class. They must make sure that they show their feelings about the activity. If you like, demonstrate a mime yourself, e.g. mime ironing clothes while yawning to show that you don't like ironing. Facial expressions and gestures can also be used to show feelings.
- Students take turns to mime. The rest of the class makes guesses, e.g. 'He hates travelling by boat.' 'She likes flying.'

VARIATION
- Students can work in pairs. Each of them has their own sentence, but they help their partner with their mime. For example, if the sentence is 'I hate flying', their partner can play the part of an air steward or another passenger.

8B Traffic report

ACTIVITY
Pairwork. Information gap.

FOCUS
Present continuous.

PREPARATION
Photocopy one worksheet for each pair. Cut the worksheet in half.

PROCEDURE
• Hand out worksheets to students A and B.
• Ask students to read through their traffic reports. They then write in full the questions below about the missing information.
• Students take turns to ask each other their questions, starting with Student A. They complete the missing information in their reports.

EXTENSION
• Students practise the traffic report, taking turns to read different paragraphs. Ask some of the pairs to read out their traffic reports for their class.
• Stronger students can invent their own traffic reports.

ANSWERS
Student A
1 Where are the people going? (To the new shopping centre.)
2 What is blocking the road? (A car.)
3 Why are train users driving? (Because the trains aren't working.)
4 Who is sitting in the road? (A demonstrator.)

Student B
1 Where are the police going? (To London Road.)
2 Why are cars stopping? (Because the drivers can't see.)
3 Where is traffic moving slowly? (Near Queen Street station.)
4 What is the demonstrator doing? (He's singing and shouting.)

8C Sailing

ACTIVITY
Pairwork. Song.

FOCUS
Present continuous.
Listening. Understanding lyrics.

PREPARATION
Photocopy one worksheet for each pair. CD player.

 [4]

PROCEDURE
• Explain to students that they are going to listen to a song. Some of the lyrics are missing and they are going to fill in the missing lines, which are listed on the right of the page.
• Pairwork. Hand out one worksheet to each pair of students.
• Play the recording once. Students listen and fill in the gaps with the correct phrases. Play the recording again if necessary.
• Check the answers with the class. Play the recording again and go through the song line by line.

EXTENSION
• Using the completed song as a guide, students rewrite the song line by line as an open class activity. Go through each line helping the students to replace the existing verbs first, e.g. *I am running/crying/sitting/, I am running/ crying/sitting.*
In order to keep the sense of the song, students will need to choose alternative nouns and phrases at the end of the lines that follow, e.g. *home again, across the land/street/ world.* Students continue changing words and phrases, until the whole song is rewritten. Remind the students of how to keep the rhythm of the song by helping them with syllables and stress.

ANSWERS
1 I am flying, I am flying
2 I am flying, passing high clouds,
3 I am dying, forever trying
4 I am dying, forever trying
5 We are sailing, we are sailing
6 We are sailing stormy waters

Note
'Sailing' was sung by Rod Stewart in 1972.

8D Let's go by train

ACTIVITY
Pairwork. Roleplay (a night out).

FOCUS
Making arrangements.
Vocabulary: transport.

PREPARATION
Photocopy one worksheet for each pair. Cut the worksheet into three along the dotted lines. Cut up the dialogue into strips.

PROCEDURE
• Hand out a copy of the cut up dialogue to each pair. Ask them to shuffle the pieces and then work together to put the dialogue into the correct order.
• Students practise the conversation with their partners. Ask some pairs to perform it for the class.
• Students stay in their pairs. Hand out the role cards to students A and B. Student A invites student B to a party. He/she suggests each of the types of transport on the card. Student B responds using the information on his/her card. They can use the dialogue as a model.

ANSWERS

1 There's an outdoor concert tonight. Do you want to come?
2 Yes. Where is it?
3 It's in Queen's Park.
4 How do we get there?
5 We could take a taxi.
6 No. It's too expensive. Can we go on foot?
7 It's too far. Let's go by train.
8 But there isn't a station near my house.
9 OK. Let's take the bus.
10 Good idea.

9A What should I wear/do/take with me?

ACTIVITY
Pairwork. Game.

FOCUS
Should / shouldn't for giving advice.

PREPARATION
Photocopy one set of cards for each pair.

PROCEDURE
- Explain to students that they are going to play a card game about situations where advice is needed.
- Hand out a set of cards to each pair. Ask them to shuffle them and put them face down in a pile on the table.
- Demonstrate the activity with a student at the front of the class.
1 Ask the student to pick up the top card and read the situation to the class, e.g. 'I'm going to an important interview'.
2 Elicit offers of advice about what to wear, do or take along in this situation, e.g. 'You should wear clean and neat clothes.' 'You shouldn't wear a very short skirt.' 'You should arrive on time'. Encourage students to give as much advice as possible.
3 Take the next card, and repeat the procedure, but with only the student offering advice.
- Pairwork. Students now do the activity, taking turns to take a card and receive advice from their partner.
- The game continues until all of the cards have been used.

EXTRA IDEAS
- Stronger students could also offer advice about how to behave in these situations, e.g. 'If you're meeting your girlfriend's parents, you must be polite. Shake her father's hand …'

9B Stand on one foot!

ACTIVITY
Groupwork. Action game.

FOCUS
Responding to imperatives.
Vocabulary: body parts.

PREPARATION
Photocopy two sets of cards for the class.

PROCEDURE
- Divide the class into two groups. Each group chooses one player to be a leader.
- Give each group a set of cards. The leader shuffles them.
- Students stand facing towards the leader. The leader picks up the first card and reads the instruction. Students adopt the appropriate pose.
- The leader then reads the second instruction. Students must move from the first pose to the second without losing their balance. If they have to break their pose, they are out. Students can relax only when the 'stand comfortably' card is read.
- The game continues until there is only one player remaining, or until all the cards have been read.
- Students choose a new leader and play again.

VARIATION
- This game can also be played as a whole class activity, with one leader reading the instructions to the rest of the students.

9C Who is it?

ACTIVITY
Pairwork. Guessing game.

FOCUS
Vocabulary: physical characteristics.
Personal pronouns.
Describing people.

PREPARATION
Photocopy one worksheet for each student.

PROCEDURE
- Explain to students that they are going to play a describing game.
- Hand out a worksheet to each student. Demonstrate the activity by going though the example statements with the class. After each statement, ask the class who fits that description.
- Pairwork. Ask students to choose a face. They must not tell their partner who it is.
- Students take turns to give each other clues about their chosen person. They should use possessive pronouns when describing the person's physical characteristics, as in the examples.
- The student in each pair who guesses correctly in the shortest time wins.
- Students play the game twice more to find an overall winner.

9D At the doctor's

ACTIVITY
Pairwork. Roleplay (at the doctor's).

FOCUS
Asking/saying how you feel.
Giving advice.

PREPARATION
Copy and cut up one set of cards for each pair.

PROCEDURE
- Hand out the two top role cards for the first conversation to students A and B.
- Explain that each student must follow the instructions on their cards, i.e. the doctor asks the questions listed, and the patient replies using the information on his/her card. The doctor listens and then decides what advice to give. He/she begins with 'You should …'
- Students practise the conversation together. When they have finished, give them the second pair of role cards and repeat the exercise.

EXTENSION
- Stronger students can elaborate on the information given to them to make a fuller dialogue, e.g. 'What's the matter?' 'I've got a stomachache. My stomach hurt last night and it still hurts today …'
- Ask some of the pairs to perform their roleplay for the class.

10A Rules dominoes

ACTIVITY
Pairwork. Game.

FOCUS
Must, mustn't & needn't.

PREPARATION
Photocopy one worksheet for each pair. Cut up the domino pieces.

PROCEDURE
- Before you begin the activity, discuss rules as a class. Ask students to suggest some rules for the following situations: at school, on a train, in a car, in the kitchen and at the cinema.
- Explain to students that they are going to play a game of dominoes.
- Hand out one set of dominoes to each group.
- Ask the students to divide the dominoes evenly between them.
- Explain the rules. The first student puts down a domino. The next student must put down a domino before or after it to make a rule.
- The student says the sentence he/she has made out loud. His/her partner must agree that the sentence is acceptable before the game can continue.
- If a student can't go, they miss a turn.

- The first person to put down all their dominoes is the winner.

EXTENSION
- Ask students to categorize the sentences into rules for different places, as follows: *School, Trains, Cars, Kitchen, Cinema.*

ANSWERS
School
You needn't wear a tie to class.
You mustn't talk while the teacher is talking.
You needn't arrive ten minutes early for lessons.
You must be quiet during an exam.
You mustn't be late for lessons.
You must put your rubbish in the bin.
Trains
You mustn't smoke in 'no smoking' areas.
You mustn't open the doors while a train is moving.
You needn't use a credit card to buy a ticket.
You mustn't put your feet on the seats.
You must put your rubbish in the bin.
Cars
You mustn't drink alcohol before driving.
You must keep to the speed limit.
You needn't wash your car every day.
Kitchen
You must wash your hands before touching food.
You must cook meat properly.
You needn't wear rubber gloves to wash up.
You must put your rubbish in the bin.
Cinema
You must turn off your mobile phone before a film begins.
You mustn't talk loudly during a film.
You mustn't smoke in 'no smoking' areas.
You needn't use a credit card to buy a ticket.

Students' answers may vary. Some rules can apply to more than place.

10B Comparing capitals

ACTIVITY
Pairwork. Reading and discussion.

FOCUS
Comparatives.

PREPARATION
Photocopy one worksheet for each pair. Cut the worksheet in half.

PROCEDURE
- Explain to students that they are going to exchange information about two different capital cities and then compare the cities.
- Hand out worksheets to students A and B.
- Ask students to read through the information. They then take turns to tell their partners about their cities. They should use their own words, rather than reading directly from the sheet, e.g. 'My city is Tallinn. It's the capital of Estonia'. Demonstrate the activity if necessary.

- Students then work together to complete the sentences that compare the two cities. They must not look at each other's information. If they need to know something, they should ask their partner. Explain that they use their own opinions to answer the last question.

EXTENSION

- Ask different students around the class to say which city they think is better and why.

ANSWERS

1 London is bigger than Tallinn.
2 Tallinn is smaller than London.
3 London is more dangerous than Tallinn.
4 Tallinn is more polluted than London.
5 Tallinn is safer than London.
6 Students' own answers.

10c Which holiday?

ACTIVITY

Pairwork. Information gap and discussion.

FOCUS

Go + -ing.
Superlatives.

PREPARATION

Photocopy one worksheet for each pair. Cut the worksheet in half.

PROCEDURE

- Hand out worksheets to students A and B.
- Tell students to look at the holiday advertisements and read instruction 1. They want to do the activities listed and must find out where they can do them by asking their partner questions, e.g. 'Where can I go dancing?' 'Where can I see a musical?' They write the information in the appropriate places on their worksheets.
- When the students have filled in all of the information, they discuss the holidays together and answer the questions in 2.

EXTENSION

- Ask different students around the class to tell you which they think is the best holiday, and why.

10d Shopping for souvenirs

ACTIVITY

Groupwork. Roleplay (at the shops).

FOCUS

Buying things in shops.
Vocabulary: size and colours.

PREPARATION

Photocopy one worksheet per group of four. Cut up the cards on each worksheet.

PROCEDURE

- Explain to students that they are going to practise buying goods in shops.
- Elicit some useful shopping language and write it on the board, e.g.
  Can I help you?
  Do you have …?
  How much is/are … ?
  I'm sorry, we don't have any.
  Anything else?
  Here you are.
- Groupwork. Divide each group into 'customers' and 'shopkeepers'. Give each 'customer' a 'shopping list' and each 'shopkeeper' a 'stock list'.
- Tell 'customers' that they must buy presents for the people on their lists. They have to visit the shops and ask for what they want. The 'shopkeeper' must offer them a choice when there is more than one size or colour.
- When a 'customer' buys an item, they write down the price on their list.
- The roleplay is finished when the students have bought everything on their lists.

VARIATION/EXTENSION

- If you have a smaller class, or your group does not divide exactly into groups of four, students can play the game in threes; one student is the 'shopkeeper' and has both stock cards. The other students are the 'customers'.
- Students tell the class about what they've bought, e.g. 'I bought a large, blue T-shirt for Dad.' 'I bought a silver key ring for David'.

11a What do I do?

ACTIVITY

Pairwork. Guessing game.

FOCUS

Question words.
Vocabulary: jobs.

PREPARATION

Photocopy one worksheet for each pair.

PROCEDURE

- Hand out worksheets to each pair of students.
- Explain that students are going to play a guessing game with their partner. One student chooses a job. The other asks questions to find out what the job is. They can use the chart to help them, or ask their own questions. When they have guessed, it is their turn to choose a job.
- Repeat the activity several times.

VARIATION

- With less advanced classes, ask students to describe their jobs to their partner first. Their partner can then ask questions if they need extra information.

11B How organized are you?

ACTIVITY
Pairwork & groupwork. Questionnaire.

FOCUS
Will

PREPARATION
Photocopy one worksheet for each student.

PROCEDURE
- Explain to students that they arer going to do a questionnaire
- Pairwork. Hand out one worksheet to each student.
- Explain that students have to take it in turns to read the situations iin each square and answer Yes or No. They then read the next situation according to their previous answer. Explain that their answers will determine the route they take in the questionnaire.
- Students take turns to read each other the questionnaire.
- When they have finished, they read the analysis to their partner.
- Groupwork. Ask students to get into groups of four and tell each other about their partner, e.g. 'Mario is super organized. He ...' . Encourage them to discuss the results with the group, and whether they agree with them.

11C Life quiz

ACTIVITY
Pairwork. Questionnaire.

FOCUS
Adverbs of frequency.

PREPARATION
Photocopy one worksheet for each pair.

PROCEDURE
- Explain to students that they are going to complete a questionnaire about lifestyle.
- Hand out one worksheet to each pair of students.
- Students take turns to ask the questions with their partner. They keep a record of their partner's answers.
- When they have finished, students count up how many of each symbol their partner scored.
- Read the analysis to the class. Ask students whether they agree or disagree with what it says about them.

EXTENSION
- Ask students to give each other lifestyle advice, based on what they found out from the questionnaire.

ANSWERS
Analysis

Mostly	You need a break! You work too hard and you worry about everything. Learn to say 'no' to other people and enjoy life!
Mostly	You like excitement and adventure. There's a lot to experience in life and you want to do it all!
Mostly	It's good that you don't worry too much, but you're so relaxed that you're lazy. If you don't work, you won't get much out of life.

11D Who wants to go out with me?

ACTIVITY
Whole class. Class mingle.

FOCUS
Accepting and declining invitations.
Phrasal verbs.

PREPARATION
Photocopy one worksheet for each group of 16 students. Cut up the 'date cards' and 'answer cards'. If your class has more than 16 students, photocopy more than one worksheet.

PROCEDURE
- Before students begin the activity, revise the language we use to invite someone out. Point out that if we are asking someone to a place, we use 'to', e.g. 'Would you like to go to the cinema?' If we are inviting them to do something, we use 'for', e.g. 'Would you like to go for a coffee?'
- Divide the class into students A and students B. Allocate a 'date card' to each student A and an 'answer card' to each student B.
- Explain the rules. Students walk around the class. Students A have to invite students B to the date shown on their cards. Depending on what is on their cards, students B have to accept and ask questions or decline, giving an excuse. Everybody must talk to three people.

EXTRA IDEAS
- You could vary the game by asking students to each swap their card with another player after each conversation.

12A Pop careers

ACTIVITY
Pairwork. Guessing game.

FOCUS
Present perfect and past simple to describe achievements.

PREPARATION
Photocopy one worksheet for each pair. Cut the worksheet in half.

PROCEDURE
- Pairwork. Hand out worksheets to students A and B.
- Explain to students that they have information about two singers/bands. They also have two mystery singers/bands that they have to identify through their partner's clues.
- Demonstrate the activity. Tell the class that you are going to give them some information about a singer. Give the first piece of information below about Aretha Franklin. Ask the class if they can guess who it is. If the class guesses correctly, give them a sentence about another singer/band they all know. If they do not guess, continue giving clues until someone guesses.
1 She was born in 1942.
2 She has made more than 20 albums.
3 She recorded a song called 'Respect'.
4 She received a Lifetime Achievement Award in 1994.
5 She is called the 'Queen of Soul'.
- Student A begins. He/She looks at the notes and uses them to give their partner a clue about Singer A. The clues must be given as whole sentences. If their partner can't guess, student A gives another clue, and continues in this way. If their partner can't guess after all the clues have been given, student A can give their own clues.
- When student B has guessed the singer, it's his/her turn to give clues about Singer B.
- The activity continues until all three singers and the band have been guessed.

EXTENSION
- After the activity has finished, ask the students to turn over their worksheets and tell you what they can about the achievements of the singers/band.

12B Have you ever ...?

ACTIVITY
Groupwork. Board game.

FOCUS
Present perfect.
Talking about life experiences.

PREPARATION
- Photocopy one board for each group of three or four students. Each group will also need a dice and one counter for each person.

PROCEDURE
- Give each group a copy of the board, a dice and a set of counters.
- All players begin on the 'Have you ever ...' square. The first player throws the dice and moves around the board the right number of steps. When they land on a square, he/she looks at the question on the board and chooses another student to ask, e.g. 'Carlo, have you ever visited Australia?'. If the student answers positively ('Yes, I have.'), the player moves forward one square and asks the next question. If the student answers negatively, the next player has a turn.
- Play continues in this way around the board.
- The first player to reach the final square is the winner.

VARIATION/EXTENSION
- With a stronger class, ask students to elaborate on their answers, e.g. 'Have you ever been to a football match?' 'Yes, I went to see Real Madrid play last year'.
- Ask one person from each group to tell you what they learnt about their team during the game. Alternatively, ask students to write a text about some of their group's experiences.

12C Fields of gold

ACTIVITY
Pairwork. Song.

FOCUS
Revision of verb forms.
Listening. Understanding lyrics.

PREPARATION
Photocopy one worksheet for each pair. CD player.

 [5]

PROCEDURE
- Explain to students that they are going to listen to a song.
- Pairwork. Hand out a worksheet to each pair of students. Ask them to fold the worksheet in half and look at the picture. Use the picture to pre-teach some key vocabulary, e.g. *barley, sun, wind, field, gold* (the colour). Ask the students how this vocabulary might relate to the song. Get them to imagine some scenarios and compare ideas.
- Play the recording once. Ask the students about what is happening in the song. Who is speaking? What time of year is it? What is he talking about?
- Explain that they are going to listen to the song again but this time they are going to complete the lyrics with the correct form of the verbs in brackets.
- Students unfold their worksheets so that they can see the lyrics. Play the recording once. Students listen and write the words. Play the recording again if necessary.
- Students can check their answers with their partner.
- Play the recording again and go through the song line by line.

Note
'Fields of gold' was sung by Sting in 1993.

12D Goodbye!

ACTIVITY
Pairwork. Roleplay (parting).

FOCUS
Saying goodbye. Thanking.

PREPARATION
Photocopy one worksheet for each pair. Cut up the role cards.

PROCEDURE
- Pairwork. Hand out the role cards for Conversation 1 to students A and B.
- Ask students to read the first part of the role card. Give them a few moments to think about the things in the 'Before you start' section.
- Ask students to read the rest of the instructions and practise the roleplay with their partners.
- Ask some of the students to perform the roleplay for the class.
- Repeat with Conversation 2.

EXTENSION
- Ask students to think about a situation when they had to say goodbye to someone. How did they feel? What did they say? Did they give a card or a present? Ask some of the students to share their experiences with the class.

BASICS 1 | How do you spell that?

A

✂ ···

B

HOS	PITAL	SAND	WICH
PH	OTO	T	EA
FOOT	BALL	P	IZZA
AIR	PORT	B	US
PO	LICE	CO	FFEE
HOT	EL	TA	XI

Straightforward Elementary Teacher's Book © Macmillan Publishers Limited 2006

63	72	21
99	11	95
58	34	44
56	87	17

40	15	79
95	89	27
65	37	56
21	46	35

46	55	23
12	62	80
83	32	74
95	72	18

38	67	76
22	48	25
50	18	81
10	96	43

43	57	66
94	73	13
20	35	85
49	88	27

55	49	33
47	87	59
16	60	78
56	44	92

76	54	30
26	84	14
45	68	77
92	23	16

70	88	24
36	61	51
98	97	17
43	79	63

11	10	21	22	23	24	25	26	27
12	20	32	33	34	35	36	37	38
13	30	43	44	45	46	47	48	49
14	40	54	55	56	57	58	59	51
15	50	65	66	67	68	62	61	63
16	60	76	77	78	79	73	72	74
17	70	87	88	89	81	84	83	85
18	80	98	99	97	92	95	94	96

1A | This is her credit card

pen

desk

earrings

computer

sandwich

chair

coffee

paper

mobile phone

taxi

wallet

credit card

CD player

TV

book

apple

1B | Worldwide dominoes

Brazil	Polish	Italy	Chinese
France	British	Russia	American
Japan	Irish	Argentina	Scottish
Poland	French	Turkey	Brazilian
America	Canadian	Australian	English
Greece	Italian	Scotland	Mexican
Britain	Japanese	Australia	Turkish
Canada	Greek	Ireland	Russian
England	Portuguese	Mexico	German
Portugal	Germany	China	Argentinian

 Straightforward Elementary Teacher's Book © Macmillan Publishers Limited 2006

1c | What's this?

B

Your name is _____
You are from _____

You would like …

a glass of beer
a glass of mineral water
a cup of tea

Your name is _____
You are from _____

You would like …

a glass of red wine
a glass of beer
a cup of tea

Your name is _____
You are from _____

You would like …

a glass of beer
a glass of white wine
an orange juice

Your name is _____
You are from _____

You would like …

a glass of red wine
an apple juice
an orange juice

Your name is _____
You are from _____

You would like …

a glass of white wine
an orange juice
a cup of coffee

Your name is _____
You are from _____

You would like …

a glass of red wine
a glass of apple juice
a cup of coffee

Your name is _____
You are from _____

You would like …

a glass of white wine
a glass of mineral water
a cup of coffee

Your name is _____
You are from _____

You would like …

a cup of tea
a cup of coffee
a glass of mineral water

A

WAITER

WAITER

WAITER

WAITER

WAITER

WAITER

WAITER

WAITER

2A Expat lifestyle profiles

A

	Frank	Maria	Tom	Lindy
works ...	in an office		in a school	
speaks ...		Spanish		Italian
goes to ...	language classes		football matches	
drinks ...		red wine		coffee
eats ...	a lot of pizza		Chinese food	
lives in ...		a house in London		a flat in Paris
has ...	a car		a small dog	
reads ...		books		English newspapers

✂ ··

B

	Frank	Maria	Tom	Lindy
works ...		in a hospital		in a shop
speaks ...	Chinese		German	
goes to ...		evening classes		university
drinks ...	beer		mineral water	
eats ...		Mexican food		chocolate
lives in ...	a flat in New York		a flat in Malaga	
has ...		a cat		a bicycle
reads ...	American newspapers		magazines	

2B Do you play football?

Activity	Me	Partner 1 _____	Partner 2 _____
go to restaurants alone			
play football			
listen to music alone			
talk about your feelings			
have lots of friends			
go dancing with friends			
drink beer			
speak Turkish			
have women friends			
go to the cinema alone			
watch sport on TV			
have a dog			
live in a house			
go shopping with friends			

1 🔊 **1** Listen to the song. Are the words in **bold** right or wrong? Correct the wrong words.

Girls just wanna have fun

I come home in the morning light
My ¹ **mother** says when you gonna live your life right
Oh ² **mummy** dear, we're not the fortunate ones
And ³ **boys** they wanna have fun
Oh girls just wanna have fun

The phone rings in the middle of the night
My ⁴ **brother** yells what you gonna do with your life
Oh ⁵ **daddy** dear, you know you're still number one
And girls they wanna have fun
Oh girls just wanna have fun

That's all they really want
Some fun
When the working day is done
Oh ⁶ **sisters** they wanna have fun
Oh ⁷ **girls** just wanna have fun

Some boys take a beautiful girl
And hide her away from the rest of the world
I wanna be the ⁸ **girl** to walk in the sun
Oh girls they wanna have fun
Oh girls just wanna have fun

That's all ⁹ **parents** really want
Some fun
When the working day is done
Oh ¹⁰ **girls** they wanna have fun
Oh ¹¹ **women** just wanna have fun
They wanna have fun
They wanna have fun
Girls just wanna have fun

2 🔊 **1** Listen to the song again and answer these questions.

1 Who does the girl live with?
2 What does she want?
3 Does she have a boyfriend?
4 Does she have a job?

2D | Find your double

You are tall and thin. You wear glasses.

Age: young, about 24 years old
Hair: blonde hair
Eyes: green eyes

You are tall and thin. You wear glasses.

Age: young, about 24 years old
Hair: blonde hair
Eyes: green eyes

You are short and thin. You have glasses.

Age: middle-aged, about 52 years old
Hair: dark hair Eyes: brown eyes

You are short and thin. You have glasses.

Age: middle-aged, about 52 years old
Hair: dark hair Eyes: brown eyes

You are tall and fat.

Age: old, about 65 years old
Hair: brown hair
Eyes: brown eyes

You are tall and fat.

Age: old, about 65 years old
Hair: brown hair
Eyes: brown eyes

You are tall and thin. You have glasses.

Age: old, about 69 years old
Hair: black hair
Eyes: brown eyes

You are tall and thin. You have glasses.

Age: old, about 69 years old
Hair: black hair
Eyes: brown eyes

You are tall and thin.

Age: young, about 34 years old
Hair: dark hair
Eyes: blue eyes

You are tall and thin.

Age: young, about 34 years old
Hair: dark hair
Eyes: blue eyes

You are tall and fat. You have glasses.

Age: middle aged, about 56 years old
Hair: dark hair
Eyes: green eyes

You are tall and fat. You have glasses.

Age: middle aged, about 56 years old
Hair: dark hair
Eyes: green eyes

You are medium height and thin. You have glasses.

Age: young, about 22 years old
Hair: blonde hair
Eyes: blue eyes

You are medium height and thin. You have glasses.

Age: young, about 22 years old
Hair: blonde hair
Eyes: blue eyes

You are medium height and fat.

Age: young, about 29 years old
Hair: black hair
Eyes: green eyes

You are medium height and fat.

Age: young, about 29 years old
Hair: black hair.
Eyes: green eyes

3A | A flat by the river

A

Gerry Thompson lives in London. He has a flat close to _____ and a small house in Windsor. During the week he lives in his _____. The flat is opposite a small shop and a café. He likes it because it's near _____. It's only ten minutes from all the shops and restaurants. His flat is next to the river on the _____ floor. It's a great place to live.

At the weekend he lives in his house in Windsor. It's a small cottage at the end of _____. There's a garden in front of the house but there isn't a garage. He parks his car _____ the house. His house is opposite a church. There's a small _____ behind the church and he often goes there with his dog. There are some _____ next to the park. It's very quiet here but he likes it.

✂ ....

B

Gerry Thompson lives in _____. He has a flat close to Chelsea and a small house in _____. During the week he lives in his flat. The _____ is opposite a small shop and a café. He likes it because it's near the Kings Road. It's only ten minutes from all the shops and restaurants. His flat is next to the _____, on the fourth floor. It's a great place to live.

At the weekend he lives in his _____ in Windsor. It's a small cottage at the end of St Mark's Road. There's a _____ in front of the house but there isn't a garage. He parks his car near to the house. His house is opposite a _____. There's a small park behind the church and he often goes there with his dog. There are some shops next to the _____. It's very quiet here but he likes it.

3c | There are two lamps

A

✂ ....

B

3D | Finding the hotel shop

A

1 Ask your partner how to get to these places. Mark them on your plan.

- the café • the hairdresser • the spa • the first floor lift
- the telephones • the gym • the shop

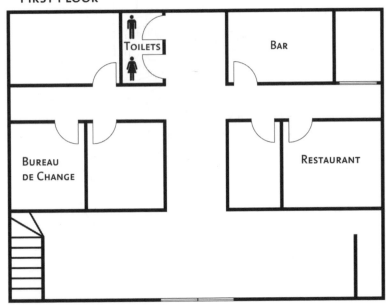

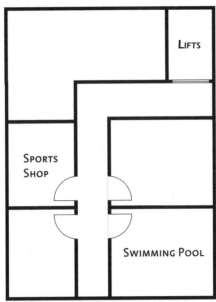

B

2 Ask your partner how to get to these places. Mark them on your plan.

- the toilets • the sports shop • the restaurant • the stairs
- the Bureau de Change • the swimming pool • the bar

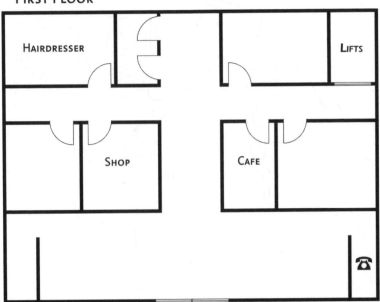

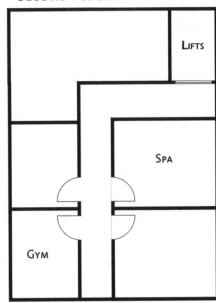

I say a little prayer

1 💿 **2** Listen to the song and tick (✓) these words when you hear them.

think ☐   run ☐   wake up ☐   live ☐   answer ☐   put ☐   love ☐   believe ☐   say ☐

⟋FOLD⟍ ─

2 💿 **2** Listen again. Complete the song with the words from the box in 1.

I SAY A LITTLE PRAYER

The moment I ^{1} _____ , before
 I ^{2} _____ on my make up
I ^{3} _____ a little prayer for you
While combing my hair now
And wonderin' what dress to wear now
I say a little prayer for you.

Chorus

 Forever, forever you'll stay in my heart
And I will love you forever and ever
We never will part, oh how I love you
Together, together that's how it must be
To ^{4} _____ without you would only be heartbreak
  for me

 I ^{5} _____ for the bus dear, while running I
  ^{6} _____ of us, dear
And say a little prayer for you
At work I just take time, and all through my coffee break time
I say a little prayer for you

Chorus (twice)

My darlin' ^{7} _____ me, for there is no one
  but you
Please ^{8} _____ me true
'Cause I'm in love with you
Answer my prayer
Say you love me true
Just ^{9} _____ my prayer now

Chorus

A

✂ .... ✂ ....

I go swimming at	People don't eat Christmas cake at
My birthday isn't on	My family doesn't go on holiday in
Our school isn't open in	I have a shower in
The school holidays are in	My friends and I go to pop concerts in
My baby brother doesn't sleep at	I don't play tennis at
My sister's birthday is in	I walk the dog at

✂ ....

B

✂ .... ✂ ....

July.	quarter past eleven.
the weekend.	the afternoon.
Saturdays.	May.
night.	the evening.
half past seven.	summer.
Easter.	5th October.

4c | How often do you ...?

Find someone who ...	Name
... always reads in the bath.	_____
... is rarely late for class.	_____
... never takes out the rubbish.	_____
... usually goes to bed after 11.00 p.m.	_____
... sometimes talks on the phone every day.	_____
... often eats fast food.	_____
... never cleans the bathroom.	_____
... never sees his/her grandparents at the weekend.	_____
... hardly ever goes on holiday in April.	_____
... always has a shower before breakfast.	_____
... never makes his/her bed.	_____
... hardly ever washes the dishes.	_____
... usually works on Saturdays.	_____
... sometimes watches television in the morning.	_____
... often plays football in the park.	_____

4D | Just a minute, please.

A

1 Read the cards and make these telephone calls.

> **1**
>
> **Name: Mr Roberts**
> **Telephone number: 07960 488322**
> **Call your friend Bella at work. She works at the Corner Café.**
> **You don't want to leave a message.**
> **You want her to call you back.**

> **2**
>
> Name: Mrs Lewis
> Telephone number: 07780 387005
> Call the travel agent and ask to speak to Maria.

2 Read the cards and answer the phone.

> **3**
>
> Your name is Michelle.
> You work with the manager at the City Museum. The manager, Mr Lawson, is not at work with you today.
> Answer the phone.

> **4**
>
> **Your name is David.**
> **You work at the Regal Cinema. Answer the phone.**
> **Your boss Mr Jenkins can't come to the phone. You don't offer to take a message.**
> **Mr Jenkins wants callers to call him back.**

✂ ┄┄

B

1 Read the cards and answer the phone.

> **1**
>
> You work at the Corner Café.
> Answer the phone. Your boss, Bella, is busy and can't come to the phone now.
> Offer to take a message.

> **2**
>
> You work at Pizza Parlour Restaurant.
> Your telephone number is 0845 92821611
> Answer the phone. The caller has the wrong number.

2 Read the cards and make these telephone calls.

> **3**
>
> Name: Mr Wilson
> Telephone number: 0192 838382
> Call the City Museum. Ask to speak to Mr Lawson.

> **4**
>
> Name: Mrs Jenkins
> Telephone number: 0800 48219128
> Call the Regal Cinema. Ask to speak to Mr Jenkins. You don't want to leave a message.
> You want Mr Jenkins to call you back.

5A | I believe I can fly

1 🔵 **3** Listen to the song. Some of the lines are missing. Complete the song with the correct lines.

- Sometimes silence can seem so loud
- I believe I can fly
- then I can do it
- then I can be it
- I believe I can soar
- If I can see it
- I believe I can touch the sky

I believe I can fly

I used to think that I could not go on
And life was nothing but an awful song
But now I know the meaning of true love
I'm leaning on the everlasting arms

If I can see it, ¹ _____
If I just believe it, there's nothin' to it

² _____
I believe I can touch the sky
I think about it every night and day
Spread my wings and fly away
³ _____
I see me runnin' through that open door
I believe I can fly
I believe I can fly
I believe I can fly

See, I was on the verge of breaking down
⁴ _____
There are miracles in life I must achieve
But first I know it starts inside of me, oh

If I can see it, ⁵ _____
If I just believe it, there's nothin' to it

I believe I can fly
⁶ _____
I think about it every night and day
Spread my wings and fly away
I believe I can soar
I see me runnin' through that open door
I believe I can fly
I believe I can fly
I believe I can fly

Hey, 'cause I believe in you

⁷ _____ *, then I can do it*
If I just believe it, there's nothin' to it

5B What was the weather like?

A

1 Ask your partner questions about his/her holiday and complete the holiday profile.

A: *Where were you?*
B: *I was on holiday in ...*

Your partner's holiday profile
• Where / you? _____
• Who / with? _____
• What / weather like? _____
• What / hotel like? _____
• / it expensive? _____
• How many days / you there? _____
• / tour guide friendly? _____
• / a good holiday? _____

2 Read about your holiday and answer your partner's questions.

> I was on holiday in Sydney, Australia. I was with my best friend, Sam. The weather was very hot and sunny, and the temperature was about 32 degrees. We were there for five days. Our hotel was really fantastic. There was a beautiful swimming pool and the rooms were really big, but it was very expensive. Our tour guide was called Jason. He was very handsome but he wasn't very friendly. That was OK. It was still a great holiday!

✂ ┄┄

B

1 Read about your holiday and answer your partner's questions.

> I was on holiday in the French Alps. I was with my family. The weather was very cold and snowy. It was brilliant! The temperature was about minus 5 degrees. On the last three days it was really sunny! We were there for seven days. We weren't in a hotel. We were in an apartment and it was great! There were three bedrooms and a balcony, but it wasn't expensive. Our tour guide was called Sally. She was very pretty and really friendly. She was a great skier. It was a fantastic holiday!

2 Ask your partner questions about his/her holiday and complete the holiday profile.

A: *Where were you?*
B: *I was on holiday in ...*

Your partner's holiday profile
• Where / you? _____
• Who / with? _____
• What / weather like? _____
• What / hotel like? _____
• / it expensive? _____
• How many days / you there? _____
• / tour guide friendly? _____
• / a good holiday? _____

5c | My ideal holiday

Imagine you were on your ideal holiday last week. What did you do?

❶ Clothes

a You packed a swimming costume, a guide book and a digital camera. [2]
b Your packed a swimming costume, shorts and trainers. [3]
c You packed a swimming costume, T-shirts and sunglasses. [1]

❷ Transport

a You travelled by plane. [1]
b You travelled by car. [3]
c You travelled by train. [2]

❸ Accommodation

a You stayed in a small hotel in town. [2]
b You stayed on a campsite. [3]
c You stayed in a very expensive hotel by the sea. [1]

❹ Activities

a You stayed on the beach all day, every day. [1]
b You played tennis and went to the hotel gym. [3]
c You visited the local museums and art galleries. [2]

❺ The weather

a It was hot, hot, hot! [1]
b It was cool and windy. [2]
c It was warm and sunny. [3]

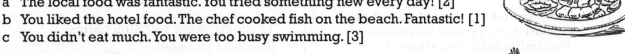

❻ Food

a The local food was fantastic. You tried something new every day! [2]
b You liked the hotel food. The chef cooked fish on the beach. Fantastic! [1]
c You didn't eat much. You were too busy swimming. [3]

❼ Entertainment

a You watched the beautiful sunset
   every night. [1]
b The local disco was great. You danced
   every night. [3]
c You didn't go out much in the evening.
   You watched lots of old films in
   your hotel room. [2]

5D | A weekend away

1 You want to stay in Winchester for the weekend. Consider these details before you book your accommodation, and make notes.

arriving by train or car? _____

one or two rooms? _____

smoking / non-smoking? _____

American Express / Visa / Mastercard?

_____

telephone? _____

breakfast? dinner? _____

room service? _____

private or shared bathroom? _____

children? _____

animals? _____

evening entertainment? _____

2 Book your room. Ask questions about the facilities.

Is it OK if I ...?   Are there ...?   Can I ...?   May I ...?

Bridge Guest House

**8 rooms. Non-smoking.
Breakfast included.
TV. Shared and private
bathrooms.
Visa and Mastercard.
Extra charge for dogs.
Room service. No parking.
Payphone in Reception.
5 min walk to city centre.**

MANOR HOTEL

24 rooms. Some smoking rooms.
Breakfast and dinner included.
TV and private bathroom. All credit cards.
Dogs allowed. Free parking.
Gardens and children's play area.
Phones in all rooms. Views of countryside.
5 min taxi ride to city centre.

Home Farm Bed & Breakfast

4 rooms. Non-smoking. Breakfast included.
TV. Shared and private bathroom.
No credit cards. Pets allowed.
No room service. Free parking. No telephone.
10 min taxi ride to city centre.

THE GEORGE HOTEL

12 rooms. Some smoking rooms.
Breakfast included.
TV and en-suite
bathroom.
Visa and Mastercard
credit cards.
No pets.
No parking.
Small garden.
Phones in all rooms.
5 min walk to town
centre.

Straightforward Elementary Teacher's Book © Macmillan Publishers Limited 2006

A

1 Last night you and your partner celebrated your birthdays, but you did different things.
Ask and answer questions to find five differences between the pictures.

Where / go?   What / do?   Who / be / with?   What / they give / you?

What / eat?   What / drink?   What / do next?   What time / go to bed?

✂ ··

B

1 Last night you and your partner celebrated your birthdays, but you did different things.
Ask and answer questions to find five differences between the pictures.

Where / go?   What / do?   Who / be / with?   What / they give / you?

What / eat?   What / drink?   What / do next?   What time / go to bed?

6B Who's the actor?

A

1 Write the questions.

2 Take turns to ask the questions and write the missing information.

3 Guess who it is.

1 Where / she / born?_____

2 When / she / act in / first film? _____

3 What / most famous film? _____

4 Who / she marry / 2003? _____

5 What film / act in / 2004? _____

She was born in ¹ _____ in 1975.

In ² _____, she acted in her first film, *Heavenly Creatures*.

She made her most famous film in 1997. It was called ³ _____.

In 1998, she married Jim Threapleton and they had a daughter called Mia. But after three years, the couple divorced.

In 2003, she married ⁴ _____. They have a son called Joe.

In 2004, she acted in ⁵ _____, with Johnny Depp.

B

1 Write the questions.

2 Take turns to ask the questions and write the missing information.

3 Guess who it is.

1 When / she / born?_____

2 What / first film? _____

3 When / make / most famous film? _____

4 Who / she marry / 1998? _____

5 Who / she / act with / 2004? _____

She was born in England in ¹ _____.

In 1994, she acted in her first film, ² _____.

She made her most famous film in ³ _____. It was called *Titanic*.

In 1998, she married ⁴ _____ and they had a daughter called Mia. But after three years, the couple divorced.

In 2003, she married Sam Mendes. They have a son called Joe.

In 2004, she acted in *Finding Neverland*, with ⁵ _____.

Straightforward Elementary Teacher's Book © Macmillan Publishers Limited 2006

6c | Do you sing badly?

1 Write an adverb to describe how you do each activity in the table. Choose from this list.

| carefully | beautifully | angrily | fast | quietly | well | noisily | slowly | badly |

2 Guess how your partner does things. Write the adverbs.

3 Ask questions to find out if you are right.

Do you drive carefully?   **Yes, I do.**
Do you swim well?   **No, I don't.**

4 Count how many guesses you got right.

Activity	Me	My partner	✓ / X
drive			
speak English			
eat			
cry			
sleep			
swim			
cook			
type			
draw			
sing			
play football			
read			

6D | Can't stand coffee

Walk around the class. Ask and answer questions about the things below. Find one person for each thing.

Do you like coffee?
☺ Yes, I do.
☺☺ I love it!

Do you like shopping?
☺ It's OK. / I don't mind it.

Do you like exams?
☹ No, I don't.
☹☹ I hate them. / I can't stand them.

Find someone who ...	Name
... can't stand coffee	_____
... doesn't mind loud music	_____
... likes champagne	_____
... doesn't like the internet	_____
... likes English food	_____
... loves football	_____
... doesn't mind exams	_____
... loves parties	_____
... hates shopping	_____
... loves TV	_____
... doesn't like mobile phones	_____
... doesn't mind hospitals	_____

7A Which diet?

1 Choose a diet. Don't tell your partner what it is. Answer your partner's questions.

Can you eat any chocolate?
Yes.
Can you drink any tea?
No.

2 Ask questions about your partner's diet.

Cold food diet
bread
cheese
egg (cold)
lettuce
tomatoes
cold meat
chocolate

Sweet dream diet
Eat: chocolate (50g a day)
    fruit
    cake

Drink: fruit juice
      tea with sugar
      wine

THE GREEN DIET

You can eat	You can drink
apples	water
lettuce	fruit juice
tomatoes	
carrots	

The juice diet
orange juice
apple juice
water
tomato juice
carrot juice

Don't eat any food.
Just drink juice.

Eat well diet
Eat as much as you like of these:
meat • fish
chicken • cheese
apples • egg
chocolate

The good egg diet
Eat one egg with every meal.
egg and bread
egg and meat
egg and potatoes
egg and soup
egg and cheese

7B Recipes

A

1 Complete the lists of ingredients. Ask your partner questions.

How many potatoes do you need?   How much butter do you need?

Spanish Omelette
_____ of potatoes
4 spoonfuls of oil
_____ onion
2 tomatoes
_____ eggs

Chocolate soufflé
200 grams of chocolate
_____ of milk
100 grams of sugar
_____ of butter
3 eggs

2 Work with your partner. Which of the ingredients are countable and which are uncountable?

countable		uncountable	
_____	_____	_____	_____
_____	_____	_____	_____
_____		_____	

✂ ···

B

1 Complete the lists of ingredients. Ask your partner questions.

How many tomatoes do you need?   How much oil do you need?

Spanish Omelette
1 kg of potatoes
_____ of oil
1 onion
_____ tomatoes
6 eggs

Chocolate soufflé
_____ of chocolate
3 spoonfuls of milk
_____ of sugar
20 grams of butter
_____ eggs

2 Work with your partner. Which of the ingredients are countable and which are uncountable?

countable		uncountable	
_____	_____	_____	_____
_____	_____	_____	_____
_____		_____	

Straightforward Elementary Teacher's Book © Macmillan Publishers Limited 2006

7c Are you a fussy eater?

1 You go to a restaurant. When your food arrives, it's very spicy. What do you say to the waiter?
Mmm. I love spicy food. (2)
This is spicy, but I like it. (1)
This is too spicy. I can't stand spicy food. (0)

2 Your friend makes you some gazpacho – cold soup! What do you say?
Thanks. How interesting! (1)
Great! Gazpacho is my favourite. (2)
I'm sorry. I can't eat this. I don't like cold soup. (0)

3 What do you think of sushi?
It's horrible – it's raw fish! (0)
It's OK, but I like to cook fish. (1)
I like it. (2)

4 How often do you try new food?
Sometimes – when I go to a restaurant. (1)
Often. I like to try new things. (2)
Never! I know what I like. (0)

5 How do you eat your vegetables?
Sometimes raw, sometimes cooked. (2)
Always cooked. I don't like raw vegetables. (1)
I never eat vegetables. I hate them! (0)

6 Where's the best place to eat?
In a Mexican restaurant. (2)
At home. (0)
In a hamburger restaurant. (1)

7 Do you ever put garlic in your food?
No. It smells awful! (0)
Yes. It makes food taste great! (2)
Sometimes, but I don't like a lot of garlic. (1)

8 Your friend makes you a cup of tea. It isn't very hot. What do you say?
A nice cup of tea. Thanks. (2)
Thanks, but it's too cold. (1)
I can't drink this. I don't like tea or coffee. (0)

Menu

Paella
Seafood paella
Vegetable paella
Mushroom paella

Pizza
Cheese and tomato
Spicy beef
Ham and mushroom

Pasta
Spaghetti Bolognese
Meat lasagne
Vegetarian lasagne

Salads
Tomato and onion
Lettuce and tomato
Chicken and lettuce

Drinks
Orange juice
Apple juice
Beer
Red wine
White wine

Problem!
There isn't any salt. Ask the waiter.

Problem!
Your food is cold. Tell the waiter.

Problem!
You've got the wrong drink. Tell the waiter.

Waiter
Greet the customers and take their orders.
Be careful – you haven't got some of the things on the menu:

- You haven't got any orange juice. Offer a different drink.
- You haven't got any tomato and onion salad. Offer a different salad.
- You haven't got any seafood paella. Offer a different paella.

Check everything is OK. Help the customers with their problems.

8A | He loves playing football

___ drinking beer.	___ talking on a mobile phone.	___ going to hospital.	___ travelling by underground.
___ driving fast cars.	___ eating apples.	___ travelling by boat.	___ waiting for a bus.
___ writing exams.	___ doing the ironing.	___ playing football.	___ flying.
___ listening to hard rock.	___ eating hamburgers.	___ playing golf.	___ watching horror films.

8B Traffic report

A

1 Read the traffic report and write the questions.

2 Ask and answer the questions to complete the report.

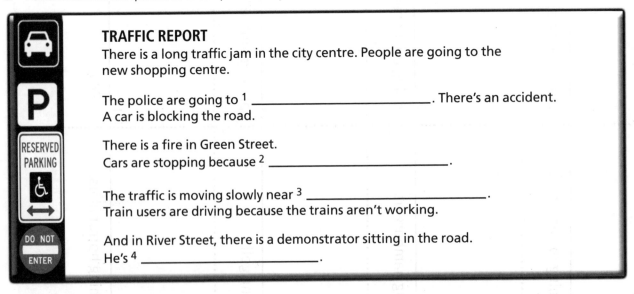

TRAFFIC REPORT

There is a long traffic jam in the city centre. People are going to
1 _____.

The police are going to London Road. There's an accident.
A 2 _____ is blocking the road.

There is a fire in Green Street.
Cars are stopping because the drivers can't see.

The traffic is moving slowly near Queen Street station.
Train users are driving because 3 _____.

And in River Street, there is a 4 _____ sitting in the road.
He's singing and shouting.

1 Where / the people / go

_____

2 What / block / the road

_____

3 Why / train users / drive

_____

4 Who / sit / in the road

_____

✂ ··

B

1 Read the traffic report and write the questions.

2 Ask and answer the questions to complete the report.

TRAFFIC REPORT

There is a long traffic jam in the city centre. People are going to the
new shopping centre.

The police are going to 1 _____. There's an accident.
A car is blocking the road.

There is a fire in Green Street.
Cars are stopping because 2 _____.

The traffic is moving slowly near 3 _____.
Train users are driving because the trains aren't working.

And in River Street, there is a demonstrator sitting in the road.
He's 4 _____.

1 Where / police / go

_____

2 Why / cars / stop

_____

3 Where / traffic / move slowly

_____

4 What / demonstrator / do

_____

8c | Sailing

💿 4 Listen and complete the song with the correct lines.

Sailing

I am sailing, I am sailing
Home again, across the sea
I am sailing stormy waters
To be near you, to be free

1 _____

like a bird across the sky.

2 _____

to be with you, to be free.

Can you hear me, can you hear me
thro' the dark night, far away,

3 _____

to be with you, who can say.

Can you hear me, can you hear me
thro' the dark night, far away,

4 _____

to be with you, who can say.

5 _____

home again across the sea.

6 _____

to be near you, to be free.

Oh Lord, to be near you, to be free.
Oh Lord, to be near you, to be free,
Oh Lord.

I am dying, forever trying

We are sailing stormy waters

I am flying, passing high clouds,

I am dying, forever trying

I am flying, I am flying

We are sailing, we are sailing

8D | Let's go by train

✂ There's an outdoor concert tonight. Do you want to come?

✂ Yes. Where is it?

✂ It's in Queen's Park.

✂ How do we get there?

✂ We could take a taxi.

✂ No. It's too expensive. Can we go on foot?

✂ It's too far. Let's go by train.

✂ But there isn't a station near my house.

✂ OK. Let's take the bus.

✂ Good idea.

✂ --

A

Invite your friend to a party in the city centre.
Suggest travelling by:

• bicycle
• underground
• car

✂ --

B

Listen to your partner and reply to his/her suggestions, using the information below.

• **You don't have a bicycle.**
• **You don't like the underground.**
• **You like travelling by car.**

going to an
important interview

visiting a relative
in hospital

going on a long
plane journey

going to a wedding

going to a school /
college meeting

going to a disco

going to the theatre

going cycling

meeting new boyfriend's /
girlfriend's parents

going to a beach party

going cycling

going to a barbecue

9B | Stand on one foot!

Put your hands behind your back	Stand on one foot.
Open your fingers.	Hold your elbow behind your head.
Move your knees together.	Touch your right foot with your left hand.
Turn your head to the right.	Turn your head to the left.
Move your eyes to the left.	Put your hands on your waist.
Put your hands behind your back.	Touch your knees with your elbows.
Hold your left elbow with your right hand.	Close your eyes.
Put your left hand on your stomach.	Stand comfortably.

9c | Who is it?

Choose a face. Don't tell your partner who it is. Take turns to give clues.

His chin is big.
Her eyes are small.
His cheeks are red.
Her glasses are round.

Claire

Paul

Pam

John

Ellen

Amy

Martin

Bryan

Liz

Andrew

A

You are the patient.
Say hello.
Answer the doctor's questions. Use this information.
• You don't feel very well.
• You've got a stomachache.
• You ate shellfish last night, but your husband's fine.
• You're very tired.

Listen to the doctor's advice.
Thank the doctor. Say goodbye.

B

You are the doctor.
Greet the patient.
Ask these questions.
• What's the matter?
• What's wrong?
• Was it something you ate last night?
• Are you tired?

Give advice: You should ...
Say goodbye to the patient.

A

You are the doctor.
Greet the patient.
Ask these questions.
• How are you today?
• Have you got a stomachache?
• Have you got a headache?
• Did you drink too much last night?

Give advice: You should ...
Say goodbye to the patient.

B

You are the patient.
Say hello.
Answer the doctor's questions. Use this information:
• You feel sick.
• You haven't got a stomachache.
• You've got a headache.
• You don't drink wine.

Listen to the doctor's advice.
Thank the doctor. Say goodbye.

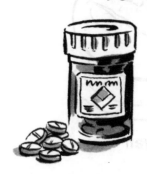

wear a tie to class.	You mustn't	put your feet on the seats.	You mustn't
talk while the teacher is talking.	You needn't	drink alcohol before driving.	You needn't
arrive ten minutes early for lessons.	You must	keep to the speed limit.	You mustn't
be quiet during an exam.	You must	wash your car every day.	You must
be late for lessons.	You must	wash your hands before touching food.	You mustn't
put your rubbish in the bin.	You mustn't	cook meat properly.	You needn't
smoke in 'no smoking' areas.	You needn't	wear rubber gloves to wash up.	You must
open the doors while a train is moving.	You must	turn off your mobile phone before a film begins.	You mustn't
use a credit card to buy a ticket.	You mustn't	talk loudly during a film.	You needn't

10B | Comparing capitals

A

1 Read the notes about the capital city. Tell your friend about it.

London, England

Population: 7.2 million people live in London

Attractions: You can visit the London Eye, Buckingham Palace and many museums, theatres and restaurants.

Weather: In the summer, the average temperature is 22°C. The average temperature in the winter is 7°C. It rarely snows.

Crime: London is a big city and violent crime is a problem. Some areas aren't safe for tourists.

Pollution: London has a lot of cars, but the government is trying to reduce pollution. The River Thames is much cleaner today than it was in the past.

2 Work with your partner. Complete the sentences.

1 _____ is bigger than _____.

2 _____ is smaller than _____.

3 _____ is more dangerous than _____.

4 _____ is more polluted than _____.

5 _____ is safer than _____.

6 _____ is more interesting than _____.

B

1 Read the notes about the capital city. Tell your friend about it.

Tallinn, Estonia

Population: 430,000

Attractions: Tourists come to visit the beautiful old town with its buildings from the 13th and 14th Centuries.

Weather: The average temperature in summer is 20°C. In winter, it's -5°C. Occasionally parts of the sea around Tallinn freeze.

Crime: There is some violent crime, but visitors to the area are usually safe.

Pollution: Oil pollution from the Baltic Sea travels to Estonia's rivers. Sometimes drinking water isn't safe.

2 Work with your partner. Complete the sentences.

1 _____ is bigger than _____.

2 _____ is smaller than _____.

3 _____ is more dangerous than _____.

4 _____ is more polluted than _____.

5 _____ is safer than _____.

6 _____ is more interesting than _____.

Straightforward Elementary Teacher's Book © Macmillan Publishers Limited 2006

10c | Which holiday?

A

1 You want to do these things.

go dancing   go on a boat trip   go swimming   go diving

Ask questions to find out where you can do them.
Complete the missing information.

2 Discuss the holidays with your partner. Which do you think is ...

- the cheapest?
- the most expensive?
- the most popular with young couples?
- the most popular with families?
- the most dangerous?
- the safest?
- the best?

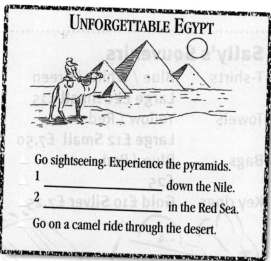

UNFORGETTABLE EGYPT

Go sightseeing. Experience the pyramids.

1 _____ down the Nile.

2 _____ in the Red Sea.

Go on a camel ride through the desert.

THE GREEK ISLANDS

3 _____ in clear blue seas.

Relax on sandy beaches.

Go walking in the mountains.

Visit traditional Greek villages.

☆ The New York Experience ☆

☆ See a musical on Broadway.

☆ Go shopping in the world's most famous stores.

☆ 4 .... all night.

☆ Eat at some of the best restaurants in the world.

✂ -

B

1 You want to do these things.

go walking   go sightseeing   see a musical   go on a camel ride

Ask questions to find out where you can do them.
Complete the missing information.

2 Discuss the holidays with your partner. Which do you think is ...

- the cheapest?
- the most expensive?
- the most popular with young couples?
- the most popular with families?
- the most dangerous?
- the safest?
- the best?

UNFORGETTABLE EGYPT

1 _____ . Experience the pyramids.

Go on a boat trip down the Nile.

Go diving in the Red Sea.

2 _____ through the desert.

THE GREEK ISLANDS

Go swimming in clear blue seas.

Relax on sandy beaches.

3 _____ in the mountains.

Visit traditional Greek villages.

☆ The New York Experience ☆

☆ 4 .... on Broadway.

☆ Go shopping in the world's most famous stores.

☆ Go dancing all night.

☆ Eat at some of the best restaurants in the world.

Sally's Souvenirs

T-shirts	Blue / White / Green **Large £20 Small £15**
Towels	Yellow / Red **Large £12 Small £7.50**
Bags	Blue / Red £25
Key rings	**Gold £10 Silver £7.25**

Greg's Gifts

Teddy bears	**Large £18 Small £11**
Pens	Blue / Black / Green £2.50
Mugs	Orange / Blue / White **Large £5 Small £3.50**
Towels	Blue / White **Large £10 Small 7.50**

Shopping list
Customer A

Teddy bear (Mum) _____

Key ring (David) _____

Bag (Celia) _____

Mug (Dad) _____

Shopping list
Customer B

T-shirt (Dad) _____

Pen (Barbara) _____

Key ring (Thomas) _____

Towel (Mum) _____

11A What do I do?

1 Choose one of the jobs below.

2 Your partner will ask you questions about your job.

Where	do you work?
What time	do you start work?
	do you finish work?
Who	do you work with?
What	do you do every day?

3 Answer your partner's questions.

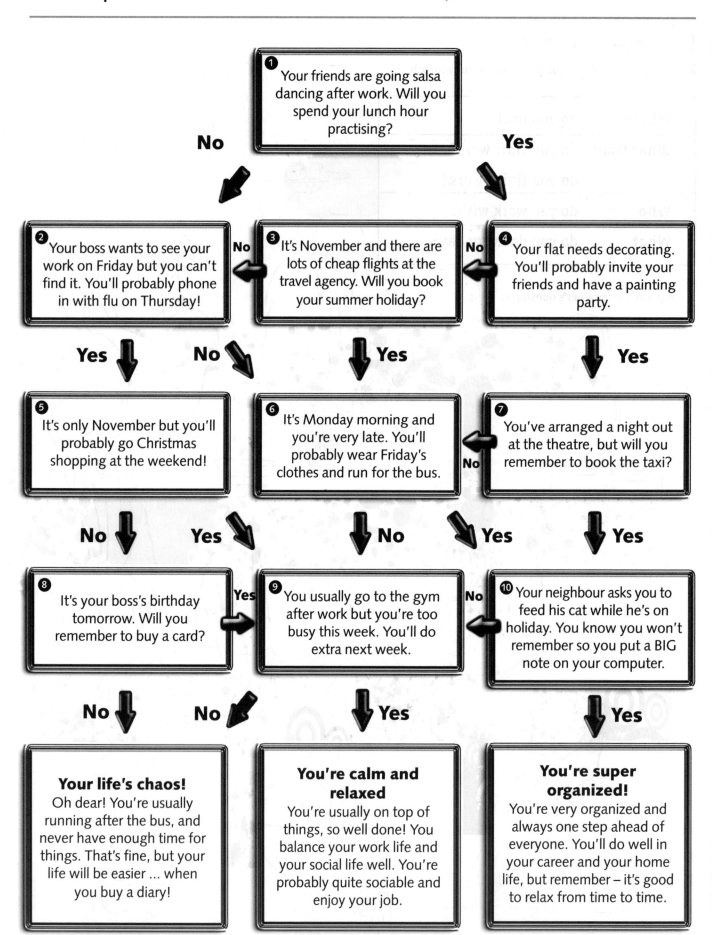

1 Your friends are going salsa dancing after work. Will you spend your lunch hour practising?

No → **Yes**

2 Your boss wants to see your work on Friday but you can't find it. You'll probably phone in with flu on Thursday!

No ←

3 It's November and there are lots of cheap flights at the travel agency. Will you book your summer holiday?

No ←

4 Your flat needs decorating. You'll probably invite your friends and have a painting party.

Yes ↓ **No** ↓ **Yes** ↓ **Yes** ↓

5 It's only November but you'll probably go Christmas shopping at the weekend!

6 It's Monday morning and you're very late. You'll probably wear Friday's clothes and run for the bus.

7 You've arranged a night out at the theatre, but will you remember to book the taxi?

No ←

No ↓ **Yes** ↓ **No** ↓ **Yes** ↓ **Yes** ↓

8 It's your boss's birthday tomorrow. Will you remember to buy a card?

Yes →

9 You usually go to the gym after work but you're too busy this week. You'll do extra next week.

No ←

10 Your neighbour asks you to feed his cat while he's on holiday. You know you won't remember so you put a BIG note on your computer.

No ↓ **No** ↓ **Yes** ↓ **Yes** ↓

Your life's chaos!
Oh dear! You're usually running after the bus, and never have enough time for things. That's fine, but your life will be easier ... when you buy a diary!

You're calm and relaxed
You're usually on top of things, so well done! You balance your work life and your social life well. You're probably quite sociable and enjoy your job.

You're super organized!
You're very organized and always one step ahead of everyone. You'll do well in your career and your home life, but remember – it's good to relax from time to time.

Is it difficult to say 'no' to people?

Not at all. 'No' is my favourite word.

Yes. I can't say 'no' to anyone.

It depends. Sometimes 'Yes' is the best answer.

How do you feel when you make mistakes?

If it's a serious mistake, I worry.

I feel angry with myself.

I make too many mistakes to worry.

Do you worry about small problems?

Yes. I worry all the time.

No. Life is full of more important things.

No. I never worry about anything.

How often do you have a good laugh?

All the time. I'm never serious about anything.

Sometimes. Some situations are funny and others are serious.

I never laugh.

Do you work too hard?

Yes. I never rest.

Never!

I work hard when I'm interested in something.

How often do you exercise?

I'm very active. I do a lot of exercise.

I never exercise. It's a waste of time.

I exercise if I have time.

How often do you get a good night's sleep?

Never. I'm awake all night.

Often, but I don't sleep if I'm excited about something.

I sleep all night (and sometimes all day).

What's the best advice for life?

You only live once. Experience everything!

Don't do anything dangerous.

Take it easy.

11D | Who wants to go out with me?

party	dinner	theatre	beach
concert	**coffee**	**picnic**	**cinema**

NO. You broke up with your girlfriend / boyfriend last week.	**NO. You're busy. You have to wash up and take the rubbish out.**
NO. You don't think it's a good idea to go out with people from work.	**YES. Ask when and where to meet.**
NO. You don't think you'll get along well.	**YES. Ask what to wear.**
NO. You don't think you'll get along well.	**YES. Ask for his / her phone number.**

12A | Pop careers

A

Singer A: Kylie Minogue

- Began her career as an actress
- Made her first record in 1988
- Has made nine albums
- Has worked with other singers, including Robbie Williams in a duet called *Kids*
- Has had health problems; in 2005, doctors told her she had cancer

Singer C: Paul McCartney

- Has been making music for over 40 years
- Received Grammy Lifetime Achievement Award in 1990
- Belonged to the most famous pop band in the world
- Over 3,000 people have made their own versions of his song *Yesterday*
- Has been married twice; his first wife, Linda, died of cancer in 1998

Singer B: _____

Band D: _____

- -

B

Singer A: _____

Singer C: _____

Singer B: Madonna

- Has sold over 100 million records
- Has had 12 number one records and 35 top ten records
- Has done many sell-out concerts, including four world tours
- Has done some acting; appeared in *Dick Tracy* and *Evita*
- Has been married twice. Her present husband is Guy Ritchie

Band D: U2

- Have been together for 30 years
- Have made 12 albums
- Lead singer has been involved in campaigning for human rights and working with AIDS charities
- Played at the original Live Aid concert in 1985
- Are from Dublin

Have you ever ...

driven a bus?

spoken to a politician?

been to a football match?

visited Australia?

had a boring holiday?

called the police?

read an English newspaper?

taken a difficult exam?

met a beautiful singer?

studied psychology?

met a handsome film star?

given flowers to your teacher?

cooked spicy food?

gone to sleep in class?

written a book?

broken an expensive present?

slept outside?

been on a miracle diet?

made a big mistake?

written poetry?

been on an underground train?

12c | Fields of gold

1 Look at
the picture.

✂️ FOLD -

2 🌐 **5** Listen and complete the song with the correct form of the verbs in brackets. Use these tense forms.

• present simple • *can* • past simple • future (*will*) • present perfect

Fields of gold

You ¹ _____ (remember) me
when the west wind ² _____ (move)
Upon the fields of barley
You ³ _____ (forget) the sun in his jealous sky
As we ⁴ _____ (walk) in fields of gold.

So she ⁵ _____ (take) her love
For to gaze awhile
Upon the fields of barley
In his arms she ⁶ _____ (fall)
as her hair ⁷ _____ (come) down
Among the fields of gold

Will you stay with me, ⁸ _____ (be) my love
Among the fields of barley
We ⁹ _____ (forget) the sun in his jealous sky
As we ¹⁰ _____ (lie) in fields of gold

See the west wind ¹¹ _____ (move)
like a lover so
Upon the fields of barley
Feel her body rise when you
¹² _____ (kiss) her mouth
Among the fields of gold

I never ¹³ _____ (make) promises lightly
And there ¹⁴ _____ (be) some that
I ¹⁵ _____ (break)
But I swear in the days still left
We ¹⁶ _____ (walk) in fields of gold
We'll walk in fields of gold

Many years ¹⁷ _____ (pass)
since those summer days
Among the fields of barley
See the children run as the sun
¹⁸ _____ (go) down
Among the fields of gold

You ¹⁹ _____ (remember) me
when the west wind ²⁰ _____ (move)
Upon the fields of barley
You ²¹ _____ (tell) the sun in his jealous sky
When we ²² _____ (walk) in fields of gold
When we walked in fields of gold
When we walked in fields of gold

12D | Goodbye!

A

Conversation 1

You are Student B's teacher. You are leaving to go to a new school.

Before you start

Think of all the things that make someone a good student.
Think of what advice a teacher can give to a student.

Roleplay

- Say goodbye and thank Student B for being a good student.
- Thank him / her for your present.
- Give him / her some advice for the future.

B

Conversation 1

Student A is your teacher. He / She is leaving to go to a new school.

Before you start

Think of all the things a good teacher helps you with.
Choose a gift for your teacher. Write it here. _____

Roleplay

- Thank Student A for some of the things he / she has done for you.
- Give Student A your present.
- Listen to Student A's advice for the future.

A

Conversation 2

Student B is your neighbour. He / she is moving to a new house.

Before you start

Think of all the things that neighbours do for each other.

Roleplay

- Thank Student B for some of the things he / she has done for you.
- Give Student B a card.
- Wish Student B good luck in his / her new house.

B

Conversation 2

You are Student A's neighbour. You are moving to a new house.

Before you start

Think of all the things that neighbours do for each other.

Roleplay

- Say goodbye to Student A. Thank him / her for some being a good neighbour.
- Say thank you for your card.
- Invite Student A to visit you in your new house.

Straightforward Elementary Teacher's Book © Macmillan Publishers Limited 2006